MEMOIR AND REMAINS

OF THE

REV. ROBERT MURRAY McCHEYNE

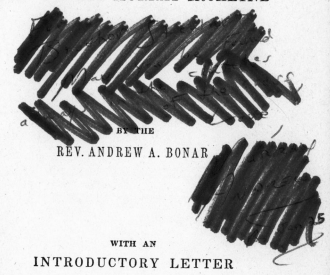

BY THE

REV. ANDREW A. BONAR

WITH AN

INTRODUCTORY LETTER

BY THE

Rev. SAMUEL MILLER, D.D.

BAKER BOOK HOUSE
Grand Rapids, Michigan

Reprinted 1978 by
Baker Book House
from the edition issued by the
Presbyterian Board of Publication

ISBN: 0-8010-0728-3

PHOTOLITHOPRINTED BY CUSHING - MALLOY, INC.
ANN ARBOR, MICHIGAN, UNITED STATES OF AMERICA
1978

CONTENTS

		Page
Introductory Letter,		vii
Chap. I. His Youth and Preparation for the Ministry,		19
... II. His Labours in the Vineyard before Ordination,		54
... III. First Years of Labour in Dundee,		80
... IV. His Mission to Palestine and the Jews,		117
... V. Days of Revival,		156
... VI. The Latter Days of his Ministry,		189
Concluding Memorials,		218
Private Correspondence,		225
Pastoral Letters,		316
To Members of a Prayer Meeting,		371
Evidence on Revivals,		375
Songs of Zion.		386
The Barren Fig Tree,		ib.
They sing the Song of Moses,		387
Jehovah Tsidkenu,		389
On Mungo Park's finding a tuft of moss,		390
I am Debtor,		392
Children called to Christ,		394
Thy Word is a Lamp unto my Feet,		395
The Fountain of Siloam,		396
The Sea of Galilee,		397
To Yonder Side,		398
On the Mediterranean Sea, at Acre,		400
The Child coming to Jesus,		401
Oil in the Lamp,		402

INTRODUCTORY LETTER

TO THE CHAIRMAN OF THE EXECUTIVE COMMITTEE
OF THE BOARD OF PUBLICATION OF THE PRESBY-
TERIAN CHURCH IN THE UNITED STATES.

REV. AND DEAR BROTHER.—I have received, within
a few days, from a valued correspondent in Scotland,
a biographical work which I have read with peculiar
pleasure, and which I could earnestly wish might be
circulated throughout the bounds of our beloved
Church. The work to which I refer is entitled,
"Memoir and Remains of the Reverend ROBERT
MURRAY MCCHEYNE, Minister of St. Peter's Church,
Dundee, by the Rev. *Andrew A. Bonar*, Minister of
the Free Church of Scotland, Collace."

Although Mr. McCheyne was a young man, not
extensively known to fame, who died last year at the
early age of twenty-nine, yet he was so highly esteemed and confided in by his brethren of the Church
of Scotland, that in 1838, when in the twenty-fourth
year of his age, he was chosen, in connection with
three older ministers, on a delegation to the Jews of
Europe and Asia; to inquire into their condition, and
to report on the prospects and best means of calling
their attention to the character and claims of the reli
gion of Christ. This commission he fulfilled with an
ability and faithfulness which, together with the preceding and subsequent character of his ministry, caused

his death, which took place in 1843, to be regarded as a great calamity to the cause of truth and of vital piety in North Britain.

The impression left by Mr. McCheyne on the minds of those who were most intimately acquainted with his person and ministry, is strongly portrayed in the following representation, found in a review of this memoir, contained in a periodical published in Edinburgh, and evidently written by one who had the best opportunity of knowing the whole character of the deceased, in all its aspects. The extract will speak for itself. Such language could not have been prompted by an ordinary man.

"ROBERT MURRAY McCHEYNE! To dwell on his saintly character would be a pleasant theme. At this realizing moment to produce his effigy seems a possible task. That countenance so benevolently earnest, with its gleams of brightness flitting over its settled pensiveness;—that eye so mild and penetrating, as of one who had seen through the world's vanity before he had discerned the Saviour's beauty;—that forehead familiar with high and holy thoughts;—that disentangled pilgrim-look which showed plainly that he 'sought a city;'—the serene self-possession of one who walked by faith;—and the sequestered musing gait such as we might suppose the meditative Isaac had;—that aspect of compassion, in such unison with the remonstrating and entreating tones of his melodious and tender voice;—that entire appearance as of one who had been with Jesus, and who would never be right at home till, where Jesus is, there he should also be:—these things we think we could delineate; for associated as they are with some of the most solemn and delightful hours of personal history, they come back on memory with a vividness which annihilates the interval since last we saw them, and with that air of immortality about them, which says, joyfully, ' He is not dead, but sleepeth.' To know him was the best interpretation of many texts. At least, we have a clearer conception of what is meant by a ' hidden life,' and a ' living sacrifice,' and can better understand the sort of life which Enoch led, since we made the acquaintance of Robert McCheyne.

" Happy would it have been for Scotland had all its churches and manses witnessed the scenes with which St. Peter's, Dundee, and the abode of its minister had become familiar. So heart-deep and humbling were the confessions of sin in Mr. McCheyne's family prayers and in public worship; so far did he descend into the inward abysses of atheism, and carnality, and hypocrisy; and so faithfully and mournfully did he lay before the Lord these hidden plagues, the perversities of motive, and the intricacies of self-righteousness, that nothing was so fitted to convince of sin and destroy confidence in the flesh. Then in his prayers he held such reverential and endearing communion with a reconciled God ;—he pressed so near the throne ; there was something so filial in his ' Abba, Father ;' it was so obvious even to lookers-on, that he was putting his petitions and praises into the golden censer ;—so express, and urgent, and hopeful were his supplications, that it was awakening to hear him pray. It was enough to make some Christians feel, ' Hitherto we have asked nothing in Jesus' name;' and enough to prick the heart of prayerless worldlings. His preaching was a continuation of his prayers. In both he spoke from within the veil, his hand on the mercy seat, and his eye fixed on the things invisible. His usual address was calm and evenly, but arresting and enchanting. His hold of the truth gave him a hold of his hearers. He was at home in the pulpit. He did not need to bestow that care on composition which is incumbent on less gifted men. His poetic fancy and instinctive taste, with a steady flow of thoughts and words, saved him much trouble in this respect. But that was all. He did not avail himself of his fine genius and happy power of language, to procure a name for eloquence. He was content that the subordinate end was answered, and that even in extempore addresses he could proceed without embarrassment or hesitation. His eye was single ; his aim was souls—souls for Jesus' sake. He had some other use for his bow than to entertain his hearers with the twang of the sonorous string. The salvation of souls was his object ; and in his study preparing for the pulpit, and in the pulpit looking down upon his people, all his anxiety was to find truth that would penetrate the conscience—the unawakened consciences of all kinds of people, and truth which would lead anxious souls to the desired landing place of peace with God. This unity of purpose gave a continuous earnestness and solemnity to his ministry. His feeblest appeal was more personal and importunate than the most pointed exhortations of vaguer ministers in their most faithful moods. His solicitude for the salvation of his hearers made him affectionate even beyond his natural tenderness. Sometimes a smile of momentary bitterness would be provoked when depicting the absurdity of sin, and the infatuation of sinners; but it instantly subsided into the habitual compassion with which he yearned over souls. So well understood was his errand ;—so accustomed were they to the entreating voice and expostulating attitude of this ambassador of Christ ;—so thoroughly aware that he was seeking their immediate conversion were the most careless in his congregation, that any disquisition which had not a present and practical bearing, a sermon without Christ or without earnestness, would have astonished the most indifferent among them, and made them fear that their minister was no longer himself.

" Commending the truth to every man's conscience in the sight of God, a demonstration of the Spirit seldom failed to accompany his preaching. His ministry at Dundee was a constant awakening, and he seldom addressed an auditory elsewhere without its proving to some a time much to be remembered. Nay, a demonstration of the Spirit accompanied his presence. His visits to pious families were hallowing, and his casual contact with secular men was solemnizing ; and even those who only ' wondered and perished ' knew that a prophet had been among them indeed.

" But his character has been so often delineated already, and the materials for knowing him better which these volumes supply, are so abundant, that we shall not pursue this personal portraiture any further. Nor shall we fill our pages with extracts from a book which we hope every reader of this Review has, by this time, either read or begun to read. His school-companion, his fellow-pilgrim to Palestine, his near neighbour in the ministry, and most frequent coadjutor in each labour of love, is his biographer. No one who knew how undivided in his life Mr. McCheyne and Mr. A. Bonar were, thought that any other should attempt the record of that life ; no one that reads it could wish that any other had. By natural talent fitted to notice the finer features of character, and to fathom some of its abstruser depths, and by a better taste accustomed to observe the rise and progress of religion in the souls of men, and peculiarly happy in describing things as he sees them, Mr. Bonar is a fit biographer in any case where eminent piety reigned in a delicate and accomplished mind. In the present case, so intimate and like-minded were they, that the narrative derives much of its beauty from the congeniality between the subject and its narrator. The only fault is one, into which a stranger could not have fallen. Some of the more obvious features of Mr. McCheyne's character are hardly noticed. To Mr. Bonar they were so habitual that they had ceased to be observable. They would have impressed a stranger. The ordinary aspect of the man, his in-door life and daily walk, his manner of conversation in the world, and among his Christian friends, such scenes as have seldom transpired, except in the prayer meetings and at the communions of St. Peter's, more of his sayings and deep remarks on Scripture, and, if possible, more of the special instances of his success in winning souls, we should have gladly obtained, and some of these a distant on-looker would have been apt to give. The work does not absolutely lack these things, and it possesses the surpassing value of revealing the interior growth of that eminent piety which produced his eminent usefulness. And altogether, the memoir is a faithful and affecting record of as beauteous a character, and as effective a ministry as He who holds the seven stars has exhibited to the Church in these last days.

" To give this article a practical tendency, we may be allowed to mention what we believe to have been the secret of Mr. McCheyne's uncommon usefulness. The subject is seasonable, at this time when so many ministers, and elders, and private Christians are inquiring by what means they may extend their personal efficiency, and become, in the hands of the Spirit, the agents in adding to the Church of such as shall be saved. From what we know of Mr. McCheyne, and have read in these Memoirs, we are persuaded that next to his habitual dependence on the Spirit of God, the occasion of his uncommon success was the consistency and conspicuousness of his Christian character. He lived in the eye of his people. Though his house had been a glass-fronted cabinet, they could scarcely have been more minutely cognizant of his movements and whole manner of life. They knew that his week days were but a sequel to his Sabbaths, and what they saw him in the pulpit, they found him in his study and among his friends, by the way-side, and in their own houses. He was every where ' the man of God.' His preaching was impressive, for his life applied it. His every day demeanour exemplified and adorned his doctrine."*

Such is the attestation of the contemporaries and intimate friends of this extraordinary man, who had marked his spirit, and listened to his instructions, in public and in private for years together, in all the various circumstances which " try men's souls." Can any one who appreciates the value of Christian character, doubt that such an example ought to be portrayed for the benefit of the Church and of the world; and that such a spirit ought to be studied as deeply, and recommended as widely as possible?

One of the most promising and gratifying features in the present aspect of the Free Church of Scotland, and one of the most precious pledges of the blessing of God on her noble enterprise, is the evident revival of a

---

* The Presbyterian Review and Rel. Journal. No LXV. July, 1844. Edinburgh.

spirit of vital piety among her members, and especially among her ministers and elders. This revival has gone hand in hand with her faithful struggle for maintaining the truth and order of Christ's house. Nor is the connection between these two objects of attention either remote or unimportant. For as, on the one hand, the prevalence of vital piety cannot be expected to be found in any church in which the pure doctrines of the gospel are not held fast and faithfully preached; so, on the other, where a sound faith at present exists, it will assuredly not long continue to be maintained, after vital piety declines. As men are "sanctified by the truth," so none but sanctified men will be disposed for any length of time together, to "contend for the truth," and to preach it with simplicity and clearness. In the early history of the Reformed churches of France, we find orthodoxy and vital piety maintaining a joint reign to an extent as benign and happy as in any other portion of Protestant Christendom. One of the first symptoms of a departure from their original purity, was a disposition manifested by some of their ministers of questionable piety, to explain some of the articles of the Confession of Faith which they had solemnly subscribed, in a latitudinarian manner. Deviation followed deviation; Synodical bodies began to tolerate serious error; an evangelical spirit declined with evangelical truth; until, at length, they ceased to occupy the place and to maintain the character of "witnesses" for "the faith once delivered to the saints." The history of the Church of Scotland, is in melancholy accordance with the same great principle. With the growth of "Moderatism," orthodoxy and piety sunk together; until "the things which remained were ready to die." At this juncture God was pleased to interpose for her help. Faithful men were raised up; men "full of faith, and of the Holy Ghost;" men who remembered the orthodoxy and piety of their fathers; men trained in the school of experience and of sound doctrine, and willing to give up all for Christ. The sublime spectacle which these devoted men have since exhibited, in abandoning all the endowments and comforts of the established church, for the sake of fidelity to their Master in heaven has been, since the era of its occurrence, the admiration and joy of a large part of the Protestant world. Of this blessed revival and triumph of Christian principle, McCheyne, and his memoir may be considered at once as a fruit and a specimen.

I write these lines, and recommend this work, my dear brother, under the deep impression that we cannot pray for a greater blessing to our beloved Church, than that the mantle of this holy man may rest upon all our Pastors and Elders, exciting them to the zeal, the unceasing diligence, and the entire consecration to their Master in heaven which were so conspicuous in his short course. We need—greatly need large additions to the number of our ministers; but we still more urgently need a higher standard of piety among those that we have. Often, in reading this delightful memoir, have I said to myself, "O if all the Pastors of our Church, or a large portion of them, were such as McCheyne, as dead to the world as he was; as full of sanctified unceasing ardour to do good to the souls of men; as watchful to instruct and edify the young and the old; as much like Christ in all their habits and efforts—what a different aspect would our portion of the religious community wear! How much more elevated would be the eloquence of our pulpits! An eloquence not growing out of the principles and rules of art, but governed and animated by that heart-felt sense of the infinite importance and preciousness of evangelical truth, which never fails to reach the heart. How much more frequent would be revivals of religion! or rather, how much would most of our congregations resemble that of the subject of this memoir, in which those who knew it best have told us there was a gentle, noiseless, but almost constant awakening! If such men presided over all our churches, what a hallowed impulse would be given to the missionary cause, and to all the Scriptural plans for diffusing the knowledge of salvation throughout the world! How easy would it be to do without public agents for stirring up the people to sustain the cause of Christian benevolence! The Pastor and the Eldership of every church would be a source of hallowed influence in regard to that great cause, adapted under God, to keep every church awake and alive to its claims. McCheyne, while he lived needed no body to come in and remind the people of his charge, that the church was bound to send the gospel to every creature; and that every individual member of the church was under obligation to take an active part in this work. The habitual preaching, the public and private prayers, and the daily example of this heavenly minded pastor were at once a constant memento of their duty, and a powerful stimulus to its performance.

While I lament that there is not more of this spirit reigning among the ministers and elders, and members of our beloved church, I consider the appearance and the popularity of such works as this memoir, as a pledge that the gracious King of Zion will revive us. Some of us who are old and grey headed, and have been permitted to preach the gospel for more than half a century, so far as the eye of man can discern, have been instrumental in winning much fewer souls, and have done far, far less for the honour of our blessed Master, than this youthful servant of Christ in a ministry of less than a fifth part of the same length. Surely the contemplation of such a portrait as that presented in this memoir, ought to fill us with humiliation and shame.

My hope is, that the great Head of the Church will speedily raise up a race of ministers more holy, more zealous, more wise, more diligent, and more entirely devoted to their work than their fathers have ever been.

Blessed day! when the watchmen on the walls of Zion "shall never hold their peace day nor night; when they that make mention of the Lord shall not keep silence, nor give Him any rest, until he establish and make Jerusalem a praise in the earth; until the righteousness thereof go forth as brightness, and the salvation therof as a lamp that burneth." Come, Lord Jesus, come quickly thus to bless thy church and people; even so, come, Lord Jesus!

With fervent prayers that we may all lay to heart our duty and our responsibility more deeply than we have ever yet done,

  I am, Rev. and Dear Brother,
    Your fellow servant
      In the Gospel of Christ,

          SAMUEL MILLER

PRINCETON, *September* 19, 1844

MEMOIR, &c.

CHAPTER I

Many shall rejoice at his birth; for he shall be great in the sight
of the Lord.—LUKE i. 14.

IN the midst of the restless activity of such a day as
ours, it will be felt by ministers of Christ to be useful,
in no common degree, to trace the steps of one who
but lately left us, and who, during the last years of
his short life, walked calmly in almost unbroken fellowship with the FATHER and the SON.

The date of his birth was May 21, 1813. About
that time, (it is now evident to us who can look back
on the past,) the Great Head had a purpose of blessing
for the Church of Scotland. Eminent men of God
appeared to plead the cause of Christ. The cross was
lifted up boldly in the midst of Church Courts which
had long been ashamed of the Gospel of Christ. More
spirituality and deeper seriousness began a few years
onward to prevail among the youth of our divinity
halls. In the midst of such events, whereby the Lord
was secretly preparing a rich blessing for souls in all
our borders, the subject of this memoir was born.
" Many were to rejoice at his birth;" for he was one
of the blessings which were beginning to be dropped
down upon Scotland, though none then knew that
one was born whom hundreds would look up to as
their spiritual father.

The place of his birth was Edinburgh, where his

(19)

parents resided. He was the youngest child of the family, and was called Robert Murray, after the name of some of his kindred.

From his infancy, his sweet and affectionate temper was remarked by all who knew him. His mind was quick in its attainments; he was easily taught the common lessons of youth, and some of his peculiar endowments began early to appear. At the age of four, while recovering from some illness, he selected as his recreation the study of the Greek alphabet, and was able to name all the letters, and write them in a rude way upon a slate. A year after, he made rapid progress in the English class, and at an early period became somewhat eminent among his school-fellows for his melodious voice and powers of recitation. There were at that time catechetical exercises held in the Tron Church, in the interval between sermons; and some friends remember the interest often excited in the hearers by his correct and sweet recitation of the Psalms and passages of Scripture. But as yet he knew not the Lord; he lived to himself, "having no hope, and without God in the world." (Eph. ii. 12.)

In October 1821, he entered the High School, where he continued his literary studies during the usual period of six years. He maintained a high place in his classes; and, in the Rector's class, distinguished himself by eminence in geography and recitation. It was during the last year of his attendance at the High School that he first ventured on poetical composition, the subject being, "Greece, but living Greece no more." The lines are characterized chiefly by enthusiasm for liberty and Grecian heroism, for in these days his soul had never soared to a higher region. His companions speak of him as one who had even then peculiarities that drew attention—of a light, tall form—full of elasticity and vigour—ambitious, yet noble in his dispositions, disdaining every thing like meanness or deceit. Some would have been apt to regard him as exhibiting many traits of a Christian character; but his susceptible mind had not, at that time, a relish for any higher joy than the refined gayeties of society, and for such pleasures as the song and the dance could yield. He himself regarded these as days of ungodliness—days wherein he cherished a pure morality, but lived in heart a Pharisee. I have heard him say that there was a correctness and propriety in his demeanour at times of devotion, and in public worship which some, who knew not his heart, were ready to put to the account of real feeling. And this experience of his own heart made him look with jealousy on the mere outward signs of devotion, in dealing with souls. He had learned in his own case how much a soul, unawakened to a sense of guilt, may have satisfaction in performing, from the proud consciousness of integrity toward man, and a sentimental devotedness of mind that chastens the feelings, without changing the heart.

He had great delight in rural scenery. Most of his summer vacations used to be spent in Dumfriesshire, and his friends in the parish of Ruthwell and its vicinity retain a vivid remembrance of his youthful days. His poetic temperament led him to visit whatever scenes were fitted to stir the soul. At all periods of his life, also, he had a love of enterprise. During the summer months he occasionally made excursions with his brother, or some intimate friend, to visit the lakes and hills of our Highlands, cherishing thereby, unawares, a fondness for travel, that was most useful to him in after days. In one of these excursions, a somewhat romantic occurrence befel the travellers, such as we might rather have expected to meet with in the records of his Eastern journey. He and his friend had set out on foot to explore, at their leisure, Dunkeld and the Highlands in its vicinity. They spent a day at Dunkeld, and about sunset set out again with the view of crossing the hills to Strathardle. A dense mist spread over the hills soon after they began to climb. They pressed on, but lost the track that might have guided them safely to the glen. They knew not how to direct their steps to any dwelling. Night came on, and they had no resource but to couch among the heath, with no other covering than the clothes they wore. They felt hungry and cold; and, awaking at midnight, the awful stillness of the lonely mountains spread a strange fear over them. But, drawing close together, they again lay down to rest, and slept soundly till the cry of some wild birds and the morning dawn aroused them.

Entering the Edinburgh University in November, 1827, he gained some prize in all the various classes he attended. In private he studied the modern languages; and gymnastic exercises at that time gave him unbounded delight. He used his pencil with much success, and then it was that his hand was prepared for sketching the scenes of the Holy Land. He had a very considerable knowledge of music, and himself sang correctly and beautifully. This, too, was a gift which was used to the glory of the Lord in after days—wonderfully enlivening his secret devotions, and enabling him to lead the song of praise in the congregation wherever occasion required. Poetry also was a never-failing recreation; and his taste in this department drew the attention of Professor Wilson, who adjudged him the prize in the Moral Philosophy class for a poem, " On the Covenanters."

In the autumn of 1831, he commenced his studies in the Divinity Hall, under Dr. Chalmers; and the study of Church History under Dr. Welsh. It may be naturally asked, What led him to wish to preach salvation to his fellow-sinners? Could he say, like Robert Bruce, " *I was first called to my grace, before I obeyed my calling to the ministry ?*" Few questions are more interesting than this; and our answer to it will open up some of the wonderful ways of Him " whose path is in the great waters, and whose footsteps are not known ;" (Psalm lxxvi. 19 :) for the same event that awakened his soul to a true sense of sin and misery, led him to the ministry.

There can be no doubt that the death of his eldest brother, David, was the event which awoke him from the sleep of nature, and brought in the first beam of divine light into his soul. By that providence the

Lord was calling one soul to enjoy the treasures of grace, while he took the other into the possession of glory.

In this brother, who was his senior by eight or nine years, the light of divine grace shone before men with rare and solemn loveliness. His classical attainments were very high; and, after the usual preliminary studies, he had been admitted Writer to the Signet. One distinguishing quality of his character was his sensitive truthfulness. In a moment would the shadow flit across his brow, if any incident were related wherein there was the slightest exaggeration; or even when nothing but truth was spoken, if only the deliverer seemed to take up a false or exaggerated view. He must not merely speak the whole truth himself, but he must have the hearer also to apprehend the whole truth. He spent much of his leisure hours in attending to the younger members of the family: tender and affectionate, his grieved look, (it is said,) when they vexed him by resisting his counsels, had something in it so persuasive that it never failed in the end to prevail on those with whom his words had not succeeded. His youngest brother, at a time when he lived according to the course of this world, was the subject of many of his fervent prayers. But a deep melancholy, in a great degree the effect of bodily ailments, settled down on David's soul. Many weary months did he spend in awful gloom, till the trouble of his soul wasted away his body; but the light broke in before his death; joy, from the face of a fully reconciled Father above, lighted up his face; and the peace of his last days was the sweet consolation left to his afflicted friends, when, July 8th, 1831, he fell asleep in Jesus.

The death of this brother, with all its circumstances, was used by the Holy Spirit to produce a deep impression on Robert's soul. In many respects—even in the gifts of a poetic mind—there had been a congeniality between him and David. The vivacity of Robert's ever active and lively mind, was the chief point of difference. This vivacity admirably fitted

him for public life; it needed only to be chastened
and solemnized, and the event that had now occurred
wrought this effect.   A few months before, the happy
family circle had been broken up by the departure of
the second brother for India, in the Bengal Medical
Service; but when, in the course of the summer,
David was removed from them for ever, there were
impressions left such as could never be effaced, at
least from the mind of Robert.   Naturally of an intensely affectionate disposition, this stroke moved his
whole soul.   His quiet hours seem to have been often
spent in thoughts of him who was now gone to glory.
There are some lines remaining in which his poetic
mind has most touchingly, and with uncommon vigour,
painted him whom he had lost—lines all the more interesting, because the delineation of character and
form which they contain, cannot fail to call up to
those who knew him, the image of the author himself.
Some time after his brother's death, he had tried to
preserve the features of his well-remembered form,
by attempting a portrait from memery; but, throwing
aside the pencil in despair, he took up the pen and
poured out the fulness of his heart.

ON PAINTING THE MINIATURE LIKENESS OF ONE DEPARTED

Alas! not perfect yet—another touch,
And still another, and another still,
Till those dull lips breathe life, and yonder eye
Lose its lack-lustre hue, and be lit up
With the warm glance of living feeling.   No—
It never can be!   Ah, poor, powerless art!
Most vaunting yet most impotent, thou seekst
To trace the thousand, thousand shades and lights
That glowed conspicuous on the blessed face
Of him thou fain wouldst imitate—to bind
Down to the fragile canvass the wild play
Of thought and mild affection, which were wont
To dwell in the serious eye, and play around
The placid mouth.   Thou seekst to give again
That which the burning soul, inhabiting
Its clay-built tenement, alone can give—
To leave on cold, dead matter the impress
Of living mind—to bid a line, a shade
Speak forth, not words, but the soft intercourse
Which the immortal spirit, while on earth

It tabernacles, breathes from every pore—
Thoughts not converted into words, and hopes,
And fears, and hidden joys, and griefs, unborn
Into the world of sound, but beaming forth
In that expression which no words, or work
Of cunning artist, can express.   In vain,
Alas! in vain!
     Come hither, Painter; come,
Take up once more thine instruments—thy brush
And palette—if thy haughty art be, as thou sayst,
Omnipotent, and if thy hand can dare
To wield creative power.   Renew thy toil,
And let my memory, vivified by love,
Which Death's cold separation has but warmed,
And rendered sacred, dictate to thy skill,
And guide thy pencil.   From the jetty hair
Take off that gaudy lustre that but mocks
The true original; and let the dry,
Soft, gently-turning locks, appear instead.
What though to fashion's garish eye they seem
Untutored and ungainly—still to me,
Than folly's foppish head-gear, lovelier far
Are they, because bespeaking mental toil,
Labour assiduous, through the golden days
(Golden if so improved) of guileless youth,
Unwearied mining in the precious stores
Of classic lore—and better, nobler still,
In God's own holy writ.   And scatter here
And there a thread of grey, to mark the grief
That prematurely checked the bounding flow
Of the warm current in his veins, and shed
An early twilight o'er so bright a dawn.
No wrinkle sits upon that brow!—and thus
It ever was.   The angry strife and cares
Of avaricious miser did not leave
Their base memorial on so fair a page.
The eye-brows next draw closer down, and throw
A softening shade o'er the mild orbs below.
Let the full eyelid, drooping, half conceal
The back-retiring eye; and point to earth
The long brown lashes that bespeak a soul
Like his who said, "I am not worthy, Lord!"
From underneath these lowly turning lids,
Let not shine forth the gaily sparkling light
Which dazzles oft and oft deceives—nor yet
The dull unmeaning lustre that can gaze
Alike on all the world.   But paint an eye
In whose half-hidden, steady light, I read
A truth-inquiring mind; a fancy, too,
That could array in sweet poetic garb
The truth he found; while on his artless harp
He touched the gentlest feelings, which the blaze

Of winter's hearth warms in the homely heart.
And O! recall the look of faith sincere,
With which that eye would scrutinize the page
That tells us of offended God appeased
By awful sacrifice upon the cross
Of Calvary—that bids us leave a world
Immersed in darkness and in death, and seek
A better country.   Ah! how oft that eye
Would turn on me, with pity's tenderest look,
And, only half-upbraiding, bid me flee
From the vain idols of my boyish heart!

It was about this same time, while still feeling the sadness of this bereavement, that he wrote the following fragment, entitled

THE RIGHTEOUS PERISHETH, AND NO MAN LAYETH IT TO HEART
Isaiah lvii. 1

A grave I know
Where earthly show
Is not—a mound
Whose gentle round
Sustains the load
Of a fresh sod.
Its shape is rude,
And weeds intrude
Their yellow flowers—
In gayer bowers
Unknown.   The grass
A tufted mass,
Is rank and strong—
Unsmoothed and long.
No rosebud there
Embalms the air;
No lily chaste
Adorns the waste,
Nor daisy's head
Bedecks the bed.
No myrtles wave
Above that grave;
No heather bell
Is there to tell
Of gentle friend
Who sought to lend
A sweeter sleep
To him who deep
Beneath the ground
Repose has found.
No stone of woe
Is there to show
The name, or tell
How passing well

He loved his God,
And how he trod
The humble road
That leads through sorrow
To a bright morrow.
Unknown in life,
And far from strife,
He lived;—and though
The magic flow
Of genius played
Around his head,
And he could weave
"The song at eve,"
And touch the heart,
With gentlest art;
Or cares beguile,
And draw the smile
Of peace from those
Who wept their woes;—
Yet when the love
Of Christ above
To guilty men
Was shown him—then
He left the joys
Of worldly noise,
And humbly laid
His drooping head
Upon the cross;
And thought the loss
Of all that earth
Contained—of mirth,
Of love, and fame,
And pleasure's name—
No sacrifice

To win the prize,
Which Christ secured,
When he endured
For us the load—
The wrath of God!
With many a tear,
And many a fear,
With many a sigh
And heart-wrung cry
Of timid faith,
He sought the Breath,
But which can give
The power to live—
Whose word alone
Can melt the stone,
Bid tumult cease,
And all be peace!
He sought not now
To wreathe his brow
With laurel bough.
He sought no more
To gather store
Of earthly lore,
Nor vainly strove
To share the love
Of heaven above,
With aught below
That earth can show.
The smile forsook
His cheek—his look
Was cold and sad;
And even the glad
Return of morn,
When the ripe corn
Waves o'er the plains,
And simple swains
With joy prepare
The toil to share
Of harvest, brought
No lively thought
To him.
*   *   *
And spring adorns
The sunny morns
With opening flowers;
And beauty showers
O'er lawn and mead;
Its virgin head
The snow-drop steeps
In dew, and peeps
The crocus forth,
Nor dreads the north—

But even the spring
No smile can bring
To him, whose eye
Sought in the sky
For brighter scenes,
Where intervenes
No darkening cloud
Of sin to shroud
The gazer's view.
Thus sadly flew
The merry spring;
And gaily sing
The birds their loves
In summer groves.
But not for him
Their notes they trim.
His ear is cold—
His tale is told.
Above his grave
The grass may wave—
*   *   *
The crowd pass by
Without a sigh
Above the spot.
They knew him not—
They could not know;
And even though,
Why should they shed
Above the dead
Who slumbers here
A single tear?
I cannot weep,
Though in my sleep
I sometimes clasp,
With love's fond grasp,
His gentle hand,
And see him stand
Beside my bed,
And lean his head
Upon my breast,
And bid me rest
Nor night nor day
Till I can say
That I have found
The holy ground
In which there lies
The Pearl of Price—
Till all the ties
The soul that bind,
And all the lies
The soul that blind,
Be   *   *   *

Nothing could more fully prove the deep impres
sion which the event made than these verses. But it
was not a transient regret, nor was it the "sorrow of
the world." He was in his eighteenth year when his
brother died: and if this was not the year of his new
birth, at least it was the year when the first streaks
of dawn appeared in his soul. From that day forward, his friends observed a change. His poetry was
pervaded with serious thought, and all his pursuits
began to be followed out in another spirit. He engaged in the labours of a Sabbath school, and began
to seek God to his soul, in the diligent reading of the
word, and attendance on a faithful ministry.

How important this period of his life appeared in
his own view, may be gathered from his allusions to
it in later days. A year after, he writes in his diary,
"On this morning last year came the first overwhelming blow to my wordliness; how blessed to me, thou,
O God, only knowest, who hast made it so." Every
year he marked this day as one to be remembered,
and occasionally its recollections seem to have come
in like a flood. In a letter to a friend (July 8th, 1842,)
upon a matter entirely local, he concludes by a post-
script—" This day eleven years ago, my holy brother
David entered into his rest, aged twenty-six." And
on that same day, writing a note to one of his flock
in Dundee, (who had asked him to furnish a preface
to a work printed 1740, "*Letters on Spiritual Subjects,*) he commends the book, and adds—"Pray for
me, that I may be made holier and wiser—less like
myself, and more like my heavenly Master; that I
may not regard my life, if so be I may finish my
course with joy. This day eleven years ago, I lost
my loved and loving brother, and began to seek a
Brother who cannot die."

It was to companions who could sympathize in his
feelings, that he unbosomed himself. At that period
it was not common for inquiring souls to carry their
case to their pastor. A conventional reserve upon
these subjects prevailed even among lively believers.
This he felt to be so great an evil, that, in after days

he was careful to encourage anxious souls to converse
with him freely. The nature of his experience, however, we have some means of knowing. On one
occasion, a few of us who had studied together were
reviewing the Lord's dealings with our souls, and
how he had brought us to himself, all very nearly at
the same time, though without any special instrumentality. He stated that there was nothing sudden in
his case, and that he was led to Christ through deep
and ever-abiding, but not awful or distracting convictions. In this we see the Lord's sovereignty. In
bringing a soul to the Saviour, the Holy Spirit invariably leads it to very deep consciousness of sin; but
then he causes this consciousness of sin to be more
distressing and intolerable to some than to others.
But in one point does the experience of all believing
sinners agree in this matter—viz. their soul presented
to their view nothing but an abyss of sin, when the
grace of God, that bringeth salvation, appeared.

The Holy Spirit carried on his work in the subject
of this memoir, by continuing to deepen in him the
conviction of his ungodliness, and the pollution of his
whole nature. And all his life long, he viewed his
original sin, not as an excuse for his actual sins, but
as an aggravation of them all. In this view he was
of the mind of David, taught by the unerring Spirit
of truth. (See Psalm li. 4, 5.)

At first the light dawned slowly; so slowly, that,
for a considerable time, he still relished an occasional
plunge into scenes of gayety. Even after entering the
Divinity Hall, he could be persuaded to indulge in
lighter pursuits, at least during the first two years of
his attendance; but it was with growing alarm. When
hurried away by such worldly joys, I find him writing
thus:—" *Sept.* 14.—May there be few such records
as this in my biography." Then, " *Dec.* 9.—A thorn
in my side—much torment." As the unholiness of
his pleasures became more apparent, he writes :—
" *March* 10th, 1832—I hope never to play cards
again." *March* 25th—" Never visit on a Sunday
evening again." *April* 10th—" Absented myself from

the dance; upbraidings ill to bear. But I must try to bear the cross." It seems to be in reference to the receding tide, which thus for a season repeatedly drew him back to the world, that on *July* 8th, 1836, he records—"This morning five years ago, my dear brother David died, and my heart for the first time knew true bereavement. Truly it was all well. Let me be dumb, for thou didst it; and it was good for me that I was afflicted. I know not that any providence was ever more abused by man than that was by me; and yet, Lord, what mountains thou comest over! none was ever more blessed to me." To us who can look at the results, it appears probable that the Lord permitted him thus to try many broken cisterns, and to taste the wormwood of many earthly streams, in order that in after days, by the side of the fountain of living waters, he might point to the world he had for ever left, and testify the surpassing preciousness of what he had now found.

Mr. Alexander Somerville (afterwards minister of Anderston Church, Glasgow,) was his familiar friend and companion in the gay scenes of his youth. And he, too, about this time, having been brought to taste the powers of the world to come, they united their efforts for each other's welfare. They met together for the study of the Bible, and used to exercise themselves in the Septuagint Greek and the Hebrew original. But oftener still, they met for prayer and solemn converse; and carrying on all their studies in the same spirit, watched each other's steps in the narrow way.

He thought himself much profited, at this period, by investigating the subject of Election, and the Free Grace of God. But it was the reading of " *The Sum of Saving Knowledge,*"* generally appended to our Confession of Faith, that brought him to a clear understanding of the way of acceptance with God. Those who are acquainted with its admirable statements of truth, will see how well fitted it was to direct an inquiring soul. I find him some years afterwards

---

* This has been published, in a small volume, by the Presbyterian Board of Publication.—Am. Ed.

recording :—*March* 11th, 1834.—Read in the ' Sum of
Saving Knowledge,' the work which I think first of
all wrought a saving change in me. How gladly
would I renew the reading of it, if that change might
be carried on to perfection." It will be observed that
he never reckoned his soul saved, notwithstanding all
his convictions and views of sin, until he really went
into the Holiest of all on the warrant of the Redeemer's work ; for assuredly a sinner is still under
wrath, until he has actually availed himself of the way
to the Father opened up by Jesus. All his knowledge
of his sinfulness, and all his sad feeling of his own
need and danger, cannot place him one step further
off from the lake of fire. It is " he that comes to
Christ" that is saved.

Before this period, he had received a bias towards
the ministry from his brother David, who used to
speak of the ministry as the most blessed work on
earth, and often expressed the greatest delight in the
hope that his younger brother might one day become
a minister of Christ. And now, with altered views—
with an eye that could gaze on heaven and hell, and
a heart that felt the love of a reconciled God, he
sought to become a herald of salvation.

He had begun to keep a register of his studies, and
the manner in which his time slipped away, some
months before his brother's death. For a considerable
time this register contains almost nothing but the
bare incidents of the diary, and on Sabbaths the texts
of the sermons he had heard. There is one gleam
of serious thought—but it is the only one—during
that period. On occasion of Dr. Andrew Thomson's
funeral, he records the deep and universal grief that
pervaded the town, and then subjoins—" Pleasing to
see so much public feeling excited on the decease of
so worthy a man. How much are the times changed
within these eighteen centuries, since the time when
Joseph besought *the body* in secret, and when he and
Nicodemus were the only ones found to bear the
body to the tomb."

It is in the end of the year that evidences of a

change appear. From that period, and ever onward his dry register of every-day incidents is varied with such passages as the following:

"*November* 12.—Reading H. Martyn's Memoirs Would I could imitate him, giving up father, mother, country, house, health, life, all for Christ. And yet, what hinders? Lord, purify me, and give me strength to dedicate myself, my all, to thee!'"

"*December* 4.—Reading Legh Richmond's Life. Pœnitentia profunda, non sine lacrymis. Nunquam me ipsum, tam vilem, tam inutilem, tam pauperem, et præcipue tam ingratum, adhuc vidi. Sint lacrymæ dedicationis meæ pignora!' ["Deep penitence, not unmixed with tears. I never before saw myself so vile, so useless, so poor, and, above all, so ungrateful. May these tears be the pledges of my self-dedication."] There is frequently at this period a sentence in Latin occurring like the above, in the midst of other matter, apparently with the view of giving freer expression to his feelings, regarding himself.

"*Dec.* 9.—Heard a street preacher: foreign voice. Seems really in earnest. He quoted the striking passage, ' The Spirit and the bride say, Come, *and let him that heareth say, Come.*' From this he seems to derive his authority. Let me learn from this man to be in earnest for the truth, and to despise the scoffing of the world."

"*Dec.* 18.—After spending an evening too lightly, he writes—" My heart must break off from all these things. What right have I to steal and abuse my Master's time? ' Redeem it,' he is crying to me."

"*Dec.* 25.—My mind not yet calmly fixed on the Rock of Ages."

"*January* 12, 1832.—Cor non pacem habet.— Quare? Peccatum apud fores manet." [" My heart has not peace. Why? Sin lieth at my door."]

"*Jan.* 25.—A lovely day. Eighty-four cases of cholera at Musselburgh. How it creeps nearer and nearer, like a snake. Who will be the first victim here? Let thine everlasting arms be around us, and we shall be safe."

"*Jan.* 29. Sabbath—Afternoon, heard Mr. Bruce, (then minister of the New North Church, Edinburgh) on Malachi i. 1—6. It constitutes the very gravamen of the charge against the unrenewed man, that he has affection for his earthly parent, and reverence for his earthly master; but none for God! Most noble discourse."

"*February* 2.—Not a trait worth remembering! And yet these four-and-twenty hours must be accounted for."

Feb. 5. Sabbath.—In the afternoon, having heard the late Mr. Martin, of St. George's,* he writes, on returning home—"O quàm humilem, sed quàm diligentissimum; quàm dejectum, sed quàm vigilem, quàm die noctuque precantem, decet me esse quum tales viros aspicio. Juva, Pater, Fili, et Spiritus!" ["O how humble yet how diligent, how lowly yet how watchful, how prayerful night and day it becomes me to be, when I see such men. Help, Father, Son, and Spirit!"]

From this date he seems to have sat, along with his friend Mr. Somerville, almost entirely under Mr. Bruce's ministry. He took copious notes of his lectures and sermons, which still remain among his papers.

"*Feb.* 28.—Sober conversation. Fain would I turn to the most interesting of all subjects. Cowardly backwardness: 'For whosoever is ashamed of me and my words,'" &c.

At this time, hearing, concerning a friend of the family, that she had said, "*that she was determined to keep by the world,*" he penned the following lines on her melancholy decision:

She has chosen the world,
    And its paltry crowd,—
She has chosen the world,
    And an endless shroud!

She has chosen the world,
    With its misnamed pleasures:
She has chosen the world,
    Before heaven's own treasures.

* He says of him on another occasion, June 8, 1834—"A man greatly beloved, of whom the world was not worthy." "An apostolic man." His own calm, deep holiness, resembled in many respects Mr. Martin's daily walk.

She hath launched her boat
  On life's giddy sea,
And her all is afloat
  For eternity.
But Bethlehem's star
  Is not in her view;
And her aim is far
  From the harbour true.

When the storm descends
  From an angry sky,
Ah! where from the winds
  Shall the vessel fly?
When the stars are concealed,
  And the rudder gone,
And heaven is sealed
  To the wandering one!

The whirlpool opes
  For the gallant prize;
And, with all her hopes,
  To the deep she hies!

But who may tell
  Of the place of woe,
Where the wicked dwell—
  Where the worldlings go?

For the human heart
  Can ne'er conceive
What joys are the part
  Of them who believe;
Nor can justly think
  Of the cup of death
Which all must drink
  Who despise the faith.

Away, then—O! fly
  From the joys of earth!
Her smile is a lie—
  There's a sting in her mirth.
Come, leave the dreams
  Of this transient night,
And bask in the beams
  Of an endless light.

"*March* 6.—Wild wind and rain all day long. Hebrew class—Psalms. New beauty in the original every time I read. Dr. Welsh—lecture on Pliny's letter about the Christians of Bithynia. Professor Jameson on quartz. Dr. Chalmers grappling with Hume's arguments. Evening—Notes and little else. Mind and body dull." This is a specimen of his register of daily study.

March 20.—After a few sentences in Latin, concluding with, "In meam animam veni, Domine Deus omnipotens," he writes, "Leaning on a staff of my own devising, it betrayed me, and broke under me. It was not thy staff. Resolving to be a god, thou showedst me that I was but a man. But my own staff being broken, why may I not lay hold of thine? —Read part of the life of Jonathan Edwards. How feeble does my spark of Christianity appear beside such a sun! But even his was a borrowed light, and the same source is still open to enlighten me."

"*April* 8.—Have found much rest in Him who bore all our burdens for us."

"*April* 26.—To-night I ventured to break the ice

of unchristian silence. Why should not selfishness be buried beneath the Atlantic in matters so sacred ?"

May 6.—Saturday evening.—This was the evening previous to the Communion, and in prospect of again declaring himself the Lord's, at his table, he enters into a brief review of his state. He had partaken of the ordinance in May of the year before for the first time ; but he was then living at ease, and saw not the solemn nature of the step he took. He now sits down and reviews the past :

" What a mass of corruption have I been ! How great a portion of my life have I spent wholly without God in the world ; given up to sense and the perishing things around me. Naturally of a feeling and sentimental disposition, how much of my religion has been, and to this day is, tinged with these colours of earth ! Restrained from open vice by educational views and the fear of man, how much ungodliness has reigned within me ! How often has it broken through all restraints, and come out in the shape of lusts and anger, mad ambition, and unhallowed words ! Though my vice was always refined, yet how subtile and how awfully prevalent it was ! How complete a test was the Sabbath—spent in weariness, as much of it as was given to God's service ! How I polluted it by my hypocrisies, my self-conceits, my worldly thoughts, and worldly friends ! How formally and unheedingly the Bible was read—how little was read— so little that even now I have not read it all ! How unboundedly was the wild impulse of the heart obeyed ! How much more was the creature loved than the Creator !——O great God, that didst suffer me to live whilst I so dishonoured thee, thou knowest the vhole, and it was thy hand alone that could awaken me from the death in which I was, and was contented to be. Gladly would I have escaped from the Shepherd that sought me as I strayed ; but he took me up in his arms and carried me back ; and yet he took me not for any thing that was in me. I was no more fit for his service than the Australian, and no more worthy to be called and chosen. Yet, why should I doubt? not God's unwillingness, not his ability—of both I am assured. But, perhaps, my old sins are too fearful, and my unbelief too glaring. Nay; I come to Christ not *although* I am a sinner, but just *because* I am a sinner, even the chief." He then adds, "And though sentiment and constitutional enthusiasm may have a great effect on me, still I believe that my soul is in sincerity desirous and earnest about having all its concerns at rest with God and Christ—that his kingdom occupies the most part of all my thoughts, and even of my long-polluted affections. Not unto me, not unto me, be the shadow of praise or of merit ascribed, but let all glory be given to thy most holy name! As surely as thou didst make the mouth with which I pray, so surely dost thou prompt every prayer of faith which I utter. Thou hast made me all that I am, and given me all that I have."

Next day, after communicating, he writes: "I well remember when I was an enemy, and especially abhorred this ordinance as binding me down; but if I be bound to Christ in heart, I shall not dread any band that can draw me close to him." Evening.—"Much peace. Look back, my soul, and view the mind that belonged to thee but twelve months ago—My soul, thy place is in the dust!

" *May* 19.—Thought with more comfort than usual of being a witness for Jesus in a foreign land."

"*June* 4.—Walking with A. Somerville by Craigleith. Conversing on missions. If I am to go to the heathen to speak of the unsearchable riches of Christ, this one thing must be given me, to be out of the reach of the baneful influence of esteem or contempt. If worldly motives go with me, I shall never convert a soul, and shall lose my own in the labour."

"*June* 22.—Variety of studies. Septuagint translation of Exodus, and Vulgate. Bought Edwards' works. Drawing.—Truly there was nothing in me that should have induced God to choose me. I was but as the other brands upon whom the fire is already kindled, which shall burn for evermore! And as soon could the billet leap from the hearth and become a green tree, as my soul could have sprung to newness of life."

June 25.—In reference to the office of the holy ministry: "How apt are we to lose our hours in the vainest babblings, as do the world! How can this be with those chosen for the mighty office, fellow-workers with God, heralds of his Son, evangelists, men set apart to the work, chosen out of the chosen, as it were the very pick of the flocks, who are to shine as the stars for ever and ever? Alas, alas! my soul, where shalt thou appear? O Lord God, I am a little child! But thou wilt send an angel with a live coal from off the altar, and touch my unclean lips, and put a tongue within my dry mouth, so that I shall say with Isaiah, 'Here am I; send me.'" Then, after reading a little of Edwards' works, "O that heart and understanding may grow together, like brother and sister, leaning on one another."

"*June 27.*—Life of David Brainerd. Most wonderful man! What conflicts, what depressions, desertions, strength, advancement, victories, within thy torn bosom! I cannot express what I feel when I think of thee. To-night, more set upon missionary enterprise than ever.

"*June 28.*—O for Brainerd's humility and sin-loathing dispositions!"

"*June 30.*—Much carelessness, sin and sorrow. O wretched man that I am, who shall deliver me from this body of sin and death? Enter thou, my soul, into the rock, and hide thee in the dust for fear of the Lord and the glory of his majesty." And then he writes a few verses, of which the following are some stanzas:

> "I will arise and seek my God,
>   And bowed down beneath my load,
>   Lay all my sins before him;
>   Then he will wash my soul from sin,
>   And put a new heart me within,
>   And teach me to adore him.

"O ye that fain would find the joy—
The only one that wants alloy—
    Which never is deceiving;
Come to the Well of Life with me,
And drink, as it is proffered, free,
    The gospel draught receiving.

"I come to Christ, because I know
The very worst are called to go:
    And when in faith I find him,
I'll walk in him, and lean on him,
Because I cannot move a limb
    Until he say, 'Unbind him.'"

"*July* 3.—This last bitter root of wordliness that has so often betrayed me has this night so grossly, that I cannot but regard it as God's chosen way to make me loathe and forsake it for ever. I would vow; but it is much more like a weakly worm to pray. Sit in the dust, O my soul!" I believe he was enabled to keep his resolution. Once only, in the end of this year, was he again led back to gayety; but it was the last time.

"*July* 7.—Saturday.— After finishing my usual studies, tried to fast a little, with much prayer and earnest seeking of God's face, remembering what occurred this night last year."

"*July* 22.—Had this evening a more complete understanding of that self-emptying and abasement with which it is necessary to come to Christ—a denying of self, trampling it under foot—a recognizing of the complete righteousness and justice of God, that could do nothing else with us but condemn us utterly, and thrust us down to the lowest hell,—a feeling that, even in hell, we *should* rejoice in his sovereignty and say that all was rightly done."

"*August* 15.—Little done, and as little suffered. Awfully important question—Am I redeeming the time?"

"*Aug.* 18.—Heard of the death of James Somerville,* by fever, induced by cholera. O God, thy

---

* Son of the minister of Drummelzier—very promising and very amiable.

ways and thoughts are not as ours ! He had preached his first sermon. I saw him last on Friday, 27th July, at the College gate ; shook hands ; and little thought I was to see him no more on earth."

"*September* 2.—Sabbath evening.—Reading. Too much engrossed, and too little devotional. Preparation for a fall. Warning. We may be too engrossed with the shell even of heavenly things."

"*Sept.* 9.—O ! for true, unfeigned humility ! I know I have cause to be humble ; and yet I do not know one half of that cause. I know I am proud ; and yet I do not know the half of that pride."

"*Sept.* 30.—Somewhat straitened by loose Sabbath observance. Best way is to be explicit and manly."

"*November* 1.—More abundant longings for the work of the ministry. O that Christ would but count me faithful, that a dispensation of the Gospel might be committed to me !" And then he adds, " Much peace. *Peaceful because believing.*"

December 2.—Hitherto he used to spend much of the Sabbath evening in extending his notes of Mr. Bruce's sermons ; but now, " Determined to be brief with these for the sake of a more practical, meditative, resting, sabbatical evening."

"*Dec.* 11.—Mind quite unfitted for devotion. Prayerless prayer."

"*Dec.* 31.—God has in this past year introduced me to the preparation of the ministry—I bless him for that. He has helped me to give up much of my shame to name his name, and be on his side, especially before particular friends—I bless him for that. He has taken conclusively away friends that might have been a snare—must have been a stumbling-block—I bless him for that. He has introduced me to one Christian friend, and sealed more and more my amity with another—I bless him for that."

January 23, 1833.—On this day it had been the custom of his brother David to write a " Carmen Natale " on their Father's birth-day. Robert took up the domestic song this year ; and, in doing so, makes some beautiful and tender allusions.

"Ah! where is the harp that was strung to thy praise,
So oft and so sweetly in happier days?
When the tears that we shed were the tears of our joy,
And the pleasures of home were unmixed with alloy?

* * * * * *

Though he sparkled the gem in our circle of love,
He is even more prized in the circles above.
And though sweetly he sung of his father on earth,
When this day would inspire him with tenderest mirth,
Yet a holier tone to his harp is now given,
As he sings to his unborn Father in heaven.

February 3.—Writing to a medical friend of his brother William's, he says—"I remember long ago a remark you once made to William, which has somehow or other stuck in my head, viz., that medical men ought to make a distinct study of the Bible, purely for the sake of administering conviction and consolation to their patients. I think you also said that you had actually begun with that view. Such a determination, though formed in youth, is one which I trust riper years will not make you blush to own."

" *Feb.* 11.—Somewhat overcome. Let me see: there is a creeping defect here. Humble, purpose-like reading of the word omitted. What plant can be unwatered and not wither?"

" *Feb.* 16.—Walk to Corstorphine Hill. Exquisite clear view—blue water, and brown fields, and green firs. Many thoughts on the follies of my youth. How many, O Lord, may they be? Summed up in one—ungodliness!"

" *Feb.* 21.—Am I as willing as ever to preach to the lost heathen?"

" *March* 8.—Biblical criticism. This must not supersede heart-work. How apt it is!"

" *March* 12.—O for activity, activity, activity!"

" *March* 29.—To-day my second session (at the Divinity Hall) ends. I am now in the middle of my career. God hold me on with a steady pace!"

" *March* 31.—The bull tosses in the net! How should the Christian imitate the anxieties of the worldling?"

April 17.—He heard of the death of one whom many friends had esteemed much and lamented deeply.

This led him to touch the strings of his harp again, in a measure somewhat irregular, yet sad and sweet.

" WE ALL DO FADE AS A LEAF."

SHE LIVED—

> So dying-like and frail,
> That every bitter gale
> Of winter seemed to blow
> Only to lay her low!
> She lived to show how He
> Who stills the stormy sea,
> Can overrule the winter's power,
> And keep alive the tiniest flower—
> Can bear the young lamb in his arms,
> And shelter it from death's alarms.

SHE DIED—

> When spring with brightest flowers,
> Was freshening all the bowers.
> The linnet sung her choicest lay,
> When her sweet voice was hushed for aye!
> The snow drop rose above the ground
> When she beneath her pillow found,
> Both cold, and white, and fair—
> The fairest of the fair!
> She died to teach us all
> The loveliest must fall.
> A curse is written on the brow
> Of beauty :—and the lover's vow
> Cannot retain the flitting breath,
> Nor save from all devouring death.

SHE LIVES—

> The spirit left the earth ;
> And He who gave her birth
> Has called her to his dread abode,
> To meet her Saviour and her God.
> She lives, to tell how blest
> Is the everlasting rest
> Of those who, in the Lamb's blood laved,
> Are chosen, sanctified, and saved !
> How fearful is their doom
> Who drop into the tomb
> Without a covert from the ire
> Of Him who is consuming fire.

SHE SHALL LIVE—

> The grave shall yield his prize,
> When, from the rending skies,
> Christ shall with shouting angels come,
> To wake the slumbers of the tomb.

And many more shall rise
Before our longing eyes.
    Oh ! may we all together meet,
    Embracing the Redeemer's feet !

" *May* 20.—General Assembly. The motion regarding Chapels of Ease lost, by 106 to 103. Every shock of the ram is heavier and stronger, till all shall give way."

" *June* 4.—Evening almost lost. Music will not sanctify, though it make feminine the heart."

" *June* 22.—Omissions made way for commissions. Could I but take effective warning ! A world's wealth would not make up for that saying, ' If any man sin, we have an Advocate with the Father.' But how shall we that are dead to sin live any longer therein ?"

" *June* 30.—Self-examination. Why is a missionary life so often an object of my thoughts ? Is it simply for the love I bear to souls ? Then, why do I not show it more where I am ? Souls are as precious here as in Burmah. Does the romance of the business not weigh any thing with me—the interest and esteem I would carry with me—the nice journals and letters I should write and receive ? Why would I so much rather go to the East than to the West Indies ? Am I wholly deceiving my own heart ? and have I not a spark of true missionary zeal ? Lord, give me to understand and imitate the spirit of those unearthly words of thy dear Son, ' It is enough for the disciple that he be as his Master, and the servant as his Lord.' ' He that loveth father or mother more than me, is not worthy of me.' *Gloria in excelsis Deo.*"

" *August* 13.—Clear conviction of sin is the only true origin of dependence on another's righteousness, and therefore, (strange to say !) of the Christian's peace of mind and cheerfulness."

" *Sept.* 8.—Reading Adam's Private Thoughts. O for his heart-searching humility ! Ah, me ! on what mountains of pride must I be wandering, when all I do is tinctured with the very sins this man so deplores ;

yet where are my wailings, where my tears, over my love of praise?"

"*November* 14.—Composition—a pleasant kind of labour. I fear the love of applause or effect, goes a great way. May God keep me from preaching myself, instead of Christ crucified."

"*January* 15, 1834.—Heard of the death of J. S., off the Cape of Good Hope. O God! how thou breakest into families! Must not the disease be dangerous, when a tender-hearted surgeon cuts deep into the flesh? How much more when God is the operator, 'who afflicteth not *from his heart*, מלבו nor grieveth the children of men.' Lam. iii. 33."

"*February* 23.—Sabbath.—Rose early to seek God, and found him whom my soul loveth. Who would not rise early to meet such company? The rains are over and gone. They that sow in tears shall reap in joy."

Feb. 25.—He writes a letter to one who, he feared, was only sentimental, and not really under a sense of sin. "Is it possible, think you, for a person to be conceited of his miseries? May there not be a deep leaven of pride in telling how desolate and how unfeeling we are—in brooding over our unearthly pains—in our being excluded from the unsympathetic world—in our being the invalids of Christ's hospital?" He had himself been taught by the Spirit that it is more humbling to *take what grace offers*, than to bewail our wants and worthlessness.

Two days after, he records, with thankful astonishment, that for the first time in his life he had been blest to awaken a soul. All who find Christ for themselves are impelled, by the holy necessity of constraining love, to seek the salvation of others. Andrew findeth his brother Peter, and Philip findeth his friend Nathanael. So was it in the case before us. He no sooner knew Christ's righteousness as his own covering, than he longed to see others clothed in the same spotless robe. And it is peculiarly interesting to read the feelings of one who was yet to be blest in plucking so many brands from the fire, when for the first time he saw the Lord graciously employing him in this more than angelic work. We have his own testimony :—" *Feb.* 25. After sermon. The precious tidings that a soul has been melted down by the grace of the Saviour. How blessed an answer to prayer, if it be really so! 'Can these dry bones live? Lord, thou knowest.' What a blessed thing it is to see the first grievings of the awakened spirit, when it cries, ' I cannot see myself a sinner; I cannot pray, for my vile heart wanders.' It has refreshed me more than a thousand sermons. I know not how to thank and admire God sufficiently for this incipient work. Lord, perfect that which thou hast begun!" A few days after.—" Lord, I thank thee that thou hast shown me this marvellous working, though I was but an adoring spectator, rather than an instrument."

It is scarcely less interesting, in the case of one so gifted for the work of visiting the careless, and so singularly skilled in ministering the word by the bed side of the dying, to find a record of the occasion when the Lord led him forth to take his first survey of this field of labour. There existed at that time, among some of the students attending the Divinity Hall, a society, the sole object of which was to stir up each other to set apart an hour or two every week for visiting the careless and needy in the most neglected portions of the town. Our rule was, not to subtract any thing from our hours of study, but to devote to this work an occasional hour in the intervals between different classes, or an hour that might otherwise have been given to recreation. All of us felt the work to be trying to the flesh at the outset; but none ever repented of persevering in it. One Saturday forenoon, at the close of the usual prayer meeting, which met in Dr. Chalmers's vestry, we went up together to a district in the Castle Hill. It was Robert's first near view of the heathenism of his native city, and the effect was enduring.

" *March* 3.—Accompanied A. B. in one of his rounds through some of the most miserable habitations I ever beheld. Such scenes I never before dreamed of. Ah, why am I such a stranger to the poor in my native town? I have passed their doors thousands of times; I have admired the huge black piles of building, with their lofty chimneys breaking the sun's rays—why have I never ventured within? How dwelleth the love of God in me? How cordial is the welcome even of the poorest and most loathsome to the voice of Christian sympathy! What imbedded masses of human beings are huddled together, unvisited by friend or minister! 'No man careth for our souls,' is written over every forehead. Awake, my soul! Why should I give hours and days any longer to the vain world, when there is such a world of misery at my very door? Lord, put thine own strength in me; confirm every good resolution; forgive my past long life of uselessness and folly."

He forthwith became one of the society's most steady members, cultivating a district in the Canongate, and distributing the Monthly Visitor, along with Mr. Somerville. His experience there was fitted to give him insight into the sinner's depravity, in all its forms. His first visit in his district is thus noticed— "March 24. Visited two families with tolerable success. God grant a blessing may go with us! Began in fear and weakness, and in much trembling. May the power be of God." Soon after, he narrates the following scene:—"Entered the house of——. Heard her swearing as I came up the stair. Found her storming at three little grandchildren, whom her daughter had left with her. She is a seared, hard-hearted wretch. Read Ezekiel xxxiii. Interrupted by the entrance of her second daughter, furiously demanding her marriage-lines. Became more discreet. Promised to come back—never came. Her father-in-law entered, a hideous spectacle of an aged drunkard, demanding money. Left the house with warnings." Another case he particularly mentions of a sick woman, who, though careless before, suddenly seemed to float into a sea of joy, without being able to give any Scriptural account of the change. She continued, I believe, to her death in this state, but he feared it was a subtle delusion of satan, as an angel of light. One soul, however, was, to all appearances, brought truly to the Rock of Ages, during his and his friend's prayerful visitations. These were first-fruits.

He continues his diary, though often considerable intervals occur in the register of his spiritual state.

" *May* 9.—How kindly has God thwarted me in every instance where I sought to enslave myself. I will learn at least to glory in disappointments."

" *May* 10.—At the communion. Felt less use for the minister than ever. Let the Master of the feast alone speak to my heart." He felt at such times, as many of the Lord's people have always done, that it is not the addresses of the ministers in serving the table, but *the Supper itself*, that ought to "satiate their souls with fatness."

May 21.—It is affecting to us to read the following entry :—" This day I attained my twenty-first year. O how long and how worthlessly I have lived, Thou only knowest! *Neff* died in his thirty-first year; when shall I ?"*

May 29.—He this day wrote very faithfully, yet very kindly, to one who seemed to him not a believer, and who, nevertheless, appropriated to herself the *promises* of God. " If you are wholly unassured of your being a believer, is it not a contradiction in terms to say, that you are sure the believer's promises belong to you? Are you *an assured believer ?* If so, rejoice in your heirship ; and yet rejoice with trembling ; for that is the very character of God's heirs. But are you *unassured*—nay, *wholly unassured ?* then what mad presumption to say to your soul, that these promises,

---

* It is worthy of notice, how often the Lord has done much work by a few years of holy labour. In our church, G. Gillespie and J. Durham, died at thirty-six; Hugh Binning, at twenty-six ; Andrew Gray when scarcely at twenty-two. Of our witnesses, Patrick Hamilton was cut off at twenty-four, and Hugh McKail, at twenty-six. In other churches we might mention many, such as John Janeway at twenty-three, David Brainerd at thirty, and Henry Martyn at thirty-two. Theirs was a short life, filled up with usefulness, and crowned with glory. O to be as they !

being in the Bible, must belong indiscriminately to all? It is too gross a contradiction for you to compass, except in word." He then shows that *Christ's free offer* must be accepted by the sinner, and so the *promises* become his. "The sinner complies with the call or offer, 'Come unto me;' and thereafter, but not before, can claim the annexed *promise* as his,—' I will give thee rest.'"

"*August* 14.—Partial fast, and seeking God's face by prayer. This day thirty years my late dear brother was born. O for more love, and then will come more peace." That same evening he wrote the hymn, "*The Barren Fig-Tree.*"

"*October* 17.—Private meditation exchanged for conversation. Here is the root of the evil—forsake God, and he forsakes us."

Some evening this month he had been reading "Baxter's Call to the Unconverted." Deeply impressed with the affectionate and awfully solemn inquiry of the man of God, he wrote,—

> "Though Baxter's lips have long in silence hung,
> And death long hushed that sinner-wakening tongue ;
> Yet still, though dead, he speaks aloud to all,
> And from the grave still issues forth his "Call."
> Like some loud angel-voice from Zion Hill,
> The mighty echo rolls and rumbles still.
> O grant that we, when sleeping in the dust,
> May thus speak forth the wisdom of the just."

Mr. McCheyne was peculiarly subject to attacks of fever, and by one of these he was laid down on a sick bed, on November 15th. However, this attack was of short duration. On the 21st he writes—" Bless the Lord, O my soul, and forget not all his benefits. Learned more and more of the value of *Jehovah Tzidkenu.*" He had, three days before, written his well-known hymn, "*I once was a stranger,*" &c., entitled "Jehovah Tzidkenu, the Watchword of the Reformers." It was the fruit of a slight illness which had tried his soul, by setting it more immediately in view of the judgment seat of Christ; and the hymn he so sweetly sung, reveals the sure and solid confidence of his soul. In reference to that same illness he seems to have penned the following lines, *November* 24:—

He tenderly binds up the broken in heart,
  The soul bowed down he will raise;
For mourning the ointment of joy will impart,
  For heaviness, garments of praise.

Ah come, then, and sing to the praise of our God,
  Who giveth and taketh away;
Who first by his kindness, and then by his rod,
  Would teach us, poor sinners, to pray.

For in the assembly of Jesus' first-born,
  Who anthems of gratitude raise;
Each heart has by great tribulation been torn,
  Each voice turned from wailing to praise.

" *November* 9.—Heard of Edward Irving's death I look back upon him with awe, as on the saints and martyrs of old. A holy man in spite of all his delusions and errors. He is now with his God and Saviour, whom he wronged so much, yet, I am persuaded, loved so sincerely. How should we lean for wisdom, not on ourselves, but on the God of all grace."

" *Nov.* 21.—If nothing else will do to sever me from my sins, Lord, send me such sore and trying calamities as shall awake me from earthly slumbers. It must always be best to be alive to thee, whatever be the quickening instrument. I tremble as I write, for oh! on every hand do I see too likely occasions for sore afflictions."

" *February* 15, 1835.—To-morrow I undergo my trials before the Presbytery. May God give me courage in the hour of need. What should I fear? If God see meet to put me into the ministry, who shall keep me back? If I be not meet, why should I be thrust forward? To thy service I desire to dedicate myself over and over again."

" *March* 1.—Bodily service. What change is there in the heart! Wild, earthy affections there are here; strong, coarse passions; bands both of iron and silk. But I thank thee, O my God, that they make me cry,

'O wretched man!' Bodily weakness, too, depresses me."

" *March* 29.—College finished on Friday last. My last appearance there. Life itself is vanishing fast. Make haste for eternity."

In such records as these, we read God's dealings with his soul up to the time when he was licensed to preach the gospel. His preparatory discipline, both of heart and intellect, had been directed by the great Head of the Church in a way that remarkably qualified him for the work he was to perform in the vineyard.

His soul was prepared for the awful work of the ministry by much prayer, and much study of the word of God ; by affliction in his person ; by inward trials and sore temptations ; by experience of the depth of corruption in his own heart; and by discoveries of the Saviour's fulness of grace. He learnt experimentally to ask—" Who is he that overcometh the world, but he that believeth that Jesus is the Son of God ?" (1 John v. 5.) During the four years that followed his awakening, he was oftentimes under the many waters, but was ever raised again by the same divine hand that had drawn him out at the first ; till at length, though still often violently tossed, the vessel was able steadily to keep the summit of the wave. It appears that he learned the way of salvation experimentally, ere he knew it accurately by theory and system ; and thus no doubt it was that his whole ministry was little else than a giving out of his own inward life.

The Visiting Society noticed above was much blessed to the culture of his soul, and not less so the Missionary Association and the Prayer Meeting connected with it. None were more regular at the hour of prayer than he, and none more frequently led up our praises to the throne. He was for some time Secretary to the association, and interested himself deeply in details of missionary labours. Indeed, to the last day of his life, his thoughts often turned to foreign lands ; and one of the last notes he wrote was to the

secretary of the association in Edinburgh, expressing
his unabated interest in their prosperity.

During the first years of his college course, his
studies did not absorb his whole attention; but no
sooner was the change on his soul begun, than his
studies shared in the results. A deeper sense of
responsibility led him to occupy his talents for the
service of Him who bestowed them. There have been
few who, along with a devotedness of spirit that
sought to be ever directly engaged in the Lord's work,
have nevertheless retained such continued and unde-
caying esteem for the advantages of study. While
attending the usual literary and philosophical classes,
he found time to turn his attention to Geology and
Natural History. And often in his days of most successful preaching, when, next to his own soul, his
parish and his flock were his only care, he has been
known to express a regret that he had not laid up in
former days more stores of all useful knowledge ; for
he found himself able to use the jewels of the Egyptians in the service of Christ. His previous studies
would sometimes flash into his mind some happy illustration of Divine truth, at the very moment when he
was most solemnly applying the glorious gospel to the
most ignorant and vile.

His own words will best show his estimate of study,
and at the same time the prayerful manner in which
he felt it should be carried on. " Do get on with your
studies," he wrote to a young student in 1840. " Remember you are now forming the character of your
future ministry in great measure, if God spare you.
If you acquire slovenly or sleepy habits of study now,
you will never get the better of it. Do every thing
in its own time. Do every thing in earnest—if it is
worth doing, then do it with all your might. Above
all, keep much in the presence of God. Never see
the face of man till you have seen his face who is our
Life, our All. Pray for others: pray for your teachers,
fellow students," &c. To another he wrote—" Beware
of the atmosphere of the classics. It is pernicious
indeed ; and you need much of the south wind breath-

ing over the Scriptures to counteract it. True, we ought to know them; but only as chemists handle poisons—to discover their qualities, not to infect their blood with them." And again—" Pray that the Holy Spirit would not only make you a believing and holy lad, but make you wise in your studies also.—A ray of Divine light in the soul sometimes clears up a mathematical problem wonderfully. The smile of God calms the spirit, and the left hand of Jesus holds up the fainting head, and his Holy Spirit quickens the affection; so that even natural studies go on a million times more easily and comfortably."

Before entering the Divinity Hall, he had attended a private class for the study of Hebrew; and having afterwards attended the two sessions of Dr. Brunton's College Class, he made much progress in that language. He could consult the Hebrew original of the Old Testament with as much ease as most of our ministers are able to consult the Greek of the New.

It was about the time of his first year's attendance at the Hall that I began to know him as an intimate friend. During the summer vacations—that we might redeem the time—some of us who remained in town, when most of our fellow-students were gone to the country, used to meet once every week in the forenoon, for the purpose of investigating some point of *Systematic Divinity*, and stating to each other the amount and result of our private reading. At another time, we met in a similar way, till we had overtaken the chief points of the *Popish controversy*. Advancement in our acquaintance with the Greek and Hebrew Scriptures also brought us together; and one summer the study of *Unfulfilled Prophecy* assembled a few of us once a week, at an early morning hour, when, though our views differed much on particular points, we never failed to get food to our souls in the Scriptures we explored. But no society of this kind was more useful and pleasant to us than one which, from its object, received the name of *Exegetical*. It met during the session of the theological classes every Saturday morning at half past six. The study of

Biblical criticism, and whatever might cast light on the word of God, was our aim; and these meetings were kept up regularly during four sessions. Mr. McCheyne spoke of himself as indebted to this society for much of that discipline of mind on Jewish literature and Scripture geography, which was to be so useful in the mission of inquiry to the Jews in after days.*

But these helps in study were all the while no more than supplementary. The regular systematic studies of the Hall furnished the main provision for his mental culture. Under Dr. Chalmers for Divinity, and under Dr. Welsh for Church History, a course of four years afforded no ordinary advantages for en-

---

* The members of this Society were—Rev. *William Laughton*, now minister of St. Thomas's, Greenock, in connection with the Free Church; *Thomas Brown*, Free Church, Kinneff; *William Wilson*, Free Church, Carmylie; *Horatius Bonar*, Free Church, Kelso; *Andrew A. Bonar*, Free Church, Collace; *Robert M. McCheyne*; *Alexander Somerville*, Free Church, Anderston, Glasgow; *John Thomson*, Mariners' Free Church, Leith; *Robert R. Hamilton*, Madras; *John Burne*, for some time at Madeira; *Patrick Borrowman*, Free Church, Glencairn; *Walter Wood*, Free Church, Weststruther; *Henry Moncrieff*, Free Church, Kilbride; *James Cochrane*, Established Church, Cupar; *John Miller*, Secretary to Free Church Special Commission; *G. Smeaton*, Free Church, Auchterarder; *Robert Kinnear*, Free Church, Moffat; and *W. B. Clarke*, Free Church, Half-Morton. Every meeting was opened and closed with prayer. Minutes of the discussions were kept; and the Essays read were preserved in volumes. A very characteristic essay of Mr. McCheyne's is, "Lebanon and its Scenery," wherein he adduces the evidence of travellers for facts and customs which himself was afterwards to see. Often in 1839, pleasant remembrances of these days of youthful study were suggested by what we actually witnessed; and in the essay referred to I find an interesting coincidence. He writes—" What a refreshing sight to his eye, yet undimmed with age, after resting forty years on this monotonous scenery of the desert, now to rest on Zion's olive-clad hills, and Lebanon, with its vine-clad base and overhanging forests, and towering peaks of snow." This was the very impression on our minds when we ourselves came up from the wilderness, as expressed in the Narrative, chap. ii.—" *May* 29. Next morning we saw at a distance a range of hills, running north and south, called by the Arabs *Djebel Khalie.* After wandering so many days in the wilderness, with its vast monotonous plains of level sand, the sight of these distant mountains was a pleasant relief to the eye; and we thought we could understand a little of the feeling with which Moses, after being forty years in the desert, would pray, 'I pray thee let me go over.' Deut. iii. 25."

larging the understanding. New fields
were daily opened up. His notes and his
tify that he endeavoured to retain what
and that he used to read as much of the boo
mended by the professors as his time enabled him to
overtake. Many years after, he thankfully called to
mind lessons that had been taught in these classes.
Riding one day with Mr. Hamilton (now of Regent
Square, London,) from Abernyte to Dundee, they
were led to speak of the best mode of dividing a
sermon. " I used," said he, " to despise Dr. Welsh's
rules at the time I heard him, but now I feel I *must
use* them, for nothing is more needful for making a
sermon memorable and impressive than a logical
arrangement."

His intellectual powers were of a high order—
clear and distinct apprehension of his subject, and
felicitous illustration, characterized him among all his
companions. To an eager desire for wide acquaintance with truth in all its departments, and a memory
strong and accurate in retaining what he found, there
was added a remarkable candour in examining what
claimed to be the truth. He had, also, an ingenious
and enterprising mind—a mind that could carry out
what was suggested, when it did not strike out new
light for itself. He possessed great powers of analy-
sis; often his judgment discovered singular discrimination. His imagination seldom sought out objects
of grandeur; for, as a friend has truly said of him,
" he had a kind and quiet eye, which found out the
living and beautiful in nature, rather than the ma-
jestic and sublime."

He might have risen to high eminence in the circles
of taste and literature, but denied himself all such
hopes, that he might win souls. With such peculiar
talents as he possessed, his ministry might have, in
any circumstances, attracted many; but these attrac-
tions were all made subsidiary to the single desire of
awakening the dead in trespasses and sins. Nor
would he have expected to be blessed to the salvation
of souls, unless he had himself been a monument of

sovereign grace. In his esteem, *" to be in Christ be fore being in the ministry,"* was a thing indispensable. He often pointed to those solemn words of Jeremiah (xxiii. 21.) *" I have not sent these prophets yet they ran; I have not spoken to them, yet they prophesied. But if they had stood in my counsel, and caused my people to hear my words, then they should have turned them from their evil way, and from the evil of their doings."*

It was with faith already in his heart that he went forward to the holy office of the ministry, receiving from his Lord the rod by which he was to do signs, and which, when it had opened rocks and made waters gush out, he never failed to replace upon the ark whence it was taken, giving glory to God! He knew not the way by which God was leading him; but even then he was under the guidance of that pillar-cloud. At this very period he wrote that hymn, *" They sing the Song of Moses."* His course was then about to begin; but now that it has ended, we can look back and plainly see that the faith he therein expressed was not in vain.

CHAPTER II

HIS LABOURS IN THE VINEYARD BEFORE ORDINATION

He that goeth forth and weepeth, bearing precious seed, shall doubtless come again with rejoicing, bringing his sheaves with him.—Psa. cxxvi. 6.

WHILE he was still only undergoing a student's usual examinations before the Presbytery, in the spring and summer of 1835, several applications were made to him by ministers in the church, who desired to secure his services for their part of the vineyard. He was especially urged to consider the field of labour at Larbert and Dunipace, near Stirling, under Mr. John

Bonar, the pastor of these united parishes. This circumstance led him (as is often done in such cases) to ask the Presbytery of Edinburgh, under whose superintendence he had hitherto carried on his studies, to transfer the remainder of his public trials to another Presbytery, where there would be less press of business to occasion delay. This request being readily granted, his connection with Dumfriesshire led him to the Presbytery of Annan, who licensed him to preach the gospel, on July 1st, 1835. His feelings at the moment appear from a record of his own in the evening of the day : " Preached three probationary discourses in Annan Church, and after an examination in Hebrew, was solemnly licensed to preach the gospel, by Mr. Monylaws, the Moderator. Bless the Lord, O my soul ; and all that is within me be stirred up to praise and magnify his holy name ! What I have so long desired as the highest honour of man, Thou at length givest me—me who dare scarcely use the words of Paul, ' Unto me who am less than the least of all saints, is this grace given, that I should preach the unsearchable riches of Christ.' Felt somewhat solemnized, though unable to feel my unworthiness as I ought. Be clothed with humility."

An event occurred the week before, which cast a solemnizing influence on him, and on his after-fellow-traveller and brother in the gospel, who was licensed by another Presbytery that same day. This event was the lamented death of the Rev. John Brown Patterson, of Falkirk—one whom the Lord had gifted with pre-eminent eloquence, and learning, and who was using all for his Lord, when cut off by fever. He had spoken much before his death of the awfulness of a pastor's charge, and his early death sent home the lesson to many, with the warning that the pastor's account of souls might be suddenly required of him.

On the following Sabbath Mr. McCheyne preached, for the first time, in Ruthwell Church, near Dumfries, on " the Pool of Bethesda ;" and in the afternoon, on " the Strait Gate." He writes that evening in his diary : " Found it a more awfully solemn thing than

I had imagined to announce Christ authoritatively,
yet a glorious privilege!" The week after (Saturday
July 11,) "Lord, put me into thy service when and
where thou pleasest. In thy hand all my qualities
will be put to their appropriate end. Let me, then,
have no anxieties." Next day, also, after preaching
in St. John's Church, Leith, "Remembered, before
going into the pulpit, the confession which says,* 'We
have been more anxious about the messenger than
the message.' " In preaching that day, he states, " It
came across me in the pulpit, that if spared to be a
minister, I might enjoy sweet flashes of communion
with God in that situation. The mind is entirely
wrought up to speak for God. It is possible, then,
that more vivid acts of faith may be gone through
then, than in quieter and sleepier moments."

It was not till the 7th of November that he began
his labours at Larbert. In the interval, he preached
in various places, and many began to perceive the
peculiar sweetness of the word in his lips. In accept-
ing the invitation to labour in the sphere proposed,
he wrote : "It has always been my aim, and it is
my prayer, to have *no plans* with regard to myself—
well assured as I am, that the place where the Saviour sees meet to place me, must ever be the best
place for me."

The parish to which he had come was very large,
containing six thousand souls. The Parish Church is
at Larbert ; but through the exertions of Mr. Bonar,
many years ago, a second church was erected for the
people of Dunipace. Mr. Hanna, afterwards minister of Skirling, had preceded Mr. McCheyne in the
duties of assistant in his field of labour ; and Mr.
McCheyne now entered on it with a fully devoted
and zealous heart, although in a weak state of health.
As assistant, it was his part to preach every alternate
Sabbath at Larbert and Dunipace, and during the
week to visit among the population of both these dis-

* He here refers to the " *Full and Candid Acknowledgment of
Sin*," for Students and Ministers ; drawn up by the Commission of
Assembly, in 1651, and often reprinted since.

tricts, according as he felt himself enabled in body and soul. There was a marked difference between the two districts in their general features of character; but equal labour was bestowed on both by the minister and his assistant; and often did their prayer ascend that the windows of heaven might be opened over the two sanctuaries. Souls have been saved there. Often, however, did the faithful pastor mingle his tears with those of his younger fellow-soldier, complaining, "Lord, who hath believed our report?" There was much sowing in faith; nor was this sowing abandoned even when the returns seemed most inadequate.

Mr. McCheyne had great delight in remembering that Larbert was one of the places where, in other days, that holy man of God, Robert Bruce, had laboured and prayed. Writing at an after-period from the Holy Land, he expressed the wish, "May the Spirit be poured upon Larbert as in Bruce's days." But, more than all associations, the souls of the people, whose salvation he longed for, were ever present to his mind. A letter to Mr. Bonar, in 1837, from Dundee, shows us his yearnings over them. "What an interest I feel in Larbert and Dunipace! It is like the land of my birth. Will the Sun of righteousness ever rise upon it, making its hills and valleys bright with the light of the knowledge of Jesus!"

No sooner was he settled in his chamber here, than he commenced his work. With him, the commencement of all labour invariably consisted in the preparation of his own soul. The forerunner of each day's visitations was a calm season of private devotion during morning hours. The walls of his chamber were witnesses of his prayerfulness—I believe of his tears, as well as of his cries. The pleasant sound of psalms often issued from his room at an early hour. Then followed the reading of the word for his own sanctification; and few have so fully realized the blessing of the first Psalm. His leaf did not wither, for his roots were in the waters. It was here, too, that he began to study so closely the works of Jonathan Edwards—reckoning them a mine to be wrought, and if wrought, sure to repay the toil. Along with this author, the Letters of Samuel Rutherford were often in his hand. Books of general knowledge he occasionally perused ; but now it was done with the steady purpose of finding in them some illustration of spiritual truth. He rose from reading " Insect Architecture," with the observation, " God reigns in a community of ants and ichneumons, as visibly as among living men or mighty seraphim !"

His desire to grow in acquaintance with Scripture was very intense ; and both the Old and New Testament were his regular study. He loved to range over the wide revelation of God. " He would be a sorry student of this world," said he to a friend, " who should for ever confine his gaze to the fruitful fields and well-watered gardens of this cultivated earth. He could have no true idea of what the world was unless he had stood upon the rocks of our mountains and seen the bleak muirs and mosses of our barren land ; unless he had paced the quarter-deck when the vessel was out of sight of land, and seen the waste of waters without any shore upon the horizon. Just so, he would be a sorry student of the Bible, who would not know all that God had inspired ; who would not examine into the most barren chapters to collect the good for which they were intended ; who would not strive to understand all the bloody battles which are chronicled, that he might find 'bread out of the eater, and honey out of the lion.'"—(*June,* 1836.)

His anxiety to have every possible help to holiness led him to notice what are the disadvantages of those who are not daily stirred up by the fellowship of more advanced believers. " I have found, by some experience, that in the country here, my watch does not go so well as it used to do in town. By small and gradual changes I find it either gains or loses, and I am surprised to find myself different in time from all the world, and, what is worse, from the sun. The simple explanation is, that in town I met with a steeple in every street, and a good going clock upon it; and so any aberrations in my watch were soon noticed and easily corrected. And just so I sometimes think it may be with that inner watch, whose hands point not to time but to eternity. By gradual and slow changes the wheels of my soul lag behind, or the springs of passions become too powerful; and I have no living timepiece with which I may compare, and by which I may amend my going. You will say that I may always have the sun: and so it should be; but we have many clouds which obscure the sun from our weak eyes."—(Letters to Rev. H. Bonar, Kelso.)

From the first he fed others by what he himself was feeding upon. His preaching was in a manner the development of his soul's experience. It was a giving out of the inward life. He loved to come up from the pastures wherein the chief Shepherd had met him—to lead the flock entrusted to his care to the spots where he found nourishment.

In the field of his labour he found enough of work to overwhelm the spirit. The several collieries and the Carron Iron works furnish a population who are, for the most part, either sunk in deep indifference to the truth, or are opposed to it in the spirit of infidelity. Mr. McCheyne at once saw that the pastor whom he had come to aid, whatever was the measure of his health and zeal, and perseverance, had duties laid on him which were altogether beyond the power of man to overtake. When he had made a few weeks' trial, the field appeared more boundless, and the mass of souls more impenetrable, than he had ever conceived.

It was probably, in some degree, his experience at this time, that gave him such deep sympathy with the Church Extension Scheme, as a truly noble and Christian effort for bringing the glad tidings to the doors of a population, who must otherwise remain neglected, and were themselves willing so to live and die. He conveyed his impressions on this subject to a friend abroad, in the following terms:—" There is a soul-destroying cruelty in the cold-hearted opposition which is made to the multiplication of ministers in such neglected and overgrown districts as these. If one of our Royal Commissioners would but consent to undergo the bodily fatigue that a minister ought to undergo in visiting merely the sick and dying of Larbert, (let alone the visitation of the whole, and preparation for the pulpit,) and that for one month, I would engage that if he be able to rise out of his bed by the end of it, he would change his voice and manner at the Commission Board."

A few busy weeks passed over, occupied from morning till night in such cares and toils, when another part of the discipline he was to undergo was sent. In the end of December, strong oppression of the heart and an irritating cough caused some of his friends to fear that his lungs were affected; and for some weeks he was laid aside from public duty. On examination, it was found that though there was a dulness in the right lung, yet the material of the lungs was not affected. For a time, however, the airvessels were so clogged and irritated, that if he had continued to preach, disease would have quickly ensued. But this also was soon removed, and, under cautious management, he resumed his work.

This temporary illness served to call forth the extreme sensitiveness of his soul to the responsibilities of his office. At its commencement—having gone to Edinburgh " in so sweet a sunshine morning that God seemed to have chosen it for him "—he wrote to Mr. Bonar—"If I am not recovered before the third Sabbath, I fear I shall not be able to bear upon my conscience the responsibility of leaving you any longer to labour alone, bearing unaided the burden of six thousand souls. No, my dear sir, I must read the will of God aright in his providence, and give way, when he bids me, to fresh and abler workmen. I hope and pray that it may be his will to restore me again to you and your parish, with a heart tutored by sickness to speak more and more as dying to dying." Then, mentioning two of the sick—" Poor A. D. and C. H., I often think of them. I can do no more for their good, except pray for them. Tell them that I do this without ceasing."

The days when a holy pastor, who knows the blood-sprinkled way to the Father, is laid aside, are probably as much a proof of the kindness of God to his flock, as days of health and activity. He is occupied, during this season of retirement, in discovering the plagues of his heart, and in going in, like Moses, to plead with God face to face for his flock, and for his own soul. Mr. McCheyne believed that God had this end in view with him; and that the Lord should thus deal with him at his entrance into the vineyard, made him ponder these dealings the more. " Paul asked," says he, " What wilt thou have me *to do ?*" and it was answered, " I will show him what great things he must *suffer* for my name's sake." Thus it may be with me. I have been too anxious to do great things. The lust of praise has ever been my besetting sin; and what more befitting school could be found for me, than that of suffering alone away from the eye and ear of man ?" Writing again to Mr. Bonar, he tells him : " I feel distinctly, that the whole of my labour during this season of sickness and pain, should be in the way of prayer and *intercession.* And yet, so strongly does Satan work in our deceitful hearts, I scarcely remember a season wherein I have been more averse to these duties. I try to build myself up in my most holy faith, praying in the Holy Ghost, keeping myself in the love of God, and looking for the mercy of the Lord Jesus unto eternal life. That text of Jude has peculiar beauties for me at this season. If it be good to come under the love of God once, surely it is good to keep ourselves there. And yet how reluctant we are ! I cannot doubt that boldness is offered me to enter into the holiest of all. I cannot doubt my right and title to enter continually by the new and living way. I cannot doubt that when I do enter in, I stand not only forgiven, but accepted in the beloved. I cannot doubt that when I do enter in, the Spirit is willing and ready to descend like a dove, to dwell in my bosom as a Spirit of prayer and peace, enabling me to 'pray in the Holy Ghost;' and that Jesus is ready to rise up as my intercessor with the Father, praying for me, though not for the world ; and that the prayer-hearing God is ready to bend his ear to requests which he delights to hear and answer. I cannot doubt that thus to dwell in God is the true blessed-ness of my nature; and yet, strange, unaccountable creature! I am too often unwilling to enter in. I go about and about the sanctuary, and I sometimes press in through the rent veil, and see the blessedness of dwelling there to be far better than that in the tents of wickedness; yet it is certain that I do not dwell within."—" My prayers follow you, especially to the sick beds of A. D. and C. H. I hope they still survive, and that Christ may still be glorified in them."

On resuming his labours, he found a residence in Carronvale. From this pleasant spot he used to ride out to his work. But pleasant as the spot was, yet being only partially recovered, he was not satisfied; he lamented that he was unable to overtake what a stronger labourer would have accomplished. He often cast a regretful look at the collieries; and remember-ing them still at a later period, he reproached himself with neglect, though most unjustly. " The places which I left utterly unbroken in upon are Kinnaird and Milton. Both of these rise up against my con-science, particularly the last, through which I have ridden so often." It was not the comfort, but the positive usefulness of the ministry, that he envied; and he judged of places by their fitness to promote this great end. He said of a neighbouring parish, which he had occasion to visit—" The manse is alto-gether too sweet; other men could hardly live there without saying, ' This is my rest.' I don't think ministers' manses should ever be so beautiful."

A simple incident was overruled to promote the ease and fluency of his pulpit ministrations. From the very beginning of his ministry, he reprobated the custom of reading sermons, believing that to do so does exceedingly weaken the freedom and natural fervour of the messenger in delivering his message. Neither did he recite what he had written. But his custom was to impress on his memory the substance of what he had beforehand carefully written, and then to speak as he found liberty. One morning, as he rode rapidly along to Dunipace, his written sermons were dropped on the wayside. This accident prevented him having the opportunity of preparing in his usual manner; but he was enabled to preach with more than usual freedom. For the first time in his life, he discovered that he possessed the gift of extemporaneous composition, and learned, to his own surprise, that he had more composedness of mind, and command of language than he had believed. This discovery, however, did not in the least degree diminish his diligent preparation. Indeed, the only use that he made of the incident at the time it occurred was, to draw a lesson of dependence on God's own immediate blessing, rather than on the satisfactory preparation made. "One thing always fills the cup of my consolation, that God may work by the meanest and poorest words, as well as by the most polished and ornate—yea, perhaps, more readily, that the glory may be all his own."

His hands were again full, distributing the bread of life in fellowship with Mr. Bonar. The progress of his own soul, meanwhile, may be traced in some of the few entries that occur in his diary during this period.

"*February* 21, 1836.—Sabbath.—Blessed be the Lord for another day of the Son of Man. Resumed my diary, long broken off; not because I do not feel the disadvantages of it—making you assume feelings and express rather what you wish to be than what you are—but because the advantages seem greater. It insures sober reflection on the events of the day as seen in God's eye. Preached twice in Larbert, on the righteousness of God, Rom. i. 16. In the morning was more engaged in preparing the head than the heart. This has been frequently my error, and I have always felt the evil of it, especially in prayer. Reform it, then, O Lord."

" *Feb.* 27.—Preached in Dunipace with more heart than ever I remember to have done, on Rom. v. 10, owing to the gospel nature of the subject and prayerful preparation. Audience smaller than usual ! How happy and strange is the feeling when God gives the soul composure to stand and plead for him. O that it were altogether for him I plead, not for myself."

" *March* 5.—Preached in Larbert with very much comfort, owing chiefly to my remedying the error of 21st *Feb.* Therefore, the heart and the mouth were full. ' Enlarge my heart, and I shall run,' said David. ' Enlarge my heart, and I shall preach.' "

In this last remark we see the germ of his remarkably solemn ministry. His heart was filled, and his lips then spoke what he felt within his heart. He gave out not merely living water, but living water drawn at the springs that he had himself drunk of; and is not this a true gospel ministry ? Some venture to try what they consider a more intellectual method of addressing the conscience ; but ere a minister attempts this mode, he ought to see that he is one who is able to afford more deep and anxious preparation of heart than other men. Such intellectual men must bestow tenfold more prayerfulness on their work, if they would have either their own or their people's souls affected under their word. If we are ever to preach with compassion for the perishing, we must be moved ourselves by those same views of sin and righteousness which moved the human soul of Jesus.

About this time he occasionally contributed papers to the *Christian Herald :* one of these was *on sudden Conversions,* showing that Scripture led us to expect such. During this month, he seems to have written the " *Lines on Mungo Park,*" one of the pieces which attracted the notice of Professor Wilson. But whatever he engaged in, his aim was to honour his Master. I find him, after hearing sermon by another, remarking (*April* 3d,) " Some things powerful ; but I thirst to hear more of Christ."

On Sabbath 16, he writes, " Preached with some tenderness of heart. O why should I not weep, as Jesus did over Jerusalem? Evening.—Instructing two delightful Sabbath schools. Much bodily weariness. Gracious kindness of God in giving rest to the weary."

" *April* 13.—Went to Stirling to hear Dr. Duff once more upon his system. With greater warmth and energy than ever. He kindles as he goes. Felt almost constrained to go the whole length of his system with him. If it were only to raise up an audience, it would be defensible ; but when it is to raise up teachers, it is more than defensible. I am now made willing, if God shall open the way, to go to India. Here am I; send me !"

The missionary feeling in his soul continued all his life. The Lord had really made him willing; and this preparedness to go any where completed his preparation for unselfish, self-denied work at home. Must there not be somewhat of this missionary tendency in all true ministers? Is any one truly the Lord's messenger who is not quite willing to go when and where the Lord calls? Is it justifiable in any to put aside a call from the north, on the ground that he wishes one from the south? We must be found in the position of Isaiah, if we are to be really sent of God.

" *April* 24.—O that this day's labour may be blessed ! and not mine alone, but all thy faithful servants all over the world, till *the Sabbath* come."

" *April* 26.—Visiting in Carron-shore. Well received every where. Truly a pleasant labour. Cheered me much. Preached to them afterwards from Proverbs i."

" *May* 8.—Communion in Larbert. Served as an elder and help to the faithful. Partook with some glimpses of faith and joy. Served by a faithful old minister (Mr. Dempster of Denny,) one taught of God. This morning stood by the dying—evening, stood by the dead, poor J. F. having died last night. I laid my hand on her cold forehead, and tried to shut

her eyes. Lord, give me strength for living to thee!
—strength also for a dying hour."

" *May* 15.—This day an annular eclipse of the sun.
Kept both the services together, in order to be in time.
Truly a beautiful sight to see the shining edge of the
sun all round the dark disc of the moon. Lord, one
day thy hand shall put out those candles; for there
shall be no need of the sun to lighten the happy land;
the Lamb is the light thereof—a sun that cannot be
eclipsed—that cannot go down."

" *May* 17.—Visited thirteen families, and addressed
them all in the evening in the school, on Jeremiah
l. 4, 'going and weeping.' Experienced some enlargement of soul; said some plain things; and had
some desire for their salvation, that God might be
praised."

" *May* 21. — Preparation for the Sabbath. My
birth day. I have lived twenty-three years. Blessed
be my rock. Though I am a child in knowledge of
my Bible and of Thee, yet use me for what a child
can do, or a child can suffer. How few sufferings I
have had in the year that is past, except in my own
body. Oh! that as my day is, my strength may be.
Give me strength for a suffering, and for a dying
hour!"

" *May* 22.—O Lord, when thou workest, all dis-
couragements vanish—when thou art away, any thing
is a discouragement. Blessed be God for such a day—
one of a thousand! O why not always thus? Watch
and pray."

Being in Edinburgh this month, during the sitting
of the General Assembly, he used the opportunity of
revisiting some of his former charge in the Canongate.
" J. S., a far-off inquirer, but surely God is leading.
His hand draws out these tears. Interesting visits to
L.; near death, and still in the same mind. I cannot
but hope that some faith is here. Saw Mrs. M.;
many tears; felt much, though I am still doubtful, and
in the dark. Thou knowest, Lord!"

June 11.—Yesterday up in Dunipace. It would
seem as if I were afraid to name the name of Christ.

Saw many worldly people greatly needing a word in season, yet could not get my heart up to speak. What I did failed almost completely. I am not worthy, Lord! To-day sought to prepare my heart for the coming Sabbath. After the example of Boston, whose life I have been reading, examined my heart with prayer and fasting. 1. Does my heart really close with the offer of salvation by Jesus? Is it my choice to be saved in the way which gives him all the praise, and me none? Do I not only see it to be the Bible way of salvation, but does it cordially approve itself to my heart as delightful? Lord, search me and try me, for I cannot but answer, Yes, yes. 2. Is it the desire of my heart to be made altogether holy? Is there any sin I wish to retain? Is sin a grief to me, the sudden risings and overcomings thereof especially? Lord, thou knowest all things—thou knowest that I hate all sin, and desire to be made altogether *like thee.* It is the sweetest word in the Bible—' Sin *shall not* have dominion over you.' O then that I might lie low in the dust—the lower the better—that Jesus' righteousness and Jesus' strength alone be admired. Felt much deadness, and much grief that I cannot grieve for this deadness. Towards evening revived. Got a calm spirit through psalmody and prayer."

"*June* 12. Sabbath.—To-day a sinner preached Jesus, the same Jesus who has done all things for him, and that so lately! A day of much help, of some earnest looking up of the heart to that alone quickening power, of much temptation to flattery and pride. O for breathing gales of spiritual life! Evening— Somewhat helped to lay Jesus before little children in his beauty and excellency. Much fatigue, yet some peace. Surely a day in thy courts is better than a thousand."

"*May* 15.—Day of visiting—rather a happy one— in Carron-shore. Large meeting in the evening. Felt very happy after it, though mourning for *bitter speaking of the gospel.* Surely it is a gentle message, and should be spoken with angelic tenderness, especially by such a needy sinner."

Of this bitterness in preaching, he had little, indeed, in after days; yet so sensible was he of its being quite natural to all of us, that oftentimes he made it the subject of conversation, and used to grieve over himself if he had spoken with any thing less than solemn compassion. I remember on one occasion, when we met, he asked me what my last Sabbath's subject had been. It had been, " The wicked shall be turned into hell." On hearing this awful text, he asked, " Were you able to preach it *with tenderness?*" Certain it is that the tone of reproach and upbraiding is widely different from the voice of solemn warning. It is not saying hard things that pierces the consciences of our people; it is the voice of Divine love heard amid the thunder. The sharpest point of the two-edged sword is not *death*, but *life;* and against self-righteous souls this latter ought to be more used than the former. For such souls can hear us tell of the open gates of hell and the unquenchable fire far more unconcernedly than of the gates of heaven wide open for their immediate return. When we preach that the glad tidings *were intended to impart immediate assurance of eternal life to every sinner that believes them,* we strike deeper upon the proud enmity of the world to God, than when we show the eternal curse and the second death.

" *June* 19. Sabbath.—Wet morning. Preached at Dunipace to a small audience, on the parable of the tares. I thank God for that blessed parable.————In both discourses I can look back on many hateful thoughts of pride, and self-admiration, and love of praise, stealing the heart out of the service."

" *June* 22.—Carron-shore. My last. Some tears; yet I fear some like the messenger, not the message; and I fear I am so vain as to love that love. Lord, let it not be so. Perish *my* honour, but let *Thine* be exalted for ever.

" *June* 26.—True Sabbath-day. Golden sky. Full church, and more liveliness than sometimes. Shall I call the liveliness of this day a gale of the Spirit, or was all natural? I know that all was not of grace:

the self-admiration, the vanity, the desire of honour, the bitterness—these were all breaths of earth or hell. But was there no grace? Lord, thou knowest. I dare not wrong thee by saying—No! Larbert Sabbath school, with the same liveliness and joy. Domestic work with the same. Praised be God! O that the savour of it may last through the week! By this may I test if it be all of nature, or much of grace. Alas! how I tremble for my Monday mornings—those seasons of lifelessness. Lord, bless the seeds sown this day in the hearts of my friends, by the hand of my friends, and all over the world,—hasten the harvest!"

"*July* 3.—After a week of working and hurried preparation, a Sabbath of mingled peace and pain. Called, morning before preaching, to see Mrs. E. dying. Preached on the jailor—discomposedly—with some glimpses of the genuine truth as it is in Jesus. Felt there was much mingling of experience. At times the congregation was lightened up from their dull flatness, and then they sunk again into lethargy. O Lord, make me hang on thee to open their hearts, thou opener of Lydia's heart. I fear thou wilt not bless my preaching, until I am brought thus to hang on thee. O keep not back a blessing, for my sin! Afternoon—On the Highway of the Redeemed, with more ease and comfort. Felt the truth sometimes boiling up from my heart into my words. Some glimpses of tenderness, yet much less of that spirit than the last two Sabbaths. Again saw the dying woman. O when will I plead, with my tears and inward yearnings, over sinners! O compassionate Lord, give me to know what manner of spirit I am of! give me thy gentle spirit, that neither strives nor cries. Much weariness, want of prayerfulness, and want of cleaving to Christ." Tuesday the 5th, being the anniversary of his license to preach the gospel, he writes:—" Eventful week! One year I have preached *Jesus*, have I? or myself? I have often preached myself also, but Jesus I have preached."

About this time he again felt the hand of affliction, though it did not continue long. Yet it was plain to him now that personal trouble was to be one of the ingredients of that experience which helped to give a peculiar tone to his ministry. "*July* 8th.—Since Tuesday have been laid up with illness. Set by once more for a season to feel my unprofitableness and cure my pride. When shall this self-choosing temper be healed? 'Lord, I will preach, run, visit, wrestle,' said I. 'No, thou shalt lie in thy bed and suffer,' said the Lord. To-day missed some fine opportunities of speaking a word for Christ. The Lord saw I would have spoken as much for my own honour as his, and, therefore, shut my mouth. *I see a man cannot be a faithful minister, until he preaches Christ for Christ's sake*—until he gives up striving to attract people to himself, and seeks only to attract them to Christ. Lord, give me this! To-night some glimpses of humbling; and, therefore, some wrestling in social prayer. But my prayers are scarcely to be called prayer." Then, in the evening, "This day my brother has been five years absent from the body and present with the Lord, and knows more and loves more than all earthly saints together. Till the day break, and the shadows flee away, turn, my beloved!"

"*July* 10th.—I fear I am growing more earthly in some things. To-day I felt a difficulty in bringing in spiritual conversation immediately after preaching, when my bosom should be burning. Excused myself from dining out from other than the grand reason; though checked and corrected myself. Evening— Insensibly slid into worldly conversation. Let these things be corrected in me, O Lord, by the heart being more filled with love to Jesus; and more ejaculatory prayer."

"17th, Sabbath.—O that I may remember my own word this day: that the hour of communion is the hour for the foxes—the little foxes—to spoil the vine. Two things that defile this day in looking back, are love of praise running through all, and consenting to listen to worldly talk at all. O that these may keep me humble and be my burden, leading me to the cross. Then, satan, thou wilt be outwitted!"

"19th.—Died, this day, W. McCheyne, my cousin-german, Relief minister, Kelso. O how I repent of our vain controversies on Establishments when we last met, and that we spoke so little of Jesus. O that we had spoken more one to another. Lord, teach me to be always speaking as dying to dying."

"24th.—Dunipace Communion.—Heard Mr. Purves, of Jedburgh, preach, 'Therefore with joy shall ye draw water out of the wells of salvation.' The only way to come to ordinances, and to draw from the well, is to come with the matter of acceptance settled, believing God's anger to be turned away. Truly a precious view of the freeness of the gospel very refreshing. My soul needs to be roused much to apprehend this truth."

Above (*July* 3,) he spoke of "mingling experience with the genuine truth as it is in Jesus." It is to this that he refers again, in the last paragraph. His deep acquaintance with the human heart and passions often led him to dwell at greater length, not only on those topics whereby the sinner might be brought to discover his guilt, but also on marks that would evidence a change, than on the "Glad Tidings." And yet he ever felt that these blessed tidings, addressed to souls in the very gall of bitterness, were the true theme of the minister of Christ; and never did he preach other than a full salvation ready for the chief of sinners. From the very first, also, he carefully avoided the error of those who rather speculate or doctrinize about the gospel, than preach the gospel itself. Is not the true idea of preaching simply that of one, like Ahimaaz, coming with all-important tidings, and intent on making these tidings known? Occupied with the facts he has to tell, he has no heart to speculate on mere abstractions; nay, he is apt to forget what language he employs, excepting so far as the very grandeur of the tidings gives a glow of eloquence to his words. The glorious fact, "*By this man is preached unto you the forgiveness of sins*," is the burden of every sermon. The crier is sent to the openings of the gate by his Lord—to herald forth this one infinitely important truth through the whole creation under heaven.

He seems invariably to have applied for his personal benefit what he gave out to his people. We have already noticed how he used to feed on the word, not in order to prepare himself for his people, but for personal edification. To do so was a fundamental rule with him; and all pastors will feel that, if they are to prosper in their own souls, they must so use the word—sternly refusing to admit the idea of feeding others, until satiated themselves. And for similar ends, it is needful that we let the truth we have preached sink down into our own souls. We, as well as our people, must drink in the falling shower. Mr. McCheyne did so. It is common to find him speaking thus:— "*July* 31, Sabbath.—Afternoon, on Judas betraying Christ; much more tenderness than ever I felt before. O that I might abide in the bosom of him who washed Judas' feet, and dipped his hand in the same dish with him, and warned him, and grieved over him—that I might catch the infection of his love, of his tenderness, so wonderful, so unfathomable."

Coming home on a Sabbath evening (*Aug.* 7th) from Torwood Sabbath school, a person met him who suggested an opportunity of usefulness. There were two families of gypsies encamped in Torwood, within his reach. He was weary with a long day's labour; but instantly, as was his custom at such a call, set off to find them. By the side of their wood-fire, he opened out the parable of the Lost Sheep, and pressed it on their souls in simple terms. He then knelt down in prayer for them, and left them somewhat impressed and very grateful.

At this time a youthful parishioner, for whose soul he felt much anxiety, left his father's roof. Ever watchful for souls, he seized this opportunity of laying before him more fully the things belonging to his peace.

"My dear G——, You will be surprised to hear from me. I have often wished to be better acquainted with you; but in these sad parishes we cannot manage to know and be intimate with every one we would desire. And now you have left your father's roof and our charge; still my desires go after you, as well as the kind thoughts of many others; and since I cannot now speak to you, I take this way of expressing my thoughts to you. I do not know in what light you look upon me, whether as a grave and morose minister, or as one who might be a companion and friend; but, really, it is so short a while since I was just like you, when I enjoyed the games which you now enjoy, and read the books which you now read, that I never can think of myself as any thing more than a boy. This is one great reason why I write to you. The same youthful blood flows in my veins that flows in yours; the same fancies and buoyant passions dance in my bosom as in yours—so that, when I would persuade you to come with me to the same Saviour, and to walk the rest of your life 'led by the Spirit of God,' I am not persuading you to any thing beyond your years. I am not like a grey headed grandfather —then you might answer all I say by telling me that you are a boy. No; I am almost as much a boy as you are; as fond of happiness and of life as you are; as fond of scampering over the hills, and seeing all that is to be seen, as you are.

"Another thing that persuades me to write you, my dear boy, is, that I have felt in my own experience the want of having a friend to direct and counsel me. I had a kind brother as you have, who taught me many things: he gave me a Bible, and persuaded me to read it; he tried to train me as the gardener trains the apple tree upon the wall, but all in vain. I thought myself far wiser than he, and would always take my own way; and many a time, I well remember, I have seen him reading his Bible, or shutting his closet door to pray, when I have been dressing to go to some frolic, or some dance of folly. Well, this dear friend and brother died; and although his death made a greater impression upon me than ever his life had done, still I found the misery of being *friendless*. I do not mean that I had no relations and wordly friends, for I had many; but I had no friend *who cared for my soul*. I had none to direct me to the Saviour—none to awaken my slumbering conscience —none to tell me about the blood of Jesus washing away all sin—none to tell me of the Spirit who is so willing to change the heart, and give the victory over passions. I had no minister to take me by the hand, and say, ' Come with me, and we will do thee good.' Yes, I had one friend and minister, but that was Jesus himself, and he led me in a way that makes me give him, and him only, all the praise. Now, though Jesus may do this again, yet the more common way with him is to use earthly guides. Now, if I could supply the place of such a guide to you, I should be happy. To be a finger post is all that I want to be— pointing out the way. This is what I so much wanted myself—this is what you need not want, unless you wish.

" Tell me, dear G., would you work less pleasantly through the day—would you walk the streets with a more doleful step—would you eat your meat with less gladness of heart—would you sleep less tranquilly at night, if you had *the forgiveness of sins*— that is, if all your wicked thoughts and deeds—lies, thefts, and Sabbath breakings—were all blotted out of God's book of remembrance? Would this make you less happy, do you think? You dare not say it would. But would the forgiveness of sins not make you more happy than you are? Perhaps you will tell me that you are very happy as you are. I quite believe you. I know that I was very happy when I was unforgiven. I know that I had great pleasure in many sins—in Sabbath breaking, for instance. Many a delightful walk I have had — speaking my own words, thinking my own thoughts, and seeking my own pleasure on God's holy day. I fancy few boys were ever happier in an unconverted state than I was. No sorrow clouded my brow—no tears filled my eyes, unless over some nice story book; so that I know that you say quite true, when you say that you are happy as you are. But, ah! is not this just the saddest thing of all, that you should be happy whilst you are a child of wrath—that you should smile, and eat, and drink, and be merry, and sleep sound, when this very night you may be in *hell.* Happy while unforgiven!— a terrible happiness. It is like the Hindoo widow who sits upon the funeral pile with her dead husband, and sings songs of joy when they are setting fire to the wood with which she is to be burned. Yes, you may be quite happy in this way, till you die, my boy; but when you look back from hell, you will say, it was a miserable kind of happiness. Now, do you think it would not give you more happiness to be forgiven— to be able to put on Jesus, and say, 'God's anger is turned away?' Would not you be happier at work, and happier in the house, and happier in your bed? I can assure you, from all that ever I have felt of it, the pleasures of being forgiven are as superior to the pleasures of an unforgiven man, as heaven is higher than hell. The peace of being forgiven reminds me of the calm, blue sky, which no earthly clamours can disturb. It lightens all labour, sweetens every morsel of bread, and makes a sick bed all soft and downy— yea, it takes away the scowl of death. Now, forgiveness may be yours *now.* It is not given to those who are good. It is not given to any because they are less wicked than others. It is given *only* to those who, feeling that their sins have brought a curse on them which they cannot lift off, 'look unto Jesus,' as bearing all away.

"Now, my dear boy, I have no wish to weary you. If you are any thing like what I was, you will have yawned many a time already over this letter. However, if the Lord deal graciously with you, and touch your young heart, as I pray he may, with a desire to be forgiven, and to be made a child of God, perhaps you will not take ill what I have written to you in much haste. As this is the first time you have been away from home, perhaps you have not learned to write letters yet; but if you have, I would like to hear from you, how you come on—what convictions you feel, if you feel any—what difficulties—what parts of the Bible puzzle you; and then I would do my best to unravel them You read your Bible regularly, of course; but do try to understand it, and still more to *feel it*. Read more parts than one at a time. For example, if you are reading Genesis, read a Psalm also; or, if you are reading Matthew, read a small bit of an epistle also. *Turn the Bible into prayer.* Thus, if you were reading the first Psalm, spread the Bible on the chair before you, and kneel, and pray, ' O Lord, give me the blessedness of the man,' &c. ' Let me not stand in the counsel of the ungodly,' &c. This is the best way of knowing the meaning of the Bible, and of learning to pray. In prayer confess your sins by name—going over those of the past day, one by one. Pray for your friends by name—father, mother, &c., &c. If you love them, surely you will pray for their souls. I know well that there are prayers constantly ascending for you from your own house; and will you not pray for them back again? Do this regularly. If you pray sincerely for others, it will make you pray for yourself.

"But I must be done. Good bye, dear G. Remember me to your brother kindly, and believe me your sincere friend,   R. M. M."

It is the shepherd's duty (Ezek. xxxiv. 4,) in visiting his flock, to discriminate; "strengthening the diseased, healing that which was sick, binding up that which was broken, bringing again that which was driven away, seeking that which was lost." This Mr. McCheyne tried to do. In an after-letter to Mr. Somerville, of Anderston, in reference to the people of these parishes, whom he had had means of knowing, he wrote, "Take more heed to the saints than ever I did. Speak a word in season to S. M. S. H. will drink in simple truth, but tell him to be humble-minded. Cause L. H. to learn in silence; speak not of *religion* to her, but speak to her case always. Teach A. M. to look simply at Jesus. J. A. warn and teach. Get worldliness from the B's, if you can. Mrs. G. awake, or keep awake. Speak faithfully to the B's. Tell me of M. C., if she is really a believer, and grows? A. K., has the light visited her? M. T., I have had some doubts of. M. G. lies sore upon my conscience; I did no good to that woman; she always managed to speak of things *about the truth.* Speak boldly. What matter in eternity the slight awkwardnesses of time?"

It was about this time that the managers and congregation of the new church, St. Peter's, Dundee, invited him to preach as one of the candidates; and, in the end of August, chose him to be their pastor, with one accord. He accepted the call under an awful sense of the work that lay before him. He would rather, he said, have made a choice for himself of such a rural parish as Dunipace; but the Lord seemed to desire it otherwise. "His ways are in the sea." More than once, at a later period, he would say, "We might have thought that God would have sent a strong man to such a parish as mine, and not a feeble reed."

The first day he preached in St. Peter's as a candidate (*August* 14th,) is thus recorded: "Forenoon—Mind not altogether in a preaching frame; on the Sower. Afternoon—With more encouragement and help of the Spirit; on the Voice of the Beloved in Cant. ii. 8—17. In the evening—With all my heart; on *Ruth.* Lord, keep me humble." Returning from St. Peter's, the second time, he observed in his class of girls at Dunipace more than usual anxiety. One of them seemed to be thoroughly awakened that evening. "Thanks be to thee, Lord, for any thing," he writes that evening; for as yet he had sown without seeing fruit. It seems to have been part of the Lord's dealing with him, thus to teach him to persevere in duty and in faith, even where there was no obvious success. The arrow that was yet to wound hundreds was then receiving its point; but it lay in the quiver for a time. The Lord seemed to be touching his own heart and melting it by what he spoke to others, rather than touching or melting the hearts of those he spoke to. But from the day of his preaching in St. Peter's, tokens of success began. His first day there, especially the evening sermon on Ruth, was blessed to two souls in Dundee; and now he sees souls begin to melt under his last words in the parish where he thought he had hitherto spent his strength in vain.

As he was now to leave this sphere, he sought out with deep anxiety a labourer who would help their overburdened pastor, in true love to the people's souls. He believed he had found such a labourer in Mr. Somerville, his friend who had shared his every thought and feeling in former days, and who, with a sharp sickle in his hand, was now advancing toward the harvest field. "I see plainly," he wrote to Mr. Bonar, "that my poor attempts at labour in your dear parish will soon be eclipsed. But if at length the iron front of unbelief give way, if the hard faces become furrowed with the tears of anxiety and of faith, under whatever ministry, you will rejoice, and I will rejoice, and the angels, and the Father and God of angels will rejoice." It was in this spirit that he closed his short ten months of labour in this region.

His last sermons to the people of Larbert and Dunipace were on Hosea xiv. 1, "O Israel, return unto the Lord thy God;" and Jeremiah viii. 20, "Harvest is past." In the evening he writes, "Lord, I feel bowed down because of the little I have done for them which thou mightest have blessed! My bowels yearn over them, and all the more that I have done so little. Indeed, I might have done ten times as much as I have done. I might have been in every house; I might have spoken always as a minister. Lord, canst thou bless partial, unequal efforts?"

I believe it was about this time that some of us, first of all, began our custom of praying specially for each other on Saturday evening, with a reference to our engagements in the ministry next day. This concert for prayers we have never since seen cause to discontinue. It has from time to time been widened in its circle; and as yet his has been the only voice that has been silenced of all that thus began to go in on each other's behalf before the Lord. Mr. McCheyne never failed to remember this time of prayer. "Larbert and Dunipace are always on my heart, especially on the Saturday evenings, when I pray for a glorious Sabbath!" On one occasion, in Dundee, he was asked if the accumulation of business in his parish never led him to neglect the season of prayer on a busy Saturday; his reply was, that he was not aware that it ever did. "What would my people do, if I were not to pray?"

So steady was he in Sabbath preparations, from the first day to the last time he was with them, that though at prayer meetings, or similar occasions, he did not think it needful to have much laid up before coming to address his people; yet, anxious to give them on the Sabbath what had cost him somewhat, he never without an urgent reason, went before them without much previous meditation and prayer. His principle on this subject was embodied in a remark he made to some of us who were conversing on the matter. Being asked his view of diligent preparation for the pulpit, he replied—"*Beaten oil—beaten oil for the lamps of the sanctuary.*"* And yet his prayerfulness was greater still. Indeed, he could not neglect fellowship with God before entering the congregation. He needed to be bathed in the love of God. His ministry was so much a bringing out of views that had first sanctified his own soul, that the healthiness of his soul was absolutely needful to the vigour and power of his ministrations.

During these ten months the Lord had done much for him, but it was chiefly in the way of discipline for a future ministry. He had been taught a minister's heart; he had been tried in the furnace; he had

* See Exodus xxvii. 20.

tasted deep personal sorrow, little of which has been
recorded; he had felt the fiery darts of temptation;
he had been exercised in self-examination and in
much prayer; he had proved how flinty is the rock,
and had learned that in lifting the rod by which it
was to be smitten, success lay in Him alone who
enabled him to lift it up. And thus prepared of God
for the peculiar work that awaited him, he turned his
face towards Dundee, and took up his abode in the
spot where the Lord was so marvellously to visit him
in his ministry.

CHAPTER III

FIRST YEARS OF LABOUR IN DUNDEE

Ye know, from the first day that I came into Asia, after what manner I have been with you at all seasons, serving the Lord with
all humility of mind, and with many tears and temptations.—Acts
xx. 18, 19.

The day on which he was ordained pastor of a flock,
was a day of much anxiety to his soul. He had journeyed by Perth to spend the night preceding under
the roof of his kind friend Mr. Grierson, in the manse
of Errol. Next morning, ere he left the manse, three
passages of Scripture occupied his mind. 1. "*Thou
shalt keep him in perfect peace whose mind is stayed
on thee; because he trusteth in thee.*" Isaiah xxvi. 3.
This verse was seasonable; for, as he sat meditating
on the solemn duties of the day, his heart trembled.
2. "*Give thyself wholly to these things.*" 1 Tim. iv.
15. May that word (he prayed) sink deep into my
heart. 3. "*Here am I, send me.*" Isaiah vi. 8.
"To go or to stay—to be here till death, or to visit
foreign shores—whatsoever, wheresoever, whensoever
thou pleasest." He rose from his knees with the
prayer, "Lord, may thy grace come with the laying
on of the hands of the Presbytery."

He was ordained on November 24, 1836. The service was conducted by Mr. Roxburgh of St. John's, through whose exertions the new church had been erected, and who ever afterwards cherished the most cordial friendship towards him. On the Sabbath following, he was introduced to his flock by Mr. John Bonar, of Larbert, with whom he had laboured as a son in the Gospel. Himself preached in the afternoon upon Isaiah lxi. 1—3, " *The Spirit of the Lord is upon me,*" &c.—of which he writes, " May it be prophetic of the object of my coming here !" And truly it was so. That very sermon—the first preached by him as a pastor—was the means of awakening souls as he afterwards learned; and ever onward the impressions left by his words seemed to spread and deepen among his people. To keep up the remembrance of this solemn day, he used in all the subsequent years of his ministry to preach from this same text on the anniversary of his ordination.* In the evening of that day, Mr. Bonar again preached on " *The times of refreshing.*" " A noble sermon showing the marks of such times. Ah ! when shall we have them here ? Lord, bless this word, to help their coming ! Put thy blessing upon this day ! Felt given over to God, as one bought with a price."

There was a rapid growth in his soul, perceptible to all who knew him well, from this time. Even his pulpit preparations, he used to say, became easier from this date. He had earnestly sought that the day of his ordination might be a time of new grace.; he expected it would be so; and there was a peculiar work to be done by his hands, for which the Holy Spirit did specially prepare him.

His diary does not contain much of his feelings during his residence in Dundee. His incessant labours left him little time, except what he scrupulously spent in the direct exercises of devotion. But what we have seen of his manner of study and self-examina-

* "The Acceptable Year of the Lord" was one of these anniversary sermons preached, November, 1840.

tion at Larbert, is sufficient to show in what a constant
state of cultivation his soul was kept ; and his habits
in these respects continued with him to the last.
Jeremy Taylor recommends—" If thou meanest to
enlarge thy religion, do it rather by enlarging thine
ordinary devotions than thy extraordinary." This
advice describes very accurately the plan of spiritual
life on which Mr. McCheyne acted. He did occasionally set apart seasons for special prayer and fasting,
occupying the time so set apart exclusively in devotion.
But the real secret of his soul's prosperity lay in the
daily enlargement of his heart in fellowship with his
God.   And the river deepened as it flowed on to eternity ; so that he at last reached that feature of a holy
pastor which Paul pointed out to Timothy, (1 Tim. iv.
15.)—" His profiting did appear to all."

In his own house every thing was fitted to make
you feel that the service of God was a cheerful service, while he sought that every arrangement of the
family should bear upon eternity. His morning hours
were set apart for the nourishment of his own soul ;
not, however, with the view of laying up a stock of
grace for the rest of the day—for manna will corrupt
if laid by—but rather with the view of " giving the
eye the habit of looking upward all the day, and
drawing down gleams from the reconciled countenance." He was sparing in the hours devoted to
sleep, and resolutely secured time for devotion before
breakfast, although often wearied and exhausted when
he laid himself to rest. " A soldier of the cross," was
his remark, " must endure hardness." Often he sang
a Psalm of praise, as soon as he arose, to stir up his
soul. Three chapters of the word was his usual
morning portion. This he thought little enough, for
he delighted exceedingly in the Scriptures : they
were better to him than thousands of gold or silver.
" When you write," said he to a friend, " tell me the
meaning of Scriptures." To another, in expressing
his value for the word, he said, " One gem from that
ocean is worth all the pebbles of earthly streams."

His chief season of relaxation seemed to be breakfast-time. He would come down with a happy countenance and a full soul; and after the sweet season of family prayer, forthwith commence forming plans for the day. When he was well, nothing seemed to afford him such true delight as to have his hands full of work. Indeed, it was often remarked that in him you found—what you rarely meet with—a man of high poetic imagination and deep devotion, who nevertheless was engaged unceasingly in the busiest and most laborious activities of his office.

His friends could observe how much his soul was engrossed during his times of study and devotion. If interrupted on such occasions, though he never seemed ruffled, yet there was a kind of gravity and silence that implied—" I wish to be alone." But he farther aimed at enjoying God *all the day.* And referring on one occasion to those blank hours which so often are a believer's burden—hours during which the soul is dry and barren—he observed, " They are proofs of how little we are *filled* with the presence of God, how little we are *branch-like* in our faith." Zech. iv. 12. John xv. 5.

This careful attention to the frame of his spirit did not hinder his preparation for his people : on the contrary, it kept alive his deep conscientiousness, and kept his warm compassion ever yearning. When asked to observe a Saturday as a day of fasting and prayer, along with some others who had a special object in view, he replied—" Saturday is an awkward day for ministers ; for though I love to seek help from on high, I love also diligently to set my thoughts in order for the Sabbath. I sometimes fear that you fail in this latter duty."

During his first years in Dundee, he often rode out in an afternoon to the ruined church of Invergowrie, to enjoy an hour's perfect solitude ; for he felt meditation and prayer to be the very sinews of his work. Such notices, also, as the following show his systematic pursuit of personal holiness :

" *April* 9, 1837.—Evening.—A very pleasant quietness. Study of the Epistle to the Hebrews. Came to a more intelligent view of the first six chapters

than ever before. Much refreshed by John Newton
instructed by Edwards. Help and freedom in prayer
Lord, what a happy season is a Sabbath evening
What will heaven be !"

"*April* 16.—Sabbath evening.—Much prayer and
peace. Reading the Bible only."

"*June* 2.—Much peace and rest to-night. Much
broken under a sense of my exceeding wickedness,
which no eye can see but thine. Much persuasion of
the sufficiency of Christ, and of the constancy of his
love. O how sweet to work all day for God, and
then to lie down at night under his smiles."

"*June* 17, 1838.—At Dumbarney Communion.
Much sin and coldness two days before. Lay low at
his feet ; found peace only in Jesus."

"*September* 25.—Spent last week at Blairgowrie ;
I hope not in vain. Much sin, weakness, and uselessness ; much delight in the word also, while opening
it up at family prayer. May God make the word
fire. Opened 1 Thessalonians, the whole ; enriching to
my own mind. How true is Psalm i. ; yet observed
in my heart a strange proneness to be entangled with
the affairs of this life ; not strange because I am good,
but because I have been so often taught that bitterness
is the end of it."

"*Sept.* 27.—Devoted chief part of Friday to fasting.
Humbled and refreshed."

"*Sept.* 30.—Sabbath—Very happy in my work.
Too little prayer in the morning. Must try to get
early to bed on Saturday, that I may 'rise a great
while before day.'" These early hours of prayer on
Sabbath, he endeavoured to have all his life ; not for
study, but for prayer. He never laboured at his sermons on a Sabbath. That day he kept for its original
end, the *refreshment of his soul.* Exod. xxxi. 37.

The parish of St. Peter's, to which he had come,
was large and very destitute. It is situated at the
west end of the town, and included some part of the
adjacent country. The church was built in connection with the Church Extension Scheme. The parish
was a *quoad sacra* parish, detached from St. John's.

It contains a population of four thousand souls, very many of whom never crossed the threshold of any sanctuary. His congregation amounted, at the very outset to about one thousand one hundred hearers, one third of whom came from distant parts of the town.

Here was a wide field for parochial labour. It was also a very dead region—few, even of those who were living Christians, breathing their life on others; for the surrounding mass of impenetrable heathenism had cast its sad influence even over them. His first impressions of Dundee were severe. "A city given to idolatry and hardness of heart. I fear there is much of what Isaiah speaks of, 'The prophets prophesy lies, and the people love to have it so.'"

His first months of labour were very trying. He was not strong in bodily health, and that winter a fatal influenza prevailed for two or three months, so that most of his time in his parish was spent in visiting the sick and dying. In such cases he was always ready. "Did I tell you of the boy I was asked to see on Sabbath evening, just when I had got myself comfortably seated at home? I went and was speaking to him of the freeness and fulness of Jesus, when he gasped a little and died."

In one of his first visits to the sick, the narrative of the Lord's singular dealings with one of his parishioners greatly encouraged him to carry the glad tidings to the distressed under every disadvantage. Four years before, a young woman had been seized with cholera, and was deprived of the use of speech for a whole year. The Bible was read to her, and men of God used to speak and pray with her. At the end of the year, her tongue was loosed, and the first words heard from her lips were praise and thanksgiving for what the Lord had done for her soul. It was in her chamber he was now standing, hearing from her own lips what the Lord had wrought.

On another occasion, during the first year of his ministry, he witnessed the death bed conversion of a man who, till within a few days of his end, almost denied that there was a God. This solid conversion, as he believed it to be, stirred him up to speak with all hopefulness, as well as earnestness, to the dying.

But it was, above all, to the children of God that his visitations seemed blessed. His voice, and his very eye, spoke tenderness; for personal affliction had taught him to feel sympathy with the sorrowing. Though the following is an extract from a letter, yet it will be recognized by many as exhibiting his mode of dealing with God's afflicted ones in his visitations. " There is a sweet word in Exodus (iii. 7,) which was pointed out to me the other day by a poor bereaved child of God—' I know their sorrows.' Study that; it fills the soul. Another word like it is in Psalm ciii. 14—' He knoweth our frame.' May your own soul, and that of your dear friends, be fed by these things. A dark hour makes Jesus bright. Another sweet word—' They knew not that it was Jesus.' "

I find some specimens of his sick visits among his papers, noted down at a time when his work had not grown upon his hands. " *January* 25, 1837—Visited Mt. McBain, a young woman of twenty-four, long ill of decline. Better or worse these ten years past. Spoke of ' *the one thing needful,*' plainly. She sat quiet. *February* 14th.—Had heard she was better— found her near dying. Spoke plainly and tenderly to her, commending Christ. Used many texts. She put out her hand kindly on leaving. 15th.—Still dying-like ; spoke as yesterday. She never opened her eyes. 16th.—Showed her the dreadfulness of wrath ; free-ness of Christ ; the majesty, justice, and truth of God. Poor M. is fast going the way whence she shall not return. Many neighbours also always gather in. 17th. —Read Psalm xxii. ; showed the sufferings of Christ ; how sufficient an atonement; how feeling a high priest. She breathed loud, and groaned through pain. Died this evening at seven. I hardly ever heard her speak any thing; and I will hope that thou art with Christ in glory, till I go and see. 20th.—Prayed at her funeral. Saw her laid in St. Peter's church yard, *the first laid there,* by her own desire, in the fresh mould where man never was laid. May it be a token that she is with Him who was laid in a new tomb."

He records another case. "*January* 4, 1837— Sent for to Mrs. S——. Very ill : asthmatic. Spoke on ' *no condemnation to them that are in Christ.*' She said, ' But am I in Christ ?' seemingly very anxious —said she had often been so, and had let it go by. 5th.—Still living ; spoke to her of Christ, and of full salvation. (Myself confined in the house till the 16th.) 16th.—Much worse. Not anxious to hear, but far from rest. Dark, uneasy eye. Asked me, ' What is it to believe ? Spoke to her on ' *God who made light shine out of darkness.*' She seemed to take up nothing. Lord, help ! 17th.—Still worse ; wearing away. No smile ; no sign of inward peace. Spoke of ' *Remember me.*' Went over the whole gospel in the form of personal address. She drowsy. 18th.— Quieter. ' *My Lord and my God.*' She spoke at intervals. More cheerful ; anxious that I should not go without prayer. Has much knowledge ; complete command of the Bible. 19th.—Spoke on ' *convincing of sin and righteousness.*' Rather more heart to hear. 20th.—Psalm li. Her look and her words were lightsome. 23d.—Faintish and restless ; no sign of peace. ' *I am the way,*' and Psalm xxv. 24th.— Still silent, and little sign of any thing. 26th.—Psalm xl. ' *The fearful pit.*' Very plain. Could not get any thing out of her. *February* 1st.—Died at twelve, noon ; no visible mark of light, or comfort, or hope. The day shall declare it."

One other case. ' *February* 5, 1839.—Called suddenly in the evening. Found him near death. Careless family. Many round him. Spoke of the freeness and sufficiency of Jesus, ' *Come unto me,*' &c., and ' *The wrath of God revealed from heaven.*' Told him he was going where he would see Christ ; asked him if he wished him to be his saviour ? He seemed to answer ; his father said, ' He is saying, yes.' But it was the throe of death. One or two indescribable gasps, and he died ! I sat silent, and let God preach. 7th.—

Spoke of the ' *Widow of Nain,*' and ' *Behold, I stand at the door.*' "

Attendance at funerals was often to him a season of much exercise. Should it not be to all ministers a time for solemn inquiry? Was I faithful with this soul? Could this soul have learned salvation from me every time I saw him? And did I pray as fervently as I spoke? And if we have tender pity for souls, we will sometimes feel as Mr. McCheyne records. " *September* 24.—Buried A. M. Felt bitterly the word, 'If any man draw back,' &c. Never had more bitter feelings at any funeral."

All who make any pretension to the office of shepherd visit their flocks;* yet there is a wide difference in the kind of visits which shepherds give. One does it formally, to discharge his duty and to quiet conscience; another makes it his delight. And of those who make it their delight, one goes forth on the regular plan of addressing all in somewhat of the same style; while another speaks freely, according as the wounds of his sheep come to view. On all occasions, this difficult and trying work must be gone about with a full heart, if it is to be gone about successfully at all. There is little in it to excite, for there is not the presence of numbers, and the few you see at a time are in their calmest, every day mood. Hence there is need of being full of grace, and need of feeling as though God did visit every hearer by your means. Our object is not to get duty done, but to get souls saved. Mr. McCheyne used to go forth in this spirit; and often after visiting from house to house for several hours, he would return to some room in the place in the evening, and preach to the gathered families. " *September* 26, 1838.—Good visiting day. Twelve families; many of them go no where. It is a great thing to be well furnished by meditation and prayer before setting out; it makes you a far more full and

---

* Baxter says, "I dare prognosticate from knowledge of the nature of true grace, that all godly ministers will make conscience of this duty, and address themselves to it, unless they be, by some extraordinary accident, disabled."—*Reformed Pastor.*

faithful witness. Preached in A. F.'s house, on Job, '*I know that my Reedeemer liveth.*' Very sweet and precious to myself."

Partly from his state of health, and partly from the vast accumulation of other labours, and the calls made on him for evangelizing elsewhere, he was never able to overtake the visitation of the whole district assigned him. He was blessed to attract and reclaim very many of the most degraded; and by Sabbath schools, and a regular eldership, to take superintendence of the population, to a great extent. Still he himself often said that his parish had never fully shared in the advantages that attend an aggressive system of parochial labour. Once, when spending a day in the rural parish of Collace, as we went in the afternoon from door to door, and spoke to the children whom we met on the road side, he smiled and said, "Well, how I envy a country minister; for he can get acquainted with all his people, and have some insight into their real character." Many of us thought that he afterwards erred, in the abundant frequency of his evangelistic labours at a time when he was still bound to a particular flock.

He had an evening class every week for the young people of his congregation. The Catechism and the Bible were his text books, while he freely introduced all manner of useful illustrations. He thought himself bound to prepare diligently for his classes, that he might give accurate and simple explanations, and unite what was interesting with the most solemn and awakening views. But it was his class for young communicants that engaged his deepest care, and wherein he saw most success. He began a class of this kind previous to his first communion, and continued to form it again some weeks before every similar occasion. His tract, published in 1840, "*This do in remembrance of me,*" may be considered as exhibiting the substance of his solemn examinations on these occasions.

He usually noted down his first impressions of his communicants, and compared these notes with what he afterwards saw in them. Thus: "M. K., sprightly and lightsome, yet sensible; she saw plainly that the converted alone should come to the table, but stumbled at the question, if she was converted. Yet she claimed being awakened and brought to Christ." Another: "Very staid, intelligent-like person, with a steady kind of anxiety, but, I fear, no feeling of helplessness. Thought that sorrow and prayer would obtain forgiveness. Told her plainly what I thought of her case." Another: "Knows she was once Christless; now she reads and prays, and is anxious. I doubt not there is some anxiety, yet I fear it may be only a self-reformation to recommend herself to God and to man. Told her plainly." "A. M., I fear much for him. Gave him a token with much anxiety; warned him very much." "C. P. does not seem to have any work of anxiety. He reads prayer books, &c. Does not pray in secret. Seems not very intelligent."

He sought to encourage Sabbath schools in all the districts of his parish. The hymn, "*Oil for the Lamp,*" was written to impress the parable on a class of Sabbath scholars, in 1841. Some of his sweet, simple tracts were written for these schools. "*Reasons why Children should fly to Christ*" was the first, written at New Year, 1839; and "*The Lambs of the Flock*" was another at a later period. His heart felt for the young. One evening, after visiting some of his Sabbath schools, he writes: "Had considerable joy in teaching the children. O for real heart-work among them!" He could accommodate himself to their capacities; and he did not reckon it vain to use his talents in order to attract their attention; for he regarded the soul of a child as infinitely precious. Ever watchful for opportunities, on the blank leaf of a book which he sent to a little boy of his congregation, he wrote these simple lines:—

> Peace be to thee, gentle boy!
> Many years of health and joy!
> Love your Bible more than play—
> Grow in wisdom every day.
> Like the lark on hovering wing,
> Early rise, and mount and sing;

Like the dove that found no rest
Till it flew to Noah's breast:—
Rest not in this world of sin,
Till the Saviour take thee in.

He had a high standard in his mind as to the moral qualifications of those who should teach the young. When a female teacher was sought for to conduct an evening school in his parish for the sake of the mill-girls, he wrote to one interested in the cause—" The qualifications she should possess for sewing and knitting, you will understand far better than I. She should be able to keep up in her scholars the fluency of reading, and the knowledge of the Bible and Catechism, which they may have already acquired. She should be able to teach them to sing the praises of God, with feeling and melody. But, far above all, she should be a Christian woman, not in name only, but in deed and in truth—one whose heart has been touched by the Spirit of God, and who can love the souls of little children. Any teacher who wanted this last qualification, I would look upon as a curse rather than a blessing—a centre of blasting, and coldness, and death, instead of a centre from which life, and warmth, and heavenly influence might emanate."

It was very soon after his ordination that he began his weekly prayer meeting in the Church. He had heard how meetings of this kind had been blessed in other places, and never had he any cause to regret having set apart the Thursday evening for this holy purpose. One of its first effects was to quicken those who had already believed. They were often refreshed on these occasions even more than on the Sabbath. Some of the most solemn seasons of his ministry were at those meetings. At their commencement, he wrote to me an account of his manner of conducting them— " I give my people a scripture to be hidden in the heart—generally a promise of the Spirit, or the wonderful effects of his outpouring.* I give them the

---

* The first text he gave to be thus hidden in the heart, was Isaiah xxxiv. 15—" Until the Spirit be poured out from on high."

heads of a sermon upon it for about twenty minutes. Prayer goes before and follows. Then I read some history of revivals, and comment in passing. I think the people are very much interested in it : a number of people come from all parts of the town. But, O ! I need much the living Spirit to my own soul; I want my life to be hid with Christ in God. At present there is too much hurry, and bustle, and outward working, to allow the calm working of the Spirit on the heart. I seldom get time to meditate, like Isaac, at evening-tide, except when I am tired; but the dew comes down when all nature is at rest—when every leaf is still."

A specimen of the happy freedom and familiar illustrations which his people felt to be peculiar to these meetings, may be found in the notes taken by one of his hearers, of " *Expositions of the Epistles to the Seven Churches,*" given during the year 1838.

He had himself great delight in the Thursday evening meetings. " They will doubtless be remembered in eternity with songs of praise," said he, on one occasion ; and at another time, observing the tender frame of soul which was often manifested at these seasons, he said, " There is a stillness to the last word— not as on Sabbaths, a rushing down at the end of the prayer, as if glad to get out of God's presence." So many believing and so many inquiring souls used to attend, and so few of the worldlings, that you seemed to breathe the atmosphere of heaven.

But it was his Sabbath day's services that brought multitudes together, and were soon felt throughout the town. He was ever so ready to assist his brethren, so much engaged in every good work, and latterly so often interrupted by inquiries, that it might be thought he had no time for careful preparation, and might be excused for the absence of it. But, in truth, he never preached without careful attention bestowed on his subject. He might, indeed, have little time—often the hours of a Saturday were all the time he could obtain—but his daily study of the Scriptures stored his mind, and formed a continual preparation. Much of his Sabbath services was a drawing out of what he had carried in during busy days of the week.

His voice was remarkably clear—his manner attractive by its mild dignity. His form itself drew the eye.* He spoke from the pulpit as one earnestly occupied with the souls before him. He made them feel sympathy with what he spoke, for his own eye and heart were on them. He was, at the same time, able to bring out illustrations at once simple and felicitous, often with poetic skill and elegance. He wished to use Saxon words, for the sake of being understood by the most illiterate in his audience. And while his style was singularly clear, this clearness itself was so much the consequence of his being able thoroughly to analyse and explain his subject, that all his hearers alike reaped the benefit.

He went about his public work with awful reverence. So evident was this, that I remember a countryman in my parish observing to me—" Before he opened his lips, as he came along the passage, there was something about him that sorely affected me."

In the vestry, there was never any idle conversation; all was preparation of heart in approaching God; and a short prayer preceded his entering the pulpit. Surely in going forth to speak for God, a man may well be overawed! Surely in putting forth his hand to sow the seed of the kingdom, a man may even tremble! And surely we should aim at nothing less than to pour forth the truth upon our people through the channel of our own living and deeply affected souls.

After announcing the subject of his discourse, he used generally to show the position it occupied in the context, and then proceed to bring out the doctrines of the text in the manner of our old divines. This done, he divided his subject; and herein he was eminently skilful. "The heads of his sermons," said a friend, " were not the milestones that tell you how near you are to your journey's end, but they were nails which fixed and fastened all he said. Divisions

* "Gratior est pulchro veniens e corpore virtus."

are often dry; but not so *his* divisions—they were so
textual and so feeling, and they brought out the spirit
of a passage so surprisingly."

It was his wish to arrive nearer at the primitive
mode of expounding Scripture in his sermons. Hence
when one asked him, if he was never afraid of running short of sermons some day, he replied—" No ; I
am just an interpreter of Scripture in my sermons;
and when the Bible runs dry, then I shall." And in
the same spirit he carefully avoided the too common
mode of accommodating texts—fastening a doctrine
on the words, not drawing it from the obvious connection of the passage. He endeavoured at all times
to *preach the mind of the Spirit in a passage ;* for
he feared that to do otherwise would be to grieve the
Spirit who had written it. Interpretation was thus a
solemn matter to him. And yet, adhering scrupulously to this sure principle, he felt himself in no way
restrained from using, for every day's necessities, all
parts of the Old Testament as much as the New.
His manner was first to ascertain the primary sense
and application, and so proceed to handle it for present use. Thus, on Isaiah xxvi. 16—19, he began—
" This passage, I believe, refers *literally* to the conversion of God's ancient people." He regarded the
prophecies as *history yet to be,* and drew lessons
from them accordingly as he would have done from
the past. Every spiritual gift being in the hands of
Jesus, if he found Moses or Paul in the possession of
precious things, he forthwith was led to follow them
into the presence of that same Lord who gave them
all their grace.

There is a wide difference between preaching *doctrine* and preaching *Christ.* Mr. McCheyne preached
all the doctrines of Scripture as understood by our
Confession of Faith, dwelling upon ruin by the fall,
and recovery by the Mediator. " The things of the
human heart, and the things of the Divine mind,"
were in substance his constant theme. From personal
experience of deep temptation, he could lay open the
secrets of the heart, so that he once said, "He supposed

the reason why some of the worst sinners in Dundee had come to hear him was, because his heart exhibited so much likeness to theirs." Still it was not *doctrine* alone that he preached; it was *Christ*, from whom all doctrine shoots forth as rays from a centre. He sought to hang every vessel and flagon upon him. " It is strange," he wrote after preaching on Revelations i. 15—" It is strange how sweet and precious it is to preach directly about Christ, compared with all other subjects of preaching." And he often expressed a dislike of the phrase, " *giving attention to religion*," because it seemed to substitute doctrine, and a devout way of thinking, for *Christ himself.*

It is difficult to convey to those who never knew him a correct idea of the sweetness and holy unction of his preaching. Some of his sermons, printed from his own manuscripts, (although almost all are first copies,) may convey a correct idea of his style and mode of preaching doctrine. But there are no notes that give any true idea of his affectionate appeals to the heart and searching applications. These he seldom wrote; they were poured forth at the moment when his heart filled with his subject; for his rule was to set before his hearers a body of truth first—and there always was a vast amount of Bible truth in his discourses—and then urge home the application. His exhortations flowed from his doctrine, and thus had both variety and power. He was systematic in this; for he observed—" Appeals to the careless, &c., come with power on the back of some massy truth. See how Paul does, (Acts xiii. 40,) ' Beware, *therefore*, lest, &c., and (Hebrews ii. 1,) ' *Therefore*, we should,' &c."

He was sometimes a little unguarded in his statements, when his heart was deeply moved and his feelings stirred, and sometimes he was too long in his addresses; but this, also, arose from the fulness of his soul. " Another word," he thought, " may be blessed, though the last has made no impression."

Many will remember for ever the blessed communion Sabbaths that were enjoyed in St. Peter's. From

the very first these communion seasons were remark
ably owned of God. The awe of His presence used
to be upon the people, and the house filled with the
odour of the ointment, when His name was poured
forth, (Song i. 3.) But on common Sabbaths also
many soon began to journey long distances to attend
at St. Peter's—many from country parishes, who
would return home with their hearts burning, as they
talked of what they had heard that day.

Mr. McCheyne knew the snare of popularity, and
naturally was one that would have been fascinated by
it; but the Lord kept him. He was sometimes extra-
ordinarily helped in his preaching, but at other times,
though not perceived by his hearers, his soul felt as if
left to its own resources. The cry of Rowland Hill
was constantly on his lips, " Master, help !" and often
is it written at the close of his sermons. Much affliction, also, was a thorn in the flesh to him. He
described himself as often " strong as a giant when in
the church, but like a willow wand when all was
over." But certainly, above all, his abiding sense of
the Divine favour was his safeguard. He began his
ministry in Dundee with this sunshine on his way.
" As yet I have been kept not only in the light of his
reconciled countenance, but very much under the
guiding eye of our providing God. Indeed, as I remember good old Swartz used to say, ' I could not
have imagined that He could have been so gracious to
us.' " I believe that while he had some sorer conflicts,
he had also far deeper joy after his return from
Palestine than in the early part of his ministry;
though from the very commencement of it, he enjoyed
that sense of the love of God which keeps the heart
and mind. This was the true secret of his holy
walk, and of his calm humility. But for this, his ambition would have become the only principle of many
an action; but now the sweeter love of God constrained him, and the natural ambition of his spirit could be
discerned only as suggesting to him the idea of making
attempts which others would have declined.

What monotony there is in the ministry of many !
Duty presses on the heels of duty in an endless circle.

But it is not so when the Spirit is quickening both the pastor and his flock. Then there is all the variety of life. It was so here.

The Lord began to work by his means almost from the first day he came. There was ever one and another stricken, and going apart to weep alone.

The flocking of souls to his ministry, and the deep interest excited, drew the attention of many, and raised the wish in some quarters, to have him as their pastor. He had not been many months engaged in his laborious work, when he was solicited to remove to the parish of Skirling, near Biggar. It was an offer that presented great advantages above his own field of labour as to worldly gain, and in respect of the prospect it held out of comparative ease and comfort; for the parish was small, and the emolument great. But as it is required of a bishop, that he be " not greedy of filthy lucre;" nay, that he be " one who has no love of money" (ἀφιλαργυρος, 1 Tim. iii. 3,) at all, so was it true, that in him these qualifications eminently shone. His remarks in a letter to his father contain the honest expression of his feelings :—" I am set down among nearly four thousand people ; eleven hundred people have taken seats in my church. I bring my message, such as it is, within the reach of that great company every Sabbath day. I dare not leave this people. I dare not leave three thousand or four thousand, for three hundred people. Had this been offered me before, I would have seen it a direct intimation from God, and would heartily have embraced it. How I should have delighted to feed so precious a little flock—to watch over every family—to know every heart—' to allure to brighter worlds and lead the way !' But God has not so ordered it. He has set me down among the noisy mechanics and political weavers of this godless town. He will make the money sufficient. He that paid his taxes from a fish's mouth, will supply all my need." He had already expressed the hope, ' Perhaps the Lord will make this wilderness of chimney tops to be green and beautiful as the garden of the Lord, a field which the Lord hath blessed."

His health was delicate; and the harassing cares and endless fatigue incident to his position, in a town like Dundee, seemed unsuitable to his spirit. This belief led to another attempt to remove him to a country sphere. In the summer of this same year (1837) he was strongly urged to preach as a candidate for the vacant parish of St. Martin's, near Perth, and assured of the appointment if he would only come forward. But he declined again: "My Master has placed me here with his own hand; and I never will, directly or indirectly, seek to be removed."

There were circumstances in this latter case that made the call on him appear urgent in several points of view. In coming to a resolution, he mentions one interesting element in the decision, in a letter to me, dated *August* 8th. "I was much troubled about being asked to go to a neighbouring parish at present vacant, and made it a matter of prayer; and I mention it now because of the wonderful answer to prayer which I think I received from God. I prayed that in order to settle my own mind completely about staying, he would awaken some of my people. I agreed that that should be a sign he would wish me to stay. The next morning, I think, or at least the second morning, there came to me two young persons I had never seen before, in great distress. What brought this to mind was, that they came to me again yesterday, and their distress is greatly increased. Indeed I never saw any people in such anguish about their souls. I cannot but regard this as a real answer to prayer. I have also several other persons in deep distress, and I feel that I am quite helpless in comforting them. I would fain be like Noah, who put out his hand and took in the weary dove; but God makes me stand by and feel that I am a child. Will God never cast the scenes of our labour near each other? We are in his hand; let him do as seemeth him good. Pray for me, for my people, for my own soul, that I be not a castaway."

Few godly pastors can be willing to change the scene of their labours, unless it be plain that the

cloudy pillar is pointing them away. It is perilous
for men to choose for themselves; and too often has
it happened that the minister who, on slight grounds
moved away from his former watch-tower, has had
reason to mourn over the disappointment of his hopes
in his larger and wider sphere. But while this is
admitted, probably it may appear unwarrantable in
Mr. McCheyne to have prayed for a sign of the
Lord's will. It is to be observed, however, that he
decided the point of duty on other grounds and it
was only with the view of obtaining an additional
confirmation by the occurrences of Providence, that
he prayed in this manner, in submission to the will of
the Lord. He never held it right to decide the path
of duty by any such signs or tokens; he believed that
the written word supplied sufficient data for guiding
the believing soul; and such providential occurrences
as happened in this case he regarded as important,
only so far as they might be answers to prayer. Indeed, he himself has left us a glance of his views on
this point in a fragment, which (for it is not dated)
may have been written about this time. He had been
thinking on *" Gideon's Fleece."*

When God called Gideon forth to fight—
" Go, save thou Israel in thy might,"—
The faithful warrior sought a sign
That God would on his labour shine.
 The man who, at thy dread command,
 Lifted the shield and deadly brand,
 To do thy strange and fearful work—
 Thy work of blood and vengeance, Lord!—
 Might need assurance doubly tried,
 To prove thou wouldst his steps betide.
But when the message which we bring
Is one to make the dumb man sing;
To bid the blind man wash and see,
The lame to leap with ecstasy;
To raise the soul that's bowed down.
To wipe away the tears and frown;
To sprinkle all the heart within,
From the accusing voice of sin—
 Then, such a sign my call to prove,
 To preach my Saviour's dying love,
 I cannot, dare not, hope to find.

In the close of the same year 1837, he agreed to become Secretary to the Association for Church Extension in the county of Forfar. The Church Extension scheme, though much misrepresented and much misunderstood, had in view as its genuine, sincere endeavour, to bring to overgrown parishes the advantage of a faithful minister, placed over such a number of souls as he could readily visit. Mr. McCheyne cheerfully and diligently forwarded these objects to the utmost of his power. " It is the cause of God," said he, "and therefore I am willing to spend and be spent for it." It compelled him to ride much from place to place ; but riding was an exercise of which he was fond, and which was favourable to his health. As a specimen—" *Dec.* 4th, 1838. Travelled to Montrose. Spoke, along with Mr. Guthrie, at a Church Extension meeting ; eight or nine hundred present. Tried to do something in the Saviour's cause, both directly and indirectly. Next day at Forfar. Spoke in the same cause."

How heartily he entered into this scheme may be seen from the following extract. In a letter of an after date to Mr. Roxburgh, he says—" Every day I live, I feel more and more persuaded that it is the cause of God and of his kingdom in Scotland in our day. Many a time, when I thought myself a dying man, the souls of the perishing thousands in my own parish, who never enter any house of God, have lain heavy on my heart. Many a time have I prayed that the eyes of our enemies might be opened, and that God would open the hearts of our rulers, to feel that their highest duty and greatest glory is to support the ministers of Christ, and to send these to every perishing soul in Scotland." He felt that their misery was all the greater, and their need the deeper, that such neglected souls had no wish for help, and would never ask for it themselves. Nor was it that he imagined that, if churches were built and ministers endowed, this would of itself be sufficient to reclaim the multitudes of perishing men. But he sought and expected that the Lord would send faithful men into his vine-

yard. These new churches were to be like cisterns—
ready to catch the shower when it should fall, just as
his own did in the day of the Lord's power.

His views on the subject were summed up in the
following lines, written one day as he sat in company
with some of his zealous brethren who were deeply
engaged in the scheme :—

> " Give me a man of God the truth to preach,
> A house of prayer within convenient reach,
> Seat rents the poorest of the poor can pay,
> A spot so small one pastor can survey,
> Give these—and give the Spirit's genial shower,
> Scotland shall be a garden all in flower !"

Another public duty, to which during all the years
of his ministry he gave constant attention, was attendance at the meetings of Presbytery. His candour,
and uprightness, and Christian generosity, were felt by
all his brethren ; and his opinion, though the opinion
of so young a man, was regarded with more than
common respect. In regard to the great public questions that were then shaking the Church of Scotland,
his views were decided and unhesitating. No policy,
in his view, could be more ruinous to true Christianity,
or more fitted to blight vital godliness, than that of Moderatism. He wrote once to a friend in Ireland—" You
don't know what Moderatism is. It is a plant that
our heavenly Father never planted, and I trust it is
now to be rooted up." The great question of the
Church's independence of the civil power in all matters
spiritual, and the right of Christian people to judge
if the pastor appointed over them had the Shepherd's
voice, he invariably held to be a part of Scripture truth;
which, therefore, must be preached and carried into
practice, at all hazards. In like manner he rejoiced
exceedingly in the settlement of faithful ministers.
The appointments of Mr. Baxter to Hilltown, Mr.
Lewis to St. David's, and Mr. Miller to Wallacetown,
at a later period, are all noticed by him with expressions of thankfulness and joy ; and it occasioned the
same feelings if he heard of the destitution of any
parish in any part of the country supplied. He writes,

September 20, 1838, "Present at A. B.'s ordination at Collace with great joy. Blessed be God for the gift of this pastor. Give testimony to the word of thy grace."

Busy at home, he nevertheless always had a keenly evangelistic spirit. He might have written much, and have gained a name by his writings; but he laid every thing aside when put in comparison with preaching the everlasting gospel. He scarcely ever refused an invitation to preach on a week day; and travelling from place to place did not interrupt his fellowship with God. His occasional visits during these years were much blessed. At Blairgowrie and Collace his visits were longed for as times of special refreshment; nor was it less so at Kirriemuir, when he visited Mr. Cormick, or at Abernyte in the days when Mr. Hamilton (now of Regent Square, London,) and afterwards Mr. Manson, were labouring in that vineyard. It would be difficult even to enumerate the places which he watered at communion seasons; and in some of these it was testified of him, that not the words he spoke, but the *holy manner* in which he spoke, was the chief means of arresting souls.

Occasionally two or three of us, whose lot was cast within convenient distance, and whose souls panted for the same water brooks, used to meet together to spend a whole day in confession of ministerial and personal sins, with prayer for grace—guiding ourselves by the reading of the word. At such times we used to meet in the evening with the flock of the pastor in whose house the meeting had been held through the day, and there unitedly pray for the Holy Spirit to be poured down upon the people. The first time we held such a meeting, there were tokens of blessing observed by several of us; and the week after he wrote—"Has there been any fruit of the happy day we spent with you? I thought I saw some the Sabbath after, here. In due season we shall reap if we faint not; only be thou strong, and of a good courage." The incident that encouraged him is recorded in his diary. An elderly person came to tell him how the river of joy and peace in believing had that Sabbath most singularly flowed through her soul, so that she blessed God that she ever came to St. Peter's." He adds, " N. B.—This seems a fruit of our prayer meeting, begun last Wednesday at Collace—one drop of the shower."

It should have been remarked ere now, that during all his ministry he was careful to use not only the direct means appointed for the conversion of souls, but those also that appear more indirect, such as the key of discipline. In regard to the Lord's Supper, his little tract explains his views. He believed that to keep back those whose profession was a credible profession, even while the pastor might have strong doubts as to their fitness in his own mind, was not the rule laid down for us in the New Testament. At the same time he as steadily maintained that no unconverted person *ought* to come to the Lord's table; and on this point " they should judge themselves, if they would not be judged."

When communicants came to be admitted for the first time, or when parents that had long been communicants came for baptism to their children, it was his custom to ask them solemnly if their souls were saved. His dealing was blessed to the conversion of not a few young persons who were coming carelessly forward to the communion; and he records the blessing that attended his faithful dealing with a parent coming to speak with him about the baptism of his child. The man said that he had been taking a thought, and believed himself in the right way— that he felt his disposition better, for he could forgive injuries. Mr. McCheyne showed him that nevertheless he was ignorant of God's righteousness. The man laid it to heart; and when Mr. McCheyne said that he thought it would be better to defer the baptism, at once offered to come again and speak on the matter. On a subsequent visit, he seemed really to have seen his error, and to have cast away his own righteousness. When his child was baptized, it was joy to the pastor's heart to have the good hope that the man had received salvation.

In connection with the superstitious feeling of the most depraved as to baptism, he related an affecting occurrence. A careless parent one evening entered his house, and asked him to come with him to baptize a dying child. He knew that neither this man nor his wife ever entered the door of a church; but he rose and went with him to the miserable dwelling. There an infant lay, apparently dying; and many of the female neighbours, equally depraved with the parents, stood round. He came forward to where the child was, and spoke to the parents of their ungodly state and fearful guilt before God, and concluded by showing them that, in such circumstances, he would consider it sinful in him to administer baptism to their infant. They said, " He might at least do it for the sake of the poor child." He told them that it was not baptism that saved a soul, and that out of true concern for themselves he must not do as they wished. The friends around the bed then joined the parents in upbraiding him as having no pity on the poor infant's soul! He stood among them still, and showed them that it was they who had been thus cruel to their child; and then lifted up his voice in solemn warning, and left the house amid their ignorant reproaches.

Nor did he make light of the kirk session's power to rebuke and deal with an offender. Once from the pulpit, at an ordination of elders, he gave the following testimony upon this head :—" When I first entered upon the work of the ministry among you, I was exceedingly ignorant of the vast importance of church discipline. I thought that my great and almost only work was to pray and preach. I saw your souls to be so precious, and the time so short, that I devoted all my time, and care, and strength, to labour in word and doctrine. When cases of discipline were brought before me and the elders, I regarded them with something like abhorrence. It was a duty I shrunk from ;

and I may truly say it nearly drove me from the work of the ministry among you altogether. But it pleased God, who teaches his servants in another way than man teaches, to bless some of the cases of discipline to the manifest and undeniable conversion of the souls of those under our care; and from that hour a new light broke in upon my mind, and I saw that if preaching be an ordinance of Christ, so is church discipline. I now feel very deeply persuaded that both are of God—that two keys are committed to us by Christ, the one the key of doctrine, by means of which we unlock the treasures of the Bible, the other the key of discipline, by which we open or shut the way to the sealing ordinances of the faith. Both are Christ's gift, and neither is to be resigned without sin."

There was still another means of enforcing what he preached, in the use of which he has excelled all his brethren, namely, the holy consistency of his daily walk. Aware that one idle word, one needless contention, one covetous act, may destroy in our people the effect of many a solemn expostulation and earnest warning, he was peculiarly circumspect in his every day walk. He wished to be always in the presence of God. If he travelled, he laboured to enjoy God by the way, as well as to do good to others by dropping a word in season. In riding or walking, he seized opportunities of giving a useful tract; and, on principle, he preferred giving it to the person directly rather than casting it on the road. The former way, he said, was more open—there was no stealth in it—and we ought to be as clear as crystal in speaking or acting for Jesus. In writing a note, however short, he sought to season it with salt. If he passed a night in a strange place, he tried to bear the place specially on his soul at the mercy seat; and if compelled to take some rest from his too exhausting toils, his recreations were little else than a change of occupation, from one mode of glorifying God to another.* His beautiful

---

* Baxter's words are no less than the truth. "Recreation to a minister must be as whetting is with the mower, that is, only to be

hymn, "*I am a debtor*," was written in May, 1837, at a leisure hour.

Whatever be said in the pulpit men will not much regard, though they may feel it at the time, it the minister does not say the same in private, with equal earnestness, in speaking with his people face to face; and it must be in our moments of most familiar intercourse with them that we are thus to put the seal to all we say in public. Familiar moments are the times when the things that are most closely twined round the heart are brought out to view ; and shall we forbear, by tacit consent, to introduce the Lord that bought us, into such happy hours? We must not only speak faithfully to our people in our sermons, but live faithfully for them too. Perhaps it may be found, that the reason why many, who do certainly preach the gospel fully and in all earnestness, are not owned of God in the conversion of souls, lies in their defective exhibition of grace in these easy moments of life. " Them that honour me, I will honour;" 1 Samuel ii. 30. It was noticed long ago that men will give you leave to *preach against* their sins as much as you will, if so be you will but be friendly with them when you have done, and talk as they do, live as they live, and be indifferent with them in your conference. How much otherwise it was with Mr. McCheyne, all who knew him are witnesses !

His visits to friends were times when he sought to do good to their souls ; and never was he satisfied unless he could guide the conversation to bear upon the things of eternity. When he could not do so, he generally remained silent. And yet his demeanour was easy and pleasant to all, exhibiting at once meek-

---

used so far as is necessary for his work. May a physician in the plague time take any more relaxation or recreation than is necessary for his life, when so many are expecting his help in a case of life and death?" "Will you stand by and see sinners gasping under the pangs of death, and say, God doth not require me to make myself a drudge to save them ? Is this the voice of ministerial or Christian compassion, or rather of sensual laziness and diabolical cruelty ?"—*Reformed Pastor*, vi. 6.

ness of faith and delicacy of feeling. There was in his character a high refinement that came out in poetry and true politeness; and there was something in his graces that reminded one of his own remark, when explaining *"the spices"* of Song iv. 16, when he said that "some believers were a garden that had fruit trees, and so were useful; but we ought also to have *spices*, and so be attractive." Wishing to convey his grateful feelings to a fellow-labourer in Dundee, he sent him a Hebrew Bible, with these few lines prefixed:

> " Anoint mine eyes,   Unstop mine ear,
>   O holy Dove!   Made deaf by sin,
>   That I may prize   That I may hear
>   This book of love.   Thy voice within.
>
>   Break my hard heart,
>   Jesus, my Lord,
>   In the inmost part
>   Hide thy sweet word."

It was on a similar occasion, in 1838, that he wrote the lines, *"Thy word is a lamp unto my feet."* At another time, sitting under a shady tree, and casting his eye on the hospitable dwelling in which he found a pleasant retreat, his grateful feelings flowed out to his kind friend in the lines that follow:

"PEACE TO THIS HOUSE."

> Long may peace within this dwelling
>   Have its resting place;
> Angel shields all harm repelling—
>   God, their God of grace.
>
> May the dove-like Spirit guide them
>   To the upright land!
> May the Saviour-shepherd feed them
>   From his gentle hand!

Never was there one more beloved as a friend, and seldom any whose death could cause so many to feel as if no other friend could ever occupy his room. Some, too, can say that so much did they learn from his holy walk, "that it is probable a day never passes wherein they have not some advantage from his friendship.''*

I find written on the leaf of one of his note books, a short memorandum, *" Rules worth remembering.—* When visiting in a family, whether ministerially or otherwise, speak particularly to *the strangers* about eternal things. Perhaps God has brought you together just to save that soul." And then he refers to some instances which occurred to himself, in which God seemed to honour a word spoken in this incidental way.

In this spirit, he was enabled for nearly three years to give his strength to his Master's service. Sickness sometimes laid him aside, and taught him what he had to suffer; but he rose from it to go forth again to his joyful labours. Often, after a toilsome day, there were inquirers waiting for him, so that he had to begin work afresh in a new form. But this was his delight; it was a kind of interruption which he allowed even on a Saturday, in the midst of his studies. He was led to resolve not to postpone any inquirers till a future time, by finding that having done so on one occasion at a pressing moment, the individuals never returned; and so alive was he to the responsibilities of his office, that he ever after feared to lose such an opportunity of speaking with souls at a time when they were aroused to concern. Busy one evening with some extra-parochial work, he was asked if any person should be admitted to see him that night. " Surely—what do we live for?" was his immediate reply. It was his manner, too, on a Saturday afternoon, to visit one or two of his sick who seemed near the point of death, with the view of being thus stirred up to a more direct application of the truth to his flock on the morrow, as dying men on the edge of eternity.

We have already observed that in his doctrine there

* Ἐγὼ μὲν δὴ κατανοῶν τοῦ ἀνδρὸς τήν τε σοφίαν καὶ τὴν γενναιότητα, οὔτε μὴ μεμνῆσθαι δύναμαι αὐτῶν, οὔτε μεμνημένος μὴ οὐκ ἐπαινεῖν. Εἰ δέ τις τῶν ἀρετῆς ἐφιεμένων ὠφελιμωτέρῳ τινὶ Σωκράτους συνεγένετο ἐκεῖνον ἐγὼ τὸν ἄνδρα ἀξιομακαριστότατον νομίζω.

was nothing that differed from the views of truth laid
down in the standards of our Church. He saw no
inconsistency in preaching an electing God, who
" calleth whom he will;" and a salvation free to
" whosoever will;" nor in declaring the absolute sovereignty of God, and yet the unimpaired responsibility
of man. He preached Christ as a gift laid down by
the Father for every sinner freely to take. In the
beginning of his ministry, as he preached the fulness
of the glad tidings, and urged on his people that there
was enough in the glad tidings to bring direct and
immediate assurance to every one who really believed
them, some of his flock were startled. For he ever
preached that while it is true that there are believers
who do not enjoy full assurance of the love of God,
yet certainly no true believer should remain satisfied
in the absence of this blessed peace. Not a few had
hitherto been accustomed to take for granted that
they might be Christians, though they knew of no
change ; and had never thought of enjoying the knowledge of the love of God as their present portion.
They heard that others, who were reckoned believers,
had doubts ; so they had come to consider fears and
doubts as the very marks of a believing soul. The
consequence had been that, in past days, many concluded themselves to be Christians, because they
seemed to be in the very state of mind of which those
who were reputed to be believers spoke, viz., doubt
and alarm. Alas ! in *their* case there could be nothing
else, for they had only a name to live.

Some one wrote to him, putting several questions
concerning conversion, assurance, and faith, which
had been stirred up by his ministry. The import of
the questions may be gathered from his reply, which
was as follows :—

" 1. *I doubt if there are many saints who live and
die without a comfortable sense of forgiveness, and
acceptance with God.* The saints of whom the Bible
speaks seem to have enjoyed it richly both in life and
death. See the murderers of our Lord, Acts ii. 41 ;
the Ethiopian, Acts viii. 39 ; the jailor, Acts xvi. 35.

David also felt it, sinful man though he was, Romans iv. 6. Paul also prayed that the Romans might have it; Romans xv. 13. I fear this objection is generally made by those who are living in sin, and do not wish to know the dangerous road they are on.

"2. *A sense of forgiveness does not proceed from marks seen in yourself, but from a discovery of the beauty, worth, and freeness of Christ*; Psa. xxxiv. 5. We look *out* for peace, not *in*. At the same time there is also an assurance rising from what we see in ourselves: the seal of the Spirit, love to the brethren, &c., are the chief marks.

"3. *Feeling a body of sin is a mark that we are like Paul, and that we are Christ's ;* Rom. vii. ; Gal. v. 17. Paul was cheerful with a body of sin ; and so ought we to be. So was David, and all the saints.

"4. *I do not think there is any difference between those converted within these few years, and those who were Christians before.* Many of those converted since I came, are, I fear, very unholy. I fear this more than any thing. I fear there is too much talk and too little reality. Still there are many good figs—many of whom I am persuaded better things, and things that accompany salvation. The answer to your question I fear is this, that many used to be taken for Christians before, who had only a name to live, and were dead. I think there is more discrimination now. But take care and be not proud, for that goes before a fall. Take care of censorious judging of others, as if all must be converted in the same way. " God moves in a mysterious way. He hath mercy on whom he will have mercy. To him alone be glory."

He thus stated his views on another occasion. Referring to Song vi. 3, " My Beloved is mine," following " My Beloved is gone down into his garden," he said, "This is the faith of assurance—a complete, unhesitating embracing of Christ as my righteousness and my strength and my all. A common mistake is that this clear conviction that Christ is mine, is an attainment far on in the divine life, and that it springs from evidences seen in my heart. When I see myself a new creature, Christ on the throne in my heart, love to the brethren, &c., it is often thought that I may begin then to say ' My Beloved is mine.' How different this passage. The moment Jesus comes down into the garden to the beds of spices—the moment he reveals himself, the soul cries out, ' My Beloved is mine.' So saith Thomas : John xx. 27, 28. The moment Jesus came in and revealed his wounds, Thomas cried out, ' My Lord and my God.' He did not look to see if he was believing, or if the graces of love and humility were reigning ; but all he saw and thought of was Jesus and he crucified and risen." At a subsequent period, when preaching on Matt. xi. 28, " Come unto me," he said, " I suppose it is almost impossible to explain what it is to come to Jesus, it is so simple. If you asked a sick person who had been healed, what it was to come and be healed, he could hardly tell you. As far as the Lord has given me light in this matter, and looking at what my own heart does in like circumstances, I do not feel that there is any thing more in coming to Jesus than just believing what God says about his Son to be true. I believe that many people keep themselves in darkness by expecting something more than this. Some of you will ask, ' Is there no *appropriating* of Christ ? no *putting out the hand of faith ?* no touching the hem of his garment ?' I quite grant, beloved, there is such a thing, but I do not think it is inseparable from believing the record. If the Lord persuades you of the glory and power of Immanuel, I feel persuaded that you cannot but choose him. It is like opening the shutters of a dark room ; the sun that moment shines in. So, the eye that is opened to the testimony of God, receives Christ that moment."

In the case of a faithful ministry, success is the rule; want of it the exception. For it is written, " In doing this thou shalt both save thyself and them that hear thee ;" 1 Tim. iv. 16. Mr. McCheyne expected it, and the Lord exceeded all his hopes.

It was not yet common for persons in anxiety to go

to their pastor for advice; but soon it became an almost weekly occurrence. While it was yet rare, two of his young people wrote a joint note, asking liberty to come and speak with him, "For we are anxious about our souls." Among those who came there were those who had striven against the truth—persons who used to run out of hearing when the Bible was read—throw down a tract if the name of God was in it—go quickly to sleep after a Sabbath's pleasure in order to drown the fear of dropping into hell. There were many whose whole previous life had been but a threadbare profession. There were some open sinners too. In short, the Lord glorified himself by the variety of those whom his grace subdued, and the variety of means by which his grace reached its object.

One could tell him that the reading of the chapter in the church with a few remarks, had been the time of her awakening. Another had been struck to the heart by some expression he used in his first prayer before sermon one Sabbath morning. But most were arrested in the preaching of the word. An interesting case was that of one who was aroused to concern during his sermon on " *Unto whom coming as unto a living stone.*" As he spoke of the Father taking the gem out of his bosom, and laying it down for a foundation stone, she felt in her soul, "I know nothing of this precious stone; I am surely not converted." This led her to come and speak with him. She was not under deep conviction; but before going away he said, " You are a poor, vile worm; it is a wonder the earth does not open and swallow you up." These words were blessed to produce a very awful sense of sin. She came a second time with the arrows of the Almighty drinking up her spirit. For three months she remained in this state, till having once more come to him for counsel, the living voice of Jesus gave life to her soul while he was speaking of Christ's words— " If thou knewest the gift of God," &c., and she went away rejoicing. Some awakened souls told him that since they were brought under concern, very many sermons which they had heard from him before and completely forgotten, had been all brought back to mind. He used to remark that this might show what the resurrection day would awaken in the souls of gospel hearers.

In dealing with souls, he used to speak very plainly. One came to him who assented to his statements of the gospel, and yet refused to be comforted, always looking upon *coming to Christ* as something in addition to really believing the record God has given of his Son. He took John iii. 16, 17—" For God so loved the world that," &c. The woman said that " God did not care for her." Upon this he at once convicted her of making God a liar; and as she went away in deep distress his prayer was—" Lord, give her light."

To another person, who spoke of having times of great joy, he showed that these were times for worshipping God in the Spirit. " You would come to a king when you are full dressed; so come to God, and abide in his presence as long as you can."

Sometimes he would send away souls, of whom he entertained good hope, with a text suited to their state. " If ye live after the flesh, ye shall die; but if ye, through the Spirit, do mortify the deeds of the body, ye shall live." Or he would say, " I hear of you that God has opened your heart; but remember not to trust in man's opinion. Remember an all-seeing Christ will be the judge at the great day." To another he said, " I have long hoped you were really under the wings of the Saviour; if it be so, abide there; do not be like Demas."

To a prayer meeting, consisting of a few young men that had been awakened to flee from wrath, he gave this advice, " Guard against all ambition to excel one another in expression. Remember the most spiritual prayer is a 'groan which cannot be uttered,' Rom. viii. 26; or a cry of ' Abba, Father,' Gal. iv. 6."

There is very little recorded in his diary during these years; but what does exist will be read with deepest interest.

"*March* 28, 1838, Thursday.—I think of making this more a journal of my people, and the success, or otherwise, of my ministry. The first success among my people was at the time of my first sacrament: then it appeared, my first sermon on Isaiah lxi. 1, was blessed to —— and some others. That on Ezek. xxii. 14, 'Can thine heart endure,' &c., was blessed to awaken M. L. That on Song v. 2, 'Open to me,' &c., the Sabbath after the sacrament, was blessed to another. These were happy days. M. D. was awakened by coming to the communicants' class. Another by the action sermon. At the words, 'I know thee, Judas,' she trembled, and would have risen from the table. These were glad days when one and another were awakened. The people looked very stirred and anxious, every day coming to hear the words of eternal life—some inquiring in private every week. Now, there is little of this. About fifteen cases came to my knowledge the first sacrament, and two awakened who seem to have gone back. About eleven last sacrament—four of these young men. Several Christians seemed quickened to greater joy, and greater love one to another. Now it appears to me there is much falling off: few seem awakened— few weep as they used to do.

"*April* 1.—Sacrament day. Sweet season we have had. Never was more straitened and unfurnished in myself, and yet much helped. Kept in perfect peace, my mind being stayed on Thee. Preached on 'My God, my God,' &c.; Psalm xxii. 1. Not fully prepared, yet found some peace in it. Fenced the tables from 'Christ's eyes of flame.' Little helped in serving the tables. Much peace in communion. Happy to be one with Christ! *I,* a vile worm; *He,* the Lord my righteousness. Mr. Cumming of Dumbarney served some tables; Mr. Somerville of Anderston served three, and preached in the evening on, 'Thou art all fair, my love.' Very full and refreshing. All sweet, sweet services. Come, thou north wind, and blow, thou south, upon this garden! May this time be greatly blessed. It is my third communion; it may be my last. My Lord may come, or I may be sitting at another table soon. Moody, Candlish, and Mellis, were a goodly preparation for this day; and the sweet word from Cumming yesterday, ' When the poor and needy seek water,' &c. Lord, grant some awakening this day—to some bringing peace—comfort to mourners—fulness to believers—an advance in holiness in me and my children ! 3 John iv. Lord, wean me from my sins, from my cares, and from this passing world. May Christ be all in all to me."

" Admitted about twenty-five young communicants; kept two back, and one or two stayed back. Some of them evidently brought to Christ. May the Lord be their God, their comforter, their all ! May the morrow bring still richer things to us, that we may say as of to-night, ' Thou hast kept the good wine until now.' "

Toward the close of this same year, some of his notices are as follows:—

" *October* 7.—Evening.—In the Gaelic Chapel, on ' I know that my Redeemer liveth,' with more seeming power on the people than for a while. I never remember of compelling souls to come in to Christ so much as in that discourse."

" *Oct.* 8.—A person of the name of —— came ; I hope really awakened by last night's work ; rather, by *thee*. I do not know, however, whether *grace* is begun or not."

" *Oct.* 14.—Preached on ' Forgiving injuries.' Afternoon.—On the Second coming : ' Let your loins be girded about,' &c. Felt its power myself more than ever before, how the sudden coming of the Saviour constrains to a holy walk, separate from sin. Evening.—Preached it over in the Ferry."

" *Oct.* 21.—Met young communicants in the evening. Good hope of all but one."

" *Oct.* 22.—A Jew preached in my church, Mr. Frey, to a crowded house. Felt much moved in hearing an Israelite after the flesh."

" *Oct.* 23.—Preached to sailors aboard the ' Dr

Carey,' in the Docks. About 200. Very attentive and impressed-like, on 'I know that my Redeemer liveth.' May the seed sown on the waters be found after many days."

"*November* 1.—Fast-day.—Afternoon.—Mr. C., on 'The Thief on the Cross.' A most awakening and engaging sermon, enough to make sinners fly like a cloud, and as doves to their windows. The offers of Christ were let down very low, so that those low of stature might take hold."

"*Nov.* 5.—Mr. —— died this morning at seven o'clock. O that I may take warning, lest, after preaching to others, I myself be a castaway. Love of popularity is said to have been his besetting sin."

"*December* 2.—Errol communion. Heard Mr. Grierson preach on Christ's entry into Jerusalem. Served two tables. Evening.—Preached to a large congregation, on 'Unto you, O men, I call,' &c. The free visitation of the Saviour. May some find him this day!"

In addition to the other blessings which the Lord sent by his means to the place where he laboured, it was obvious to all that the tone of Christians was raised as much by his holy walk as by his heavenly ministry. Yet, during these pleasant days, he had much reproach to bear. He was the object of supercilious contempt to formal, cold-hearted ministers, and of bitter hatred to many of the ungodly. At this day, there are both ministers and professing Christians of whom Jesus would say, "The world cannot hate you," (John vii. 7,) for the world cannot hate itself; but it was not so with Mr. McCheyne. Very deep was the enmity borne to him by some—all the deeper, because the only cause of it was his likeness to his Master. But nothing turned him aside. He was full of ardour, yet ever gentle, and meek and generous; full of zeal, yet never ruffled by his zeal; and not only his strength of " first love " (Rev. ii. 4.,) but even its warm glow, seemed in him to suffer no decay.

Thus he spent the first years of his ministry in

Dundee. The town began to feel that they had a peculiar man of God in the midst of them; for he lived as a true son of Levi. " My covenant was with him of life and peace, and I gave them to him for the fear wherewith he feared me, and was afraid before my name. The law of truth was in his mouth, and iniquity was not found on his lips: he walked with me in peace and equity; and did turn many away from iniquity." (Mal. ii. 5, 6.)

CHAPTER IV

HIS MISSION TO PALESTINE AND THE JEWS

Here am I; send me.—ISAIAH vi. 8

THOUGH engaged night and day with his flock in St. Peter's, Mr. McCheyne ever cherished a missionary spirit. " This place hardens me for a foreign land," was his remark on one occasion. This spirit he sought to kindle yet more by reading missionary intelligence for his own use, and often to his people at his weekly prayer meeting. The necessities both of his own parish, and of the world at large, lay heavy on his soul; and when an opportunity of evangelizing occurred, there was none in Scotland more ready to embrace it. He seemed one who stood with his loins girt—" Here am I; send me."

Another motive to incessant activity, was the decided impression on his mind that his career would be short. From the very first days of his ministry he had a strong feeling of this nature; and his friends remember how his letters used to be sealed with this seal, " *The night cometh.*" At a time when he was apparently in his usual health, we were talking together on the subject of the Premillennial Advent. We had begun to speak of the practical influence which the belief of that doctrine might have. At length he said, " that he saw no force in the arguments generally urged against it, though he had difficulties of his own in regard to it. And, perhaps (he added,) it is well for you, who enjoy constant health, to be so firmly persuaded that Christ is thus to come; but my sickly frame makes me feel every day that my time may be very short."

He was, therefore, in some measure prepared when, in the midst of his laborious duties, he was compelled to stand still and see what the Lord would do.

In the close of 1838, some symptoms appeared that alarmed his friends. His constitution, never robust, began to feel the effects of unremitting labour; for occasionally he would spend six hours in visiting, and then, the same evening, preach in some room to all the families whom he had that day visited. Very generally, too, on Sabbath, after preaching twice to his own flock, he was engaged in ministering somewhere else in the evening. But now, after any great exertion, he was attacked by violent palpitation of heart. It soon increased, affecting him in his hours of study ; and at last it became almost constant. Upon this, his medical advisers insisted on a total cessation of his public work; for though, as yet, there was no organic change on his lungs, there was every reason to apprehend that that might be the result. Accordingly, with deep regret, he left Dundee to seek rest and change of occupation, hoping it would be only for a week or two.

A few days after leaving Dundee he writes from Edinburgh, in reply to the anxious inquiries of his friend Mr. Grierson, " The beating of the heart is not now so constant as it was before." The pitcher draws more quietly at the cistern ; so that, by the kind providence of our Heavenly Father, I may be spared a little longer before the silver cord be loosed, and the golden bowl be broken."

It was found that his complaints were such as would be likely to give way under careful treatment, and a temporary cessation from all exertion. Under his father's roof, therefore, in Edinburgh, he resigned himself to the will of his Father in heaven. But deeply did he feel the trial of being laid aside from his loved employment, though he learnt of Him who was meek and lowly, to make the burden light in his own way, by saying, "Even so, Father, for so it seemeth good in thy sight." He wrote to Mr. Grierson again, *January* 5, 1839, "I hope this affliction will be blessed to me. I always feel much need of God's afflicting hand. In the whirl of active labour there is so little time for watching, and for bewailing, and seeking grace, to oppose the sins of our ministry, that I always feel it a blessed thing when the Saviour takes me aside from the crowd, as he took the blind man out of the town, and removes the veil, and clears away obscuring mists; and by his word and Spirit leads to deeper peace and a holier walk. Ah! there is nothing like a calm look into the eternal world to teach us the emptiness of human praise, the sinfulness of self-seeking and vain glory—to teach us the preciousness of Christ, who is called 'The Tried Stone.' I have been able to be twice at College to hear a lecture from Dr. Chalmers. I have also been privileged to smooth down the dying pillow of an old school companion, leading him to a fuller joy and peace in believing. A poor, heavy laden soul, too, from Larbert, I have had the joy of leading toward the Saviour. So that even when absent from my work, and when exiled as it were, God allows me to do some little things for his name."

He was led to look more carefully into this trying dispensation, and began to anticipate blessed results from it to his flock. He was well aware how easily the flock begin to idolize the shepherd, and how prone the shepherd is to feel somewhat pleased with this sinful partiality of his people, and to be uplifted by his success. "I sometimes think," is his remark in a letter, dated *January* 18, "that a great blessing may come to my people in my absence. Often God does not bless us when we are in the midst of our labours, lest we should say, 'My hand and my eloquence have done it.' He removes us into silence, and then pours 'down a blessing so that there is no room to receive it;' so that all that see it cry out, 'It is the Lord!' This was the way in the South Sea Islands. May it really be so with my dear people!" Nor did he err in this view of the dispensation. All these ends, and more also, were to be accomplished by it.

An anticipation like that which is expressed in this and other letters, especially in his Pastoral Letter of March 20, may justly be regarded as a proof from experience that the Lord teaches his people to expect and pray for what he means soon to work. And here the Lord accomplished his designs in the kindest of all ways; for he removed his servant for a season from the flock to which he had been so blessed, lest even his own children should begin to glory in man; but yet he took that servant to another sphere of labour in the meantime; and then, when the blessing was safely bestowed, brought him back to rejoice over it.

He was still hoping for, and submissively asking, from the Lord, speedy restoration to his people in Dundee, and occasionally sending to them an epistle that breathed the true pastor's soul; when one day, as he was walking with Dr. Candlish, conversing on the mission to Israel which had lately been resolved on, an idea seemed suddenly suggested to Dr. Candlish. He asked Mr. McCheyne what he would think of "being useful to the Jewish cause, during his cessation from labour, by going abroad to make personal inquiries into the state of Israel?" The idea, thus suddenly suggested, led to all the after results of the mission of inquiry. Mr. McCheyne found himself all at once called to carry salvation to the Jew, as he had hitherto done to the Gentile, and his soul was filled with joy and wonder. His medical friends highly approved of the proposal, as being likely to conduce very much to the removal of his complaints—the calm, steady excitement of such a journey being likely to restore the tone of his whole constitution.

Dr. Black of Aberdeen readily consented to use his remarkable talents as a scholar in this cause; and Dr.

Keith intimated his expectation of soon joining the deputation. I also had been chosen to go forth on this mission of love to Israel; but some difficulties stood in the way of my leaving my charge at Collace. In these circumstances, Mr. McCheyne wrote to me, March 12, from Edinburgh.

" My Dear A.—I have received so many tokens for good from God in this matter, that it were a shame indeed if I did not trust him to perfect all which concerns me. I am glad you have determined to trust all in the hands of Israel's God. I am quite ready to go this week, or next week, but am deeply anxious to be sure that you are sent with me. You know, dear A., I could not labour in this cause, nor enjoy it, if you were not to be with me in it. Would you be ready to give your Jewish lecture on the evening of Sabbath week? * * * And now, pray for us, that we may be sent of God ; and, weak as we are, that we may be made Boanerges—that we may be blessed to win some souls, and to stir up Christians to love Zion. Much interest is already excited, and I do look for a blessing. Speak to your people as on the brink of eternity. * * As to books, I am quite at a loss. My Hebrew Bible, Greek Testament, &c., and perhaps Bridge's Christian Ministry for general purposes—I mean, for keeping us in mind of our ministerial work. I do hope we shall go forth in the Spirit ; and though straitened in language, may we not be blessed, as Brainerd was, through an interpreter ? May we not be blessed also to save some English, and to stir up missionaries ? My health is only tolerable ; I would be better if we were once away. I am often so troubled, as to be made willing to go or stay, to die, or to live. Yet it is encouraging to be used in the Lord's service again, and in so interesting a manner. What if we should see the heavenly Jerusalem before the earthly ? I am taking drawing materials, that I may carry away remembrances of the Mount of Olives, Tabor, and the Sea of Galilee."

The interest that this proposed journey excited in Scotland was very great. Nor was it merely the somewhat romantic interest attached to the land where the Lord had done most of his mighty works; there were also in it the deeper feelings of a scriptural persuasion that Israel was still "beloved for the fathers' sake." For some time previous, Jerusalem had come into mind, and many godly pastors were standing as watchmen over its ruined walls, (Isa. lxii. 6,) stirring up the Lord's remembrances. Mr. McCheyne had been one of these. His views of the importance of the Jews in the eye of God, and, therefore, of their importance as a sphere of missionary labour, were very clear and decided. He agreed in the expectation expressed in one of the course of lectures delivered before the deputation set out, that we might anticipate an *outpouring of the Spirit when our Church should stretch out its hands to the Jew as well as to the Gentile.* In one letter, he says, "To seek the lost sheep of the house of Israel is an object very near to my heart, as my people know it has ever been. Such an enterprise may probably draw down unspeakable blessings on the Church of Scotland, according to the promise, 'they shall prosper who love thee.'" In another, "I now see plainly that all our views about the Jews being the chief object of missionary exertion are plain and sober truths, according to the Scripture." Again, "I feel convinced that if we pray that the world may be converted in God's way, we will seek the good of the Jews, and the more we do so, the happier we will be in our own souls. You should always keep up a knowledge of the prophecies regarding Israel." In his preaching he not unfrequently said on this subject, "We should be like God in his peculiar affections; and the whole Bible shows that God has ever had, and still has, a peculiar love to the Jews."

The news of his proposed absence alarmed his flock at Dundee. They manifested their care for him more than ever; and not a few wrote expostulatory letters. To one of these well meant remonstrances, he replied, "I rejoice exceedingly in the interest you take in me, not so much for my own sake as that I hope it is a sign you know and love the Lord Jesus. Unless God had himself shut up the door of return to my people, and opened this new door to me, I never could have consented to go. I am not at all unwilling to spend and be spent in God's service, though I have often found that the more abundantly I love you, the less I am loved. But God has very plainly shown me that I may perform a deeply important work for his ancient people, and at the same time be in the best way of seeking a return of health."—" A minister will make a poor saviour in the day of wrath. It is not knowing a minister, or loving one, or hearing one, or having a name to live, that will save. You need to have your hand on the head of the Lamb for yourselves; Lev. i. 4. You need to have your eye on the brazen serpent for yourselves; John iii. 14, 15. I fear I will need to be a swift witness against many of my people in the day of the Lord, that they looked to me, and not to Christ, when I preached to them. I always feared that some of you loved to hear the word, who do not love to do it. I always feared there were many of you who loved the Sabbath meetings, and the class, and the Thursday evenings, who yet were not careful to walk with God, to be meek, chaste, holy, loving, harmless, Christ-like, Godlike. Now God wants you to think that the only end of a gospel ministry is, that you may be holy. Believe me, God himself could not make you happy, except you be holy."

At this crisis in his people's history, he sought from the Lord, one to supply his place—one who would feed the flock and gather in wanderers during their own pastor's absence. The Lord granted him his desire by sending Mr. William C. Burns, son of the minister of Kilsyth. In a letter to him, dated *March* 12th, the following remarkable words occur:—" You are given in answer to prayer, and these gifts are, I

believe, always without exception blessed. I hope
you may be a thousand times more blessed among
them than ever I was. Perhaps there are many souls
that would never have been saved under my ministry,
who may be touched under yours; and God has taken
this method of bringing you into my place. *His
name is Wonderful.*"

This done, and being already disengaged from his
flock, he set out for London to make arrangements
for the rest of the deputation, who soon after were
all sent forth by the brethren with many prayers.
None had more prayers offered in their behalf than
he—and they were not offered in vain. During all
his journeyings the Lord strengthened him, and saved
him out of all distresses.

It was a singular event—often still it looks like a
dream—that four ministers should be so suddenly
called away from their quiet labours in the towns and
villages of Scotland, and be found in a few weeks
traversing the land of Israel, with their Bibles in their
hands, eye-witnesses of prophecy fulfilled, and spies of
the nakedness of Israel's worship and leanness of soul.
The details of that journey need not be given here.
They have been already recorded in the " Narrative
of a Mission of Inquiry to the Jews, from the Church
of Scotland, in 1839." But there are some incidents
worthy to be preserved, which could find a place only
in such a record of private life and feelings as we are
now engaged in.

When Mr. McCheyne was on board the vessel that
carried him to London, he at once discovered an interesting young Jew, who seemed, however, unwilling
to be recognized as belonging to the seed of Abraham.
He made several attempts to draw this young Israelite
into close conversation; and before parting, read with
him the 1st Psalm in Hebrew, and pressed home the
duty of meditating on the word of the Lord. In
visiting Bethnal Green, he has noted down that it
was very sweet to hear Jewish children sing a hymn
to Jesus, the burden of which was טבוח עלינו " slain
for us!"

The awful profanation of the holy Sabbath which we witnessed on the streets of Paris, called forth the following appeal, in a letter to Mr. Macdonald of Blairgowrie. His spirit had been stirred in him when he saw the city wholly given to idolatry. "Stand in the breach, dear friend, and lift up your voice like a trumpet, lest Scotland become another France. You know how many in our own parishes trample on the holy day. They do not know how sweet it is to walk with God all that holy day. Isaiah lviii. 11—14 is a sweet text to preach from. Exodus xxxi. 13, is also very precious, showing that the real sanctifying of the Sabbath is one of God's signs or marks which he puts upon his people. It is one of the letters of the new name, which no one knoweth but they who receive it."

In his brief notes during the first part of the journey, he has seldom failed to mark our seasons of united prayer, such as those in the cabin of the vessel on the passage to Genoa; for these were times of refreshing to his spirit. And his feelings, as he stood in that city, and surveyed its palaces, are expressed in a few lines, which he sent homeward from the spot. "A foreign land draws us nearer God. He is the only one whom we know here. We go to him as to one we know: all else is strange. Every step I take, and every new country I see, makes me feel more that there is nothing real, nothing true, but what is everlasting. The whole world lieth in wickedness: its judgments are fast hastening. The marble palaces, among which I have been wandering to-night, shall soon sink like a mill-stone in the waters of God's righteous anger; but he that doth the will of God abideth for ever!"

At Valetta, in the island of Malta, he wrote—"My heart beats a little to day, but another sail will do me good. One thing I know, that I am in the hands of my Father in heaven, who is all love to me—not for what I am in myself, but for the beauty he sees in Immanuel."

The classic shores of Italy and Greece are invested with a peculiar interest, such as may raise deep emotions even in a sanctified soul. "We tried to recollect many of the studies of our boyhood. But what is classic learning to us now? I count all things but loss for the excellency of the knowledge of Christ Jesus my Lord. And yet these recollections tinged every object, and afforded us a most lawful pleasure."

During our voyage, it was his delight to search into the Scriptures, just as at home. And so much did he calculate on an unceasing study of the word during all our journey, that he took with him some notes I had written on each chapter of the Book of Leviticus, observing it would be suitable meditation for us while busy with Jewish minds. At home and abroad he had an insatiable appetite for all the word—both for the types of the Old Testament, and the plain text of the New. On one occasion, before leaving home, in studying Numbers iv., he fixed the different duties assigned to the priests on his memory, by means of the following lines :—

> "The *Kohathites* upon their shoulders bear
> The holy vessels, covered all with care ;
> The *Gershonites* receive an easier charge,
> Two wagons full of cords and curtains large ;
> *Merari's* sons four ponderous wagons load
> With boards and pillars of the house of God."

He acted on the principle, that whatever God has revealed, must deserve our study and prayerful investigation.

Arrived at Alexandria, in Egypt, and thence proceeding onward to Palestine by the way of the Desert, we found ourselves set down on a new stage of experience. Mr. McCheyne observed on the silence of the desert places—"It is a remarkable feeling to be quite alone in a desert place ; it gives similar feelings to fasting ; it brings God near. Living in tents, and moving among such lonely scenes for many days, awake many new ideas. It is a strange life we lead in the wilderness. Round and round there is a complete circle of sand and wilderness shrubs ; above, a blue sky without a cloud, and a scorching sun which often made the thermometer stand at 96° in our tents.

When evening came, the sun went down as it does in the ocean, and the stars came riding forth in their glory ; and we used to pitch all alone, with none but our poor ignorant Bedouins and their camels, and our all-knowing, all-loving God beside us. When morning began to dawn, our habitations were taken down. Often we have found ourselves shelterless before being fully dressed. What a type of the last of our body ! Ah ! how often taken down before the soul is made meet for the inheritance of the saints in light." To Mr. Bonar of Larbert he writes : " I had no idea that travelling in the wilderness was so dreadful a thing as it is. The loneliness, I often felt, quite solemnized me. The burning sun over head—round and round a circle of barren sand, chequered only by a few prickly shrubs (' the heath of the wilderness,' of which Jeremiah speaks)—no rain, not a cloud, the wells often like that of Marah, and far between. I now understand well the murmurings of Israel. I feel that our journey proved and tried my own heart very much." When we look back, and remember that he who thus stands on the sandy desert road between Egypt and Palestine, and looks on its singular scenery, is one who but lately was to be found busy night and day in dealing with the souls of men in the densely peopled streets of the town teeming with population, we are led to wonder at the ways of the Lord. But is it not a moment that may remind us that the God who sent Elijah to the brook at Cherith, is the same God still ? and the wise, considerate, loving Master, who said, " Come into a desert place and rest awhile," is as loving, considerate, and wise as he was then ?

At Balteen, a small village in Egypt, I well remember the indignation that fired his countenance when our Arab attendants insisted on our travelling onward on the Sabbath day, rather than sitting under a few palm trees, breathing a sultry, furnace-like atmosphere, with nothing more than just such supply of food as sufficed. He could not bear the thought of being deprived of the Sabbath rest ; it was needful for our souls as much in the wilderness as in the crowded city ; and if few glorify God in that desolate land, so much the more were we called on to fill these solitudes with our songs of praise. It was in this light he viewed our position; and when we had prevailed, and were seated under the palms, he was excited to deep emotion, though before quite unnerved by the heat, at the sight of a row of poor wretched Egyptians, who gathered round us. " O that I could speak their language, and tell them of salvation !" was his impassioned wish.

An event occurred at that time in which the hand of God afterwards appeared very plain, though it then seemed very dark to us. Dr. Black fell from his camel in the midst of the sandy desert, and none of all our company could conjecture what bearing on the object of our Mission this sad occurrence could have. Is it a frown on our undertaking ? or can it really be a movement of His kind, guiding hand ? We often spoke of it ; in our visit to Galilee we thought we saw some purposes evolving; but there was still something unexplained. Now, however, the reason appears ; even that event was of the Lord, in wise and kind design.   But for that fall, our fathers in the deputation would not have sailed up the Danube on their way to Vienna, and Pesth would not have been visited.   This accident, which mainly disabled Dr. Black, from undertaking the after fatigue of exploring Galilee, was the occasion of directing the steps of our two fathers to that station, where a severe stroke of sickness was made the means of detaining Dr. Keith till they had learned that there was an open door among the Jews.   And there, accordingly, it has been that the Lord has poured down his Spirit on the Jews that have come to our missionaries, so remarkably that no Jewish mission seems ever to have been blessed with deeper conversions.   There is nothing but truth in the remark made by one of our number : " Dr. Black's fall from the camel was the first step toward Pesth."   " Whoso is wise, and will observe these things, even they shall understand the loving-kindness of the Lord ;" Psalm cvii. 42.   Indeed, whether it was that we were prepared to expect, and therefore, were peculiarly ready to observe, or whether it was really the case that the watchful eye of our Lord specially guided us, certain it is that we thought we could perceive the whole course we took signally marked by Providence. There were many prayers in Scotland ascending up in our behalf, and the High Priest gave the answer by shining upon our path. Mr. McCheyne has stated—" For much of our safety I feel indebted to the prayers of my people, I mean the Christians among them, who do not forget us. If the veil of the world's machinery were lifted off, how much we would find is done in answer to the prayers of God's children !"

Many things lost somewhat of their importance in our view when examined amid the undistracted reflections of the long desert journey, where for many days we had quiet, like the quiet of death, around us all night long, and even during the bright day. It is the more interesting, on this very account, to know his feelings there on the subject of the ministry. As his camel slowly bore him over the soft sandy soil, much did he ruminate on the happy days when he was permitted to use all his strength in preaching Jesus to dying men. " Use your health while you have it, my dear friend and brother. Do not cast away peculiar opportunities that may never come again. You know not when your last Sabbath with your people may come. Speak for eternity. Above all things, cultivate your own spirit. A word spoken by you when your conscience is clear, and your heart full of God's Spirit, is worth ten thousand words spoken in unbelief and sin. This was my great fault in the ministry. Remember it is God, and not man, that must have the glory. It is not much speaking, but much faith, that is needed. Do not forget us. Do not forget the Saturday night meeting, nor the Monday morning thanksgiving." Thus he wrote on his way, to a fellow-labourer in Scotland.

The first Sabbath in the Holy Land our tent had been pitched in the vicinity of a colony of ants. It was in the tribe of Simeon we were encamped; it was the scenery of tne promised land we had around us; and one of the similitudes of the blessed word was illustrated within our view. He opened his Bible at Prov. vi. 6—8, and, as he read, noted—" I. *Consider her ways.* Most souls are lost for want of consideration. II. *The ant has no guide, overseer, or ruler:* no officer, no one to command or encourage her. How differently situated is the child of God. III. *Provideth her meat in the summer,* &c. Some have thought that this teaches us to heap up money; but quite the reverse. The ant lays up no store for the future. It is all for present use. She is always busy, summer and winter. The lesson is one of constant diligence in the Lord's work."

Many a time in these days, when our attendants in the evening were driving in the stakes of our tent and stretching its cords, he would lie down on the ground under some tree that sheltered him from the dew. Completely exhausted by the long day's ride, he would lie almost speechless for half an hour; and then, when the palpitation of his heart had a little abated, would propose that we two should pray together. Often, too, did he say to me, when thus stretched on the ground—not impatiently, but very earnestly—" Shall I ever preach to my people again?" I was often reproved by his unabated attention to personal holiness; for this care was never absent from his mind, whether he was at home in his quiet chamber, or on the sea, or in the desert. Holiness in him was manifested, not by efforts to perform duty, but in a way so natural, that you recognized therein the easy outflowing of the indwelling Spirit. The fountain springing up unto everlasting life (John iv. 14,) in his soul, welled forth its living waters alike in the familiar scenes of his native Scotland, and under the olive trees of Palestine. Prayer and meditation on the word were never forgotten; and a peace that the world could not give, kept his heart and mind. When we were detained a day at Gaza, in very tantalizing circumstances, his remark was, " *Je-*

hovah Jireh; we are at that mount again." It was sweet at any time to be with him, for both nature and grace in him drew the very heart; but there were moments of enjoyment in these regions of Palestine that drew every cord still closer, and created unknown sympathies. Such was that evening when we climbed Samson's Hill together. Sitting there, we read over the references to the place in the word of God; and then he took out his pencil and sketched the scene, as the sun was sinking in the west. This done, we sang some verses of a Psalm, appropriate to the spot, offered up prayer, and, slowly descending, conversed of all we saw, and of all that was brought to mind by the scenery around us, till we reached our tent.

In approaching Jerusalem, we came up the Pass of Latroon. He writes, "The last day's journey to Jerusalem was the finest I ever had in all my life. For four hours we were ascending the rocky pass upon our patient camels. It was like the finest of our Highland scenes, only the trees and flowers, and the voice of the turtle, told us that it was Immanuel's land." Riding along, he remarked, that to have seen the Plain of Judea and this mountain pass, was enough to reward us for all our fatigue; and then began to call up passages of the Old Testament Scriptures which might seem to refer to such scenery as that before us.

During our ten days at Jerusalem, there were few objects within reach that we did not eagerly seek to visit. "We stood at the turning of the road where Jesus came near, and beheld the city, and wept over it. And if we had had more of the mind that was in Jesus, I think we should have wept also." This was his remark in a letter homeward; and to Mr. Bonar of Larbert, he expressed his feelings in regard to the Mount of Olives and its vicinity : " I remember, the day when I saw you last, you said, that there were other discoveries to be made than those in the physical world—that there were sights to be seen in the spiritual world, and depths to be penetrated,

of far greater importance. I have often thought of
the truth of your remark. But if there is a place on
earth where physical scenery can help us to discover
divine things, I think it is Mount Olivet. Gethsemane
at your feet leads your soul to meditate on Christ's
love and determination to undergo divine wrath for
us. The cup was set before him there, and there he
said, 'Shall I not drink it?' The spot where he
wept makes you think of his divine compassion,
mingling with his human tenderness—his awful justice that would not spare the city, his superhuman
love that wept over its coming misery! Turning the
other way, and looking to the southeast, you see
Bethany, reminding you of his love to his own—that
his name is love—that in all our afflictions he is
afflicted—that those who are in their graves shall
one day come forth at his command. A little further
down you see the Dead Sea, stretching far among the
mountains its still and sullen waters. This deepens
and solemnizes all, and makes you go away saying,
'How shall we escape, if we neglect so great salvation?'"

He wrote to another friend in Scotland, from Mount
Zion, where we were then dwelling.

"Mount Zion, *June* 12, 1839.

"My Dear Friend,—Now that we are in the most
wonderful spot in all this world—where Jesus lived,
and walked, and prayed, and died, and will come
again—I doubt not you will be anxious to hear how
we come on. I am thankful that ever he privileged
us to come to this land. I heard of my flock yesterday by a letter from home—the first I have received,
dated 8th May.   *   *   *   We are living
in one of the missionaries' houses on Mount Zion.
My window looks out upon where the temple was,
the beautiful Mount of Olives rising behind. The
Lord that made heaven and earth bless thee out of
Zion.—Yours," &c.

One evening, after our visit to Sychar, he referred
to the Bible which I had dropped into Jacob's Well.

We were then resting from our journey in our tents Soon after, he penned on a leaf of his note-book the following fragment :

> " My own loved Bible, must I part from thee,
> Companion of my toils by land and sea;
> Man of my counsels, soother of distress;
> Guide of my steps through this world's wilderness !
> In darkest nights, a lantern to my feet ;
> In gladsome days, as dropping honey sweet.
> When first I parted from my quiet home,
> At thy command, for Israel's good to roam,
> Thy gentle voice said, ' For Jerusalem pray,
> So shall Jehovah prosper all thy way.'
> When through the lonely wilderness we strayed,
> Sighing in vain for palm trees' cooling shade,
> Thy words of comfort hushed each rising fear,
> ' The shadow of thy mighty Rock is near.'
> And when we pitched our tent on Judah's hills,
> Or thoughtful mused beside Siloa's rills ;
> Whene'er we climbed Mount Olivet, to gaze
> Upon the sea, where stood in ancient days
> The heaven-struck Sodom——
>   Sweet record of the past, to faith's glad eyes,
>   Sweet promiser of glories yet to rise !"*

At the foot of Carmel, during the seven days we were in quarantine under the brow of the hill, there was time to recall many former scenes ; and in these circumstances, he wrote the hymn, " *The Fountain of Siloam.*"

Here, too, he had leisure to write home ; and most graphically does he describe our journey from Alexandria onward.

"CARMEL, *June* 26, 1839.

MY DEAR FATHER, MOTHER, &c.,—It is a long time since I have been able to write to you—this being the very first time since leaving Egypt that any one has appeared to carry letters for us. I must therefore, begin by telling you that, by the good hand of our God upon me, I am in excellent health, and have been ever since I wrote you last. Fatigues we have had many, and much greater than I anticipated ,

* It is a somewhat curious occurrence, that the remnants of this Bible were found, and drawn up from the bottom of the well, in July 1843, by Dr. Wilson and his fellow-traveller, who employed a Samaritan from Sychar to descend and examine the well.

hardships and dangers we have also encountered, but God has brought us all safely through and in fully better condition than when we began. You must no imagine that I have altogether lost the palpitation of my heart, for it often visits me to humble and prove me; still I believe it is a good deal better than it was, and its visits are not nearly so frequent. I hope very much, that in a cold bracing climate, and with less fatigue, I may, perhaps, not feel it at all. I was very thankful to receive your letter, dated 8th May—the first since leaving home. I was delighted to hear of your health and safety, and of the peaceful communion at St. Peter's. The public news was alarming and humbling.* I suppose I had better begin at the beginning, and go over all our journeyings from the land of Egypt through the howling wilderness to this sweet land of promise. I would have written *journalwise* (as my mother would say) from time to time, so that I might have had an interesting budget of news ready; but you must remember it is a more fatiguing thing to ride twelve or fourteen hours on a camel's back in a sandy wilderness, than in our home excursions; and I could often do nothing more than lie down on my rug and fall asleep.

" We left Alexandria on 16th *May*, 1839, parting from many kind friends in that strange city. We and our baggage were mounted on seventeen donkeys, like the sons of Jacob when they carried corn out of Egypt. Our saddle was our bedding, viz., a rug to lie on, a pillow for the head, and a quilt to wrap ourselves in. We afterwards added a straw mat to put below all. We had procured two tents—one large, and a smaller one which Andrew and I occupy. The donkeys are nice nimble little animals, going about five miles an hour; a wild Arab accompanies each donkey. We have our two Arab servants to whom I now introduce you—Ibrahim, a handsome small made Egyptian, and Achmet the cook, a dark good natured fellow, with a white turban and bare black legs. Ibrahim speaks a little English and Italian, and

* He alludes here to the decision of the House of Lords in the Auchterarder case.

Achmet, Italian—in addition to their native Arabic. I soon made friends with our Arab donkey men, learning Arabic words and phrases from them, which pleased them greatly. We journeyed by the Bay of Aboukir, close by the sea, which tempered the air of the desert. At night we reached Rosetta, a curious half-inhabited eastern town. We saw an eastern marriage, which highly pleased us, illustrating the parables. It was by torch light. We slept in the convent. 17th.—Spent morning in Rosetta : gave the monk a New Testament. Saw some of Egyptian misery in the bazaar. Saw the people praying in the mosque, Friday being the Moslem's day of devotion. In the evening we crossed the Nile in small boats. It is a fine river ; and its water, when filtered, is sweet and pleasant. We often thought upon it in the desert. We slept that night on the sand, in our tents, by the sea shore. 18th.—In six hours we came to Bourlos (you will see it in the map of the Society for diffusing Useful Knowledge :) were ferried across. Watched the fishermen casting their nets into the sea: hot—hot. In two hours more, through a palmy wilderness, we came to Balteen—" the Vale of Figs"— an Arab village of mud huts. You little know what an Arab house is. In general, in Egypt, it is an exact square box, made of mud, with a low hole for a door. The furniture is a mat and cooking things ; and an oven made of mud. 19th.—Spent our Sabbath unoccupied in midst of the village ; the poor Arabs have no Sabbath. The thermometer 84° in tent. The governor called in the evening and drank a cup of tea with great relish. The heat we felt much all day ; still it was sweet to rest and remember you all in the wilderness. 20th.—At twelve at night, left Balteen by beautiful moonlight. Proceeding through a pleasant African wild of palms and brushwood, we reached the sea in two hours, and rode along, its waves washing our feet—very sleepy. We got a rest at mid-day, if rest it could be called, under that scorching sun, which I never will forget. Proceeding onward, at three o'clock we left the sea shore, and perceived the minarets of Damietta. Before us the mirage cheated us often when we were very thirsty. We crossed the Nile again, a much smaller branch—the only remaining one—and soon found ourselves comfortably reclining on the divan of the British Consul, an Egyptian gentleman of some fortune and manners. He entertained us at supper in true Egyptian style; provided a room for us, where we spread our mats in peace. We spent the whole of the next day here, having sent off a Bedouin to have camels ready for us at San. The consul entertained us in the same Egyptian style of hospitality, and sent us away the next day on board of a barge upon Lake Menzaleh. 22d.—Even E—— would not have been afraid to sail upon that lake. It is no where more than ten feet deep, and in general only four or five. We made an awning with our mats, and spent a very happy day. At evening we entered a canal among immense reeds. In moonlight the scene was truly romantic: we slept moored to the shore all night. Next morning (23d) we reached San about ten. This evening and next morning we spent in exploring the ruins of the ancient Zoan, for this we find is the very spot.

"Wandering along we were quite surprised to find great mounds of brick, and pottery, and vitrified stones. Andrew at last came upon beautiful obelisks. Next morning we examined all carefully, and found two sphinxes and many Egyptian obelisks. How wonderful to be treading over the ruins of the ancient capital of Egypt! Isaiah xix. 12, "Where are the princes of Zoan?" Ezek. xxx. 14, "God has set fire in Zoan." This is the very place where Joseph was sold as a slave, and where Moses did his wonders, Psalm lxxviii. 43. This was almost the only place where we have been in danger from the inhabitants. They are a wild race; and our Arabs were afraid of them. You would have been afraid too, if you had seen, out of the door of our tent, our Bedouins keeping watch all night with their naked sabres gleaming in the moonlight, firing off their guns now and then, and keeping up a low chant to keep one another awake. No evil happened to us, and we feel that many pray for us, and that God is with us. 24th.— This day our journeyings on camels commenced, and continued till we came to Jerusalem. It is a strange mode of conveyance. You have seen a camel kneeling; it is in this condition that you mount; suddenly it rises first on its fore feet, and then on its hind feet. It requires great skill to hold yourself on during this operation; one time I was thrown fairly over its head, but quite unhurt. When you find yourself exalted on the hunch of a camel, it is somewhat of the feeling of an aëronaut, as if you were bidding farewell to sublunary things; but when he begins to move, with solemn pace and slow, you are reminded of your terrestrial origin, and that a wrong balance or turn to the side will soon bring you down from your giddy height. You have no stirrup, and generally only your bed for your saddle; you may either sit as on horseback, or as on a side-saddle—the latter is the pleasanter, though not the safer of the two. The camel goes about three miles an hour, and the step is so long that the motion is quite peculiar. You bend your head toward your knees every step. With a vertical sun above and a burning sand below, you may believe it is a very fatiguing mode of journeying. However, we thought of Rebecca and Abraham's servant, (Gen. xxiv.) and listened with delight to the wild Bedouins' plaintive song. That night, 24th, we slept at Menagie, a Bedouin mud village—palm trees and three wells, and an ocean of sand, formed the only objects of interest. 25th.—Up by sunrise, and proceeded as before. The only event this day was Dr. Black's fall from his camel, which greatly alarmed us. He had fallen asleep, which you are very apt to do: we encamped and used every restorative, so that we were able to proceed the same evening to Gonatre, a miserable Arab post, having a governor; not a tree. 26th.— The Sabbath dawned sweetly; thermometer 92° in tent; could only lie on the mat and read Psalms. Evening.—Gathered governor and Bedouins to hear some words of eternal life, Ibrahim interpreting.

27th.—Two very long stages brought us to Katieh; thankful to God for his goodness while we pitched by the date trees. 28th.—Spent the day at Katieh; interesting interviews with the governor, a kind Arab; thermometer 96° in tent. Same evening, proceeded through a greener desert, among flocks of goats and sheep, and encamped by a well, Bir-el-Abd. 29th.—Another hot day in the desert; came in sight of the sea, which gave us a refreshing breeze; bathed in a salt lake as hot as a warm bath. Evening.—Encampment at Abugilbany. 30th.—This was our last day in the Egyptian wilderness. We entered on a much more mountainous region. The heat very great; we literally panted for a breath of wind. The Bedouins begged handkerchiefs to cover their heads, and often cast themselves under a bush for shade. Towards sunset, we came down on the old ruins of Rhinocolura, now buried in the sand; and soon after our camels kneeled down at the gates of El Arish, the last town on the Egyptian frontier. 31st.—We spent in El Arish, being unable to get fresh camels. We bought a sheep for five shillings; drank freely of their delightful water; what a blessing after the desert. Found out the river of Egypt, the boundary of Judah mentioned in the Bible, quite dry. *June 1st.* —Visited the school, a curiosity; all the children sit cross-legged on the floor, rocking to and fro, repeating something in Arabic. We had a curious interview with the governor, sitting in the gate in the ancient manner. We are quite expert now at taking off our shoes and sitting in the Eastern mode. Smoking, and coffee in very small cups, are the constant accompaniments of these visits. Left the same evening, and did not reach Sheikh Juidhe, in the land of the Philistines, till the sun was nearly bursting into view. 2d.—Spent a happy Sabbath here; sung " In Judah's land God is well known." Singing praises in our tents is very sweet, they are so frail, like our mortal bodies; they rise easily into the ears of our present Father. Our journey through the land of the Philistines was truly pleasant. 3d.—We went through a fine pasture country; immense straths; flocks of sheep and goats, and asses and camels, often came in sight. This is the very way up out of Egypt. little changed from the day that the Ethiopian went on his way rejoicing, and Joseph and Mary carried down the babe from the anger of Herod. Little changed, did I say? it is all changed; no more is there one brook of water. Every river of Egypt— Wady Gaza, Eshcol, Sorek—every brook we crossed, was dried up, not a drop of water. The land is changed; no more is it the rich land of Philistia. The sand struggles with the grass for mastery. The cities are changed—where are they? The people are changed—no more the bold Philistines—no more the children of Simeon—no more Isaac and his herdsmen—no more David and his horsemen; but miserable Arab shepherds—simple people, without ideas—poor, degraded, fearful. Khanounes was the first town we entered—Scripture name unknown. The burying ground outside the town. The well, and people coming to draw, were objects of great interest to us. The people were highly entertained with us in return. We sat down in the bazaar, and were a spectacle to all. How much we longed to have the Arabic tongue, that we might preach the unsearchable riches of Christ in God's own land. Same evening, we heard the cry of the wolf, and encamped two miles from Gaza. The plague was raging, so we did not enter, but spent a delightful day in comparing its condition with God's word concerning it—"Baldness is come upon Gaza." The old city is buried under sand hills, without a blade of grass, so that it is bald indeed. The herds and flocks are innumerable, fulfilling Zeph ii.; Andrew and I climbed the hill up which Samson carried the gates. 5th.—Passed through a fine olive grove for many miles, and entered the vale of Eschol. The people were all in the fields cutting and bringing in their barley. They reap with the hook as we do. They seem to carry in at the same time upon camels. No vines in Eshcol now—no pomegranates; but some

green fig trees. Crossed the brook Sorek—dry.
Spent the mid-day under the embowering shade of a
fig tree; tasted the apricots of the good land. Same
evening we came to Doulis, which we take to be
Eshtaol, where Samson was born. 6th.—We went due
east, and, after a mountain pass, saw the hills of
Judah—an immense plain intervening, all studded
with little towns. From their names, we found out
many Bible spots. This valley or plain is the very
vale of Zephathah, of which you read in 2 Chronicles
chap. xiv—"in the plain of Sephela." Before night
we entered among the hills of Judah—very like
our own highlands—and slept all night among
the mountains, at a deserted village called Latroon.
7th.—One of the most privileged days of our life.
We broke up our tents by moonlight; soon the sun
was up; we entered a defile of the most romantic
character: wild rocks and verdant hills,—wild flowers
of every colour and fragrance scented our path. Sometimes we came upon a clump of beautiful olive trees,
then wild again. The turtle's voice was heard in the
land, and singing birds of sweetest note. Our camels
carried us up this pass for four hours; and our turbaned Bedouins added by their strange figures to the
scene. The terracing of all the hills is the most remarkable feature of Judean scenery. Every foot of
the rockiest mountains may, in this way, be covered
with vines. We thought of Isaiah wandering here,
and David and Solomon. Still all was wilderness.
The hand of man had been actively employed upon
every mountain, but where were these labourers now?
Judah is gone into captivity before the enemy. There
are few men left in the land; not a vine is there.
"The vine languisheth." We came down upon
Garieh, a village embosomed in figs and pomegranates.
Ascending again, we came down into the valley
of Elah, where David slew Goliath. Another long
and steep ascent of a most rugged hill, brought us
into a strange scene—a desert of sun burnt rocks. I
had read of this, and knew that Jerusalem was near.
I left my camel and went before, hurrying over the

burning rocks. In about half an hour Jerusalem came in sight. "How doth the city sit solitary that was full of people!" Is this the perfection of beauty? "How hath the Lord covered the daughter of Zion with a cloud in his anger!" It is, indeed, very desolate. Read the first two chapters of Lamentations, and you have a vivid picture of our first sight of Jerusalem. We lighted off our camels within the Jaffa gate. Among those that crowded round us, we observed several Jews. I think I had better not attempt to tell you about Jerusalem. There is so much to describe, and I know not where to begin. The consul, Mr. Young, received us most kindly, provided us a house where we might spread our mats, and helped us in every way. Mr. Nicolayson called the same evening, and insisted on our occupying one of the mission houses on Mount Zion. The plague is still in Jerusalem, so that we must keep ourselves in quarantine. The plague only communicates by contact, so that we are not allowed to touch any one, or let any one touch us. Every night we heard the mourners going about the streets with their dismal wailings for the dead. On Sabbath, Mr. Nicolayson read the prayers, and Dr. Black preached from Isaiah ii. 2. Dr. Keith in the evening. Three converted Jews were among the hearers. On Monday 10th we visited the sepulchre, and a painful sight, where we can find no traces of Calvary. Same evening rode up to the Mount of Olives; past Gethsemane, a most touching spot. Visited Sir Moses Montefiore, a Jew of London, encamped on Mount Olivet; very kind to us. 11th.—Went round the most of the places to be visited near Jerusalem—Rephaim, Gihon, Siloa's Brook "that flowed fast by the Oracle of God;" the Pool of Siloam—the place where Jesus wept over the city — Bethany, of all places my favourite—the tombs of the kings. Such a day we never spent in this world before. The climate is truly delightful—hot at mid-day, but delightful breezes at morn and even. 12th.—A business day, getting information about Jews. In the evening, walked to Aceldama — a

dreadful spot. Zion is ploughed like a field. I
gathered some barley, and noticed cauliflowers planted
in rows. See Micah iii. 12. Jerusalem is, indeed,
heaps. The quantities of rubbish would amaze you—
in one place higher than the walls. 13th.—We went
to Hebron, twenty miles south; Mr. Nicolayson, his
son, the consul, and ladies, accompanying us, all on
mules and horses. Judah's cities are all waste. Except Bethlehem, we saw none but ruins till we reached
Hebron. The vines are beautifully cultivated here,
and make it a paradise. The hills all terraced to the
top. We spent a delightful evening and all next day.
We met the Jews and had an interesting interview
with them. We read Genesis xviii., and many other
Bible passages, with great joy. Saw the mosques
where the tomb of Abraham and Sarah is. 14th.—
Returned by Bethlehem to Jerusalem. Bethlehem is
a sweet village, placed on the top of a rocky hill—
very white and dazzling. You see it on both sides of
the hill. At Rachel's sepulchre you see Jerusalem on
one hand and Bethlehem on the other, an interesting
sight—six miles apart. On Sabbath we enjoyed the
Lord's Supper in an upper chamber in Jerusalem. It
was a time much to be remembered. Andrew preached
in the evening from John xiv. 2, 3. 17th.—The
plague has been increasing, so that we think it better
to depart. Last visit to Gethsemane, and Bethany,
and Siloam. Evening.—Took farewell of all our
friends in Jerusalem, with much sorrow, you may
believe. Went due north to Ramah, by Gibeon, and
slept at Beer, again in our tent, in Benjamin. 19th.—
Passed Bethel where Jacob slept. Passed through
the rich and rocky defile of Ephraim, by Lebonah, to
Sychar. You cannot believe what a delightsome land
it is. We sought anxiously for the well where Jesus
sat. Andrew alone found it, and lost his Bible in it.
20th.—Had a most interesting morning with the Jews
of Sychar. Saw many of them; also the Samaritans,
in their synagogue. Same evening visited Samaria,
a wonderful place, and encamped at Sanour. 21st.—
Arrived at Carmel, where we now are, encamped

within two yards of the sea. We have been in quarantine here seven days, as there is no plague north of this. Several English are encamped here—Lord R., Lord H., &c. We have daily conversations sitting on the sand. We are not allowed to touch even the rope of a tent. Acre is in sight across the bay. We have delightful bathing. To-morrow Lord H. leaves, and kindly offers to take this. Carmel's rocky brow is over us. We are all well and happy. On Monday, we propose leaving for Tiberias and Saphet. Soon we shall be in Beyrout, and on our way to Smyrna. Do not be anxious for me. Trust us to God, who goes with us where we go. I only pray that our mission may be blessed to Israel. Sir Moses M. has arrived, and pitched his tent within fifty yards of us. Kindest regards to all that inquire after me, not forgetting dear W.—Your affectionate son," &c.

When the two elder brethren of the deputation left us for Europe, we turned southward again from Beyrout to visit the regions of Phœnicia and Galilee. Never did Mr. McCheyne seem more gladsome than in gazing on these regions.

At Tyre, he remembered the request of an elder in the parish of Larbert, who had written to him before his departure, stating a difficulty in the usual expositions of the prophecies in regard to that renowned city. With great delight, he examined the difficulty on the spot; and it is believed that his testimony on such points as these, when it reached some men of sceptical views in that scene of his early labours, was not unblest.

From Saphet he writes:—"I sat looking down upon the lake this morning for about an hour. It was just at our feet—the very water where Jesus walked, where he called his disciples, where he rebuked the storm, where he said, 'Children, have ye any meat?' after he rose from the dead. Jesus is the same still." To his early and familiar friend, Mr. Somerville, he thus describes the same view:—"O what a view of the Sea of Galilee is before you, at your feet! It is above three hours' descent to the water's edge, and yet it looks as if you could run down in as many minutes. The lake is much larger than I had imagined. It is hemmed in by mountains on every side, sleeping as calmly and softly as if it had been the sea of glass which John saw in heaven. We tried in vain to follow the course of the Jordan running through it. True, there were clear lines, such as you see in the wake of a vessel, but then these did not go straight through the lake. The hills of Bashan are very high and steep, where they run into the lake. At one point, a man pointed out to us where the tombs in the rocks are, where the demoniacs used to live; and near it the hills were exactly what the Scriptures describe, 'a steep place,' where the swine ran down into the sea. On the northeast of the sea, Hermon rises very grand, intersected with many ravines full of snow."

The day we spent at the lake—at the very water side—was ever memorable; it was so peculiarly sweet. We felt an indescribable interest even in lifting a shell from the shore of a sea where Jesus had so often walked. It was here that two of the beautiful hymns in "*The Songs of Zion*," were suggested to him. The one was, "*How pleasant to me*," &c., the other, "*To yonder side;*" but the latter lay beside him unfinished till a later period.

His complaint was now considerably abated; his strength seemed returning; and often did he long to be among his people again, though quieting his soul upon the Lord. Not a few pastors of another church have, from time to time, come forth to this land, compelled by disease to seek for health in foreign regions; but how rarely do we find the pastor's heart retained —how rarely do we discover that the shepherd yearns still over the flock he left! But so deep were Mr. McCheyne's feelings toward the flock over which the Holy Ghost had made him overseer, that his concern for them became a temptation to his soul. It was not in the mere desire to preach again that he manifested this concern; for this desire might have been selfish,

as he said—" No doubt there is pride in this anxiety
to preach; a submissive soul would rejoice only in
doing the present will of God." But his prayers for
them went up daily to the throne. We had precious
seasons of united prayer also for that same end—
especially one morning at sun rise in Gethsemane, and
another morning at Carmel, where we joined in supplication on the silent shore at the foot of the hill as
soon as day dawned, and then again at evening on the
top, where Elijah prayed.

Distance of place, or peculiarities of circumstance,
never altered his views of duty, nor changed his feelings as a minister of Christ. In Galilee he meditated
upon the aspect of ecclesiastical affairs in our beloved
Scotland, and the principles he had maintained appeared to him as plainly accordant with the word of
God when tried there, apart from excitement, as they
did when he reviewed them in connection with their
effects at home. "I hope," were his words to a brother in the ministry, "I hope the church has been
well guided and blessed; and if times of difficulty
are to come, I do believe there is no position so proper
for her to be in, as the attitude of a missionary church,
giving freely to Jew and Gentile, as she has freely received—so may she be found when the Lord comes."

At the foot of Lebanon, in the town of Beyrout,
he was able to expound a chapter (Acts x.) at a
prayer meeting of the American brethren. This quite
rejoiced his heart; for it seemed as if the Lord were
restoring him, and meant again to use him in preaching the glad tidings. But shortly after, during
the oppressive heat of the afternoon, he felt himself
unwell. He had paid a visit to a young man from
Glasgow in the town, who was ill of fever: and it is
not unlikely that this visit, at a time when he was in
a state of debility from previous fatigue, was the
immediate occasion of his own illness. He was very
soon prostrated under the fever. But his medical
attendant apprehended no danger, and advised him
to proceed to Smyrna, in the belief that the cool air
of the sea would be much more in his favour than

the sultry heat of Beyrout. Accordingly, in company
with our faithful Hebrew friend, Erasmus Calman,
we embarked; but as we lay off Cyprus, the fever
increased to such a height, that he lost his memory
for some hours, and was racked with excessive pain
in his head. When the vessel sailed, he revived
considerably, but during three days no medical aid
could be obtained. He scarcely ever spoke; and
only once did he for a moment, on a Saturday night,
lift his languid eye, as he lay on deck enjoying the
breeze, to catch a distant sight of Patmos. We
watched him with agonizing anxiety till we reached
Smyrna and the village of Bouja. Though three
miles off, yet for the sake of medical aid he rode
to this village upon a mule after sunset, ready to drop
every moment with pain and burning fever. But
here the Lord had prepared for him the best and
kindest help. The tender and parental care of Mr.
and Mrs. Lewis, in whose house he found a home, was
never mentioned by him but with deepest gratitude;
and the sight of the flowering jessamine, or the mention of the deep green cypress, would invariably call
up in his mind associations of Bouja and its inmates.
He used to say it was his second birth place.

During that time, like most of God's people who
have been in sickness, he felt that a single passage of
the word of God was more truly food to his fainting
soul than any thing besides. One day his spirit revived,
and his eye glistened, when I spoke of the Saviour's
sympathy, adducing as the very words of Jesus,
Psalm xli. 1—*" Blessed is he that considereth the
poor, the Lord will deliver him in time of trouble,'*
&c.; it seemed so applicable to his own case, as a
minister of the glad tidings; for often had he " considered the poor," carrying a cup of cold water to a
disciple. Another passage, written for the children of
God in their distress, was spoken to him when he
seemed nearly insensible—*" Call upon me in the day
of trouble."* This word of God was as the drop of
honey to Jonathan.

He himself thus spoke of his illness to his friends

at home :—" I left the foot of Lebanon when I could hardly see, or hear, or speak, or remember. I felt my faculties going, one by one, and I had every reason to expect that I would soon be with my God. It is a sore trial to be alone and dying, in a foreign land, and it has made me feel, in a way that I never knew before, the necessity of having unfeigned faith in Jesus and in God. Sentiments, natural feelings, glowing fancies of Divine things, will not support the soul in such an hour. There is much self-delusion in our estimation of ourselves when we are untried and in the midst of Christian friends, whose warm feelings give a glow to ours, which they do not possess in themselves." Even then he had his people in his heart. " When I got better, I used to creep out in the evenings about sunset. I often remembered you all then. I could not write, as my eyes and head were much affected ; I could read but very little ; I could speak very little, for I had hardly any voice ; and so I had all my time to lay my people before God, and pray for a blessing on them. About the last evening I was there, we all went to the vintage, and I joined in gathering the grapes." To Mr. Somerville he wrote : " My mind was very weak when I was at the worst, and therefore, the things of eternity were often dim. *I had no fear to die, for Christ had died.* Still I prayed for recovery, if it was the Lord's will. You remember you told me to be humble among your last advices. You see God is teaching me the same thing. I fear I am not thoroughly humbled. I feel the pride of my heart, and bewail it." To his kind medical friend, Dr. Gibson, in Dundee, he wrote :—" I really believed that my Master had called me home, and that I would sleep beneath the dark green cypresses of Bouja till the Lord shall come, and they that sleep in Jesus come with him ; and my most earnest prayer was for my dear flock, that God would give them a pastor after his own heart."

When we met, after an eight days' separation, on board the vessel at Constantinople, he mentioned as one of the most interesting incidents of the week, that one evening, while walking with Mr. Lewis, they met a young Greek and his wife, both of whom were believed to be really converted souls. It created a thrill in his bosom to meet with these almost solitary representatives of the once faithful and much tried native church of Smyrna.

Meanwhile there were movements at home that proved the Lord to be him who "alone doeth wondrous things." The cry of his servant in Asia was not forgotten; the eye of the Lord turned towards his people.—It was during the time of Mr. McCheyne's sore sickness, that his flock in Dundee were receiving a blessing from the opened windows of heaven. Their pastor was lying at the gate of death, in utter helplessness. But the Lord had done this on very purpose; for he meant to show that he needed not the help of any: he could send forth new labourers, and work by new instruments, when it pleased Him. We little knew that during the days when we were waiting at the foot of Lebanon for a vessel to carry us to Smyrna, the arm of the Lord had begun to be revealed in Scotland. On the 23d of July the great revival at Kilsyth took place.

Mr. W. C. Burns, the same who was supplying Mr. McCheyne's place in his absence, was on that day preaching to his father's flock; and while pressing upon them immediate acceptance of Christ with deep solemnity, the whole of the vast assembly were overpowered. The Holy Spirit seemed to come down as a rushing mighty wind, and to fill the place. Very many were that day struck to the heart; the sanctuary was filled with distressed and inquiring souls. All Scotland heard the glad news that the sky was no longer as brass—that the rain had begun to fall. The Spirit in mighty power began to work from that day forward in many places of the land.

Mr. Burns returned to Dundee to Mr. McCheyne's flock on August 8th—one of the days when Mr. McCheyne was stretched on his bed, praying for his people under all his own suffering. The news of the work at Kilsyth had produced a deep impression in

Dundee; and two days after, the Spirit began to work in St. Peter's, at the time of the prayer meeting in the church, in a way similar to Kilsyth. Day after day, the people met for prayer and hearing the word; and the times of the Apostles seemed returned, when "the Lord added to the church daily of such as should be saved." All this time, Mr. McCheyne knew not how gracious the Lord had been in giving him his heart's desire. He continued, like Epaphras, "labouring fervently for them in prayer;" but it was not till we were within sight of home that the glad news of these revivals reached our ears.

Our journey led us through Moldavia, Wallachia, and Austria—lands of darkness and of the shadow of death. Profound strangers to the truth as it is in Jesus, the people of these lands, nevertheless, profess to be Christians. Superstition and its idolatries veil the glorious object of faith from every eye. In these regions, as well as in those already traversed, Mr. McCheyne's anxiety for souls appeared in the efforts he made to leave at least a few words of Scripture with the Jews whom we met, however short the time of our interview. His spirit was stirred in him; and, with his Hebrew Bible in his hand, he would walk up thoughtfully and solemnly to the first Jew he could get access to, and begin by calling the man's attention to some statement of God's word. In Palestine, if the Jew did not understand Italian, he would repeat to him such texts in Hebrew as, "In that day there shall be a fountain opened to the house of David," &c., (Zech. xiii. 1.) And one evening, at the well of Doulis, when the Arab population were all clustered round the water troughs, he looked on very wistfully, and said, "If only we had Arabic, we might sow beside all waters!"

At Jassy, after a deeply interesting day, spent in conversation with Jews who came to the inn, he said, "I will remember the faces of those men at the Judgment seat." When he came among the more educated Jews of Europe, he rejoiced to find that they could converse with him in Latin. His heart was bent on doing what he could (Mark xiv. 8,) in season and out of season. "One thing," he writes, "I am deeply convinced of, that God can make the simplest statement of the gospel, effectual to save souls. If only it be the true gospel, the good tidings, the message that God loved the world, and provided a ransom free to all, then God is able to make it wound the heart, and heal it too. There is deep meaning in the words of Paul, ' I am not ashamed of the gospel of Christ.' "

The abominations of Popery witnessed in Austrian Poland, called forth many a prayer for the destruction of the Man of Sin. "The images and idols by the way side are actually frightful, stamping the whole land as a kingdom of darkness. I do believe that a journey through Austria would go far to cure some of the Popery-admirers of our beloved land." He adds —"These are the marks of the beast upon this land." And in like manner our privileges in Scotland used to appear to him the more precious, when, as at Brody, we heard of Protestants who were supplied with sermon only once a year. "I must tell this to my people," said he, "when I return, to make them prize their many seasons of grace."

He estimated the importance of a town or country by its relation to the house of Israel; and his yearnings over these lost sheep resembled his bowels of compassion for his flock at home. At Tarnapol, in Galicia, he wrote home—"We are in Tarnapol, a very nice clean town, prettily situated on a winding stream, with wooded hills around. I suppose you never heard its name before; neither did I till we were there among the Jews. I know not whether it has been the birth place of warriors, or poets, or orators; its flowers have hitherto been born to blush unseen, at least by us barbarians of the north; but if God revive the dry bones of Israel that are scattered over the world, there will arise from this place an exceeding great army."

Our friend and brother in the faith, Erasmus Calman, lightened the tediousness of a long day's journey, by repeating to us some Hebrew poetry. One piece was on Israel's present state of degradation, it began—

צור · גואל ·

מחר וחיש פרות

As the vehicle drove along, we translated it line by line, and soon after Mr. McCheyne put it into verse. The following lines are a part:—

> Rock and Refuge of my soul,
> Swiftly let the season roll,
> When thine Israel shall arise
> Lovely in the nations' eyes!

> Lord of glory, Lord of might,
>   As our ransomed fathers tell;
> Once more for thy people fight,
>   Plead for thy loved Israel.
> Give our spoilers' towers to be
> Waste and desolate as we.

> Hasten, Lord, the joyful year,
>   When thy Zion, tempest-tossed,
> Shall the silver trumpet hear,
>   Bring glad tidings to the lost!
> Captive, cast thy cords from thee,
> Loose thy neck—be free—be free!

> Why dost thou behold our sadness?
>   See the proud have torn away
> All our years of solemn gladness,
>   When thy flock kept holy day!
> Lord, thy fruitful vine is bare,
> Not one gleaning grape is there!

> Rock and refuge of my soul,
> Swiftly let the season roll,
> When thine Israel shall be,
> Once again, beloved and free!

In his notes, he has one or two subjects marked for hymns. One of these is—Isaiah ii. 3—"Come ye," &c., *A loving call to the Jews.* Another is to the same effect—Isaiah i. 15—"Come, let us reason together." But these he never completed. In Cracow, having heard of the death of a friend, the wife of an English clergyman, in the midst of her days and in the full promise of usefulness, he began to pen a few sweet lines of comfort.

Oft as she taught the little maids of France
To leave the garland, castanet, and dance,
And listen to the words which she would say
About the crowns that never fade away,
A new expression kindled in her eye,
A holy brightness, borrowed from the sky.
And when returning to her native land,
She bowed beneath a Father's chastening hand;
When the quick pulse and flush upon the cheek,
A touching warning to her friends would speak,
A holy cheerfulness yet filled her eye;
Willing she was to live, willing to die.
As the good Shunammite (the Scriptures tell,)
When her son died, said meekly, "It is well,"
So when Sophia lost her infant boy,
And felt how dear-bought is a mother's joy,
When with green turf the little grave she spread,
"Not lost, but gone before," she meekly said.
And now they sleep together 'neath the willow,
The same dew drops upon their silent pillow.

Return, O mourner, from this double grave,
And praise the God who all her graces gave,
Follow her faith, and let her mantle be
A cloak of holy zeal to cover thee.

The danger which he incurred from the shepherds
in this region, and other similar perils to which he
was exposed in company with others, have been
recorded in the Narrative. Out of them all the Lord
delivered him; and not from these perils only did He
save him, but from many severe trials to his health,
to which variety of climate and discomforts of accom-
modation subjected him. And now we were traversing Prussia, drawing nearer our own land. It was
about five months since we had received letters from
Scotland, our route having led us away from places
which we had anticipated visiting, and where com-
munications had been left for us. We pressed homeward somewhat anxiously, yet wondering often at
past mercies. In a letter from Berlin, Mr. McCheyne
remarked, "Our heavenly Father has brought us
through so many trials and dangers that I feel persuaded he will yet carry us to the end. Like John,
we shall fulfil our course. 'Are there not twelve
hours in the day?' Are we not all immortal till our
work is done."

His strength was rapidly increasing; the journey had answered the ends anticipated to a great extent, in his restoration to health. He was able to preach at Hamburgh to the English congregation of Mr. Rheder, from whom it was that the first hint of a revival in Dundee reached his ears. He heard just so much both of Kilsyth and Dundee as to make him long to hear more. A few days after, on board the vessel that conveyed us to England, he thus expressed his feelings:

" Sailing up the Thames, Nov. 6, 1839.

"MY DEAR FATHER AND MOTHER,—You will be glad to see by the date that we are once more in sight of the shores of happy England. I only wish I knew how you all are. I have not heard of you since I was in Smyrna. In vain did I inquire for letters from you at Cracow, Berlin and Hamburgh. You must have written to Warsaw, and the Resident there has not returned them to Berlin, as we desired. Andrew and I and Mr. Calman are all quite well, and thankful to God, who has brought us through every danger in so many countries. I trust our course has not been altogether fruitless, and that we may now resign our commission with some hope of good issuing from it to the Church and to Israel. I preached last Sabbath in Hamburgh, for the first time since leaving England, and felt nothing the worse of it; so that I do hope it is my heavenly Father's will to restore me to usefulness again among my beloved flock. We have heard something of a reviving work at Kilsyth. We saw it noticed in one of the newspapers. I also saw the name of Dundee associated with it; so that I earnestly hope good has been doing in our church, and the dew from on high watering our parishes, and that the flocks whose pastors have been wandering may also have shared in the blessing. We are quite ignorant of the facts, and you may believe we are anxious to hear. . . . . . . We are now passing Woolwich, and in an hour will be in London. We are anxious to be home, but I suppose will not get away till next week. I never thought to have seen you again in this world, but now I hope to meet you once more in peace.—Believe me, your affectionate son," &c.

The day we arrived on the shores of our own land was indeed a singular day. We were intensely anxious to hear of events that had occurred at home a few months before—the outpouring of the Spirit from on high—while our friends were intensely interested in hearing tidings of the land of Israel and the scattered tribes. The reception of the deputation on their return, and the fruits of their mission, are well known, and have been elsewhere recorded.

Mr. McCheyne listened with deepest interest to the accounts given of what had taken place in Dundee during the month of August, when he lay at the gates of death in Bouja. The Lord had indeed fulfilled his hopes, and answered his prayers. His assistant, Mr. Burns, had been honoured of God to open the flood-gate at Dundee, as well as at Kilsyth. For some time before, Mr. Burns had seen symptoms of deeper attention than usual, and of real anxiety in some that had hitherto been careless. But it was after his return from Kilsyth that the people began to melt before the Lord. On Thursday, the second day after his return, at the close of the usual evening prayer meeting in St. Peter's, and when the minds of many were deeply solemnized by the tidings which had reached them, he spoke a few words about what had for some days detained him from them, and invited those to remain who felt the need of an outpouring of the Spirit to convert them. About a hundred remained; and at the conclusion of a solemn address to these anxious souls, suddenly the power of God seemed to descend, and all were bathed in tears. At a similar meeting, next evening, in the church, there was much melting of heart and intense desire after the Beloved of the Father; and on adjourning to the vestry, the arm of the Lord was revealed. No sooner was the vestry door opened to admit those who might feel anxious to converse, than a vast number pressed in with awful eagerness. It was like a pent-up flood breaking forth; tears were streaming from the eyes of many, and some fell on the ground groaning, and weeping, and crying for mercy. Onward from that evening, meetings were held every day for many weeks; and the extraordinary nature of the work justified and called for extraordinary services. The whole town was moved. Many believers doubted; the ungodly raged ; but the word of God grew mightily and prevailed. Instances occurred where whole families were affected at once, and each could be found mourning apart, affording a specimen of the times spoken of by Zechariah (xii. 2.) Mr. Baxter of Hilltown, Mr. Hamilton, then assistant at Abernyte, and other men of God in the vicinity, hastened to aid in the work. Mr. Roxburgh of St. John's, and Mr. Lewis of St. David's, examined the work impartially and judiciously, and testified it to be of God. Dr. McDonald of Ferintosh, a man of God well experienced in revivals, came to the spot and put to his seal also ; and continued in town, preaching in St. David's church to the anxious multitudes, during ten days. How many of those who were thus awfully awakened were really brought to the truth, it was impossible to ascertain. When Mr. McCheyne arrived, drop after drop was still falling from the clouds.

Such in substance were the accounts he heard before he reached Dundee. They were such as made his heart rejoice. He had no envy at another instrument having been so honoured in the place where he himself had laboured with many tears and temptations. In true Christian magnanimity, he rejoiced that the work of the Lord was done, by whatever hand. Full of praise and wonder, he set his foot once more on the shore of Dundee.

CHAPTER V

They shall spring up as among the grass, as willows by the water courses.—ISAIAH xliv. 4

His people, who had never ceased to pray for him, welcomed his arrival among them with the greatest joy. He reached Dundee on a Thursday afternoon; and in the evening of the same day—being the usual time for prayer in St. Peter's—after a short meditation, he hastened to the church, there to render thanks to the Lord, and to speak once more to his flock. The appearance of the church that evening, and the aspect of the people, he never could forget. Many of his brethren were present to welcome him, and to hear the first words of his opened lips. There was not a seat in the church unoccupied, the passages were completely filled, and the stairs up to the pulpit were crowded, on the one side with the aged, on the other with eagerly listening children. Many a face was seen anxiously gazing on their restored pastor; many were weeping under the unhealed wounds of conviction; all were still and calm, intensely earnest to hear. He gave out Psalm lxvi., and the manner of singing, which had been remarked since the revival began, appeared to him peculiarly sweet—"so tender and affecting, as if the people felt that they were praising a present God." After solemn prayer with them, he was able to preach for above an hour. Not knowing how long he might be permitted to proclaim the glad tidings, he seized that opportunity, not to tell of his journeyings, but to show the way of life to sinners. His subject was 1 Cor. ii. 1—4,—the matter, the manner, and the accompaniments of Paul's preaching. It was a night to be remembered.

On coming out of the church, he found the road to his house crowded with old and young, who were waiting to welcome him back. He had to shake hands with many at the same time; and before this happy multitude would disperse, had to speak some words of life to them again, and pray with them where they stood. "To thy name, O Lord," said he that night when returned to his home, "To thy name, O Lord, be all the glory." A month afterwards, he was visited by one who had hitherto stood out against all the singular influence of the revival, but who that night was deeply awakened under his words, so that the arrow festered in her soul, till she came crying, "O my hard, hard heart!"

On the Sabbath, he preached to his flock in the afternoon. He chose 2 Chron. v. 13, 14, as his subject; and in the close, his hearers remember well how affectionately and solemnly he said—"Dearly beloved and longed for, I now begin another year of my ministry among you; and I am resolved, if God give me health and strength, that I will not let a man, woman, or child among you alone, until you have at least heard the testimony of God concerning his Son, either to your condemnation or salvation. And I will pray, as I have done before, that, if the Lord will, indeed, give us a great outpouring of his Spirit, he will do it in such a way that it will be evident to the weakest child among you, that it is the Lord's work, and not man's. I think I may say to you, as Rutherford said to his people, 'Your heaven would be two heavens to me.' And if the Lord be pleased to give me a crown from among you, I do here promise in his sight, that I will cast it at his feet, saying, 'Worthy is the Lamb that was slain! Blessing, and honour, and glory, and power, be unto Him that sitteth upon the throne, and to the Lamb, for ever and ever.'"

It was much feared for a time that a jealous spirit would prevail among the people of St. Peter's, some saying, "I am of Paul, and others, I of Cephas." Those recently converted were apt to regard their spiritual father in a light in which they could regard none besides. But Mr. McCheyne had received from the Lord a holy disinterestedness that suppressed every feeling of envy. Many wondered at the single heartedness he was enabled to exhibit. He could sincerely say, " I have no desire but the salvation of my people, by whatever instrument."

Never, perhaps, was there one placed in better circumstances for testing the revival impartially, and seldom has any revival been more fully tested. He came among a people whose previous character he knew. He found a work wrought among them during his absence, in which he had not had any direct share. He returned home to go out and in among them, and to be a close observer of all that had taken place; and, after a faithful and prayerful examination, he did most unhesitatingly say, that the Lord had wrought great things, whereof he was glad; and, in the case of many of those whose souls were saved in that revival, he discovered remarkable answers to the prayers of himself, and of those who had come to the truth, before he left them. He wrote to me his impressions of the work, when he had been a few weeks among his people.

2d Dec. 1839.

" Rev. AND. A. BONAR, Collace.

" My dear A.—I begin upon note paper, because I have no other on hand but our thin travelling paper. I have much to tell you, and to praise the Lord for. I am grieved to hear that there are no marks of the Spirit's work about Collace during your absence ; but if Satan drive you to your knees, he will soon find cause to repent it. Remember how fathers do to their children when they ask bread. How much more shall our heavenly Father give (ἀγαθὰ) all good things to them that ask him. Remember the rebuke which I once got from old Mr. Dempster of Denny, after preaching to his people—' I was highly pleased with your discourse, but in prayer it struck me that you thought God *unwilling to give.*' Remember Daniel— ' At the beginning of thy supplications the commandment came forth.' And do not think you are forgotten by me as long as I have health and grace to pray.

" Every thing here I have found in a state better than I expected. The night I arrived I preached to such a congregation as I never saw before. I do not think another person could have got into the church, and there was every sign of the deepest and tenderest emotion. R. Macdonald was with me, and prayed. Affliction and success in the ministry have taught and quickened him. I preached on 1 Cor. ii. 1—4, and felt what I have often heard, that it is easy to preach where the Spirit of God is. On the Friday night, Mr. Burns preached; on the Sabbath I preached on that wonderful passage, 2 Chron. v. 13, 14; Mr. Burns preached twice, morning and evening. His views of Divine truth are clear and commanding. There is a great deal of substance in what he preaches, and his manner is very powerful,—so much so, that he sometimes made me tremble. In private, he is deeply prayerful, and seems to feel his danger of falling into pride.

I have seen many of the awakened, and many of the saved; indeed, this is a pleasant place compared with what it was once. Some of the awakened are still in the deepest anxiety and distress. Their great error is exactly what your brother Horace told me. They think that coming to Christ is some strange act of their mind, different from believing what God has said of his Son; so much so, that they will tell you with one breath, I believe all that God has said, and yet with the next, complain that they cannot come to Christ, or close with Christ. It is very hard to deal with this delusion.

" I find some old people deeply shaken; they feel insecure. One confirmed drunkard has come to me, and is, I believe, now a saved man. Some little children are evidently saved. All that I have yet seen are related to converts of my own. One, eleven years old, is a singular instance of Divine grace. When I asked if she desired to be made holy, she said, ' Indeed I often wish I was awa', that I might sin nae mair.' A. L., of fifteen is a fine tender hearted believer. W. S., ten years of age, is also a happy boy.

" Many of my own dear children in the Lord are much advanced; much more full of joy—their hearts lifted up in the ways of the Lord. I have found many more savingly impressed under my own ministry than I knew of. Some have come to tell me. In one case, a whole family saved. I have hardly met with any thing to grieve me. Surely the Lord had dealt bountifully with me. I fear, however, that the great Spirit has in some measure passed by—I hope soon to return in greater power than ever. The week meetings are thinner now. I will turn two of them into my classes soon, and so give solid, regular instruction, of which they stand greatly in need. I have not met with one case of extravagance or false fire, although doubtless there may be many. At first they used to follow in a body to our house, and expected many an address and prayer by the road. They have given up this now. I preached last Sabbath twice, first on Isaiah xxviii. 14—18, and then on Rev. xii. 11, 'Overcame by the blood of the Lamb.' It was a very solemn day. The people willingly sat till it was dark. Many make it a place of Bochim. Still there is nothing of the power which has been. I have tried to persuade Mr. Burns to stay with us, and I think he will remain in Dundee. I feel fully stronger in body than when I left you. Instead of exciting me, there is every thing to solemnize and still my feelings. Eternity sometimes seems very near.

" I would like your advice about prayer meetings; —how to consolidate them; what rules should be followed, if any; whether there should be mere reading of the word and prayer, or free converse also on the passage ? We began to day a ministerial prayer meeting, to be held every Monday at eleven for an hour and a half. This is a great comfort, and may be a great blessing. Of course, we do not invite the colder ministers; that would only damp our meeting. Tell me if you think this right.

" And now, dear A., I must be done, for it is very late. May your people share in the quickening that has come over Dundee. I feel it a very powerful argument with many—' Will you be left dry when others are getting drops of heavenly dew ?' Try this with your people.

" I think it probable we shall have another communion again before the regular one. It seems very desirable. You will come and help us; and perhaps Horace too.

"I thought of coming back by Collace from Errol, if our Glasgow meeting had not come in the way.

" Will you set a going your Wednesday meeting again immediately?

" Farewell, dear A. 'O man, greatly beloved, fear not; peace be to thee; be strong: yea, be strong.' Yours, ever," &c.

To Mr. Burns he thus expresses himself, on *December* 19th:—" My Dear Brother, I shall never be able to thank you for all your labours among the precious souls committed to me; and what is worse, I can never thank God fully for his kindness and grace, which every day appears to me more remarkable. He has answered prayer to me in all that has happened in a way which I have never told any one." Again, on the 31st, " Stay where you are, dear brother, as long as the Lord has any work for you to do.* If I know my own heart, its only desire is that Christ may be glorified, by souls flocking to him, and abiding in him, and reflecting his image; and whether it be in Perth or Dundee should signify little to us. You know I told you my mind plainly, that I thought the Lord had so blessed you in Dundee that you were called to a fuller and deeper work there; but if the Lord accompanies you to other places, I have nothing to object. The Lord strengthened my body and soul last Sabbath, and my spirit also was glad. The people were much alive in the Lord's service. But O dear brother, the most are Christless still. The rich are almost untroubled."

His evidence on this subject is given fully in his answers to the queries put by a committee of the Aberdeen Presbytery; and, in a note to a friend, he incidentally mentions a pleasing result of this wide-

---

* Mr. Burns was at that time in Perth, and there had begun to be some movement among the dry bones.

spread awakening. "I find many souls saved under my own ministry, whom I never knew of before. They are not afraid to come out now, it has become so common a thing to be concerned about the soul." At that time, also, many came from a distance—one came from the north, who had been a year in deep distress of soul, to seek Christ in Dundee.

In his brief diary he records, on *December* 3d, that twenty anxious souls had that night been conversing with him; many of them very deeply interesting. He occasionally fixed an evening for the purpose of meeting with those who were awakened; and in one of his note books there are at least *four hundred* visits recorded, made to him by inquiring souls, in the course of that and the following years. He observed, that those who had been believers formerly had got their hearts enlarged, and were greatly established; and some seemed able to feed upon the truth in a new manner—as when one related to him how there had for some time appeared a glory in the reading of the word in public quite different from reading it alone.

At the same time he saw backslidings, both among those whom believers had considered really converted, and among those who had been deeply convicted, though never reckoned among the really saved. He notes in his book—" Called to see ——. Poor lad, he seems to have gone back from Christ, led away by evil company. And yet I felt sure of him at one time. What blind creatures ministers are : man looketh at the outward appearance." One morning he was visited by one of his flock, proposing a concert for prayer on the following Monday, in behalf of those who had fallen back, that God's Spirit might re-awaken them," —so observant were the believers as well as their pastor of declensions. Among those who were awakened, but never truly converted, he mentions one case. " *January* 9, 1840.—Met with the case of one who had been frightened during the late work, so that her bodily health was injured. She seems to have no care now about her soul. It has only filled her mouth with evil speaking."

That many, who promised fair, drew back and walked no more with Jesus, is true. Out of about eight hundred souls, who, during the months of the revival, conversed with different ministers in apparent anxiety, no wonder surely if many proved to have been impressed only for a time. President Edwards considered it likely that in such cases, the proportion of real conversions might resemble the proportion of blossoms in spring, and fruit in autumn. Nor can any thing be more unreasonable than to doubt the truth of all, because of the deceit of some. The world itself does not so act in judging of its own. The world reckons upon the possibility of being mistaken in many cases, and yet does not cease to believe that there is honesty and truth to be found. One of themselves, a poet of their own, has said with no less justice than beauty—

> "Angels are bright still, though the brightest fell;
> And though foul things put on the brows of grace,
> Yet grace must still look so."

But, above all, we have the authority of the word of God, declaring that such backslidings are the very tests of the true Church—"For there must be also heresies among you, that they which are approved may be made manifest among you." 1 Cor. xi. 19. It is not, however, meant that any who had really believed, went back to perdition. On the contrary, it is the creed of every sound evangelical church, that those who do go back to perdition, were persons who never really believed in Jesus. Their eyes may have been opened to see the dread realities of sin and of the wrath to come, but if they saw not righteousness for their guilty souls in the Saviour, there is nothing in all Scripture to make us expect that they will continue awake. "Awake, thou that sleepest, and *Christ will give thee light*," is the call and the invitation. One who, for a whole year, went back to folly, said— "Your sermon on the corruption of the heart made me despair, and so I gave myself up to my old ways— attending dances, learning songs," &c. A knowledge

of our guilt, and a sense of danger, will not of themselves keep us from falling; nay, these, if alone, may
(as in the above case) thrust us down the slippery
places.   We are truly secure only when our eye is on
Jesus, and our hand locked in his hand.   So that the
history of backslidings, instead of leading us to doubt
the reality of grace in believers will only be found to
teach us two great lessons, viz., the vast importance
of pressing immediate salvation on awakened souls,
and the reasonableness of standing in doubt of all,
however deep their convictions, who have not truly
fled to the hope set before them.

There was another ground of prejudice against the
whole work, arising from the circumstance that the
Lord had employed in it young men not long engaged
in the work of the ministry, rather than the fathers
in Israel.   But herein it was that sovereign grace
shone forth the more conspicuously.   Do such objec-
tors suppose that God ever intends the honour of man
in a work of revival?   Is it not the honour of his own
name that he seeks?   Had it been his wish to give
the glory to man at all, then indeed, it might have
been asked, "Why does he pass by the older pastors,
and call for the inexperienced youth?"   But when
sovereign grace was coming to bless a region in the
way that would redound most to the glory of the
Lord, can we conceive a wiser plan than to use the
sling of David in bringing down the Philistine?   If,
however, there be some whose prejudice is from the
root of envy, let such hear the remonstrance of Richard
Baxter to the jealous ministers of his day.   "What!
malign Christ in gifts for which he should have the
glory, and all because they seem to hinder our glory!
Does not every man owe thanks to God for his brethren's gifts—not only as having himself part in them,
as the foot has the benefit of the guidance of the eye,
but also because his own ends may be attained by his
brethren's gifts as well as by his own? . . . .
A fearful thing that any man, that hath the least of
the fear of God, should so envy at God's gifts, that
he would rather his carnal hearers were unconverted

and the drowsy not awakened, than that it should be done by another who may be preferred before them."*

The work of the Spirit went on, the stream flowing gently; for the heavy showers had fallen, and the overflowing of the waters had passed by. Mr. McCheyne became more than ever vigilant and discriminating in dealing with souls. Observing, also, that some were influenced more by feelings of strong attachment to their pastor personally, than by the power of the truths he preached, he became more reserved in his dealings with them, so that some thought there was a little coldness or repulsiveness in his manner. If there did appear any thing of this nature to some, certainly it was no indication of diminished compassion; but, on the contrary, proceeded from a scrupulous anxiety to guard others against the deceitful feelings of their own souls. A few notes of his work occur at this period.

" *November* 27, 1839.—A pleasant meeting in the Cross church on Wednesday last, for the seamen. All that spoke seemed to honour the Saviour. I had to move thanksgiving to God for his mercies. This has been a real blessing to Dundee. It should not be forgotten in our prayers and thanksgivings."

" *Nov.* 28.—Thursday evening.—Much comfort in speaking. There was often an awful stillness. Spoke on Jerem. vi. 14—' They have healed also the hurt of the daughter of my people slightly.' " &c.

" *December* 1.—This evening came a tender Christian, so far as I can see; an exposition of that text, ' *I will go softly,*' or of that other, ' *Thou shalt not open thy mouth any more.*' A child of shame made one of honour. Her sister was awakened under Mr. Baxter's words in St. Peter's, at whom he asked, ' Would you like to be holy?' She replied, ' Indeed, I often wish I were dead that I might sin no more.' "

" *Dec.* 3.—Preached six times within these two days."

" *Dec.* 8.—Saw J. T. in fever. She seems really

* Reformed Pastor, iv. 2.

in Christ now; tells me how deeply my words sunk into her soul when I was away. A. M. stayed to tell me her joy. J. B. walked home with me, telling me what God had done for his soul, when one day I had stopped at the quarry on account of a shower of rain, and took shelter with my pony in the engine house." He had simply pointed to the fire of the furnace, and said, "What does that remind you of?" and the words had remained deep in the man's soul.

Dec. 11. — A woman awakened that night I preached in J. D.'s green, about two years ago, on Ezek. xx. 43. For twenty years she had been out of church privileges, and now, for the first time, came trembling to ask restoration. Surely Immanuel is in this place, and even old sinners are flocking to him. I have got an account of about twenty prayer meetings connected with my flock. Many open ones; many fellowship meetings; only one or two have any thing like exhortation superadded to the word. These, I think, it must be our care to change, if possible, lest error and pride creep in. The only other difficulty is this. In two of the female meetings, originally fellowship meetings, anxious female inquirers have been admitted. They do not pray, but only hear. In one M. and J. had felt the rising of pride to a great degree; in the other M. could not be persuaded that there was any danger of pride. This case will require prayerful deliberation. My mind at present is, that there is great danger from it, the praying members feeling themselves on a different level from the others, and any thing like female teaching, as a public teacher, seems clearly condemned in the word of God."

"*Dec.* 12.—Felt very feeble all day, and as if I could not do any more work in the vineyard. Evening.—Felt more of the reality of Immanuel's intercession. The people also were evidently subdued by more than a human testimony. One soul waited, sobbing most piteously. She could give no more account of herself than that she was a sinner, and did not believe that God would be merciful to her. When

I showed how I found mercy, her only answer was—
' But you were not sic a sinner as me.'

" *Dec.* 18.—Went to Glasgow along with A. B.
Preached in St. George's to a full audience, in the
cause of the Jews. Felt real help in time of need."
This was one of his many journeys from place to place
in behalf of Israel, relating the things seen and heard
among the Jews of Palestine and other lands.

" *Dec.* 22.—Preached in Anderston church with a
good deal of inward peace and comfort."

" *Dec.* 23.—Interesting meeting with the Jewish
Committee. In the evening met a number of God's
people. The horror of some good people in Glasgow
at the Millenarian views is very great, while at the
same time their objections appear very weak."

" *Dec.* 31.--Young communicants. Two have made
application to be admitted under eleven years of age ;
four that are only fourteen ; three who are fifteen or
sixteen."

" *January* 1, 1840.—Awoke early by the kind
providence of God, and had uncommon freedom and
fervency in keeping the concert for prayer this morning before light. Very touching interview with M.
P., who still refuses to be comforted. Was enabled
to cry after a glorious Immanuel along with her.
How I wish I had her bitter convictions of sin !
Another called this evening, who says she was
awakened and brought to Christ during the sermon
on the morning of December 1st, on the *covenant with
death.* Gave clear answers, but seems too unmoved
for one really changed."

" *Jan.* 2.—Visited six families. Was refreshed and
solemnized at each of them. Spoke of the Word
made flesh, and of all the paths of the Lord being
mercy and truth. Visited in the evening by some
interesting souls : one a believing little boy ; another
complaining she cannot come to Christ for the hardness of her heart ; another once awakened under my
ministry, again thoroughly awakened and brought to
Christ under Horace Bonar's sermon at the communion. She is the only saved one in her family—awfully

persecuted by father and mother. Lord, stand up for thine own! Make known, by their constancy under suffering, the power and beauty of thy grace! Evening.—Mr. Miller preached delightfully on ' The love of Christ constraineth us.' His account of the Protestants of France was very interesting—the work of God at Nismes, where it is said they are no more fishing with line, but dragging with the nets. Read a letter from Mr. Cumming, describing the work at Perth, and entreating the prayers of God's children."

The last reference is to the awakening which took place in St. Leonard's church, Perth, on the last night of the year, when Mr. Burns, along with their pastor, Mr. Milne, was preaching. Mr. B. had intended to return to Dundee for the Sabbath, but was detained by the plain indications of the Lord's presence. At one meeting, the work was so glorious that one night about one hundred and fifty persons at one time seemed bowed down under a sense of their guilt, and above two hundred came next day to the church in the forenoon to converse about their souls. This awakening was the commencement of a solid work of grace, both in that town and its neighbourhood, much fruit of which is to be found there at this day in souls that are walking in the fear of the Lord, and the comfort of the Holy Ghost. And it was in the spring of this same year, that, in Collace, at our weekly prayer meeting, when two brethren were ministering, we received a blessed shower from the Lord.

His journal proceeds:—

" *Jan.* 3.—An inquirer came, awakened under my ministry two years and a half ago."

" *Jan.* 5.—Two came ; M. B. sorely wounded with the forenoon's discourse."

" *Jan.* 12.—Intimated a concert for prayer, that unworthy communicants might be kept back, the Lord's children prepared for the feast, and ministers furnished from on high."

" *Jan.* 13.—Kept concert of prayer this morning with my dear people. Did not find the same enlargement as usual."

"*March* 5.—Thursday evening.—Preached on Zech. iii.—Joshua. Was led to speak searchingly about making Christ the minister of sin. One young woman cried aloud very bitterly. M. B. came to tell me that poor M. is like to have her life taken away by her parents. A young woman also, who is still concerned, and persecuted by her father. A young man came to tell me that he had found Christ. Roll on, thou river of life ! visit every dwelling ! save a multitude of souls. Come, Holy Spirit ! come quickly !"

"*March* 25.—Last night at Forfar speaking for Israel to a small band of friends of the Jews. Fearfully wicked place—the cry of it ascends up before God like that of Sodom."

"*March* 31.—Met with young communicants on Wednesday and Friday. On the latter night especially, very deep feeling, manifested in sobbings. Visits of several. One dear child nine years old. Sick bed."

"*April* 1.—Presbytery day. Passed the constitution of two new churches—blessed be God !—may he raise up faithful pastors for them both—Dudhope and Wallace-Feus. Proposal also for the Mariners' church. A fast day fixed for the present state of the church."

"*April* 5.—Sabbath evening.—Spoke to twenty-four young persons, one by one ; almost all affected about their souls."

"*April* 6.—Lovely ride and meditation in a retired grove."

"*April* 7.—Impressed to-night with the complete necessity of preaching to my people in their own lanes and closes ; in no other way will God's word ever reach them. To-night spoke in St. Andrew's church to a very crowded assembly in behalf of Israel. Was helped to speak plainly to their own consciences. Lord, bless it ! Shake this town !"

"*April* 13.—Spoke in private to nearly thirty young communicants, all in one room, going round each, and advising for the benefit of all."

" *April* 22.—Rode to Collessie (Fife) and Kirkaldy Sweet time alone in Collessie woods."

" *July* 30.—One lad came to me in great distress wishing to know if he should confess his little dishonesties to his master." About this time, he has noted down, " I was visiting the other day, and came to a locked door. What did this mean ? ' Torment me, torment me not.' Ah, satan is mighty still."— referring to Mark v. 7.

A few of his communion seasons are recorded. We could have desired a record of them all. The first of which he has detailed any particulars, is the one he enjoyed soon after returning home.

" *January* 19, 1840.—Stormy morning with gushing torrents of rain, but cleared up in answer to prayer. Sweet union in prayer with Mr. Cumming, and afterwards with A. Bonar. Found God in secret. Asked especially that the very sight of the broken bread and poured out wine might be blessed to some souls ; then pride will be hidden from man. Church well filled—many standing. Preached the action sermon on John xvii. 24, 'Father, I will,' &c. Had considerable nearness to God in prayer—more than usual—and also freedom in preaching, although I was ashamed of such poor views of Christ's glory. The people were in a very desirable frame of attention— hanging on the word. Felt great help in fencing the tables, from Acts v. 3, 'Lying to the Holy Ghost.' Came down and served the first table, with much more calmness and collectedness than ever I remember to have enjoyed. Enjoyed a sweet season while A. B. served the next table. He dwelt chiefly on believing the words of Christ about his fulness, and the promise of the Father. There were six tables altogether. The people more and more moved to the end. At the last table, every head seemed bent like a bulrush while A. B. spoke of the ascension of Christ. Helped a little in the address, ' Now to him who is able to keep you,' &c., and in the concluding prayer. One little boy, in retiring, said, ' This has

been another bonnie day.' Many of the little ones
seemed deeply attentive. Mr. Cummings and Mr.
Burns preached in the school the most of the day. In
the evening Mr. C., preached on the pillar of cloud on
every dwelling, Isaiah iv. 5, some very sweet, powerful words. Mr. Burns preached in the school room.
When the church emptied, a congregation formed in
the lower school, and began to sing. Sang several
psalms with them, and spoke on 'Behold, I stand at
the door.' Going home, A. L. said, 'Pray for me; I
am quite happy, and so is H.' Altogether a day of
the revelation of Christ—a sweet day to myself, and,
I am persuaded, to many souls. Lord, make us meet
for the table above."

Another of these communion seasons recorded is
April 1840. "Sabbath 19.—Sweet and precious day.
Preached action sermon on Zech. xii. 10; xiii. 1. A
good deal assisted. Also in fencing the tables, on
Psa. cxxxix., 'Search me, O God.' Less at serving
the tables, on 'I will betroth thee,' and 'To him that
overcometh;' though the thanksgiving was sweet.
Communicated with calm joy. Old Mr. Burns
served two tables; H. Bonar five. There was a
very melting frame visible among the people. Helped
a good deal in the address on 'My sheep hear my
voice.' After seven before all was over. Met before
eight. Old Mr. Burns preached on 'A word in season.'
Gave three parting texts, and so concluded this blessed
day. Many were filled with joy unspeakable and full
of glory."

"*Monday* 20.—Mr. Grierson preached on, 'Ye
are come to Mount Zion' — an instructive word.
Pleasant walk with H. B. Evening sermon from
him to the little children on the 'new heart'—truly
delightful. Prayer meeting after. I began; then old
Mr. Burns; then Horace, in a very lively manner,
on the woman of Samaria. The people were brought
into a very tender frame. After the blessing, a multitude remained. One (A. N.) was like a person
struck through with a dart; she could neither stand

nor go. Many were looking on her with faces of
horror. Others were comforting her in a very kind
manner, bidding her look to Jesus. Mr. Burns went
to the desk, and told them of Kilsyth. Still they
would not go away. Spoke a few words more to
those around me, telling them of the loveliness of
Christ, and the hardness of their hearts, that they
could be so unmoved when one was so deeply
wounded. The sobbing soon spread, till many heads
were bent down, and the church was filled with sobbing. Many whom I did not know were now affected. After prayer, we dismissed, near midnight.
Many followed us. One, in great agony, prayed that
she might find Christ that very night. So ends this
blessed season."

The prayer meeting on the Monday evening following the communion was generally enjoyed by all the
Lord's people, and by the ministers who assisted, in a
peculiar manner. Often all felt the last day of the
feast to be the great day. Souls that had been enjoying the feast were then, at its conclusion, taking hold
on the arm of the Beloved in the prospect of going up
through the wilderness.

The only notice of his last communion, *January* 1,
1843, is the following:—" Sabbath.—A happy communion season. Mr. W. Burns preached on Tuesday, Wednesday, and Thursday evenings—the first
and last very solemn. Mr. Baxter (of Hilltown
church) on the Friday. A. Bonar on Saturday, on
Rom. viii.—the Spirit of adoption. I fainted on the
Sabbath morning, but revived, and got grace and
strength to preach on 1 Tim. i. 16—Paul's conversion
a pattern. There were five tables. Many godly
strangers, and a very desirable frame observable in
the people. 'While the king sitteth at his table, my
spikenard sendeth out the smell thereof.' Much sin
was covered. He restoreth my soul. *Monday* 2.—
Mr. Milne (of Perth) preached on, 'Hold fast that
thou hast;' and in the evening, to the children, on
Josh. xxiv. 'Choose ye this day whom ye will

serve.' Andrew and I concluded with Rev. v. 'Thou hast redeemed us,' &c., and 1 Cor. xv. 'Be steadfast,' &c.''

He dispensed the Lord's Supper to his flock every quarter; and though on this account his calls upon his brethren for help were frequent, yet never did a brother reckon it any thing else than a blessed privilege to be with him. His first invitation to his friend, Mr. Hamilton (then at Abernyte,) will show the nature of the intercourse that subsisted between him and his brethren who gave their services on these occasions:—" My dear friend, will you excuse lack of ceremony, and come down to-morrow and preach to us the unsearchable riches of Christ? We have the communion on Sabbath. We have no fast day, but only a meeting in the evening at a quarter past seven. Come, my dear sir, if you can, and refresh us with your company. Bring the fragrance of 'the bundle of myrrh' along with you, and may grace be poured into your lips. Yours, ever.'' (*Jan.* 15, 1840.)

Soon after his return from his mission to the Jews, a ministerial prayer meeting was formed among some of the brethren in Dundee. Mr. McCheyne took part in it, along with Mr. Lewis of St. David's, Mr. Baxter of Hilltown, Mr. P. L. Miller, afterwards of Wallacetown, and others. Feeling deep concern for the salvation of the souls under their care, they met every Monday forenoon, to pray together for their flocks, and their own souls. The time of the meeting was limited to an hour and a half, in order that all who attended might form their pastoral arrangements for the day, without fear of being hindered; and, in addition to prayer, those present conversed on some selected topic, vitally connected with their duties as ministers of Christ. Mr. McCheyne was never absent from this prayer meeting, unless through absolute necessity, and the brethren scarcely remember any occasion on which some important remark did not drop from his lips. He himself reaped great profit from it. He notes, *December* 8th—" This has been a deeply interesting week. On Monday our ministerial prayer meeting was set a going in St. David's vestry. The hearts of all seem really in earnest in it. The Lord answers prayer; may it be a great blessing to our souls and to our flocks." Another time—" Meeting in St. David's vestry. The subject of fasting was spoken upon. Felt exceedingly in my own spirit how little we feel real grief on account of sin before God, or we would often lose our appetite for food. When parents lose a child, they often do not taste a bit from morning to night, out of pure grief. Should we not mourn as for an only child? How little of the spirit of grace and supplication we have then!" On *Dec.* 30.—" Pleasant meeting of ministers. Many delightful texts on 'arguments to be used with God in prayer.' How little I have used these! Should we not study prayer more?"

Full as he was of affection and Christian kindness to all believers, he was specially so to the faithful brethren in the gospel of Christ. Perhaps there never was one who more carefully watched against the danger of undervaluing precious men, and detracting from a brother's character. Although naturally ambitious, grace so wrought in him, that he never sought to bring himself into view; and most cheerfully would he observe and take notice of the graces and gifts of others. Who is there of us that should ever feel otherwise? " For the body is not one member, but many." And " the eye cannot say unto the hand, I have no need of thee; nor, again, the head to the feet, I have no need of you."

All with whom he was intimate still remember with gratitude how faithfully and anxiously he used to warn his friends of whatever he apprehended they were in danger from. To Mr. W. C. Burns he wrote, *Dec.* 31, 1839 : " Now, the Lord be your strength, teacher, and guide. I charge you, be clothed with humility, or you will yet be a wandering star, for which is reserved the blackness of darkness for ever. Let Christ increase; let man decrease. This is my constant prayer for myself and you. If you lead sinners to yourself, and not to Christ, Immanuel will

cast the star out of his right hand into outer darkness.
Remember what I said of preaching out of the Scriptures ; honour the word both in the matter and manner.   Do not cease to pray for me."   At another time
(*Nov.* 3, 1841,) he thus wrote to the same friend :
" Now, remember, Moses wist not that the skin of his
face shone.   Looking at our own shining face is the
bane of the spiritual life and of the ministry.   O for
closest communion with God, till soul and body—
head, face, and heart—shine with divine brilliancy ;
but O for a holy ignorance of our shining.   Pray for
this ; for you need it as well as I."

To another friend in the ministry who had written
to him despondingly about his people and the times,
his reply was, " I am sure there never was a time
when the Spirit of God was more present in Scotland,
and it does not become you to murmur in your tents,
but rather to give thanks.   Remember, we may grieve
the Spirit as truly by not joyfully acknowledging his
wonders, as by not praying for him.   There is the
clearest evidence that God is saving souls in Kilsyth,
Dundee, Perth, Collace, Blairgowrie, Strathbogie,
Ross-shire, Breadalbane, Kelso, Jedburgh, Ancrum ;
and surely it becomes us to say, ' I thank my God
upon every remembrance of you.'   Forgive my presumption ; but I fear lest you hurt your own peace
and usefulness in not praising God enough for the
operation of his hands."   To another : " I have told
you that you needed trial, and now it is come.   May
you be exercised thereby, and come to that happy
' afterwards ' of which the Apostle speaks."   To the
same again : " Remember the necessity of your own
soul, and do not grow slack or lean in feeding others.
' Mine own vineyard have I not kept.'   Ah, take heed
of that !"   And in a similar tone of faithfulness at an
after period : " Remember the case of your own soul.
' What will it profit a man to gain the whole world
and lose his own soul ?'   Remember how often Paul
appeals to his holy, just, unblamable life.   O that we
may be able always to do the same !"   " Remember
the pruning knife," he says to another, " and do not

let your vine run to wood." And after a visit to Mr.
Thornton of Milnathort, in whose parish there had
been an awakening, he asks a brother, " Mr. Thornton is willing that others be blessed more than himself; do you think that you have that grace ? I find
that I am never so successful as when I can lie at
Christ's feet, willing to be used or not as seemeth good
in his sight. Do you remember David ? 'If the Lord
say, I have no delight in thee ; behold, here am I ; let
him do to me as seemeth good unto him. In his
familiar letters, as in his life, there was the manifestation of a bright, cheerful soul, without the least tendency to levity. When his medical attendant had, on
one occasion, declined any remuneration, Mr. Mc-
Cheyne peremptorily opposed his purpose ; and to
overcome his reluctance, returned the inclosure in a
letter, in which he used his poetical gifts with most
pleasant humour.

To many it was a subject of wonder that he found
time to write letters that always breathed the name
of Jesus, amid his innumerable engagements. But
the truth was, his letters cost him no expenditure of
time ; they were ever the fresh thoughts and feelings
of his soul at the moment he took up the pen ; his
habitual frame of soul is what appears in them all.
The calm, holy, tenderly affectionate style of his letters
reminds us of Samuel Rutherford, whose works he
delighted to read—excepting only that his joy never
seems to have risen to ecstasies. The selection of
his letters which I have made for publication, may
exhibit somewhat of his holy skill in dropping a word
for his Master on all occasions. But what impressed
many yet more, was his manner of introducing the
truth, most naturally and strikingly, even in the
shortest note he penned ; and there was something so
elegant, as well as solemn, in his few words at the
close of some of his letters, that these remained deep
in the receiver's heart. Writing to Mr. G. S. on
July 28, 1841, he thus draws to a close : " Remember me to H. T. I pray he may be kept abiding in
Christ. Kindest regards to his mother. Say to her

from me, ' Pass the time of your sojourning here in fear, forasmuch as ye know ye were not redeemed with corruptible things such as silver and gold;' 1 Peter i. 17, 18. Keep your own heart, dear brother, ' in the love of God' (Jude 21,) in his love to you, and that will draw your love to him. Kindest remembrances to your brother. Say to him, ' Be sober and hope to the end.' (1 Peter i. 13.) To your own dear mother say, ' He doth not afflict willingly.' Write me soon.—Ever yours, till time shall be no more." In a note to the members of his own family :—" The Tay is before me now like a resplendent mirror, glistening in the morning sun. May the same sun shine sweetly on you, and may He that makes it shine, shine into your hearts to give you the knowledge of the glory of God in the face of Jesus Christ. In haste, your affectionate son and brother." There were often such last words as the following—" O for drops in the pastures of the wilderness ! The smiles of Jesus be with you, and the breathings of the Holy Ghost. Ever yours." (To Rev. J. Milne,) "May we have gales passing from Perth to this, and from here to you, and from heaven to both. Ever yours." (To the same.) " The time is short ; eternity is near ; yea, the coming of Christ the second time is at hand. Make sure of being one with the Lord Jesus, that you may be glad when you see him. Commending you all to our Father in heaven," &c. (To his own brother.) " I have a host of letters before me, and therefore, can add no more. I give you a parting text, ' Sorrowful, yet always rejoicing.' " Another —" Farewell ! yours till the day dawn." (Rev. Hor. Bonar.) " I am humbled and cheered by what you say of good done in Kelso. Roll on, roll on, river of God, that art full of water. A woman came to me, awakened under your sermon to the children in the Cross church, very bitterly convinced of sin. Glory to the Divine Archer, who bringeth down the peo ple !" (To a student.) " Grace be with you, and much of the knowledge of Jesus—much of his likeness. I thrist for the knowledge of the word, but most of all of Jesus himself, the true Word. May he abide in you, and you in him! The fear of Isaac watch over you." In concluding a letter to Mr. Bonar of Larbert, in Feburary 1843, some weeks before his last illness, he writes—" My soul often goes out at the throne of grace in behalf of Larbert and Dunipace. May the disruption be more blessed to them than days of peace! How sweet to be in the ark when the deluge comes down. Ever yours in gospel bonds."

The Jewish mission continued near his heart, " the nearest," said he to Mr. Edwards, who is now at Jassy, " of all missionary enterprises. Were it not for my own unfitness, and also the success the Lord has given me where I am, I would joyfully devote myself to it." In connection with this cause, he was invited to visit Ireland, and be present at the meeting of the Synod of our Presbyterian brethren in the summer of 1840. While preparing to set out, he notices the hand of his Master guiding him:—" *July* 2.—Expected to have been in Ireland this day. Detained by not being able to get supply for Sabbath. In the good providence of God, for this evening there was a considerable awakening in the church while I was preaching upon Philip. iii. 18, ' Enemies of the cross of Christ.' When that part was expounded, there was a loud and bitter weeping—probably thirty or forty seemed to share in it; the rest deeply impressed—many secretly praying." On the Sabbath following, one person was so overcome as to be carried out of the church.

He set out for Ireland on the 7th, and on the 10th witnessed at Belfast the union between the Synod of Ulster and the Secession. He speaks of it as a most solemn scene—five hundred ministers and elders present. During his stay there, he pleaded the cause of the Jews in Mr. Morgan's church, Mr. Wilson's, and some others; and also visited Mr. Kirkpatrick at Dublin. He preached the way of salvation to the Gentiles, in all his pleadings for Israel. His visit was blessed to awaken a deep interest in the cause of the Jews, and his words sunk into the consciences of some.

His sermon on Ezekiel xxxiv. 16, was felt by some
to be indescribably impressive; and when he preached
on Rom. i. 16, 17, many ministers, as they came out,
were heard saying, " How was it we never thought
of the duty of remembering Israel before ?" On another occasion, the people to whom he had preached
entreated their minister to try and get him again, and
if he could not preach to them, that at least he should
pray once more with them.

He was not, however, long absent from home on
this occasion. On the 25th, I find him recording—
" Reached home. Entirely unprepared for the evening. Spoke on Psalm li. 12, 13, ' Restore unto me
the joy,' &c. There seemed much of the presence of
God—first one crying out in extreme agony, then another. Many were deeply melted, and all solemnized.
Felt a good deal of freedom in speaking of the glory
of Christ's salvation. Coming down, I spoke quietly
to some whom I knew to be under deep concern.
They were soon heard together, weeping bitterly;
many more joined them. Mr. Cumming spoke to
them in a most touching strain, while I dealt privately
with several in the vestry. Their cries were often
very bitter and piercing, bitterest when the freeness
of Christ was pressed upon them, and the lion's nearness. Several were offended ; but I felt no hesitation
as to our duty to declare the simple truth impressively,
and leave God to work in their hearts in his own way.
If he save souls in a quiet way, I shall be happy ; if
in the midst of cries and tears, still I will bless his
name. One painful thing has occurred : a man who
pretends to be a missionary for Israel, and who brings
forward the Apocryphal book of Enoch, has been
among my people, in my absence, and many have
been led after him. How humbling is this to them
and to me ! Lord, what is man ! This may be blessed,
1st. To discover chaff which we thought to be wheat ;
2d. To lead some to greater distrust of themselves,
when their eyes are opened ; 3d. To teach me the
need of solidly instructing those who seem to have
grace in their hearts."

The work of God went on, so much so at this time
that he gave it as his belief, in a letter to Mr. Purves
of Jedburgh, that for some months about this period,
no minister of Christ had preached in a lively manner,
without being blessed to some soul among his flock.

In other places of Scotland also the Lord was then
pouring out his Spirit. Perth has been already mentioned, and its vicinity. Throughout Ross-shire,
whole congregations were frequently moved as one
man, and the voice of the minister drowned in the
cries of anxious souls. At Kelso, where Mr. Horace
Bonar laboured, and at Jedburgh, where Mr. Purves
was pastor, a more silent, but very solid work of conversion was advancing. At Ancrum (once the scene
of John Livingston's labours,) the whole parish, but
especially the men of the place, were awakened to
the most solemn concern. On *Lochtay* side, where
Mr. Burns was for a season labouring, there were
marks of the Spirit every where; and the people
crossing the lake in hundreds, to listen to the words
of life on the hill side, called to mind the people of
Galilee in the days when the Gospel began to be
preached. At Lawers, their pastor, Mr. Campbell,
spoke of the awakening as "like a resurrection,"
so great and sudden was the change from deadness
to intense concern. On several occasions, the Spirit
seemed to sweep over the congregations like wind
over the fields, which bends the heavy corn to the
earth. It was evident to discerning minds, that the
Lord was preparing Scotland for some crisis not far
distant.

Several districts of Strathbogie had shared to some
extent in a similar blessing. Faithful ministers were
now every where on the watch for the shower, and
were greatly strengthened to go forward boldly in
seeking to cleanse the sanctuary. It was their fond
hope that the Established Church of Scotland would
soon become an example and pattern to the nations
of a pure Church of Christ, acknowledged and upheld
by the State, without being trammelled in any degree,

far less controlled by civil interference. But Satan was stirring up adversaries on every side.

The Court of Session had adopted a line of procedure that was at once arbitrary and unconstitutional. And now that Court interdicted, under the penalty of fine or imprisonment, all the ministers of the Church of Scotland from administering ordinances or preaching the word in any of the seven parishes of Strathbogie, whose former incumbents had been suspended from office by the General Assembly, for ecclesiastical offences. The Church saw it to be her duty to refuse obedience to an interdict, which hindered the preaching of Jesus, and attempted to crush her constitutional liberties. Accordingly, ministers were sent to these districts, fearless of the result; and under their preaching the gross darkness of the region began to give way to the light of truth.

In the month of August, Mr. McCheyne was appointed, along with Mr. Cumming of Dumbarney, to visit Huntly, and dispense the Lord's Supper there. As he set out he expressed the hope, that " the dews of the Spirit there might be turned into the pouring rain." His own visit was blessed to many. Mr. Cumming preached the action sermon in the open air at the meadow well; but the tables were served within the building where the congregation usually met. Mr. McCheyne preached in the evening to a vast multitude at the well; and about a hundred waited after sermon for prayer, many of them in deep anxiety.

He came to Edinburgh on the 11th, to attend the meeting of ministers and elders who had come together to sign the *Solemn Engagement* in defence of the liberties of Christ's Church. He hesitated not to put his hand to the engagement. He then returned to Dundee ; and scarcely had he returned, when he was laid aside by one of those attacks of illness with which he was so often tried. In this case, however, it soon passed away. " My health," he remarked, " has taken a gracious turn, which should make me

look up." But again, on September 6th, an attack
of fever laid him down for six days. On this occasion, just before the sickness came on, three persons
had visited him, to tell him how they were brought
to Christ under his ministry some years before.—
" Why," he noted in his journal, " why has God
brought these cases before me *this week?* Surely
he is preparing me for some trial of faith." The
result proved that his conjecture was just. And
while his Master prepared him beforehand for these
trials, he had ends to accomplish in his servant by
means of them. There were other trials also, besides
these, which were very heavy to him; but in all he
could discern the husbandman pruning the branch,
that it might bear more fruit. As he himself said one
day in the church of Abernyte, when he was assisting
Mr. Manson, " If we only saw the whole, we would
see that the Father is doing little else in the world but
training his vines."

His preaching became more and more to him a
work of faith. Often I find him writing at the close
or beginning of a sermon :—" Master, help ;" " Help,
Lord, help ;" " send showers ;" " Pardon, give the
Spirit, and take the glory ;" " May the opening of my
lips be right things." The piercing effects of the word
preached on this season may be judged of,
from what one of the awakened, with whom he was
conversing, said to him, " *I think hell would be some
relief from an angry God.*"

His delight in preaching was very great. He himself used to say that he could scarcely ever resist an
invitation to preach. And this did not arise from the
natural excitement there is in commanding the attention of thousands; for he was equally ready to proclaim Christ to small country flocks. Nay, he was
ready to travel far to visit and comfort even one soul.
There was an occasion this year on which he rode
far to give a cup of cold water to a disciple, and his
remark was, " I observe how often Jesus went a long
way for one soul, as for example the maniac, and the
woman of Canaan."

In February, 1841, he visited Kelso and Jedburgh at the communion season; and gladly complied with an invitation to Ancrum, also, that he might witness the hand of the Lord. "Sweet are the spots," he wrote, "where Immanuel has ever shown his glorious power in the conviction and conversion of sinners. The world loves to muse on the scenes where battles were fought and victories won. Should not we love the spot where our great Captain has won his amazing victories? Is not the conversion of a soul more worthy to be spoken of than the taking of Acre?" At Kelso, there were some who will long remember his remarks in visiting a little girl, to whom he said, "Christ gives last knocks. When your heart becomes hard and careless, then fear lest Christ may have given a *last knock*." At Jedburgh, the impression left was chiefly that there had been among them a man of peculiar holiness. Some felt, not so much his words, as his presence and holy solemnity, as if one spoke to them who was standing in the presence of God; and to others his prayers appeared like the breathings of one already within the veil.

I find him proposing to a minister who was going up to the General Assembly that year, "that the Assembly should draw out a *Confession of Sin*, for all its ministers." The state, also, of parishes under the direful influence of Moderatism, lay much upon his spirit. In his diary he writes—"Have been laying much to heart the absolute necessity laid upon the Church of sending the gospel to our dead parishes, during the life of the present incumbents. It is confessed that many of our ministers do not preach the gospel—alas! because they know it not. Yet they have complete control over their own pulpits, and may never suffer the truth to be heard there during their whole incumbency. And yet our Church consigns these parishes to their tender mercies for perhaps fifty years, without a sigh! Should not certain men be ordained as Evangelists, with full power to preach in every pulpit of their district—faithful, judicious, lively preachers, who may go from parish to

parish, and thus carry life into many a dead corner?"
This was a subject he often reverted to; and he
eagerly held up the example of the Presbytery of
Aberdeen, who made a proposal to this effect. From
some of his later letters, it appears that he had sometimes seriously weighed the duty of giving up his fixed
charge, if only the Church would ordain him as an
Evangelist. So deep were his feelings on this matter,
that a friend relates of him, that as they rode together
through a parish where the pastor "clothed himself
with wool, but fed not the flock," he knit his brow
and raised his hand with vehemence as he spoke of
the people left to perish under such a minister.

He was invited to visit Ireland again this year, his
former visit having been much valued by the Presbyterian brethren there. He did so in July. Many were
greatly stirred up by his preaching, and by his details
of God's work in Scotland. His sermon on Song viii.
5, 6, is still spoken of by many. His prayerfulness
and consistent holiness left enduring impressions on
not a few ; and it was during his visit that a memorial
was presented to the Irish Assembly in behalf of a
Jewish mission. His visit was in a great measure the
means of setting that mission on foot.

Cordially entering into the proposal of the concert
for prayer, he took part, in September of this year, in
the preliminary meetings in which Christians of all
denominations joined. "How sweet are the smallest
approximations to unity," is his remarks in his diary.
Indeed, he so much longed for a scriptural unity, that
some time after, when the General Assembly had re-
pealed the statute of 1799, he embraced the opportunity of showing his sincere desire for unity by inviting
two dissenting brethren to his pulpit, and then writing
in defence of his conduct when attacked. In reference
to this matter, he observed, in a note to a friend—" I
have been much delighted with the 25th and 26th
chapters of the Confession of Faith. O for the grace
of the Westminster divines to be poured out upon this
generation of lesser men !"

As it was evident that his Master owned his labour

abundantly, by giving him seals of his apostleship, there were attempts made occasionally by zealous friends to induce him to remove to other spheres. In all these cases, he looked simply at the apparent indications of the Lord's will. Worldly interest seemed scarcely ever to cross his mind in regard to such a matter, for he truly lived a disinterested life. His views may be judged of by one instance—a letter to Mr. Heriot of Ramornie, in reference to a charge which many were anxious to offer him.

DUNDEE, 24*th December*, 1841.

"DEAR SIR,—I have received a letter from my friend, Mr. McFarlane of Collessie, asking what I would do if the people of Kettle were to write desiring me to be their minister. He also desires me to send an answer to you. I have been asked to leave this place again and again, but have never seen my way clear to do so. I feel quite at the disposal of my Divine Master. I gave myself away to him when I began my ministry, and he has guided me as by the pillar of cloud from the first day till now. I think I would leave this place to-morrow if he were to *bid* me; but as to *seeking removal*, I dare not and *could not*. If my ministry were unsuccessful — if God frowned upon the place and made my message void— then I would willingly go; for I would rather beg my bread than preach without success: but I have never wanted success. I do not think I can speak a month in this parish without winning some souls. This very week, I think, has been a fruitful one, more so than many for a long time, which, perhaps, was intended graciously to free me from all hesitation in declining your kind offer. I mention these things, not, I trust, boastfully, but only to show you the ground upon which I feel it to be my duty not for a moment to entertain the proposal. I have four thousand souls here hanging on me. I have as much of this world's goods as I care for. I have full liberty to preach the gospel night and day; and the Spirit of God is often with us. What can I desire more? ' I dwell among my own people.' Hundreds look to me as a father; and I fear I would be but a false shepherd if I were to leave them when the clouds of adversity are beginning to lower. I know the need of Kettle, and its importance ; and also the dark prospect of your getting a godly minister. Still that is a future event in the hand of God. My duty is made plain and simple according to God's word.

"Praying that the Lord Jesus may send you a star from his own right hand, believe me to be," &c.

It was during this year that the Sabbath question began to interest him so much. His tract, "I love the Lord's day," was published December 18th ; but he had already exerted himself much in this cause, as Convener of the Committee of Presbytery on Sabbath Observance, and had written his well known letter to one of the chief defenders of the Sabbath desecration. He continued unceasingly to use every effort in this holy cause. And is it not worth the prayers and self-denying efforts of every believing man ? Is not that day set apart as a season wherein the Lord desires the refreshing rest of his own love to be offered to a fallen world ? Is it not designed to be a day on which every other voice and sound is to be hushed, in order that the silver trumpets may proclaim atonement for sinners ? Nay, it is understood to be a day wherein God himself stands before the altar and pleads with sinners to accept the Lamb slain from morning to evening ! Who is there that does not see the deep design of Satan in seeking to effect an inroad on this most merciful appointment of God our Saviour ?

Mr. McCheyne's own conduct was in full accordance with his principles in regard to strict yet cheerful Sabbath observance. Considering it the summit of human privilege to be admitted to fellowship with God, his principle was, that the Lord's day was to be spent wholly in the enjoyment of that sweetest privilege. A letter, written at a later period, but bearing on this subject, will show how he felt this day to be better than a thousand. An individual near Inver-

ness had consulted him on a point of Sabbatical casu
istry : the question was, Whether or not it was sinful to
spend time in registering meteorological observations
on the Sabbath? His reply was the following,
marked by a holy wisdom, and discovering the place
which the Lord held in his inmost soul.

"December 7, 1842.

"DEAR FRIEND,—You ask me a hard question.
Had you asked me *what I would do in the case,* I
could easily tell you. I love the Lord's day too well
to be marking down the height of the thermometer
and barometer every hour. I have other work to do,
higher and better, and more like that of angels above.
The more entirely I can give my Sabbaths to God,
and half forget that I am not before the throne of the
Lamb, with my harp of gold, the happier am I, and
I feel it my duty to be as happy as I can be, and as
God intended me to be. The joy of the Lord is my
strength. But whether another Christian can spend
the Sabbath in his service, and mark down degrees
of heat and atmospheric pressure, without letting
down the warmth of his affections, or losing the
atmosphere of heaven, I cannot tell. My conscience
is not the rule of another man. One thing we may
learn from these men of science, namely, to be as
careful in marking the changes and progress of our
own spirit as they are in marking the changes of the
weather. An hour should never pass without our
looking up to God for forgiveness and peace. This
is the noblest science, to know how to live in hourly
communion with God in Christ. May you and I
know more of this, and thank God that we are not
among the wise and prudent from whom these things
are hid!—The grace of the Lord of the Sabbath be
with you," &c.

Up to this period, *the Narrative of our Mission
to Israel* had not been given to the public. Interruptions, arising from multiplicity of labours and constant calls of duty, had from time to time come in our

way. Mr. McCheyne found it exceedingly difficult
to spare a day or two at a time in order to take part.
" I find it hard work to carry on the work of a diligent
pastor and that of an author at the same time. How
John Calvin would have smiled at my difficulties!"
At length, however, in the month of March 1842, we
resolved to gain time by exchanging each other's pastoral duties for a month. Accordingly, during four or
five weeks, he remained in Collace, my flock enjoying
his Sabbath day services and his occasional visits,
while he was set free from what would have been the
never ceasing interruptions of his own town.

Many a pleasant remembrance remains of these
days, as sheet after sheet passed under the eyes of
our mutual criticism. Though intent on accomplishing his work, he kept by his rule, " that he must first
see the face of God before he could undertake any
duty." Often would he wander in the mornings among
the pleasant woods of Dunsinnan, till he had drunk
in refreshment to his soul by meditation on the word
of God; and then he took up the pen. And to a
brother in the ministry, who had one day broken in
upon his close occupation, he afterwards wrote—" You
know you stole away my day; yet I trust all was not
lost. I think I have had more grace ever since that
prayer among the fir trees. O to be *like* Jesus, and
with him to all eternity." Occasionally, during the
same period, he wrote some pieces for the " Christian's Daily Companion." The narrative was finished
in May, and the Lord has made it acceptable to the
brethren.

When this work was finished the Lord had other
employment ready for him in his own parish. His
diary has this entry : " *May* 22d.—I have seen some
very evident awakenings of late. J. G. awakened
partly through the word preached, and partly through
the faithful warnings of her fellow-servant. A. R.,
who has been for about a year in the deepest distress,
seeking rest, but finding none. B. M. converted last
winter at the Tuesday meeting in Annfield. She was
brought very rapidly to peace with God, and to a

calm, sedate, prayerful state of mind. I was surprised at the quickness of the work in this case, and pleased with the clear tokens of grace ; and now I see God's gracious end in it. She was to be admitted at last communion, but caught fever before the Sabbath. On Tuesday last, she died in great peace and joy. When she felt death coming on, she said, ' O death, death, come ! let us sing !' Many that knew her have been a good deal moved homeward by this solemn providence. This evening, I invited those to come who are leaving the parish at this term. About twenty came, to whom I gave tracts and words of warning. *I feel persuaded that if I could follow the Lord more fully myself, my ministry would be used to make a deeper impression than it has yet done.*"

CHAPTER VI.

THE LATTER DAYS OF HIS MINISTRY

My meat is to do the will of Him that sent me, and to finish his work. JOHN iv. 34

DURING the summer of 1842, he was exposed to several attacks of illness, experienced some severe personal trials, and felt the assaults of sore temptation. His own words will best express his state. "*July* 17th. —I am myself much tempted, and have no hope, but as a worm on the arm of Jesus." "*August* 4th.— Often, often, would I have been glad to depart, and be with Christ. I am now much better in body and mind, having a little of the presence of my beloved, whose absence is death to me." The same month— " I have been carried through deep waters, bodily and spiritual, since last we met." It was his own persuasion that few had more to struggle with in the inner man. Who can tell what wars go on within ?

During this season of trial, he was invited to form

one of a number of ministers from Scotland, who were to visit the north of England, with no other purpose than to preach the glad tidings. This scheme was planned by a Christian gentleman, who has done much for Christ in his generation. When the invitation reached him, he was in the heat of his furnace. He mentioned this to the brother who corresponded with him on the subject, Mr. Purves of Jedburgh, whose reply was a balm to his spirit. . . . "I have a fellow-feeling with you in your present infirmity, and you know for your consolation that another has, who is a brother indeed. In all our afflictions, he is afflicted. He is, we may say, the common heart of his people; for they are one body, and an infirmity in the very remotest and meanest member is felt *there*, and borne *there*. Let us console, solace, yea, satiate ourselves in him, as, amid afflictions especially, brother does in brother. It is blessed to be like him in every thing, even in suffering. There is a great want about all Christians who have not suffered. Some flowers must be broken or bruised before they emit any fragrance. All the wounds of Christ send out sweetness—all the sorrows of Christians do the same. Commend me to a bruised brother, a broken reed— one like the Son of man. The man of sorrows is never far from him. To me there is something sacred and sweet in all suffering; it is so much akin to the Man of Sorrows." It was thus he suffered, and thus that he was comforted. He wrote back, agreeing to go, and added, " Remember me especially, who am heavy laden oftentimes. My heart is all of sin; but Jesus lives."

They set out for England. Mr. Purves, Mr. Somerville, of Anderston, Mr. Cumming, of Dumbarney, and Mr. Bonar, of Kelso, formed the company. Their chief station was Newcastle, where Mr. Burns had been recently labouring with some success, and where he had seen " a town giving itself up to utter ungodliness—a town, where Satan's trenches were deep and wide, his wall strong and high, his garrison great and fearless, and where all that man could do seemed but as arrows shot against a tower of brass." But those who went knew that the Spirit of God was omnipotent, and that he could take the prey from the mighty.

They preached both in the open air and in the places of worship belonging to the Presbyterians and to the Wesleyan Methodists. The defenders of the Sabbath cause were specially prepared to welcome Mr. McCheyne, whose tract on the Lord's day had been widely circulated and blessed. Many were attracted to hear; interesting congregations assembled in the market place, and there is reason to believe many were impressed. A person in the town describes Mr. McCheyne's last address as being peculiarly awakening. He preached in the open air, in a space of ground between the corn market and St. Nicholas' Church. Above a thousand souls were present, and the service continued till ten, without one person moving from the ground. The moon shone brightly, and the sky was spangled with stars. His subject was, "The great white Throne," (Rev. xx. 11.) In concluding his address, he told them, "that they would never meet again till they all met at the judgment seat of Christ; but the glorious heavens over their heads, and the bright moon that shone upon them, and the old venerable church behind them, were his witnesses that he had set before them life and death." Some will have cause to remember that night through eternity.*

His preaching at Gilsland also was not without effect; and he had good cause to bless the Lord for bringing him through Dumfries-shire in his way homeward. He returned to his people in the beginning of September, full of peace and joy. "I have returned much stronger, indeed quite well. I think I have got some precious souls for my hire on my way home. I earnestly long for more grace and personal holiness, and more usefulness."

* He afterwards preached the same subject with equal impressiveness in the Meadows at Dundee. It was in the open air, and the rain fell heavy, yet the dense crowd stood still to the last.

The sunsets during that autumn were peculiarly beautiful. Scarcely a day passed but he gazed upon the glowing west after dinner; and as he gazed he would speak of the Sun of Righteousness, or the joy of angels in his presence, or the blessedness of those whose sun can no more go down, till his face shone with gladness as he spoke. And during the winter, he was observed to be peculiarly joyful, being strong in body, and feeling the near presence of Jesus in his soul. He lived in the blessed consciousness that he was a child of God, humble and meek, just because he was fully assured that Jehovah was his God and Father. Many often felt that in prayer the name "Holy Father" was breathed with peculiar tenderness and solemnity from his lips.

His flock in St. Peter's began to murmur at his absence when again he left them for ten days in November, to assist Mr. Hamilton of Regent Square. London, at his communion. But it was his desire for souls that thus led him from place to place, combined with a growing feeling that the Lord was calling him to evangelistic more than to pastoral labours. This visit was a blessed one, and the growth of his soul in holiness was visible to many. During the days of his visit to Mr. Hamilton, he read through the song of Solomon at the time of family worship, commenting briefly on it with rare gracefulness and poetic taste, and yet rarer manifestation of soul-filling love to the Saviour's person. The sanctified affections of his soul, and his insight into the mind of Jesus, seemed to have much affected his friends on these occasions.

Receiving while here an invitation to return by the way of Kelso, he replied:—

"LONDON, *Nov.* 5, 1842.

"MY DEAR HORATIUS.—Our friends here will not let me away till the Friday morning, so that it will require all my diligence to reach Dundee before the Sabbath. I will thus be disappointed of the joy of seeing you, and ministering a word to your dear flock. O that my soul were new moulded, and I were effectnally called a second time, and made a vessel full of the Spirit, to tell only of Jesus and his love. I fear I shall never be in this world what I desire. I have preached three times here; a few tears also have been shed. O for Whitefield's week in London, when a thousand letters came ! The same Jesus reigns; the same Spirit is able. Why is he restrained ? Is the sin ours ? Are we the bottle-stoppers of these heavenly dews ? Ever yours till glory."

" P. S.—We shall meet, God willing, at the Convocation."

The memorable Convocation met at Edinburgh on November 17th. There were five hundred ministers present from all parts of Scotland. The encroachment of the civil courts upon the prerogatives of Christ, the only Head acknowledged by our Church, and the negligent treatment hitherto given by the legislature of the country to every remonstrance on the part of the Church had brought on a crisis. The Church of Scotland had maintained from the days of the Reformation that her connection with the state was understood to imply no surrender whatsoever of complete independence in regulating all spiritual matters; and to have allowed any civil authority to control her in doctrine, discipline, or any spiritual act, would have been a daring and flagrant act of treachery to her Lord and King. The deliberations of the Convocation continued during eight days, and the momentous results are well known in the land.

Mr. McCheyne was never absent from any of the diets of this solemn assembly. He felt the deepest interest in every matter that came before them, got great light as to the path of duty in the course of the consultations, and put his name to all the resolutions, heartily sympathizing in the decided determination that, as a Church of Christ, we must abandon our connection with the State, if our " Claim of Rights" were rejected. These eight days were times of remarkable union and prayerfulness. The proceedings, from time to time, were suspended till the brethren had again asked counsel of the Lord by prayer; and none present will forget the affecting solemnity with which, on one occasion, Mr. McCheyne poured out our wants before the Lord.

He had a decided abhorrence of Erastianism. When the question was put to him, "Is it our duty to refuse ordination to any one who holds the views of Erastianism?" he replied—"Certainly, whatever be his other qualifications." He was ever a thorough Presbyterian, and used to maintain the necessity of abolishing lay patronage, because, 1. It was not to be found in the word of God; 2. It destroyed the duty of "trying the spirits;" 3. It meddled with the headship of Christ, coming in between him and his people, saying, "I will place the stars." But still more decided was he in regard to the spiritual independence of the Church. This he reckoned a vital question; and in prospect of the disruption of the Church of Scotland, if it were denied, he stated at a public meeting—1st. That it was to be deplored in some respects, viz., because of the sufferings of God's faithful servants, the degradation of those who remained behind, the alienation of the aristocracy, the perdition of the ungodly, and the sin of the nation. But, 2d. It was to be hailed for other reasons—viz., Christ's kingly office would be better known, the truth would be spread into desolate parishes, and faithful ministers would be refined. And when, on March 7th of the following year, the cause of the Church was finally to be pleaded at the bar of the House of Commons, I find him writing—"Eventful night this in the British Parliament! Once more King Jesus stands at an earthly tribunal, and they know him not!"

An interesting anecdote is related of him by a copresbyter, who returned with him to Dundee after the Convocation. This co-presbyter, Mr. Stewart, was conversing with him as to what it might be their duty to do in the event of the disruption, and where they might be scattered. Mr. Stewart said he could preach Gaelic, and might go to the Highlanders in Canada, if it were needful. Mr. McCheyne said—"I think of going to the many thousand convicts that are transported beyond seas, for no man careth for their souls."

We have not many records of his public work after this date. Almost the last note in his diary is dated *December* 25. "This day ordained four elders, and admitted a fifth, who will all, I trust, be a blessing in this place when I am gone. Was graciously awakened a great while before day, and had two hours alone with God. Preached with much comfort on 1 Tim. v. 17, "Let the elders that rule well," &c. At the end of the sermon and prayer, proposed the regular questions; then made the congregation sing standing; during which time I came down from the pulpit and stood over the four men, then prayed, and all the elders gave the right hand of fellowship, during which I returned to the pulpit, and addressed them and the congregation on their relative duties. Altogether a solemn scene."

The last recorded cases of awakening, and the last entry in his diary, is dated *January* 6, 1843. "Heard of an awakened soul finding rest—true rest, I trust. Two new cases of awakening; both very deep and touching. At the very time when I was beginning to give up in despair, God gives me tokens of his presence returning."

He here speaks of discouragement, when God for a few months or weeks seemed to be withholding his hand from saving souls. If he was not right in thus hastily forgetting the past for a little, still this feature of his ministry is to be well considered. He entertained so full a persuasion that a faithful minister has every reason to expect to see souls converted under him, that when this was withheld he began to fear that some hidden evil was provoking the Lord and grieving the Spirit. And ought it not to be so with all of us? Ought we not to suspect, either that we are not living near to God, or that our message is not a true transcript of the glad tidings in both matter and manner, when we see no souls brought to Jesus? God may certainly hide from our knowledge much of what he accomplishes by our means, but as certainly

will he bring to our view some seals of our ministry,
in order that our persuasion of being thus sent by him
may solemnize and overawe us, as well as lead us on
to unwearied labour. Ought it not to be the inscrip-
tion over the doors of our Assembly and college halls:
—" *Thanks be unto God, which always causeth us
to triumph in Christ, and maketh manifest the
savour of his knowledge by us in every place;*"
2 Corinthians ii. 14.

About this time in one of his MSS., there occurs
this sentence—" As I was walking in the fields, the
thought came over me with almost overwhelming
power, that every one of my flock must soon be in
heaven or hell. O how I wished that I had a tongue
like thunder, that I might make all hear; or that I had
a frame like iron, that I might visit every one, and
say, ' Escape for thy life!' Ah, sinners! you little
know how I fear that you will lay the blame of your
damnation at my door."

He was never satisfied with his own attainments in
holiness; he was ever ready to learn, and quick to
apply, any suggestion that might tend to his greater
usefulness. About this period, he used to sing a
psalm or hymn every day after dinner. It was often,
" The Lord's my shepherd," &c., or " O may we stand
before the Lamb," &c. Sometimes it was that hymn,
" O for a closer walk with God;" and sometimes the
psalm, " O that I like a dove had wings," &c. A
friend said of him, " I have sometimes compared him
to the silver and graceful ash, with its pensile branches,
and leaves of gentle green, reflecting gleams of happy
sunshine. The fall of its leaf, too, is like the fall of
his—it is green to-night, and gone to-morrow—it does
not sere, nor wither."

An experienced servant of God has said, that, while
popularity is a snare that few are not caught by, a
more subtile and dangerous snare is to be *famed for
holiness*. The fame of being a godly man is as great
a snare as the fame of being learned or eloquent. It
is possible to attend with scrupulous anxiety even to
secret habits of devotion, in order to get a name for

holiness.* If any were exposed to this snare in his day, Mr. McCheyne was the person. Yet nothing is more certain than that, to the very last, he was ever discovering, and successfully resisting, the deceitful tendencies of his own heart, and a tempting devil. Two things he seems never to have ceased from—the cultivation of personal holiness, and the most anxious efforts to save souls.

About this time he wrote down, for his own use, an examination into things that ought to be amended and changed. I subjoin it entire. How singularly close and impartial are these researches into his soul! How acute is he in discovering his variations from the holy law of God! O that we all were taught by the same Spirit thus to try our reins! It is only when we are thus thoroughly experiencing our helplessness, and discovering the thousand forms of indwelling sin, that we really sit as disciples at Christ's feet, and gladly receive him as all in all! And at each such moment we feel in the spirit of Ignatius, "Νυν γαρ αρχηι εχω του μαθητευεσθαι"—"It is only now that I begin to be a disciple."

Mr. McCheyne entitles the examination of his heart and life "Reformation," and it commences thus—

"It is the duty of ministers in this day to begin the reformation of religion and manners with themselves, families, &c., with confession of past sin, earnest prayer for direction, grace, and full purpose of heart. Mal. iii. 3. 'He shall purify the sons of Levi.' Ministers are probably laid aside for a time for this very purpose.

"I. PERSONAL REFORMATION.

"I am persuaded that I shall obtain the highest amount of present happiness, I shall do most for God's

---

* How true, yet awful, is the language of Dr. Owen (quoted in Bridges' Christian Ministry, p. 168,) "He that would go down to the pit in peace, let him obtain a great repute for religion; let him preach and labour to make others better than he is himself, and, in the meantime, neglect to humble his heart, to walk with God in manifest holiness and usefulness, and he will not fail of his end."

glory and the good of man, and I shall have the fullest reward in eternity, by maintaining a conscience always washed in Christ's blood, by being filled with the Holy Spirit at all times, and by attaining the most entire likeness to Christ in mind, will, and heart, that it is possible for a redeemed sinner to attain to in this world.

"I am persuaded that whenever any one from without or my own heart from within, at any moment, or in any circumstances, contradicts this—if any one shall insinuate that it is not for my present and eternal happiness, and for God's glory, and my usefulness, to maintain a blood-washed conscience, to be entirely filled with the Spirit, and to be fully conformed to the image of Christ in all things—that is the voice of the devil, God's enemy, the enemy of my soul, and of all good—the most foolish, wicked, and miserable of all the creatures. See Proverbs ix. 17. 'Stolen waters are sweet.'

"1. *To maintain a conscience void of offence*, I am persuaded that I ought to confess my sins more. I think I ought to confess sin the moment I see it to be sin; whether I am in company, or in study, or even preaching, the soul ought to cast a glance of abhorrence at the sin. If I go on with the duty, leaving the sin unconfessed, I go on with a burdened conscience, and add sin to sin. I think I ought at certain times of the day—my best times—say, after breakfast and after tea—to confess solemnly the sins of the previous hours, and to seek their complete remission.

"I find that the devil often makes use of the confession of sin to stir up again the very sin confessed, into new exercise, so that I am afraid to dwell upon the confession. I must ask experienced Christians about this. For the present, I think I should strive against this awful abuse of confession, whereby the devil seeks to frighten me away from confessing. I ought to take all methods for seeing the vileness of my sins. I ought to regard myself as a condemned branch of Adam—as partaker of a nature opposite to God from the womb, Psa. li.—as having a heart full of all wickedness, which pollutes every thought, word, and action, during my whole life, from birth to death. I ought to confess often the sins of my youth, like David and Paul—my sins before conversion, my sins since conversion—sins against light and knowledge— against love and grace—against each person of the Godhead. I ought to look at my sins in the light of the holy law—in the light of God's countenance—in the light of the Cross—in the light of the Judgment- seat—in the light of hell—in the light of eternity. I ought to examine my dreams—my floating thoughts —my predilections—my often recurring actions—my habits of thought, feeling, speech, and action—the slanders of my enemies—and the reproofs, and even banterings of my friends—to find out traces of my prevailing sin—matter for confession. I ought to have a stated day of confession, with fasting—say, once a month. I ought to have a number of Scriptures marked, to bring sin to remembrance. I ought to make use of all bodily affliction, domestic trial, frowns of Providence on myself, house, parish, church, or country, as calls from God to confess sin. The sins and afflictions of other men should call me to the same. I ought, on Sabbath evenings, and on com- munion Sabbath evenings, to be especially careful to confess the sins of holy things. I ought to confess the sins of my confessions—their imperfection, sin- ful aims, self-righteous tendency, &c.—and to look to Christ as having confessed my sins perfectly over his own sacrifice.

" I ought to go to Christ for the forgiveness of each sin. In washing my body, I go over every spot, and wash it out: should I be less careful in washing my soul? I ought to see the stripe that was made on the back of Jesus by each of my sins. I ought to see the infinite pang thrill through the soul of Jesus equal to an eternity of my hell for my sins, and for all of them. I ought to see that in Christ's bloodshed- ding there is an infinite overpayment for all my sins. Although Christ did not suffer more than infinite justice demanded, yet he could not suffer at all without laying down an infinite ransom.

"I feel, when I have sinned, an immediate reluctance to go to Christ. I am ashamed to go. I feel as if it would do no good to go—as if it were making Christ a minister of sin, to go straight from the swine trough to the best robe—and a thousand other excuses; but I am persuaded they are all lies, direct from hell. John argues the opposite way—' If any man sin, we have an advocate with the Father;' Jeremiah iii. 1, and a thousand other Scriptures are against it. I am sure there is neither peace nor safety from deeper sin, but in going directly to the Lord Jesus Christ. This is God's way of peace and holiness. It is folly to the world and the beclouded heart, but it is *the way*.

"I must never think a sin too small to need immediate application to the blood of Christ. If I put away a good conscience, concerning faith I make shipwreck. I must never think my sins too great, too aggravated, too presumptuous—as when done on my knees, or in preaching, or by a dying bed, or during dangerous illness—to hinder me from fleeing to Christ. The weight of my sins should act like the weight of a clock, the heavier it is, it makes it go the faster.

"I must not only wash in Christ's blood, but clothe me in Christ's obedience. For every sin of omission in self, I may find a divinely perfect obedience ready for me in Christ. For every sin of commission in self, I may find not only a stripe or a wound in Christ, but also a perfect rendering of the opposite obedience in my place, so that the law is magnified—its curse more than carried—its demand more than answered.

"Often the doctrine of *Christ for me* appears common, well known, having nothing new in it; and I am tempted to pass it by, and go to some Scripture more taking. This is the devil again—a red hot lie. *Christ for us* is ever new, ever glorious. ' Unsearchable riches of Christ'—an infinite object, and the only one for a guilty soul. I ought to have a number of

Scriptures ready, which lead my blind soul directly to Christ, such as Isaiah xlv., Romans iii.

" 2. *To be filled with the Holy Spirit*, I am persuaded that I ought to study more my own weakness. I ought to have a number of Scriptures ready to be meditated on, such as Romans vii., John xv., to convince me that I am a helpless worm.

" I am tempted to think that I am now an established Christian—that I have overcome this or that lust so long—that I have got into the habit of the opposite grace—so that there is no fear; I may venture very near the temptation—nearer than other men. This is a lie of Satan. I might as well speak of gunpowder getting by habit a power of resisting fire, so as not to catch the spark. As long as powder is wet it resists the spark; but when it becomes dry, it is ready to explode at the first touch. As long as the Spirit dwells in my heart he deadens me to sin, so that, if lawfully called through temptation, I may reckon upon God carrying me through. But when the Spirit leaves me, I am like dry gunpowder. O for a sense of this!

" I am tempted to think that there are some sins for which I have no natural taste, such as strong drink, profane language, &c., so that I need not fear temptation to such sins. This is a lie—a proud, presumptuous lie. The seeds of all sin are in my heart, and perhaps, all the more dangerously that I do not see them.

" I ought to pray and labour for the deepest sense of my utter weakness and helplessness that ever a sinner was brought to feel. I am helpless in respect of every lust that ever was, or will be, in the human heart. I am a worm—a beast—before God. I often tremble to think that this is true. I feel as if it would not be safe for me to renounce all indwelling strength as if it would be dangerous for me to feel (what is the truth) that there is nothing in me keeping me back from the grossest and vilest sin. This is a delusion of the devil. My only safety is to know, feel, and confess my helplessness, that I may hang upon the arm of Omnipotence. . . . . I daily wish that sin had been rooted out of my heart. I say, 'Why did God leave the roots of lasciviousness, pride, anger, &c., in my bosom? He hates sin, and I hate it; why did he not take it clean away?' I know many answers to this which completely satisfy my judgment; but still I do not *feel* satisfied. This is wrong. It is right to be weary of the being of sin, but not right to quarrel with my present 'good fight of faith.' . . . . The falls of professors into sin make me tremble. I have been driven away from prayer, and burdened in a fearful manner by hearing or seeing their sin. This is wrong. It is right to tremble and to make every sin of every professor a lesson of my own helplessness, but it should lead me the more to Christ. . . . . If I were more deeply convinced of my utter helplessness, I think I would not be so alarmed when I hear of the falls of other men. . . . . I should study those sins in which I am most helpless, in which passion becomes like a whirlwind, and I like a straw. No figure of speech can represent my utter want of power to resist the torrent of sin. . . . I ought to study Christ's omnipotence more; Heb. vii. 25; 1 Thess. v. 23; Rom. vi. 14; Rom. v. 9, 10; and such Scriptures should be ever before me. . . . . Paul's thorn, 2 Cor. xii., is the experience of the greater part of my life. It should be ever before me. . . . . There are many subsidiary methods of seeking deliverance from sins, which must not be neglected—thus, marriage, 1 Cor. vii. 2; fleeing, 1 Tim. vi. 11, 1 Cor. vi. 18; watch and pray, Matt. xxvi. 41; the word, 'It is written, It is written.' So Christ defended himself; Matt. iv. . . . . But the main defence is casting myself into the arms of Christ like a helpless child, and beseeching him to fill me with the Holy Spirit; 'This is the victory that overcometh the world, even our faith,' 1 John v. 4, 5—a wonderful passage.

" I ought to study Christ as a living Saviour more— as a Shepherd carrying the sheep he finds—as a King reigning in and over the souls he has redeemed—as a Captain fighting with those who fight with me, Psal.

xxxv.—as one who has engaged to bring me through all temptations and trials, however impossible to flesh and blood.

" I am often tempted to say, How can this man save us ?   How can Christ in heaven deliver me from lusts which I feel raging in me, and nets I feel enclosing me ?   This is the father of lies again !   ' He is able to save unto the uttermost.'

" I ought to study Christ as an Intercessor.   He prayed most for Peter who was to be most tempted.   I am on his breastplate.   If I could hear Christ praying for me in the next room, I would not fear a million of enemies.   Yet the distance makes no difference ; he is praying for me.

" I ought to study the Comforter more—his God-head, his love, his almightiness.   I have found by experience that nothing sanctifies me so much as meditating on the Comforter, as John xiv. 16.   And yet how seldom I do this.   Satan keeps me from it.   I am often like those men who said, they knew not if there be any Holy Ghost. . . . . . .   I ought never to forget that my body is dwelt in by the Third Person of the Godhead.   The very thought of this should make me tremble to sin ; 1 Cor. vi. . . . . I ought never to forget that sin grieves the Holy Spirit—vexes and quenches him. . . . . . If I would be filled with the Spirit, I feel I must read the Bible more, pray more, and watch more.

" 3. *To gain entire likeness to Christ,* I ought to get a high esteem of the happiness of it.   I am persuaded that God's happiness is inseparably linked in with his holiness.   Holiness and happiness are like light and heat.   God never tasted one of the pleasures of sin.

" Christ had a body such as I have, yet he never tasted one of the pleasures of sin.   The redeemed, through all eternity, will never taste one of the pleasures of sin ; yet their happiness is complete.   It would be my greatest happiness to be from this moment entirely like them.   Every sin is something away from my greatest enjoyment. . . . .   The devil strives night and day to make me forget this, or disbelieve it. He says, Why should you not enjoy this pleasure as much as Solomon or David? You may go to heaven also. I am persuaded that this is a lie—that my true happiness is to go and sin no more.

" I ought not to delay parting with sins. Now is God's time. ' I made haste and delayed not.' . . . I ought not to spare sins because I have long allowed them as infirmities; and others would think it odd if I were to change all at once. What a wretched delusion of Satan that is !

" Whatever I see to be sin, I ought from this hour to set my whole soul against it, using all scriptural methods to mortify it — as, the Scriptures, special prayer for the Spirit, fasting, watching.

" I ought to mark strictly the occasions when I have fallen, and avoid the occasion as much as the sin itself.

" Satan often tempts me to go as near to temptations as possible, without committing the sin. This is fearful—tempting God and grieving the Holy Ghost. It is a deep laid plot of Satan.

" I ought to flee all temptation, according to Prov. iv. 15—' Avoid it, pass not by it, turn from it, and pass away.' . . . . I ought constantly to pour out my heart to God, praying for entire conformity to Christ—for the whole law to be written on my heart. . . . . I ought stately and solemnly to give my heart to God—to surrender my all into his everlasting arms, according to the prayer—Ps. xxxi., ' Into thine hand I commit my spirit '—beseeching him not to let any iniquity, secret or presumptuous, have dominion over me, and to fill me with every grace that is in Christ in the highest degree that it is possible for a redeemed sinner to receive it, and at all times till death.

"I ought to meditate often on heaven as a world of holiness—where all are holy, where the joy is holy joy, the work holy work; so that without personal holiness, I can never be there. . . . . . I ought to avoid the appearance of evil. God commands me;

and I find that Satan has a singular art in linking the appearance and reality together.

" I find that speaking of some sins defiles my mind and leads me into temptation; and I find that God forbids even saints to speak of the things that are done in secret. I ought to avoid this.

" Eve, Achan, David, all fell through the lust of the eye. I should make a covenant with mine, and pray, ' Turn away mine eyes from viewing vanity.' . . . . Satan makes unconverted men like the deaf adder to the sound of the gospel. I should pray to be made deaf by the Holy Spirit to all that would tempt me to sin.

" One of my most frequent occasions of being led into temptation is this — I say it is needful to my office that I listen to this, or look into this, or speak of this. So far this is true; yet I am sure Satan has his part in this argument. I should seek divine direction to settle how far it will be good for my ministry, and how far evil for my soul, that I may avoid the latter.

" I am persuaded that nothing is thriving in my soul unless it is growing. ' Grow in grace.' ' Lord, increase our faith.' ' Forgetting the things that are behind.' . . . . . . I am persuaded that I ought to be inquiring at God and man what grace I want and how I may become more like Christ. . . . . . . I ought to strive for more purity, humility, meekness, patience under suffering, love. ' Make me Christ-like in all things,' should be my constant prayer. ' Fill me with the Holy Spirit.'

" II. REFORMATION IN SECRET PRAYER.

" I ought not to omit any of the parts of prayer— confession, adoration, thanksgiving, petition, and intercession.

" There is a fearful tendency to omit *confession*, proceeding from low views of God and his law—slight views of my heart and the sins of my past life. This must be resisted. There is a constant tendency to omit *adoration*, when I forget to whom I am speak. ing—when I rush heedlessly into the presence of Jehovah, without remembering his awful name and character—when I have little eyesight for his glory, and little admiration of his wonders. 'Where are the wise!' I have the native tendency of the heart to omit *giving thanks*. And yet it is specially commanded, Phil. iv. 6. Often when the heart is selfish—dead to the salvation of others—I omit *intercession*. And yet it especially is the spirit of the Great Advocate, who has the name of Israel always on his heart.

"Perhaps every prayer need not have all these; but surely a day should not pass without some space being devoted to each.

"I ought to pray before seeing any one. Often when I sleep long, or meet with others early, and then have family prayer, and breakfast, and forenoon callers, often it is eleven or twelve o'clock before I begin secret prayer. This is a wretched system. It is unscriptural. Christ rose before day, and went into a solitary place. David says, 'Early will I seek thee; thou shalt early hear my voice.' Mary Magdalene came to the sepulchre while it was yet dark. Family prayer loses much of its power and sweetness; and I can do no good to those who come to seek from me. The conscience feels guilty, the soul unfed, the lamp not trimmed. Then, when secret prayer comes, the soul is often out of tune. I feel it is far better to begin with God—to see his face first—to get my soul near him before it is near another. 'When I awake, I am still with thee.'

"If I have slept too long, or am going an early journey, or my time is any way shortened, it is best to dress hurriedly, and have a few minutes alone with God, than to give it up for lost.

"But, in general, it is best to have at least one hour *alone with God*, before engaging in any thing else. At the same time, I must be careful not to reckon communion with God by minutes or hours, or by solitude. I have pored over my Bible, and on my knees for hours, with little or no communion; and my times of solitude have been often times of greatest temptation.

"As to *intercession*, I ought daily to intercede for my own family, connections, relatives, and friends; also for my flock—the believers, the awakened, the careless; the sick, the bereaved; the poor, the rich; my elders, Sabbath school teachers, day school teachers, children, tract distributers—that all means may be blessed—Sabbath day preaching and teaching; visiting of the sick, visiting from house to house; providences, sacraments. I ought daily to intercede briefly for the whole town, the Church of Scotland, all faithful ministers; for vacant congregations, students of divinity, &c.; for dear brethren by name; for missionaries to Jews and Gentiles; and for this end I must read missionary intelligence regularly, and get acquainted with all that is doing throughout the world. It would stir me up, to pray with the map before me. I must have a scheme of prayer, also the names of missionaries marked on the map. I ought to intercede at large for the above on Saturday morning and evening from seven to eight. Perhaps also I might take different parts for different days; only I ought daily to plead for my family and flock. I ought to pray in every thing. 'Be careful for nothing, but in *every thing*,' &c. Often I receive a letter asking to preach, or some such request. I find myself answering before having asked counsel of God. Still oftener a person calls and asks me something, and I do not ask direction. Often I go out to visit a sick person in a hurry, without asking his blessing, which alone can make the visit of any use. I am persuaded that I ought never to do any thing without prayer, and, if possible, special, secret prayer.

"In reading the history of the Church of Scotland, I see how much her troubles and trials have been connected with the salvation of souls and the glory of Christ. I ought to pray far more for our church, for our leading ministers by name, and for my own clear guidance in the right way, that I may not be led aside, or driven aside, from following Christ. Many difficult questions may be forced on us for which I am not fully prepared, such as the lawfulness of covenants. I should pray much more in peaceful days, that I may be guided rightly when days of trial come.

"I ought to spend the best hours of the day in communion with God. It is my noblest and most fruitful employment, and is not to be thrust into any corner. The morning hours, from six to eight, are the most uninterrupted, and should be thus employed, if I can prevent drowsiness. A little time after breakfast might be given to intercession. After tea is my best hour, and that should be solemnly dedicated to God, if possible.

"I ought not to give up the good old habit of prayer before going to bed; but guard must be kept against sleep; planning what things I am to ask is the best remedy. When I awake in the night, I ought to rise and pray, as David and as John Welsh did.

"I ought to read three chapters of the Bible in secret every day, at least.

"I ought on Sabbath morning to look over all the chapters read through the week, and especially the verses marked. I ought to read in three different places; I ought also to read according to subjects, times," &c.

He has evidently left this unfinished, and now he knows even as he is known.

Toward the end of his ministry, he became peculiarly jealous of becoming an idol to his people; for he was loved and revered by many who gave no evidence of love to Christ. This often pained him much. It is indeed right in a people to regard their pastor with no common love, 2 Cor. ix. 14, but there is ever a danger ready to arise. He used to say, "Ministers are but the pole; it is to the brazen serpent you are to look."

The state of his health would not permit him to be laborious in going from house to house, whereas preaching and evangelistic work in general was less exhausting; but of course, while he was thus engaged, many concerns of the parish would be unattended to; accordingly his Session offered him a stated assistant to help him in his parochial duty. With this proposal he at once concurred. Mr. Gatherer, then at Caraldstone, was chosen, and continued to labour faithfully with him during the remaining days of his ministry.

In the beginning of the year he published his *"Daily Bread,"* an arrangement of Scripture, that the Bible might be read through in the course of a year. He sought to induce his people to meditate much on the written word in all its breadth. His last publication was, *" Another Lily Gathered,"* or the account of James Laing, a little boy in his flock, brought to Christ early, and carried soon to glory.

In the middle of January 1843, he visited Collace, and preached on 1 Cor. ix. 27, " A Castaway "—a sermon so solemn that one said it was like a blast of the trumpet that would awaken the dead. Next day he rode on to Lintrathen, where the people were willing to give up their work at mid day, if he would come and preach to them. All this month he was breathing after glory. In his letters there are such expressions as these : " I often pray, Lord, make me as holy as a pardoned sinner can be made." " Often, often I would like to depart and be with Christ—to mount to Pisgah top and take a farewell look of the Church below, and leave my body and be present with the Lord. Ah, it is far better !" Again : " I do not expect to live long. I expect a sudden call some day—perhaps soon—and therefore, I speak very plainly." But, indeed, he had long been persuaded that his course would be brief. His hearers remember well how often he would speak in such language as that with which he one day closed his sermon. " Changes are coming ; every eye before me shall soon be dim in death. Another pastor shall feed this flock ; another singer lead the psalm ; another flock shall fill this fold."

In the beginning of February, by appointment of the committee of the convocation, he accompanied

Mr. Alexander, of Kirkaldy, to visit the districts of
Deer and Ellon—districts over which he yearned, for
Moderatism had held undisputed sway over them for
generations. It was to be his last evangelistic tour.
He exemplified his own remark, "The oil of the
lamp in the temple burnt away in giving light; so
should we."

He set out, said one that saw him leave town, as
unclouded and happy as the sky that was above his
head that bright morning. During the space of
three weeks, he preached or spoke at meetings in
four-and-twenty places, sometimes more than once in
the same place. Great impression was made upon
the people of the district. One who tracked his footsteps a month after his death states, that sympathy
with the principles of our suffering church was
awakened in many places; but, above all, a thirst
was excited for the pure word of life. His eminently
holy walk and conversation, combined with the deep
solemnity of his preaching, was specially felt. The
people loved to speak of him. In one place, where
a meeting had been intimated, the people assembled,
resolving to cast stones at him as soon as he should
begin to speak; but no sooner had he begun, than his
manner, his look, his words, riveted them all, and they
listened with intense earnestness; and before he left
the place, the people gathered round him, entreating
him to stay and preach to them. One man, who had
cast mud at him, was afterwards moved to tears on
hearing of his death.

He wrote to Mr. Gatherer, *February* 14th, "I had
a nice opportunity of preaching in Aberdeen; and in
Peterhead our meeting was truly successful. The
minister of St. Fergus I found to be what you described. We had a solemn meeting in his church.
In Strichen, we had a meeting in the Independent
meeting house. On Friday evening, we had two
delightful meetings, in a mill at Crechie, and in the
church of Clola. The people were evidently much
impressed, some weeping. On Saturday evening, we
met in the Brucklay barn. I preached on Sabbath,

a. New Deer in the morning, and at Fraserburgh in the evening—both interesting meetings. To-night, we meet in Pitsligo church. To-morrow we trust to be in Aberdour; and then we leave for the Presbytery of Ellon. The weather has been delightful till now. To-day, the snow is beginning to drift. But God is with us, and he will carry us to the very end. I am quite well, though a little fatigued sometimes." On the 24th, he writes to another friend, " To-day is the first we have rested since leaving home, so that I am almost overcome with fatigue. Do not be idle; improve in all useful knowledge. You know what an enemy I am to idleness."

Never was it more felt that God was with him than in this journey. The Lord seemed to show in him the meaning of the text, " Out of his belly shall flow rivers of living water." John vii. 38. Even when silent, the near intercourse he held with God left its impression on those around. His *constant holiness* touched the consciences of many.

Returning to his beloved flock on March 1st, in good health, but much exhausted, he related next evening at his prayer meeting, what things he had seen and heard. During the next twelve days, he was to be found going out and in among his people, filling up, as his manner was, every inch of time. But he had been much weakened by his unceasing exertions when in the north, and so was more than ordinarily exposed to the typhus fever that was then prevailing in his parish, several cases of which he visited in his enfeebled state.

On Sabbath the 5th, he preached three times; and two days after, I find him writing to his father: " All domestic matters go on like a placid stream—I trust not without its fertilizing influence. Nothing is more improving than the domestic altar, when we come to it for a daily supply of soul nourishment." To the last we get glances into his soul's growth. His family devotions were full of life and full of gladness to the end. Indeed, his very manner of reading the chapter reminded you of a man poring into the sand for

pieces of fine gold, and from time to time holding up
to you what he was delighted to have found.

On Sabbath the 12th, he preached upon Heb. ix. 15,
in the forenoon, and Rom. ix. 22, 23, in the afternoon,
with uncommon solemnity; and it was observed, both
then and on other late occasions, he spoke with pecu
liar strength upon the sovereignty of God. These
were his last discourses to his people in St. Peter's.
That same evening, he went down to Broughty
Ferry, and preached upon Isaiah lx. 1, "Arise, shine,"
&c. It was the last time he was to be engaged
directly in proclaiming Christ to sinners; and as he
began his ministry with souls for his hire, so it appears that his last discourse had in it saving power to
some, and that, rather from the holiness it breathed,
than from the wisdom of its words. After his death,
a note was found unopened, which had been sent to
him in the course of the following week when he lay
in the fever. It ran thus: I hope you will pardon a
stranger for addressing to you a few lines. I heard
you preach last Sabbath evening, and it pleased God
to bless that sermon to my soul. It was not so much
what you said, as your manner of speaking, that
struck me. I saw in you a beauty in holiness that I
never saw before. You also said something in your
prayer that struck me very much. It was, ' *Thou
knowest that we love thee.*' O sir, what would I give
that I could say to my blessed Saviour, 'Thou knowest
that I love thee.' "

Next evening he held a meeting in St. Peter's, with
the view of organizing his people for collecting in
behalf of the Free Protesting Church—the disruption
of the Establishment being now inevitable. He spoke
very fervently; and after the meeting felt chilled and
unwell. Next morning he felt that he was ill; but
went out in the afternoon to the marriage of two of
his flock. He seemed, however, to anticipate a serious
attack, for, on his way home, he made some arrangements connected with his ministerial work, and left a
message at Dr. Gibson's house, asking him to come
and see him. He believed that he had taken the fever,

and it was so. That night he lay down upon the bed from which he was never to rise. He spoke little, but intimated that he apprehended danger.

On Wednesday, he said he thought that he would never have seen the morning, he felt so sore broken, and had got no sleep; but afterwards added, " Shall we receive good at the hand of the Lord, and shall we not receive evil also?" He seemed clouded in spirit, often repeating such passages as—" My moisture is turned into the drought of summer ;" " My bones wax old, through my roaring all day long." It was with difficulty that he was able to speak a few words with his assistant, Mr. Gatherer. In the forenoon Mr. Miller of Wallacetown found him oppressed with extreme pain in his head. Among other things they conversed upon Psalm cxxvi. On coming to the 6th verse, Mr. McCheyne said he would give him a division of it. 1. *What is sowed*—" Precious seed." 2. *The manner of sowing it*—"Goeth forth and weepeth." He dwelt upon " *weepeth*," and then said, " Ministers should go forth at all times." 3. *The fruit*—" Shall doubtless come again with rejoicing." Mr. Miller pointed to the *certainty* of it; Mr. McCheyne assented, " Yes—*doubtless*." After praying with him, Mr. Miller repeated Matthew xi. 28, upon which Mr. McCheyne clasped his hands with great earnestness. As he became worse, his medical attendants forbade him to be visited. Once or twice he asked for me, and was heard to speak of " *Smyrna*," as if the associations of his illness there were recalled by his burning fever now. I was not at that time aware of his danger; even the rumour of it had not reached us.

Next day, he continued sunk in body and mind, till about the time when his people met for their usual evening prayer meeting, when he requested to be left alone for half an hour. When his servant entered the room again, he exclaimed with a joyful voice, " My soul is escaped, as a bird out of the snare of the fowler; the snare is broken, and I am escaped." His countenance, as he said this, bespoke inward peace. Ever after, he was observed to be happy; and at supper time that evening, when taking a little refreshment, he gave thanks, "for strength in the time of weakness—for light in the time of darkness—for joy in the time of sorrow—for comforting us in all our tribulations, that we may be able to comfort those that are in any trouble, by the comfort wherewith we ourselves are comforted of God."

On Sabbath, when his servant expressed a wish that he had been able to go forth as usual to preach, he replied, "My thoughts are not your thoughts, neither are my ways your ways, saith the Lord;" and added, "I am preaching the sermon that God would have me to do."

On Tuesday (the 21st) his sister read to him several hymns. The last words he heard, and the last he seemed to understand, were those of Cowper's hymn, "Sometimes a light surprises the Christian as he sings." And then the delirium came on.

At one time, during the delirium, he said to his attendant, "Mind the text, 1 Corinth. xv. 58. Be steadfast, unmovable, always abounding in the work of the Lord;" dwelling with much emphasis on the last clause, "*forasmuch as ye know that your labour is not in vain in the Lord.*" At another time, he seemed to feel himself among his brethren, and said, "I don't think much of policy in church courts; no, I hate it; but I'll tell you what I like, faithfulness to God, and a holy walk." His voice, which had been weak before, became very strong now; and often was he heard speaking to or praying for his people. "You must be awakened in time, or you will be awakened in everlasting torment, to your eternal confusion!" "You may soon get me away, but that will not save your souls!" Then he prayed, "This parish, Lord, this people, this whole place!" At another time, "Do it thyself, Lord, for thy weak servant!" And again, as if praying for the saints, "Holy Father, keep through thine own name those whom thou hast given me!"

Thus he continued, most generally engaged while

the delirium lasted, either in prayer or in preaching to his people, and always apparently in happy frame, till the morning of Saturday the 25th. On that morning, while his kind medical attendant, Dr. Gibson, stood by, he lifted up his hands, as if in the attitude of pronouncing the blessing, and then sank down. Not a groan or a sigh, but only a quiver of the lip, and his soul was at rest.

As he was subject to frequent sickness, it was not till within some days of his death that serious alarm was generally felt, and hence the stroke came with awful suddenness upon us all. That same afternoon, while preparing for Sabbath duties, the tidings reached me. I hastened down, though scarce knowing why I went. His people were that evening met together in the church, and such a scene of sorrow has not often been witnessed in Scotland. It was like the weeping for King Josiah. Hundreds were there, the lower part of the church was full : and none among them seemed able to contain their sorrow. Every heart seemed bursting with grief, so that the weeping and the cries could be heard afar off. The Lord had most severely wounded the people whom he had before so peculiarly favoured ; and now, by this awful stroke of his hand, was fixing deeper in their souls all that his servant had spoken in the days of his personal ministry.

Wherever the news of his departure came, every Christian countenance was darkened with sadness. Perhaps, never was the death of one, whose whole occupation had been preaching the everlasting gospel, more felt by all the saints of God in Scotland. Not a few also of our Presbyterian brethren in Ireland felt the blow to the very heart. He used himself to say, " Live so as to be missed ;" and none that saw the tears that were shed over his death would have doubted that his own life had been what he recommended to others. He had not completed more than twenty-nine years when God took him.

On the day of his burial, business was quite suspended in the parish. The streets, and every window,

from the house to the grave, were crowded with
those who felt that a prince in Israel had fallen; and
many a careless man felt a secret awe creep over his
hardened soul as he cast his eye on the solemn
spectacle.

His tomb may be seen on the pathway at the north-
west corner of St. Peter's burying ground. He has
gone to the "mountain of myrrh and the hill of frank-
incense, till the day break and the shadows flee away."
His work was finished! His heavenly Father had
not another plant for him to water, nor another vine
for him to train; and the Saviour who so loved him
was waiting to greet him with his own welcome—
"Well done, good and faithful servant, enter thou into
the joy of thy Lord."

But what is the voice to us? Has this been sent
as the stroke of wrath, or the rebuke of love? "His
way is in the sea, and his path in the great waters,
and his footsteps are not known." Only this much
we can clearly see, that nothing was more fitted to
leave his character and example impressed on our
remembrance for ever than his early death. There
might be envy while he lived; there is none now.
There might have been some of the youthful attrac-
tiveness of his graces lost had he lived many years;
this cannot be impaired now. It seems as if the
Lord had struck the flower from its stem, ere any of
the colours had lost their bright hue, or any leaf its
fragrance.

Well may the flock of St. Peter's lay it to heart.
They have had days of visitation. Ye have seen the
right hand of the Lord plucked out of his bosom!
What shall the unsaved among you do in the day of
the Lord's anger? "If thou hadst known, even thou,
at least in this thy day, the things which belong to thy
peace!"

It has been more than once the lot of Scotland (as
was said in the days of Durham,) to enjoy so much
of the Lord's kindness, as to have men to lose whose
loss has been felt to the very heart—witnesses for
Christ, who saw the King's face and testified of his

beauty. We cannot weep them back; but shall we not call upon Him with whom is the residue of the Spirit, that ere the Lord come, he would raise up men, like Enoch or like Paul, who shall reach nearer the stature of the perfect man, and bear witness with more power to all nations! Are there not (as he who has left us used to hope) " better ministers in store for Scotland than any that have yet arisen?"

Ministers of Christ, does not the Lord call upon us especially? Many of us are like the angel of the Church of Ephesus: we have " works, and labour, and patience, and cannot bear them that are evil, and we have borne, and for his name's sake we labour, and have not fainted;" but we want the fervour of "first love." O how seldom now do we hear of fresh supplies of holiness arriving from the heavenly places (Eph. i. 3,)—new grace appearing among the saints, and in living ministers! We get contented with our old measure and kind, as if the windows of heaven were never to be opened. Few among us see the lower depths of the horrible pit; few ever enter the inner chambers of the house of David.

But there has been one among us who, ere he had reached the age at which a priest in Israel would have been entering on his course, dwelt at the mercy seat as if it were his home—preached the certainties of eternal life with an undoubting mind—and spent his nights and days in ceaseless breathings after holiness, and the salvation of sinners. Hundreds of souls were his reward from the Lord, ere he left us; and in him have we been taught how much one man may do who will only press further into the presence of his God, and handle more skilfully the unsearchable riches of Christ, and speak more boldly for his God. We speak much against unfaithful ministers, while we ourselves are awfully unfaithful! Are we never afraid that the cries of souls whom we have betrayed to perdition through our want of personal holiness, and our defective preaching of Christ crucified, may ring in our ears for ever? Our Lord is at the door. In the twinkling of an eye our work will be done.

" Awake, awake, O arm of the Lord, awake as in
the ancient days," till every one of thy pastors be
willing to impart to the flock, over which the Holy
Ghost has made him overseer, not the gospel of God
only, but also his own soul.   And, O that each one
were able, as he stands in the pastures feeding thy
sheep and lambs, to look up and appeal to thee—
" *Lord, thou knowest all things! thou knowest that
I love thee!*"

CONCLUDING MEMORIALS

It is, perhaps right, at the close of this memoir, to
preserve a specimen of the many tributes to his memory which appeared at the time of his decease. One
of these, written in his own town, after a brief review
of his life, concluded thus :

" Whether viewed as a son, a brother, a friend, or
a pastor, often has the remark been made, by those
who knew him most intimately, that he was the most
faultless and attractive exhibition of the true Christian which they had ever seen embodied in a living
form. His great study was to be Christ-like. He
was a man of remarkable singleness of heart. He
lived but for one object—the glory of the Redeemer
in connection with the salvation of immortal souls.
Hence he carried with him a kind of hallowing influence into every company into which he entered, and
his brethren were accustomed to feel as if all were
well when their measures met with the sanction and
approval of Mr. McCheyne. He was, indeed, the
object of an esteem and reverence altogether singular
toward so young a man, and which had their foundation in the deep and universal conviction of his perfect integrity of purpose—his unbending sincerity and
truthfulness—his Christian generosity of spirit—and
in the persuasion that he was a man who lived near
to God, as was evident from his holy walk, his spiritual and heavenly-minded frame, and his singularly
amiable and affectionate temper and disposition. In

his zeal in the cause in which the Church is engaged he was most exemplary. His spiritual mind had a quick and strong perception of the connection of the great principles for which she is contending, with the interests of vital godliness in the land. His views concerning the issues of the controversy, as regards the fate of the Establishment, and the guilt and consequent danger of the country, were remarkably dark ; but, as respects the imperishable interests of the Gospel, he rejoiced in the assurance, 'We have a strong city; salvation will God appoint for walls and bulwarks.' The example of his zeal and growing devotion in this cause has been bequeathed by him as a precious legacy to his attached and weeping flock. His death has spread a general gloom among the friends of religion throughout this town, and bitter are the tears that have been wrung from many eyes all unused to weep. Every one feels as if bereaved of a personal friend, and is at a loss for language to convey his sense of the loss which himself and the cause of truth have sustained—' sorrowing most of all that they shall see his face no more.' 'There is a prince and a great man fallen this day in Israel.' May the Lord increase the measures of his grace and strength to his surviving servants, who are called to occupy the breach thus left in the walls of our Zion ! ' Help, Lord ; for the godly man ceaseth ; for the faithful fail from among the children of men.'

" It is impossible to describe the grief which pervades his flock. The lane in which his residence was situated was constantly crowded with anxious inquirers, and numerous prayer meetings were held during the progress of his illness On Thursday there was the usual meeting in the church ; and it was then agreed, by many present, to meet for prayer the next evening in the school house. This they accordingly did, but it proved all too small to contain the crowds who flocked to it, and an adjournment to the church was necessary. Towards the close, it became known that increasing fears for their pastor's life were entertained, and the mourning people were with difficulty persuaded against remaining in the church throughout the night; and when, the next morning, the news spread among them, the voice of weeping might have been heard in almost every household. On Sabbath, Mr. Bonar of Collace, the dear friend of the deceased, and his companion in Palestine, preached in the forenoon and afternoon, and Mr. Miller, of Wallacetown in the evening.* On each occasion the church (including the passages) was crowded in every part; and it was remarked by those who were present, that they never before saw so many men in tears. It was truly a weeping congregation."

The funeral took place on the Thursday following. " Business was almost totally suspended throughout the bounds of his parish, and, hours before the time appointed for the funeral arrived, crowds began to draw towards the scene of the mournful obsequies from all parts of the town, anxious to pay the last sad token of respect to the remains of one whom living they had esteemed so highly. Long before the hour arrived, the whole line of road intervening between the dwelling house and the church yard was crowded with men, women, and children, principally of the working classes. Every window overlooking the procession, and the church itself, were likewise densely filled with females, almost all attired in deep mourning, and the very walls and house tops were surmounted with anxious on-lookers. Altogether not fewer than six or seven thousand people must have assembled. The funeral procession itself was followed by nearly every man in the parish and congregation who could command becoming attire; by the brethren of the Presbytery, and many ministers from the surrounding districts, as well as from a distance; by the great body of the elders, by most of the Dissenting ministers in town, and by multitudes of all ranks and persuasions besides, who thus united in testifying their sense of the loss which their common Christianity had sustained in the untimely death of him in whom all

* The texts were these: After reading 2 Kings ii. 1—15, the subject in the forenoon was Romans viii. 38, 39—in the afternoon, Romans viii. 28-30—in the evening, Rev. viii. 13—17.

recognized one of its brightest ornaments. The grave was dug in the pathway, near the southwest corner of the church, and within a few yards of the pulpit from which he had so often and so faithfully proclaimed the word of life; and in this his lowly resting place all that is mortal of him was deposited, amid the tears and sobs of the crowd. There his flesh rests in that assured hope of a blessed resurrection, of the elevating and purifying influences of which, his life and his ministry were so beauteous an example. His memory will never perish.

" The church was opened for public worship every evening during the week, and was on each occasion filled to overflowing. On Sabbath, according to the appointment of the Presbytery, funeral sermons were preached by the Rev. Messrs. Roxburgh, Somerville, and Burns. Mr. Roxburgh preached from Philippians iii. 17, 20, and 21; Mr. Somerville from Hebrews iv. 14; and Mr. Burns from Romans viii. 30. So early as nine o'clock on Sabbath morning, a crowd, many of them from distant country parishes, had assembled outside the church, and when the doors were opened at ten o'clock, the church was instantly densely filled in every part, lobbies included. Unfortunately, they were chiefly strangers, very few of the congregation having succeeded in obtaining admission; and by the time the ordinary hour for commencing divine service had arrived, another large congregation had assembled outside. To these Mr. Somerville volunteered to preach, and there was service, therefore, both within and without the church, and the same in the afternoon. In the afternoon, arrangements were made to secure the admission within the church of the proper congregation, being all, male and female, habited in deep mourning—the poorest amongst them having contrived, by a black ribbon, or some other inexpensive mode within their reach, to give outward token of their inward grief of heart."

Another tribute, from the pen of Mr. Hamilton, Regent Square, London, is too precious to be forgotten though only a small part is inserted here.

" A striking characteristic of his piety was absorbing love to the Lord Jesus. This was his ruling passion. It lightened all his labours, and made the reproaches which for Christ's sake sometimes fell on him, by identifying him more and more with his suffering Lord, unspeakably precious. He cared for no question unless his Master cared for it ; and his main anxiety was to know the mind of Christ. He once told a friend, 'I bless God every morning I awake that I live in witnessing times.' And, in a letter six months ago, he says, 'I fear lest the enemy shall so contrive his measures in Scotland as to divide the godly. May God make our way plain ! It is comparatively easy to suffer when we see clearly that we are suffering members of Jesus.' It were wrong not to mention the fact, that his public actings were a direct emanation from the most heavenly ingredient in his character—his love and gratitude to the Divine Redeemer. In this he much resembled one whose *Letters* were almost daily his delight, Samuel Rutherford ; and, like Rutherford, his adoring contemplations naturally gathered round them the imagery and language of the Song of Solomon. Indeed, he had preached so often on that beautiful book, that at last he had scarcely left himself a single text of its ' good matter' which had not been discoursed on already. It was very observable that, though his deepest and finest feelings clothed themselves in fitting words, with scarcely any effort, when he was descanting on the glory or grace of Immanuel, he despaired of transferring to other minds the emotions which were overfilling his own ; and after describing those excellencies which often made the careless wistful, and made disciples marvel, he left the theme with evident regret that where he saw so much he could say so little. And so rapidly did he advance in scriptural and experimental acquaintance with Christ, that it was like one friend learning more of the mind of another. And we doubt not that, when his hidden life is revealed, it will be found that his progressive holiness and usefulness coincided with those new aspects of endear-

ment or majesty which, from time to time, he beheld
in the face of Immanuel, just as the 'authority' of his
'gracious words,' and the impressive sanctity of his
demeanour, were so far a transference from Him who
spake as no man ever spake, and lived as no man
ever lived. In his case the words had palpable meaning; 'Beholding as in a glass, the glory of the Lord,
we are changed into the same image from glory to
glory, as by the Spirit of the Lord.'

" More than any one whom we have ever known,
had he learned to do every thing in the name of the
Lord Jesus. Amidst all his humility, and it was very
deep, he had a prevailing consciousness that he was
one of those who belong to Jesus; and it was from
Him, his living Head, that he sought strength for the
discharge of duty, and through Him, his Righteousness, that he sought the acceptance of his perform-
ances. The effect was to impart habitual tranquillity
and composure to his spirit. He committed his ways
to the Lord, and was sure that they would be brought
to pass; and though his engagements were often numerous and pressing, he was enabled to go through
them without hurry or perturbation. We can discern
traces of this uniform self-possession in a matter so
minute as his hand writing. His most rapid notes
show no symptoms of haste or bustle, but end in the
same neat and regular style in which they began; and
this quietness of spirit accompanied him into the most
arduous labours and critical emergencies. His effort
was to do all in the Surety; and he proved that promise, 'Great peace have they which love thy law, and
nothing shall offend them.'

" To speak with a plainness which such a solemn
occasion justifies, or rather to make the confession
which this heavy visitation calls for, it must be owned
that, while the possession of such a bright and shining
light was the Church of Scotland's privilege, the rarity
of such is the Church of Scotland's sin. When we
consider the ability and orthodoxy of the pious portion
of our ministry, it is mournful how little progress the
work of God has made. It certainly has not stood

still; but taking the labours and success of the sever. short and feeble years allotted to this faithful evangelist for our standard, we almost feel as if the work had been going back. If few congregations have witnessed the scenes with whch St. Peter's had become happily familiar, one reason is that few ministers preach with the fervour, the Christ-exalting simplicity, and the prayerful expectancy of Robert McCheyne; and few follow out their preaching with the yet more impressive urgency of his gracious intercourse and consistent example. The voice of this loud providence shall not have been uttered in vain, if it impart new instancy to the ministers, and new eagerness and solemnity to hearers—if it break up that conventional carnality which would restrain matters of eternal import to pulpits and Sabbath days, and make it henceforth the business of the gospel ministry to win souls and tend them. Hireling shepherds will not regret the brother who is gone. His life and labours were a reproof to them. But if the many devout men who, now that Stephen has been carried to his burial, are making lamentation over him, would arise and follow him even as he followed Christ, the present judgment would end in unprecedented blessing. Coming at this conjuncture, the death of this faithful witness is a striking call to ministerial disinterestedness and devotedness. 'Be thou faithful unto death, and I will give thee a crown of life.' And while some are crying mournfully, 'Where is the Lord God of Elijah?' we pray that many may find the answer in a double portion of Elijah's spirit descending on themselves.

"LONDON, April 3, 1843."

Even so, Lord! Amen

PRIVATE CORRESPONDENCE

~~~~~~~~

TO REV. R. MACDONALD, BLAIRGOWRIE

Written when first laid aside by that illness which afterwards led to the Jewish Mission.

EDINBURGH, *January 12th,* 1839.

MY DEAR FRIEND.—The very day I received your kind letter, I intended to have written you that you might provide some one to stand in my place on Monday evening next. I am ashamed at not having answered your kind inquiries sooner, but am not very good at the use of the pen, and I have had some necessary letters to write. However, now I come to you. This is Saturday, when you will be busy preparing to feed the flock of God with food convenient. Happy man! It is a glorious thing to preach the unsearchable riches of Christ. We do not value it aright till we are deprived of it; and then Philip Henry's saying is felt to be true—that he would beg all the week in order to be allowed to preach on the Sabbath day.

I have been far from alarmingly ill—my complaint is all unseen, and sometimes unfelt. My heart beats by night and day; but especially by night, too loud and too strong. My medical friends have tried several ways of removing it—hitherto without complete success. As long as it lasts, I fear I shall be unfit for the work of the ministry; but I do hope that God has something more for me to do in the vineyard, and that a little patient rest, accompanied by his blessing, may quiet and restore me. O! my dear friend, I need it all to keep this proud spirit under. Andrew Bonar was noticing the providence of "Elijah in the wilderness " being my allotted part at our next meeting. I read it in the congregation the Sabbath after, with an envious feeling in my own heart, though I did not like to express it, that I would not be sent a like day's journey to learn the same lessons as the prophet—that it is not the tempest, nor the earthquake, nor the fire, but the still small voice of the Spirit that carries on the glorious work of saving souls.

Andrew will be with you on Monday, and I am almost tempted to send this to-night to the post office; but it is not right to encourage the Sabbath mail, so I will defer it till Monday. May you have a time of refreshing from the presence of the Lord! May He be the third with you who joined the two disciples on the way to Emmaus, and made their hearts burn by opening to them the Scriptures concerning himself! I hope your evening meeting may be as delightful as the last. May your mind be solemnized, my dear friend, by the thought that we are ministers but for a time, that the Master may summon us to retire into silence, or may call us to the temple above; or the midnight cry of the great bridegroom may break suddenly on our ears, Blessed is the servant that is found waiting! Make all your services tell for eternity; speak what you can look back upon with comfort when you must be silent.

I am persuaded that I have been brought into retirement to teach me the value and need of prayer. Alas! I have not estimated aright the value of near access unto God. It is not the mere daily routine of praying for certain things that will obtain the blessing. But there must be the need within—the real filial asking of God the things which we need, and which he delights to give. We must study prayer more. Be instant in prayer You will be thinking my affliction is teaching me much, by my saying these things. O! I wish it were so. Nobody ever made less use of affliction than I do. I feel the assaults of Satan most when I am removed into a corner; every evil thought and purpose rushes over my soul, and it is only at times that I can find Him whom my soul loveth.

Monday, January 14, 1839.—I now sit down to finish this, and send it away. I am much in my usual state to-day, perhaps, if any thing, a little better. Still I have no hope at present of resuming my labours. Will you give me a Sabbath day's labour? I had no intention of asking you when I began this; but I feel that I had better not close it without asking this favour. I would fain be back, but I do not feel that I would be justified in so doing. When I give a short prayer in the family, it often quite knocks me up. I heard of my people to day; they are going on as well as can be expected. Death is busy among them, and Satan too. I try to lean them all on Him who entrusted them to me. I did hear of your brother's illness, and sympathized with you in it, though I heard no particulars. Write me particularly how he is. I hope and believe that he has an anchor within the veil, and therefore, we need not fear for him whatever storms may blow. Remember me to him when you write him or see him. May we both be made better men, and holier, by our affliction.

Take care of your health. Redeem the time, because the days are evil. Does the work of God still go on among your people? There is a decided improvement in the ministers here—more prayer, and faith, and hope. There are marks of God's Spirit not having left us. Remember me to Gillies and Smith, your fellow-labourers. May their names be in the book of life. Yours, ever,

ROBT. MURRAY MCCHEYNE.

———◆———

TO MRS. THAIN, HEATHPARK

During the continuance of the same illness.

EDINBURGH, *February 9th,* 1839.

MY DEAR MRS. THAIN,—I was happy to receive your and Mr. Thain's kind letter. It is very cheering to me, in my exile from my flock, to hear of them.

I send you a short line, as I am not good at writing I am glad you are keeping pretty well, and still more that your spiritual health seems to prosper. The spring is advancing—I feel already the softness of the wind—so that we may hope the winter is past, the rain over and gone. I know the summer revives you, and the doctor gives me good hope that it will revive me. In spiritual things, this world is all winter time as long as the Saviour is away. To them that are in Christ there are some sweet glistenings of his countenance, there are meltings of his love, and the sweet song of the turtle dove when his Holy Spirit dwells in the bosom; still it is but winter time till our Lord shall come. But then, "to you that fear his name, shall the Sun of Righteousness arise with healing in his wings." And if before he comes we should go away to be where he is, still we shall enter into a world of perpetual summer—we shall behold his glory which the Father gave him.

I feel much better than usual to-day, but I have returns of my beating heart occasionally. Jesus stands at the door and knocks, and sometimes I think the door will give way before his gentle hand. I am bid to try the sea water hot bath, which I hope will do me good. I have good hope of being restored to my people again, and only hope that I may come in the fulness of the blessing of the gospel of Christ, that this time of silent musing may not be lost.

I am thankful indeed at the appointment of Mr. Lewis. I hope he has been given in answer to prayer, and then he will be a blessing. We must pray that he may be furnished from on high for his arduous work. I have great hope that he will be the means of raising many more churches and schools in our poor town—I mean poor in spiritual things.

I hope Mr. Macdonald was happy, and made others so. "Apollos watered." May great grace be upon you all. Your affectionate friend, &c.

TO THE SAME

Before going forth on the Mission to Israel.

EDINBURGH, *March* 15*th*, 1839.

MY DEAR MRS. THAIN,—You will think me very unkind in breaking my word to Mr. Thain, in not writing you in answer to your kind letter by him. But I did too much the week he was in Edinburgh, and fairly knocked myself up, so that I had just to lay aside my pen and suffer quietly. My friendly monitor is seldom far away from me, and when I do any thing too much, he soon checks me. However, I feel thankful that I am better again this week, and was thinking I would preach again. This is always the way with me. When my heart afflicts me, I say to myself—Farewell, blessed work of the gospel ministry! happy days of preaching Christ and him crucified! winning jewels for an eternal crown! And then again, when it has abated, I feel as if I would stand up once more to tell all the world what the Lord of glory has done for sinners.

You have sent me a pocket companion (a Bible) for Immanuel's land. I shall, indeed, be very happy to take it with me, to remind me of you and your kind family, at the time when I am meditating on the things that concern our everlasting peace. All my ideas of peace and joy are linked in with my Bible; and I would not give the hours of secret converse with it for all the other hours I spend in this world.

Mr. M—— is the bearer of this, and I have told him he is to call on you with it. He is one much taught of God, and though with much inward corruption to fight against, he still holds on the divine way, a burning and a shining lamp.

I knew you would be surprised at the thought of my going so far away; and, indeed, who could have foreseen all that has happened? I feel very plainly that it is the Lord's doing, and this has taken away the edge of the pain. How many purposes God has in view of which we know nothing! Perhaps we do not see the hundredth part of his intentions toward us in sending me away. I am contented to be led blindfold, for I know that all will redound, through the thanksgiving of many, to the glory of our heavenly Father. I feel very plainly that towards many among my people this separation has been a most faithful chastisement. To those that liked the man but not the message—who were pleased with the vessel but not with the treasure—it will reveal the vanity of what they thought their good estate. To some, I hope, it has been sent in mercy. To some, I fear, it has been sent in judgment. Above all, none had more need of it than myself; for I am naturally so prone to make an ill use of the attachment of my people, that I need to be humbled in the dust, and to see that it is a very nothing. I need to be made willing to be forgotten. O! I wish that my heart were quite refined from all self-seeking. I am quite sure that our truest happiness is not to seek our own—just to forget ourselves—and to fill up the little space that remains; seeking only, and above all, that our God may be glorified. But when I would do good, evil is present with me.

I am not yet sure of the day of my going away. There is to be a meeting on Monday to arrange matters. Andrew Bonar and Dr. Black can hardly get away till the first week of April; but I may probably go before to London next week. I know you will pray for me in secret and in the family, that I may be kept from evil, and may do good. Our desire is to save sinners—to gather souls, Jew or Gentile, before the Lord come. O! is it not wonderful how God is making people take an interest in the Jews? Surely the way of these Kings of the East will be soon prepared.

I shall be quite delighted if J—— is able to take a small part in the Sabbath school. She knows it is what I always told her, not to be a hearer of the word only, but a doer. It is but a little time, and we shall work no more here for him. O that we might glorify him on the earth! I believe there are better

ministers in store for Scotland than any that have yet
appeared. Tell J—— to stay herself upon God.
Jesus continueth ever, he hath an unchangeable priesthood. Others are not suffered to continue by reason
of death.

You expected me in Dundee before I go; but I dare
not. You remember Paul sailed past Ephesus—he
dared not encounter the meeting with his people.
Indeed, I do not dare to think too much on my going
away, for it often brings sadness over my spirit, which
I can ill bear just now. But the will of the Lord be
done.

Kindest regards to you all. Christ's peace be left
with you. I shall remember you all, and be glad
to write you a word when I am far away. Yours,
ever, &c.

TO MISS COLLIER, DUNDEE

How his silence may be useful to his people and himself.

EDINBURGH, *March* 14, 1839.

MY DEAR MISS COLLIER.—I feel it very kind your
writing to me, and rejoice in sending you a word in
answer by my excellent friend Mr. Moody. Indeed, I
was just going to write to you when I received yours,
for I heard you had been rather poorly, and I was
going to entreat of you to take care of yourself, for you
do not know how much my life is bound up in your
life, and in the life of those around you who are like
minded. I feel it quite true that my absence should
be regarded by my flock as a mark that God is
chastening them; and though I know well that I am
but a dim light in the hand of Jesus, yet there is
always something terrible where Jesus withdraws the
meanest light in such a dark world. I feel that to
many this trial has been absolutely needful. Many
liked their minister naturally, who had but little real
relish for the message he carried. God now sifts these
souls, and wants to show them that it is a looking to
Jesus that saves, not a looking to man. I think I

could name many to whom this trial should be blessed. Some also who were really on the true foundation, but were building wood, hay, and stubble upon it, may be brought to see that nothing will truly comfort in the day of the Lord but what can stand the hour of trial. You yourself, my dear friend, may be brought to cleave much more simply to the Lord Jesus. You may be made to feel that Christ continueth ever, and hath an unchangeable priesthood, that his work is perfect, and that infinitely; and poor and naked as we are, we can appear only in him—only in him. But if the trial was needed by my people, it was still more needed by *me*. None but God knows what an abyss of corruption is in my heart. He knows and covers all in the blood of the Lamb. In faithfulness thou hast afflicted me. It is perfectly wonderful that ever God could bless such a ministry. And now, when I go over all the faults of it, it appears almost impossible that I can ever preach again. But then I think again who can preach so well as a sinner, who is forgiven so much, and daily upheld by the Spirit with such a heart within ! I can truly say that the fruit of my long exile has been, that I am come near to God, and long more for perfect holiness, and for the world where the people shall be all righteous. I do long to be free from self, from pride, and ungodliness, and I know where to go, " for all the promises of God in Christ are yea and amen in Christ Jesus." Christ is my armoury, and I go to him to get the whole armour of God—the armour of light. My sword and buckler, my arrows, my sling and stone, all are laid up in Jesus. I know you find it so. Evermore grow in this truly practical wisdom. You have a Shepherd; you shall never want. What effect my long absence may have on the mass of un-converted souls I do not know. I cannot yet see God's purposes toward them; perhaps it may be judgment, as in the case of Ephesus, Rev. ii. 5 ; perhaps it may be in mercy, as in the case of Laodicea, Rev. iii. 19 ; or perhaps there are some who would not bend under my ministry, who are to flow down as wax before the fire under the ministry of the precious fellow-labourer who is to succeed me. William Burns, son of the minister of Kilsyth, has for the present agreed to supply my place ; and though there is a proposal of his being sent to Ceylon, I do hope he may be kept for us. He is one truly taught of God—young, but Christ lives in him. You know he comes of a good kind by the flesh.

Another reason of our trial, I hope, has been God's mercy to Israel. There is something so wonderful about the way in which all difficulties have been over-come, and the way opened up, that I cannot doubt the hand of Jehovah has been in it. This gives me, and should give you, who love Israel, a cheering view of this trial. The Lord meant it for great good. If God be glorified, is not this our utmost desire ? O ! it is sweet, when in prayer we can lay ourselves and all our interests along with Zion, in the hands of *Him* whom we feel to be *Abba !* And if we are thus tied ourselves in the same bundle with Zion, we must re-sign all right to ourselves, and to our wishes. May the Lord open up a way to his name being widely glorified on the earth even before we die ! I know you will pray for us on our way, that our feet may be beautiful on the mountains of Israel, and that we may say to Zion, " Thy God reigneth." Pray that your poor friend may be supplied out of His riches in glory, that he may not shrink in hours of trial, but endure hardness as a good soldier of Jesus Christ. I will remember you when far away, and pray God to keep you safe under the shadow of the Redeemer's wings till I come again in peace, if it be his holy will. Dr. Black and Andrew Bonar have both consented to go. I shall probably be sent before to London, next week, to open the way. I am not very strong yet ; often revisited by my warning friend, to tell me that I may see the New Jerusalem before I see the Jeru-salem beneath. However, I have the sentence of death in myself, and do not trust to myself, but in God, who raises the dead.

I saw Mrs. Coutts yesterday, in good health, and

full of spirit. She almost offered to go with us to Immanuel's land. I fear the Pastoral Letters are not worth printing; but I shall ask others what they think. Farewell for the present. The Lord give you all grace and peace. Your affectionate pastor, &c.

———+———

TO THE REV. W. C. BURNS

On his agreeing to undertake the charge of St. Peter's during Mr. McC.'s absence in Palestine.

EDINBURGH, *Hill Street, March* 22, 1839.

MY DEAR FRIEND,—for I trust I may now reckon you among the number in the truest sense—I haste to send you a line in answer to your last. I am glad you have made up your mind to begin your spiritual charge over my flock on the first week of April. The committee have resolved that I leave this on Wednesday next, so that you will not hear from me again till I am away. Take heed to *thyself.* Your own soul is your first and greatest care. You know a sound body alone can work with power; much more a *healthy soul.* Keep a clear conscience, through the blood of the Lamb. Keep up close communion with God. Study likeness to him in all things. Read the Bible for your own growth first, then for your people. Expound much; it is through *the truth* that souls are to be sanctified, not through *essays upon the truth.* Be easy of access, apt to teach, and the Lord teach you and bless you in all you do and say. You will not find many companions. Be the more with God. My dear people are anxiously waiting for you. The prayerful are praying for you. Be of good courage, there remaineth much of the land to be possessed. Be not dismayed, for Christ shall be with thee to deliver thee. Study Isaiah vi., and Jeremiah i., and the sending of Moses, and Psalm li. 12, 13, and John xv. 26, 27, and the connection in Luke i. 15, 16.

I shall hope to hear from you when I am away. Your accounts of my people will be a good word to make my heart glad. I am often sore cast down; but the eternal God is my refuge. Now, farewell; the Lord make you a faithful steward. Ever yours, &c.

———◆———

TO REV. JOHN ROXBURGH, OF ST. JOHN'S, DUNDEE

The Holy Land.

JERUSALEM, *June 17th*, 1839.

MY DEAR FRIEND.—I am sure you will be glad to hear from your brother in the ministry, in this land trodden by the feet of " God manifest in the flesh." My thoughts wander continually to the spot where God first counted me faithful, putting me into the ministry; where, for two years, he made me a happy minister of the gospel, and where I believe I have many praying friends who will not forget me so long as I live. In these sweet remembrances—whether in the vales of Italy, or on the mighty waters, or in the waste howling wilderness, or in this land of promise, you and your family have their constant place. I doubt not also that you often think and talk of me. When some church extension expedition has turned out well, you will say, " what would our travelling friend say to this?" Or when the liberties of our church are infringed, and the arm of unhallowed power is raised against her, you perhaps think a moment, " how will our traveller bear this?" I am thankful to Him who dwelt in the bush, that we are all here in safety, and I myself in moderate health, quite able to endure the fatigues of travelling, although these have been very great. You would hear of our swift journey through France, and our pleasant stay in Italy. Malta was the next place of interest we came to. It is a very lovely island, having customs from every nation almost under heaven. It is highly important as a centre of missionary operations, having a printing press, and some useful, excellent men employed. In riding round its rocky shore, we looked on every creek with interest, remembering *Paul's* shipwreck here, and his three months' stay in the island. The atmosphere is truly pleasant, and the sky has a peculiarly fine tinge of yellowish red. We had a pleasant sail past Greece, and among the wonderful islands of the Ægean sea. We landed on one called Syra, and saw the mission actively engaged, six hundred Greek children reading God's word in Greek. The same evening we sailed between Naxos and Paros, where the beautiful marble was found, and stretched our eyes to see Patmos, where the beloved John wrote the Revelation. We could only see the waves that washed its shore. We passed Crete, and read the Epistle to Titus with a new interest; and the next day at four (13th May) sailed into the harbour of Alexandria. The customs of the East are very striking to the eye at first. The turban, the beard, the hyke or immense plaid, the wide Arab trowsers, the black visages and legs of the men, quite arrest the attention. The close veil, the forehead ornaments, the ear-rings, the anklets, the burden carried on the head, the children carried on the shoulder, or on the side, all these in the women are striking, especially at first. They will recall to you many of the words of the prophets. The plague having broken out at Alexandria the day we arrived, we were prevented from going up to Cairo, and after having visited the Jews in the synagogues, we determined on proceeding through the desert for the Holy Land, that we might escape quarantine. We left Alexandria on the 14th May, and reached Jerusalem on the 7th June. We were about twenty-two days living after the manner of Bedouins in the wilderness.

Mount Carmel, June 24th, 1839.—I thought to have got this letter finished in Jerusalem, but we were hurried away so unexpectedly, in consequence of a considerable increase of the plague in the Holy City then, that I had to leave this and many other things undone. You will see by the date that we are now beside that mountain where God did such wonders in the days of Elijah. We are encamped in our tents within a few yards of the sea. I am now writing upon a mat on the sand. The thermometer is some where about 80°, and I am writing with my desk on my knee. For the sake of distinctness, I will take up the thread of our story where I last left it off. Our journey through the desert was a very trying one in many ways. I *now* understand the meaning of the text which says, " God led the Israelites through the wilderness to try them, and prove them, and make them know what was in their hearts." The loneliness is very great. The utter silence of all the world to you—the want of every necessary except what you carry along with you—all these try the soul in a way you can hardly imagine, whether we will cast all our care upon God or no. The first part of the desert journey we went upon asses: but the second, and longest part, upon camels—a mode of journeying of all others the most fatiguing. I have thought a hundred times what a singular picture it would make to draw our company riding through the desert exalted to the giddy height of the hunch of the camel. I have often thought also, more seriously and properly, how plainly God heard the prayers of all our dear friends in preserving us from many dangers. It is quite a miracle that I was enabled to bear the fatigue of being up before sunrise, and sailing over that burning wilderness, often twelve hours a day. We came the nearest way from Egypt, alluded to in Exod. xiii. 17, and had opportunity of seeing Rosetta and Damietta, two curious Egyptian towns. We sailed across a lake called Menzaleh, and encamped one night beside the ruins of the ancient Zoan. Amid these we could plainly trace the finger of God in the fulfilment of the word in Ezekiel xxx. 14, " I will set fire in Zoan." At El Arish, the last town of Egypt, we clearly traced what we believed to be the River of Egypt, so often spoken of as the boundary of Judah. Like all the streams in the south, it is perfectly dry, but the watercourse was very evident. By the way, this suggests the meaning of a text which I never understood before, Psalm cxxvi., "Turn our captivity as the streams in the south." In the whole of the south part of Canaan the streams dry up in the summer. I think we only came upon *one* flowing stream between the hill and Jerusalem. In the winter God restores these streams, supplying them with abundance of water. Now this is the very prayer of the Psalmist, "Do for our brethren in captivity what thou doest for the streams in the south. Restore them in all their life, and fulness and beauty." So may it be in all our parishes, in all our beloved Scotland—never so lovely or desirable as when we are far from it, and from its pleasant Sabbaths. I must tell you now about Jerusalem. It is indeed the most wonderful place I was ever in. We reached it about twelve o'clock, under a burning sun. The bleak rocky hills over which we crossed were like a heated oven, but all was forgotten when the city of the Great King came in sight. "Your house is left unto you desolate." That word was upon every tongue. Almost every approach to Jerusalem gives you this desolate feeling; but when you stay there, and wander down into its deep valleys—or climb its terraced hills—or sit beside shady Siloam, whose waters flow softly—or meditate on Mount Zion, ploughed like a field—the whole current of your feelings is made to flow, and Jerusalem presents the remains of departed beauty such as you seek for in vain in any other land. The scene which might seem of greatest interest in Jerusalem is Calvary, where the Son of God died. But God has so willed it that nothing but pain and disappointment follow the inquirer after the spot where the blood flowed which cleanses from all sin. You know there is a great church built over the place. The hole made by the cross is enclosed in a star of gold; and a marble slab covers what *they call* the sepulchre. They tell you so many heinous falsehoods, that we were all inclined to doubt the whole matter. The place in Jerusalem is now within the walls, instead of "without the gate." There is no mount—no garden—nothing to remind you of that day of awful interest. Gethsemane makes up in interest all that we want in Calvary. The very place remains, and by its simplicity convinces the mind that it was the spot that Jesus loved. Above you, on the opposite side of Kedron, the high steep brow of Moriah rises; then the wall of the city; and above it, the Mosque of Omar, which stands on the site of God's holy temple. The road to Bethany passes in front of the garden. The path up the Mount of Olives forms another boundary. It is enclosed with old stone walls, like all the walls of Judea, of rude stones, without any cement. Eight very old olives, of a thousand years at least, stand as monuments in the place. It is a sweet and sacred spot; and you will not wonder that we were often drawn to visit it, and to pray on the very spot where Jesus sweated great drops of blood. The Mount of Olives is a hill of which you never weary. As you ascend it from Gethsemane, every step gives you a new prospect. We turned round again and again to look upon Jerusalem. Jeremiah says, "From the daughter of Zion all beauty is departed." And I believe if we had seen the "perfection of beauty" in the day of its glory, we would say the same. Still, from the Mount of Olives it is most beautiful. You see "the mountains all standing round about Jerusalem." The whiteness of the buildings gives it a dazzling appearance. The deep valleys on every side are very remarkable. On the north, a rising tower marks Ramah, where Samuel was born; and on the south, the eye fixes on Herodion, a conical hill beside Bethlehem. When you come to the top of Olivet, you look to the east, and the Dead Sea seems to be stretched at your feet. The mountains of Moab look quite near; and you try to find out Pisgah, where Moses enjoyed his view of the good land. Bethany appears upon the east side of a declivity near you—a pleasant village. Twice we wandered out as far as Bethany. It was pleasant, indeed, to sit under its spreading fig trees, and to read over the xi. John. Returning by the Jericho road, we stopped at the spot where Jesus wept over the city. It is the place where

you "come near and behold the city," at the descen
of the Mount of Olives. After full consideration, .
believe it to be the very spot. *Zion* is literally
ploughed like a field. I have brought with me some
barley that I found growing on its summit. Jerusalem is become heaps. The heaps of ruins within the
city are amazing; in some parts they are higher than
the walls. "The mountain of the house is like the
high places of the forest." Mount Moriah has now
two Turkish mosques upon it. Aceldama is a peaceful spot, overhanging the pleasant valley of Hinnom,
once the scene of hideous rites. The plague was very
severe in the city during our stay there, which prevented us from having that close intercourse with the
inhabitants, and especially with the Jews, which was
so desirable. Mr. Nicolayson, the English missionary,
acted towards us like a brother. He lodged us in one
of the mission houses upon Mount Zion, and gave us
opportunity of preaching and of receiving the Lord's
Supper. It was truly pleasant to eat of that bread
and drink of that cup in an upper room in Jerusalem. There are about five thousand Jews in Jerusalem, very poor and very divided among themselves,
looked down upon as dogs by the Moslems; still they
bear in their faces and manners the proof that the
land is their own. They are entirely supported by
contributions from Europe. They devote themselves
to the study of the Law and the Talmud. I had an
interesting meeting with one Jew at the large stones,
the only remains of God's temple. He was sitting
praying, and looking very sad. I asked him what he
was reading. He showed me; it was the xxii. Psalm,
in Hebrew. I took it up and read it over to him.
He said he understood it—and that it applied to
David. I showed him that could *not* be, for David
was never pierced in hands and feet. I shortly explained to him the gospel, and showed him the only
way of forgiveness. He looked very sad sitting on
the ground.

I must hurry on. We visited Hebron, and had an
interesting meeting with the Jews there. It is a de-

ightful place. We visited Bethlehem on our return. It is curious that almost all the inhabitants of Bethlehem are Christians—that is, Greeks and Catholics. We left Jerusalem on the 18th instant, and proceeded north by Ramah, Gibeon, Bethel, Sychar, Samaria, to Carmel. I cannot tell you the delightful and solemn feelings with which we traverse this land of promise. The fulfilment of prophecy is every where remarkable. At Sychar we tried to find out *the well* where Jesus sat wearied. Mr. Bonar found it, and let his Bible fall into it. He could not get it again, " for the well is deep." Ebal on the north, is a frowning rocky hill. Gerizim is also precipitous, but smiles with verdant gardens. Sychar is a beautiful place. We spent a most interesting morning among the Jews and Samaritans—saw both their synagogues, and reasoned with them out of the Scriptures, proving that Jesus is the Christ. Oh, that the Saviour would do as he did before in this place—say plainly, " I that speak unto thee am *He.*" When we meet, if that be the will of God, I shall have many descriptions to give you of the scenes of this land. It has far surpassed all my expectations. We arrived at Carmel on Saturday, and are now in quarantine. We and all our clothes were yesterday bathed in the sea. In consequence of undergoing this process our quarantine is seven days shorter; and on Monday next we hope to proceed to Tiberias and Saphet—the only places of importance for Jews, except Tyre and Sidon, which we shall visit on our way to Beyrout. We are sorry that so much of our time is taken up, but we have gone as quickly as possible in the circumstances. We are all in good health. I suffer occasionally from my heart, but much less than I used. I do hope, if it be the will of my Master that I may yet again serve him in the gospel of his Son. This is a delicious climate. I have heard once from home. I am thankful to hear of the peace and grace given to my people on our communion day. Dear people, may the Great Shepherd feed them! I was happy to hear of Dr. Chalmers' success. Dismayed at the decision of the Lord Chancellor, but

"Jehovah nissi,"—the Lord is our banner. My kindest regards to Mrs. R., and to the brethren that ask for me. I often pray most humbly for *all*, even my enemies. Yours, ever, &c.

----◆----

TO REV. R. MACDONALD, OF BLAIRGOWRIE

The Holy Land.

MOUNT CARMEL, *June 26th*, 1839.

MY DEAR FRIEND.—I wrote to you from the land of Egypt, and now from the land of Promise. I would have written from Jerusalem, but our departure was so hurried, owing to an increase of the awful disease of plague, that I could not accomplish it. Indeed, I thought it would be more for the pleasure and advantage of all my friends if I spent my time in fully seeing the wonders of the city of the Great King. It is all deeply graven on my memory and my heart. The first sight of Jerusalem made my heart sink within me—it was so desolate; the walls appeared so low, so dark, so poor. But better acquaintance with its deep valleys and singular hills, its trees and fountains, has made it appear one of the loveliest spots Jesus visited. There is a holy beauty about Jerusalem, for you cannot walk a step without remembering the scenes that have passed there, and without looking forward to a time when it will again become the joy of the whole earth. You will be glad to know that I have stood all our great fatigues wonderfully, and even without being the worse of them, but rather the better. I may almost say I feel that God has been answering the continued prayer of those that love me; still I am not yet what I was, though I hope to be. All my companions had the privilege of preaching in Jerusalem. I felt that it was kept from me, but that it was overflowing goodness that gave us to receive the broken bread and poured out wine, in an upper chamber, where Jesus first instituted it. I wish I could recount to you all that we have seen with our eyes, so as to make you almost see it all over again. Joy is increased by spreading it to others. Thus Christ's joy and glory are increased by making us partakers of it. Our life in the wilderness was a singular one. Since the day I wrote you we have never known the luxury of a bed. We spread our mats upon the sand, and God watches over us, when we are under the cover of our frail tent, as much as if we were within brazen gates and bars. We often hear the cry of the wolves at night, and there are many lynxes and hyenas in this very mountain; but God keeps us safely. The burning heat of the desert—the long fatiguing journeys, sometimes twelve hours or fourteen in the day upon the camel—the insatiable thirst—and our weakness—were very trying to our faith and to our temper; it proved us, and made us know what was in our heart. Ah! dear friend, wherever we journey, union to Jesus and holiness from his Spirit flowing into us, is our chief and only happiness. Never cease to show your people that to be holy is to be happy; and that to bring us to perfect holiness and likeness to God was the very end for which Christ died. We entered the land of the Philistines 1st of June. You know the prophets say that the sea coast there is to be "cottages for shepherds and folds for flocks." Zeph. ii. 6. It is really so. You cannot imagine a country more completely covered with flocks and herds—camels, and asses, and oxen, and sheep, and goats. The inhabitants are Arabs—a poor and ignorant race of men. How often we have wished for the Arabian tongue to preach to them the unsearchable riches of Christ. We passed like the spies through the valley of Eshcol. We came to a small Arab town, Bet-hanoon. For illustration I will draw it.* This will give you an idea of all Arab towns. Every roof is flat; so that the people sit there, pray there, dry their corn and sift it there.

---

* Here he had sketched the village with his pen. He enlivened many of his letters with these outlines, that spoke more expressively than words.

There are no vines in Eshcol now, but immense bunches of grapes are still produced in some places of the Holy Land. The trees around the village are figs—a beautiful dark green tree. We are now tasting the first ripe figs, which are, like Jeremiah's, very good. We crossed the brook Sorek, quite dry; indeed, I think we only met with one flowing stream between the desert and Jerusalem. The streams in the south are all dry in the summer (see Psalm cxxvi.) We slept that night beside a small town, which we take to be Eshtaol, near which Samson was born. We saw there the brown tents of some Bedouin Arabs, illustrating Song i.—the brown tents of Kedar. This was in the tribe of Dan. Next day we went due east, across the vast plain Sephela, where Asa fought his battle, 2 Chron. xiv., till we entered among the lovely hills of Judah. A wonderful fulfilment of God's word was pressed on our attention all that day. The quantities of weeds in the plains are quite remarkable, and all of them are of a briery, prickly nature. I counted eleven different kinds of thistle, some of them of gigantic size. In a field where barley had been sown, there were more of these thorns and briers than of the barley. Now turn to Isaiah xxxii. 13, "Upon the land of my people shall come up thorns and briers;" and see how long (v. 15,) "Until the Spirit be poured upon us from on high." Indeed, every mountain and valley of this land is a witness for God, speaking silently but mightily, declaring that God's word abideth for ever.

We arrived at Jerusalem on 7th June, and lighted off our camels within the Jaffa gate. The first thing that struck me was the quantity of various heaps. (See Micah iii. 12.) It was two or three days before we recovered our fatigues. The first time we went out was to the two pools of Gihon; the upper pool still contains water.

Again we went to Mount Olivet. Winding round the noble walls of Jerusalem, Mount Olivet appears with its softly rounded triple point. It is a beautiful hill, of very great extent. It is composed of a pure white limestone, which appears in many places, and gives the whole a whitish appearance. Fine old olives adorn it on every side—fig trees here and there —and pomegranates, with their beautiful deep red flowers. A monastery and a mosque are on the top, and three or four small towers on different points of it. Crops of barley may be discerned here and there. It is altogether a pleasant hill. Between you and it lies the deep valley of Jehoshaphat. The bed of the Kedron, quite dry, forms the lowest part. Going along by the east wall of Jerusalem till you are nearly opposite the place where the temple stood, (now the mosque of Omar,) you then descend the steep bank of Moriah to the Kedron. A small bridge now helps you to cross. Here David went, flying from Absalom barefooted Here Jesus used to cross going to Gethsemane or to Bethany. The path before you leads right up the steepest part of Mount Olivet. It is a pleasant path. Turning every now and then, you see Jerusalem in all its faded glory, minarets and cupolas lying beneath you. Another path winds upwards round the hill to Bethany, the sweet village of Martha and Mary, two miles off. The little nook between these two paths forms all that remains of Gethsemane. It is a pleasant spot. No one that knows the Saviour can visit it, and look upon its eight old olive trees, without feeling drawn to it. We tried to pray there, where Jesus sweated blood for us. It was sweet to intercede for you and all we love in that sacred spot. Another favourite spot was the fountain of Siloam, farther down the valley of Jehoshaphat. It flows so softly from under the temple, that you cannot hear the ripple of its waters. You descend a great many steps in the rock, and drink its delightful waters. I send you a small hymn on the other side, which will imprint it on your memory. The valley of Hinnom is a deep gorge or vale to the south of Jerusalem. Mount Zion is actually ploughed like a field. It descends steeply into Hinnom, which again has a rocky barrier on the other side. Aceldama is a fearful spot above.

We left Jerusalem on 18th June, and arrived here on the 21st. Many a pleasant scene we saw between. It is a delightsome land. One only I can mention—Sychar. It was a sweet evening when we entered the valley made by Ebal, a gloomy barren hill, and Gerizim, a rocky hill, but garnished with gardens. The town lies beautiful between, keeping nearer to Gerizim. The next morning we visited the synagogue. A. B. was in time for the service at six o'clock. He had very interesting discussions with several of the Jews, all carried on in Hebrew. You may believe we are not very fluent in the holy tongue, and yet it is wonderful how we get on. We visited the Samaritans also, and, after taking off our shoes, we were admitted into their synagogue to see the MS. of the Pentateuch, three thousand six hundred years old. Andrew alone found out the well where Jesus sat, and dropped his Bible in by accident. The Jews here are far kinder and pleasanter than in Europe. They wear a beautiful dress. They are much fairer in colour than the Arabs, and every way a more noble people; and then, when you look in your Bible, and see the promises that are waiting to be fulfilled to them, how does the heart fill towards them. God will yet gather them one by one. Pray still for their in-bringing. It is not easy to pray really for Israel; it needs you to have much of the peculiar mind of God. The same evening we visited Samaria, about six or eight miles north of Sychar. It is now a poor Arab village, but the finger of God is there. It is a hill surrounded by hills on all sides. Micah i. 6, is the clearest description of it. It is like a heap of the field. Just as you have seen the stones gathered out of a field into heaps, such is Samaria. The vast ruins are all thrown down, and form just heaps in the field. It is as the plantings of a vineyard. There is but one vine on the whole hill, but it is all terraced and cleared, just as if it were to be planted with vines. " And I will pour," &c. This is wonderfully fulfilled. It filled me with holy awe to look at the heaps of stones—fragments of pillars all rolling down into the valley. The foundations are actually discovered. What a monument of the truth of God! I have only time to commend you to God, and to say —brother, pray for us. Yours, ever, &c.

P. S.—Commend me to your true yoke-fellow, Mr. Smith, and to Mr. Gillies, and to Mr. Baxter. I cease not to mention all in my prayers, and hope that they do not forget me. We are made partakers in Christ, if we hold the beginning of our confidence firm unto the end.

TO REV. WM. C. BURNS, DUNDEE

Inquiries about the revival on first coming home.

20 *Hill Street, Edinburgh,*
15th *November,* 1839.

My Dear Friend and Brother,—I last night arrived once more in my beloved home, conducted through every danger by the unseen hand of our Father in heaven. I cannot lose a moment in writing you a few lines. It was not till we arrived in Hamburg that we heard any thing of what has been doing in our beloved land for the last five months. There we heard only a rumour that God had visited his people in love, and those also that were Lo-Ammi. You may believe that it was with a thankful, joyful spirit that we read of these things. I cannot rest till I hear from you what has been done among my own dear flock. I do not like to impose a task on you; but if you have an hour's leisure, it would be truly gratifying to me to hear from you, before I come over, a minute account of all that God seems to have wrought in Dundee during my absence. You remember it was the prayer of my heart when we parted, that you might be a thousand fold more blessed to the people than ever my ministry had been. How will it gladden my heart, if you can really tell me that it has been so. My poor dear flock, hard-hearted and stiff-necked as they were, if the Lord has really opened their hearts, and brought them to a saving knowledge of Christ, and if their hearts and lives are together changed, I will bless God while I have any being.

The work at Kilsyth seems to be owned by all God's true servants as not the work of man, but indeed, divine. What a great joy to you and to your excellent father, to have your labour thus honoured of God! The Lord preserve you both from all the personal danger to your own souls which such success exposes you to!

I must not write much, having agreed to preach on Sabbath. I would often have written to you when away, but you know my weakness, and I was always uncertain as to your movements. Do write me if you have time. Tell me all the good and all the bad. I know well that when Christ is nearest, Satan also is busiest. What of my elders? Of my dear established Christians? What of those who were but lambs? And what of those whom I left in darkness and in the shadow of death?

The Lord send me good news.

I shall try to be over on Thursday evening next, if I am well, and trust to join you in praising God together for all his mercy, and grace, and faithfulness, since we parted. Whether I shall be able to resume the full work of the ministry again or no, I cannot tell. My heart still beats too much. But I shall try: and if the Lord shows me that my work in that way is done, I shall pray for submission.

Do write me speedily, for I weary to hear.

With regard to temporal things; remember I shall expect you honestly to tell how far your small salary has gone to cover your expenses. And if it has not covered them, remember I insist on your demanding as much more as will. The workman is worthy of his hire.

And now the Lord keep you humble and prayerful in secret, and may it not be needful that you be afflicted as I have been; and may your ministry be blessed stil. a thousand times more ! With kindest love to all my people, yours affectionately, &c.

TO MISS COLLIER, DUNDEE

Riches of Christ—resemblance to him.

EDINBURGH, *February 26th,* 1840.

MY DEAR MISS COLLIER,—I am sorry to leave town without seeing you, but I find myself obliged to do so. A long and interesting meeting of Presbytery took up the greater part of my time. I am delighted to hear that you are still keeping a little better, and fondly hope the Lord may restore you to us once more, to help us by your prayers in these trying but glorious times. I would like to have seen you once again before going back, but I must just content myself with casting you on the Lord on whom you believe. Precious friend and unchangeable priest is Christ—sweeter to you than honey and the honeycomb. How great is the goodness he hath *laid up* for them that fear him ! Just as the miser lays up money that he may feast his eyes upon it, so Christ has laid up unsearchable riches that he may supply all our need out of them. Unfathomable oceans of grace are in Christ for you. Dive and dive again, you will never come to the bottom of these depths. How many millions of dazzling pearls and gems are at this moment hid in the deep recesses of the ocean caves. But there are unsearchable riches in Christ. Seek more of them. The Lord enrich you with them. I have always thought it a very pitiful show when great people ornament themselves with brilliants and diamonds; but it is truest wisdom to adorn the soul with Christ and his graces. " Can a maid forget her ornaments, or a bride her attire ? yet my people have forgotten me, days without number." You see my pen runs on, though I fear you will hardly be able to read what I write. The Lord Jesus give you out of his fulness, and grace for grace. In a mirror you will observe that every feature of the face is reflected—both the large and small features. Now our soul should be a mirror of Christ; we should reflect every feature; for every grace in Christ there should be a counterpart grace in us. The Lord give you this; then I can ask no more for you. Your times are in his hand. Psalm xxxi. May you have the blessing of Asher, " As thy days, so shall thy strength be."

Farewell till we meet. Kindest regards to Miss M. and Mrs. Coutts, and believe me ever yours, in lasting bonds, &c.

TO MR. J. T. JUST

How to conduct prayer meetings.

March 17, 1840.

MY DEAR JOHN,—I was glad to receive your letter, and am happy to answer you on the matter in which you apply to me. No person can be a child of God without living in secret prayer; and no community of Christians can be in a lively condition without unity in prayer. In Daniel's time you see how it was. (Dan. ii. 17, 18.) You see what Jesus said to his disciples on it, (Matt. xviii. 19,) and what a sweet promise of his presence and a gracious answer he connects with meeting for prayer, You see how it will be in the latter day (Zech. vii. 21,) when meetings for prayer, or, at least, concerts for prayer, shall be held by different towns. One great rule in holding them is, that they be really meetings of disciples. If four or five of you, that know the Lord, would meet together regularly, you will find that far more profitable than a meeting open to all. In an open meeting you are apt to become teachers, and to be proud. In a secret meeting you feel all on a level, poor and needy, seeking water. If a young man, acquainted with any of you, becomes concerned about his soul, or a lively Christian is visiting any of you, these may be admitted, but do not make your meeting more open.

The prayer meeting I like best, is where there is only praise and prayer, and the reading of God's word. There is then least room for frail human nature to pervert the meeting to an improper end. It is well to read regularly through a book of Scripture, or at least to fix the chapter the evening before, that it may be prayed over in secret, before coming to the meeting. If you *only read*, then two chapters may be read, and then two members pray at a meeting. Each member would take his turn. Let there be no presiding of one over another, for all are brethren. When a godly minister, or elder, or experienced Christian is visiting you, he should be invited to take the whole service.

Many meetings are not contented with merely reading God's word; they fix upon some verse or two as a matter of conversation, and each gives his opinion round. Some take a question of the Shorter Catechism each evening, and speak on it in the same manner. Some propose cases of conscience, and how Christians ought to act in different cases. Now, I never forbid any of these where the members prefer this; still, I must confess I feel the danger to which they are exposed. You require more grace to be kept humble and meek, and loving, if you engage in this service. You are exposed to the danger of differing from one another—disputing, seeking admiration and pre-eminence, to all which you know, dear John, your hearts are naturally most prone. If you choose any of these, the first appears the best, that of fixing on a verse or two of the chapter read. But do seek meekness in speaking together upon it. Meet weekly, at a convenient hour. Be regular in attendance. Let nothing keep you away from your meeting. Pray in secret before going. Let your prayers in the meeting be formed as much as possible upon what you have read in the Bible. You will thus learn variety of petition, and a Scripture style. Pray that you may pray to God, and not for the ears of man. Feel his presence more than man's. Pray for the outpouring of the Spirit on the Church of Christ and for the world—for the purity and unity of God's children—for the raising up of godly ministers, and the blessing of those that are already. Pray for the conversion of your friends, of your neighbours, of the whole town. Pray for the sending of the gospel to the Jews, and to the gentile nations.

Pride is Satan's wedge for splitting prayer meetings to pieces—watch and pray against it. If you have not the Spirit of God among you, you will have the spirit of the devil. Watch against seeking to be greater than one another; watch against lip-religion. Above all, abide in Christ, and he will abide in you. He is able to keep you from falling, and to make you happy, holy young men. There is no joy like that of holiness. May Enoch's companion be yours.

Write to me how you come on, and believe me ever yours, affectionately, &c.

TO A PARISHIONER ON A SICK BED

How cares and troubles sanctify.

March 31st, 1840.

DEAR M.—I may not see you for a little, as I am not strong; and therefore I send you a line in answer to your letter. I like to hear from you, and especially when God is revealing himself to your soul. All his doings are wonderful. It is, indeed, amazing how he makes use of affliction to make us feel his love more. Your house is, I trust, in some measure like that house in Bethany, of which it is said, "Now Jesus loved Martha, and her sister, and Lazarus." They had different degrees of grace. One had more faith and another more love, still Jesus loved them all. Martha was more inclined to be worldly than Mary, yet Jesus loved them both. It is a happy house when Jesus loves all that dwell in it. Surely it is next door to heaven.

The message of Martha and Mary to Christ (John ii. 3,) teaches you to carry all your temporal as well as your spiritual troubles to his feet. Leave them there. Carry one another's case to Jesus. Is it not a wonderful grace in God to have given you *peace in Christ*, before laying you down on your long sick bed. It would have been a wearisome lying if you had been an enemy to God, and then it would have been over hell. Do you feel Rom. v. 3, to be true in your experience? You cannot love trouble for its own sake; bitter must always be bitter, and pain must always be pain. God knows you cannot love trouble. Yet for the blessings that it brings, he can make you pray for it. Does trouble work patience in you? Does it lead you to cling closer to the Lord Jesus— to hide deeper in the rock? Does it make you "be still and know that he is God?" Does it make you lie passive in his hand, and know no will but *His?* Thus does patience work experience—an experimental acquaintance with Jesus? Does it bring you a fuller taste of his sweetness, so that you know whom you have believed? And does this experience give you a further hope of glory—another anchor cast within the veil? And does this hope give you a heart that cannot be ashamed, because convinced that God has loved you, and will love you to the end? Ah! then you have got the improvement of trouble, if it has led you thus. Pray for me still, that I may get the good of all God's dealings with me. Lean all on Jesus. Pray for a time of the pouring out of God's Spirit, that many more may be saved. I hope the Lord's work is not done in this place yet. Ever your affectionate pastor, &c.

----◆----

TO A SOUL WHOM HE HAD NEVER SEEN, BUT WHOSE CASE WAS LAID BEFORE HIM BY A FRIEND

Colos. ii. 1, 2.

Looking out to Jesus.

March 20*th*, 1840.

MY DEAR FRIEND,—I do not even know your name, but I think I know something of the state of your soul. Your friend has been with me, and told me a little of your mind; and I write a few lines just to bid you to look to Jesus and live. Look at Numbers xxi. 9, and you will see your disease and your remedy. You have been bitten by the great serpent. The poison of sin is through and through your whole heart, but Christ has been lifted up on the cross that you may look and live. Now, do not look so long and so harassingly at your own heart and feelings. What will you find there but the bite of the serpent. You were shapen in iniquity, and the whole of your natural life has been spent in sin. The more God opens your eyes, the more you will feel that you are *lost in yourself.* This is your disease. Now for the remedy. Look to Christ; for the glorious Son of God so loved lost souls, that he took on him a body and died for us—bore our curse, and obeyed the law in our place. Look to him and live. You need no preparation, you need no endeavours, you need no duties, you need no strivings, you only need to look and live. Look at John xvii. 3. The way to be saved is to know God's heart and the heart of Jesus. *To be awakened*, you need to know your own heart. Look in at your own heart, if you wish to know your lost condition. See the pollution that is there—forgetfulness of God, deadness, insensibility to his love. If you are judged as you are in yourself, you will be lost. *To be saved*, you need to know the heart of God and of Christ. The four gospels are a narrative of the heart of Christ. They show his compassion to sinners and his glorious work in their stead. If you only knew that heart as it is, you would lay your weary head with John on his bosom. Do not take up your time so much with studying your own heart as with studying *Christ's heart*. " For one look at yourself, take ten looks at Christ!"

Look at Romans xv. 13. That is my prayer for you. You are looking for peace *in striving*, or peace *in duties*, or peace in *reforming* your mind; but ah! look at his word. " The God of hope fill you with all joy and *peace in believing*." All your peace is to be found in believing *God's word* about his Son. If for a moment you forget your own case altogether, and meditate on the glorious way of salvation by *Christ for us,* does your bosom never glow with a ray of peace? Keep that peace; it is joy in believing. Look as straight to Christ as you sometimes do at the rising or setting sun. Look direct to Christ.

You fear that your convictions of sin have not been deep enough. This is no reason for keeping away from Christ. You will never get a truly broken heart till you are really *in Christ.* See Ezekiel xxxvi. 25—31. Observe the order: *First,* God sprinkles clean water on the soul. This represents our being washed in the blood of Christ. *Then* he gives "a new heart also." *Thirdly,* he gives a piercing remembrance of past sins. Now, may the Lord give you all these! May you be brought as you are to the blood of the Lamb! Washed and justified, may he change your heart—give you a tender heart, and his Holy Spirit within your heart; and thus may he give you a broken heart for your past sins.

Look at Romans v. 19. By the sin of Adam, many were made sinners. We had no hand in Adam's sin, and yet the guilt of it comes upon us. We did not put out our hand to the fruit, and yet the sin and misery have been laid at our door. In the same way, " by the obedience of Christ, many are made righteous." Christ is the glorious One who stood for many. His perfect garment is sufficient to cover you. You had no hand in his obedience. You were not alive when he came into the world and lived and died; and yet, in his perfect obedience, you may stand before God righteous. This is all my covering in the sight of a holy God. I feel infinitely ungodly *in myself*—in God's eye, like a serpent or a toad—and yet, when I stand *in Christ alone,* I feel that God sees no sin in me, and loves me freely. The same righteousness is free to you. It will be as white and clean on your soul as on mine. O do not sleep another night without it. Only consent to stand in Christ, not in your poor self.

I must not weary you. One word more. Look at Rev. xxii. 17. Sweet, sweet words. "Whosoever will, let him take of the water of life freely." The last invitation in the Bible, and the freest—Christ's parting word to a world of sinners. Any one that pleases may take this glorious way of salvation. Can you refuse it? I am sure you cannot. Dear friend, be persuaded by a fellow-worm not to put off another moment. Behold the Lamb of God, that taketh away the sins of the world.

You are sitting, like Hagar, within reach of the well. May the Lord open your eyes, and show you all that is in Christ. I pray for you, that you may spiritually see Jesus, and be glad — that you may go to him and find rest. Farewell. Yours, in the Lord, &c.

REV. W. C. BURNS

A minister's afflictions to be improved.

June 10th, 1840.

MY DEAR BROTHER,—I am truly thankful that you have been raised up again—renewed, I trust, both in the inner and outer man. "I will cause you to pass under the rod, and I will bring you into the bond of the covenant." Sweet rod that drives the soul into such a precious resting place! "I will visit their iniquity with stripes; nevertheless, my loving kindness I will not take from him." This has been the experience of the greater part of my life, at least of my spiritual life. Remember Edwards' magnificent resolution, "Resolved to improve afflictions to the uttermost." Spread the sail when the breeze of adversity blows, and let it drive your vessel onwards on its course.

When I was laid aside from the ministry, I felt it was to teach me the need of prayer for my people. I used often to say, now God is teaching me the use of prayer. I thought I would never forget the lesson, yet I fear I am grown slack again when in the midst of my work.

All these remarks I have transferred to myself that you may learn in me the same things. Exhort one another daily. My object in writing now, is to say that I have engaged to be at Collessie next Wednesday, at Alloa on Thursday, and at Errol on Sabbath week. Now the people here were disappointed by your not appearing lately; and it would be very gratifying, if you are not better engaged, if the Lord would direct your steps towards us. If you would take both Thursday and the Sabbath it would be pleasant to me. I have been weakened a little by the hard labours of the Assembly, but I trust to recruit shortly for our glorious warfare. I feel there are two things it is impossible to desire with sufficient ardour —personal holiness, and the honour of Christ in the salvation of souls.

The Lord give you both more than he has given me, and may he send you to us, if it be his will. Send me a line quickly, and believe me, ever yours in sweet bonds, &c.

TO THE REV. DAN. EDWARDS

Before his ordination as missionary to the Jews—What he must seek.

DUNDEE, *June* 15*th*, 1840.

MY DEAR FRIEND— * * *
* * * The grand matter of study, however, must still be Divinity—a knowledge of divine things, a spiritual discernment of the way of pardon for the chief of sinners. I feel that the best of ministers are but babes in this. Pray for more knowledge of your own heart—of the total depravity of it—of the awful depths of corruption that are there. Pray for glorious discoveries of Christ—his person, beauty, work, and peace. But I need not tell you these things, only I feel persuaded that God will put all natural and literary qualifications in the dust, if there be not the simple exhibition of Christ for us, in the preaching of our missionaries. Yours, &c.

TO THE SAME

Holiness and success.

DUNDEE, *October 2d,* 1840.

MY DEAR FRIEND.—I trust you will have a pleasant and profitable time in Germany. I know you will apply hard to German; but do not forget the culture of the inner man—I mean of the heart. How diligently the cavalry officer keeps his sabre clean and sharp; every stain he rubs off with the greatest care. Remember you are God's sword—his instrument—I trust a chosen vessel unto him to bear his name. In great measure according to the purity and perfection of the instrument, will be the success. It is not great talents God blesses so much as great likeness to Jesus. A holy minister is an awful weapon in the hand of God. I am now almost well, but have not yet got my full strength. We had a sweet night last night, though there was no external movement. Some waited after; one from St. Andrews, awakened deeply, she knows not how. God is still working here, and I look for far greater things. I am very anxious to know how I could do more good to many people and to the whole world—and not to know only, but to do it. It is our truest happiness to live entirely for the glory of Christ—to separate between " I " and "the glory of Christ." We are always saying, what have *I* done? was it *my* preaching—*my* sermon—*my* influence? Whereas we should be asking, what hath God wrought? Strange mixed beings we are! How sweet it will be to drop our old man, and be pure as Christ is pure. I hope you will come and see us again before your departure for your mission station. The Lord direct all your steps, comfort your heart, and establish you in every good word and work, to do his will.

Yours, &c.

TO MRS. THAIN, HEATHPARK

When invited to rest a while.

DUNDEE, *June* 1840.

MY DEAR MRS. T.—You know how glad I would be of some such retreat as Elijah had by the brook Cherith, where I might learn more of my own heart, and of my Bible, and of my God; where I might while away the summer hours in quiet meditation, or talking of his righteousness all the day long. But it is only said of *the dead* in the Lord that they rest from their labours; and I fear I must not think of resting till then. Time is short, my time especially, and souls are precious; and I fear many are slumbering because I watch not with sufficient diligence, nor blow the trumpet with sufficient clearness.

I have to be away so much on business, that I feel I dare not be away on pleasure only—at least at present. I rather think I must be in Ireland next week, at the Synod of Ulster, which prevents me coming to Mr. Macdonald's communion.

There is some request as to another communion in St. Peter's also, which I shall be glad to see carried into effect, provided it be done with all the heart of the Lord's children. In these circumstances you must not think me neglectful of your kindness if I put off my visit to you a little longer.

I trust that you are keeping strong, and able to enjoy the open air, and that your souls all prosper—that you have often such times as Jacob had at Mahanaim, when the angels of God met him—or such times as that at Peniel, when God had to cry out, "Let me go, for the day breaketh." Alas, we do not weary God now with our wrestlings, but with our sins. The dark clouds gather, and the Church and we should all be entering into our chambers, and shutting our doors upon us. "In that day sing ye unto her, A vineyard of red wine." His song will be with us in the dark night. May you and yours be hid in the day of the Lord's anger. A smile of his can lighten up a thunder cloud.

Read the xxix. Psalm, and meditate on the last
verse. Live near to God, and so all things will appear
to you little in comparison with eternal realities.

Ever yours, &c.

TO A STRANGER

Intended to lead on one whose face was Zionward, but who was not fully decided

DUNDEE, *July* 1840.

MY DEAR FRIEND,—I do not even know your name,
but your cousin has been telling me about your case,
and wishes me to write you a line inviting you to lay
hold on Jesus Christ, the only refuge for a perishing
soul. You seem to have been thinking seriously of
your soul for some time. Do remember the words of
Peter (2 Peter i. 10,) "Give diligence to make your
calling and election sure." Never rest till you can
say what John says, (1 John v. 19,) "*We know* that
we are of God." The world always loves to believe
that it is impossible to know that we are converted.
If you ask them, they will say, "I am not sure—I
cannot tell;" but the whole Bible declares we may
receive, and know we have received, the forgiveness
of sins. See Psalm xxxii. 1; 1 John ii. 12. Seek
this blessedness—the joy of having forgiveness; it is
sweeter than honey and the honey comb. But where
shall I seek it? In Jesus Christ. "God hath given
to us eternal life, and this life is in his Son." "He
that hath the Son, hath life, and he that hath not the
Son, hath not life," 1 John v. 10. Get deeply acquainted with yourself, your sins and misery. Most
people are like the Laodiceans, Rev. iii. 17. Even
those that are most deeply concerned about their souls
do not see the millionth part of the blackness of their
hearts and lives. O! if we could but put our sins
where God puts them, Psalm xc. 8, how we would cry
out, Unclean, unclean! Wo is me, for I am undone!
Have you ever discovered your lost condition? Many
know that they are great sinners, but where God is
teaching he will make you feel as an *undone* sinner.

Have you felt this? What things were gain to you, those do you count loss for Christ? Do you know that no human righteousness can cover you? In his holy, pure sight, all our righteousnesses are as filthy rags, Isaiah lxiv. 6. If you have been convinced of sin, have you been convinced of righteousness? John xvi. 8. Have you heard the voice of Jesus knocking at the door of your heart? Have you opened the door and let him in? Awfully momentous question! Your eternity depends upon the answer—yes or no. " He that hath the Son hath life, and he that hath not the Son hath not life." O! what a simple thing the gospel is! How fearful to think it is hid from so many, 2 Cor. iv. 3, 4. Jesus stands at your door willing to be your shield, Psalm lxxxiv. 9, 11—your righteousness, Jer. xxiii. 6—your all in all. Now, then, throw open the door and let him in. Accept his white raiment that you may be clothed. And, O! remember, if Christ justifies you he will sanctify you. He will not save you and leave you in your sins. Why did he get the name Jesus? Mat. i. 21. Here is a prayer for every one that has been found of Christ: " Order my steps in thy word, and let not any iniquity have dominion over me." Psalm cxix. 133. If you are redeemed, you are not your own—not the world's—not Satan's. Think of this when you are tempted to sin. Now, did I not say well that you should make your calling and election sure? O, beware of being a hypocrite—a mere professor, with an unholy heart and life. That your sister is on the road to Zion, I am glad, and pray that you may go hand in hand. Be diligent—the time is short. Try and persuade your friends to go with you. It is an awful thing to separate at the throne of Christ, for that will be for eternity. Pray much for the Holy Spirit to open your eyes—to soften your heart—to make Christ lovely and precious—to come and dwell in your hearts, and fit you for glory. Come to the living stone, and you will be built up as living stones, 1 Peter ii. 4, 5. O! how sweet to be made living stones in that glorious temple. Pray much in secret

Pray for ministers, that we may speak the word boldly. Christ is doing great things in our day, which should make us wrestle at a throne of grace. O that the Lord that was pierced with many thorns, might soon be crowned with many crowns!

Praying that you and your sister may both be saved, I am your friend in the gospel, &c.

TO MISS A. S. L.

The person and heart of Jesus—consolation to believers.

August 16, 1840.

MY DEAR FRIEND,—I fear I may not be able to see you for a little time, and therefore, think of sending you a few lines to minister a little of the peace and grace of the Lord Jesus to you. I hear that you are worse in health than when I saw you; still I have no doubt you can say, " It is well," " He doeth all things well." You remember Jacob said, when they wanted to take Benjamin away from him, " All these things are against me." Gen. xlii. 36. But in a little while he saw that all these things were working together for good to him. In a little while all his lost children were restored to him, and he and his seed preserved from famine. So will it be with you. If at any time unbelief steals over your heart—if you lose sight of Jesus, our Passover sacrificed for us—if you forget the hand of the all-tender, gracious Father of Jesus and of your soul—you will be crying out, All these things are against me. But, ah! how soon you will find that every thing in your history, except *sin*, has been *for* you. Every wave of trouble has been wafting you to the sunny shores of a sinless eternity. Only believe. Give unlimited credit to our God.

Think on Jesus when your mind wanders in search of peace—think where he came from—from the bosom of his Father. He was *from the beginning*. He is the life—the life of all that truly live. He is the eternal life which was with the Father. Let the beams of the divinity of Jesus shine in upon your soul. Think how he was manifested—God manifest in flesh —to be a surety for sinners. Made sin for us, although he knew no sin—made a curse for us. O, if I could declare him unto you, you might have fellowship with apostles, and with the Father, and with his Son Jesus Christ. These things will we write unto you, that your joy may be full. Other joys do not fill the heart. But to know the Lord Jesus as our surety, satisfies the soul; it brings the soul unto rest under the eye of our pardoning God. I met,* the other day, with a thought which has filled my heart often since. It is intended to explain that wonderful verse, John xiv. 18, I will not leave you orphans—I will come to you. Jesus, at the right hand of the Father, is yet present with all his younger brethren and sisters in this vale of weeping. His *human nature* is at the right hand of God upon the throne—a lamb as it had been slain. But his divine nature is unlimited, fills all worlds, and is present in every dwelling of every disciple in this world. His divine nature thus brings in continual information to his human heart of every thing that is going on in the heart and history of his people ; so that his human heart beats towards us just as if he were sitting by our side. Hence he cried to Saul, "Why persecutest thou me?"

Dear friend, do you feel that Jesus is your surety and elder brother? Then remember that, by reason of his real divinity, he is now by your bed side, afflicted in all your afflictions, touched with a feeling of your infirmities, and able to save you to the uttermost. He is as really beside you as he was beside Mary when she sat at his feet. Tell him all your sorrows, all your doubts and anxieties. He has a willing ear. O, what a friend is Jesus, the sinner's friend ! What an open ear he has for all the wants, doubts, difficulties of his people. He has an especial care of his sick, weakly, and dying disciples. You know how it is with a kind mother, even though a

* It was in a sermon by J. B. Patterson, of Falkirk.

worldly person. In a time of danger she clasps her children to her breast. In a time of health she may often let them wander out of her sight, but in hours of sickness she will *watch* beside their bed. *Much more* will Jesus watch over you.

I trust you feel real desire after complete holiness. This is the truest mark of being born again. It is a mark that he has made us meet for the inheritance of the saints in light. If a nobleman were to adopt a beggar boy, he would not only feed and clothe him, but educate him, and fit him to move in the sphere into which he was afterwards to be brought; and if you saw this boy filled with a noble spirit, you would say he is meet to be put among the children. So may you be made meet for glory. The farmer does not cut down his corn till it is ripe. So does the Lord Jesus: He first ripens the soul, then gathers it into his barn. It is far better to be with Christ than to be in Christ. For you to live is Christ, and to die is gain. Nevertheless, I trust God will keep you a little longer for our sake, that you may pray for us, and encourage us to work on in the service of Jesus till our change come. I began this letter about two weeks ago, and now send it away to you. I was called very suddenly to Edinburgh, and then sent to the north, and am just returned again, so that I did not get it sent away. I will try and see you this week, if it be the will of God. However, you must not be disappointed if I am prevented. I pray for you, that, according as your day is, so your strength may be. Keep your eye upon Jesus and the unsearchable riches that are in him; and may the gentle Comforter fill your soul, and give you a sweet foretaste of the glory that is to follow. May he leave his deep eternal impress upon your soul, not healing you and going away, but abiding within you, keeping the image of Christ in your heart, ever fresh and full—Christ in you the hope of glory. The Comforter is able to fill you with calmness in the stormiest hour. May he fill your whole soul, and transform you into a child of light. Good bye till we meet, if it be the Lord's will; if not in this world, at least before the throne, casting our crowns at his feet. Ever yours, in the gospel, &c.

TO THE REV. W. C. BURNS

Awakenings—Personal holiness in ministers.

DUNDEE, *September*, 1840.

MY DEAR BROTHER.—I have had a severe illness, or would have answered your kind note long before this. I fear you may have left Breadalbane before this can reach it; still I write in hope. You may be sure I ever follow you with my prayers and earnest longings of heart, that God may humble, purify, and make use of you to carry glad tidings of great joy to the inmost hearts of poor, guilty, perishing sinners, wherever you go. I have been much interested by all that I have heard of the good that has attended you in the north. I long to hear still more. The very name of Moulin stirs up the inmost depths of the heart, when I remember what great things the Lord Jesus did there of old. Do write to me when you have a moment, and stir me up. You know a word to a minister is worth a word to three or four thousand souls sometimes. Nothing stirs me up so much to be instant and faithful as hearing of the triumphs of the Lord Jesus in other places. I am glad and thankful to say that we are not left quite desolate. There have been evident tokens of the presence of the Spirit of God among my dear people many nights—more I think upon the Thursday nights than on the Sabbaths. Some I have met with seemingly awakened without any very direct means. A good number of young mill girls are still weeping after the Lord Jesus. I have been out of my pulpit only one Sabbath, and I hope to be back to it next Sabbath, if the Lord will.

What Mr. T. mentioned to you was true, of some having followed after an enthusiastic kind of man, who in my absence came among them. Doubtless Satan wanted to carry off some of the sheep, and succeeded so far. Still, I trust, it will end in good. Some have been a good deal humbled in the dust on account of it, and I have been roused up to cry for more knowledge how to guide them in the right way. I think, if strength were restored to me, I will try, in name of the Lord Jesus, to catechize through my parish. I ask your advice and prayers on this. If it could be conducted humbly, and with patience, and aptness to teach, I am persuaded it would tend to ground them more deeply in divine things. Hypocrites also might be denounced and warned, and the unconverted pointedly dealt with. I feel the immense difficulty of it in a town, and such a neglected, ignorant one as this. Still, if God be with me, who can be against me ?

Every thing I meet with, and every day I study my Bible, makes me pray more that God would begin and carry on a deep, pure, widespread, and permanent work of God in Scotland. If it be not *deep and pure*, it will only end in confusion, and grieving away the Holy Spirit of God by irregularities and inconsistencies. Christ will not get glory, and the country generally will be hardened, and have their mouths filled with reproaches. If it be not *widespread*, our God will not get a large crown out of this generation. If it be not *permanent*, that will prove its impurity, and will turn all our hopes into shame. I am much more afraid of Satan than I used to be. I learned a good deal by being with Cumming in Strathbogie.

I am also deepened in my conviction, that if we are to be instruments in such a work, we must be purified from all filthiness of the flesh and spirit. O, cry for personal holiness, constant nearness to God, by the blood of the Lamb. Bask in his beams—lie back in the arms of love—be filled with his Spirit—or all success in the ministry will only be to your own everlasting confusion.

You know how I have always insisted on this with you. It is because I feel the need thereof myself. Take heed, dear friend ; do not think any sin trivial ; remember it will have everlasting consequences. O to have Brainerd's heart for perfect holiness—to be holy as God is holy—pure as Christ is pure—perfect as our Father in heaven is perfect. O! what a cursed body of sin we bear, that we should be obliged by it to break these sweet gospel rules! How much more useful might we be, if we were only more free from pride, self-conceit, personal vanity, or some secret sin that our heart knows. O! hateful sins, that destroy our peace, and ruin souls!

But I must be done. I have not attained the full use of the pen. Go on, dear brother; but an inch of time remains, and then eternal ages roll on for ever—but an inch on which we can stand and preach the way of salvation to a perishing world. May he count us faithful, keeping us in the ministry. Ever yours, &c.

TO THE REV. PATRICK L. MILLER

Then labouring in Strathbogie: on his being elected minister of Wallacetown.

DUNDEE, *Sept.* 18, 1840.

MY DEAR FRIEND,—I cannot tell you how sincerely I thank God for the event of this evening. You are unanimously chosen minister of Wallacetown. I have already been on my knees to praise God for it, and to pray that you may be filled with the Holy Spirit for this glorious work. I hope you will see your way clear in leaving your attached people at Botriphnie. Make good use of your last days among them. Warn every man. Take each aside, and tell him you will be a witness against him at the last day if he do not turn and obey the gospel. The Lord give you a spiritual family in that place; and may you come to us in the fulness of the blessing of the gospel of Christ. I am persuaded the Spirit of God is still remarkably present in this town. You could not become a minister in a more blessed season, or in a more promising field. O pray to be fitted for the arduous work. I was just praying this morning over Matt. ix. 36—38 and little thinking that God was about to answer so graciously.

I have had a severe illness of late, and been taught to look more toward the Church above. But I am better, and my heart warms again towards the Lord's work below. Now, farewell! The Lord humble, empty, satisfy, and fill you—make you a Boanerges and a Barnabas, all in one. May the Lord arise and his enemies be scattered; and may poor parched Angus become like the garden of the Lord. Ever yours, &c.

—◆—

TO MR. GEORGE SHAW, BELFAST

Prophecies concerning Israel—Revival—Conduct of studies.

DUNDEE, *September 16th*, 1840.

MY DEAR FRIEND,—It gives me great joy to be able to answer your kind letter, although I fear you have almost despaired of me. In writing your esteemed pastor, I mentioned to him my intention of writing you very soon; but I have since then been laid down upon a sick bed by a severe feverish illness, from which I am now only recovering. Like you, my dear friend, God has seen it meet to train me often by the rod, and I have always found that he doeth all things well. Indeed, who would have his own health in his own guidance! Ah! how much better to be in his all-wise, all-powerful hand, who has redeemed us, and is making us vessels to hold his praise, now and in eternal ages. I have been only twice in the open air, and cannot yet manage the pen with facility; but I cannot delay writing to you any longer. You cannot tell how much real joy your letter gave me, when you tell me of the dear brethren who meet along with you on Monday mornings, to read and pray concerning Israel. This is, indeed, a delightful fruit of my short visit among you, for which I give humble and hearty thanks to Him who has stirred up your hearts in what I have felt, by experience, to be his own blessed cause. I feel deeply persuaded, from prophecy, that it will always be difficult to stir up and maintain a warm and holy interest in outcast Israel. The lovers and pleaders of Zion's cause will, I believe, be always few. Do you not think this is hinted at in Jer. xxx. 13? "There is none to plead thy cause that thou mayest be bound up." And again, ver. 14, "All thy lovers have forgotten thee; they seek thee not." And is not this one of the very reasons why God will at last take up their cause? See ver. 17, "I will restore health unto thee, because they called thee an outcast, saying, This is Zion whom no man seeketh after." It is a sweet encouragement also to learn, that, though the friends of Zion will probably be few, so that it may almost be said no one seeketh after her, yet there always will be some who will keep watch over the dust of Jerusalem, and plead the cause of Israel with God and with man. See Isa. lxii. 6, 7. If any of your company know the Hebrew, you will see at once the true rendering, " I have set watchmen *over* thy walls, O Jerusalem, which shall never hold their peace day nor night. *Ye that are the Lord's remembrancers*, keep not silence, and give him no rest till he establish and till he make Jerusalem a praise in the earth." O! my dear brethren, into whose hearts I trust God is pouring a scriptural love for Israel, what an honour is it for us, worms of the dust, to be made watchmen by God over the ruined walls of Jerusalem, and to be made the Lord's remembrancers, to call his own promises to his mind that he would fulfil them, and make Jerusalem a blessing to the whole world! Verse 1st is supposed to be the language of our Lord himself, our glorious advocate with the Father. O what an example does he set us of unwearied intercession! Verse 2d shows the great effect which the conversion of Israel will have on the Gentile world. Verse 3d shows how converted Israel will be a glorious diadem in God's hand, held out to show forth his praise. Verse 4th shows that it is *literal Israel* that is spoken of, for there is a sweet promise to *their land*.

I think you must take these two verses, 6, 7, as the motto of your praying society, not in boasting, but in all humility of mind, and with much self-upbraiding for the neglect of the past. Indeed, you will find it a difficult matter to keep your heart in tune really to desire the salvation of Israel, and the widely extended glory of the Lord Jesus. You must keep in close union to Jesus, and much in the love of God, and be much filled with the infinite, almighty Spirit of God. He will help your infirmities. It is when you feel the sweetness of the kingdom of God within you, that you will truly fall down on your knees and pray, " Thy kingdom come." The possession of grace fills us with very different feelings from the possession of anything else. A man who has much money is not very anxious that all the world should be rich—one who has much learning does not long that all the world were learned ; but if you have tasted the grace of the gospel, the irresistible longing of your hearts will be, O that all the world might taste its regenerating waters ! And if it be true, as I think it is, that God's method of bringing in the kingdom is to be by the salvation of Israel, how can an enlightened, gracious soul but pray, " Do good in thy good pleasure unto Zion ?"

As to the mode of studying prophecy, dear friend, I am far from being a capable adviser. My advice, however, is, that you begin with the simple and more unquestioned parts, and then advance to the more difficult ground. Begin with fulfilled prophecy—you will thus gain an intimate acquaintance with the language and manner of the prophetic writings. Then advance to the marks of unfulfilled prophecy, and cautiously and prayerfully to those parts that are obviously unfulfilled. This would be a most interesting course, and, if humbly followed out, cannot but give you great light and interest in the cause of Israel, and the world's conversion. For fulfilled prophecy, you might follow the guidance of Keith on Fulfilled Prophecy, or Bishop Newton, or both.

I am delighted to hear of the thank-offering you

mention. It is sweet when thankfulness does not end in mere words, but in gifts to God and devotedness of our all to Him. I am happy to say that the Lord's cause seems still to advance in Scotland. On the very day I arrived from Ireland we had very sweet tokens of the presence of the Spirit of God in the congregation, and many Thursday evenings since.

I have been in Strathbogie also, and seen some of the Lord's wonders there. He that hath the key of David has opened the door there, for the salvation of many souls. I am still as anxious as ever that God's work should be pure, and unmixed with error and satanic delusions; and therefore, when I pray for the revival of God's work, I always add that it may be pure and permanent. I have seen two awakened since I came home, with the use of hardly any means. If they shall turn out real conversions, I think I shall never despair of any.

I trust that your own studies get on well, dear friend. Learn much of your own heart, and when you have learned all you can, remember you have seen but a few yards into a pit that is unfathomable. Jer. xvii. 9: "The heart is deceitful above all things, and desperately wicked: who can know it?" Learn much of the Lord Jesus. For every look at yourself, take ten looks at Christ. He is altogether lovely. Such infinite majesty, and yet such meekness and grace, and all for sinners, even the chief. Live much in the smiles of God. Bask in his beams. Feel his all-seeing eye settled on you in love, and repose in his almighty arms. Cry after divine knowledge, and lift up your voice for understanding. Seek her as silver, and search for her as for hid treasure, according to the word in Prov. ii. 4. See that ver. 10, be fulfilled in you. Let wisdom *enter into your heart* and knowledge *be pleasant to thy soul;* so you will be delivered from the snares mentioned in the following verses. Let your soul be filled with a heart-ravishing sense of the sweetness and excellency of Christ, and of all that is in Him. Let the Holy Spirit fill every chamber of your heart; and so there will be no room for folly, or the world, or Satan, or the flesh. I must now commend you all to God and the word of his grace. My dear people are just assembled for worship. Alas! I cannot preach to them to-night. I can only carry them and you on my heart to the throne of grace. Write me soon. Ever yours, &c.

TO HIS SABBATH SCHOOL TEACHERS, DURING A WEEK OF ABSENCE FROM THEM

(Accompanied by notes on the Scripture Lesson that was to be taught in the classes that week.)

KELSO, *Feb. 24th*, 1841.

MY DEAR FRIENDS AND FELLOW-LABOURERS,—I send you a few notes on the parable for next Sabbath evening. May you find them profitable. You cannot tell what a sweet comfort it is to me, when I am so far distant from my flock, to know that you are in the midst of the lambs, speaking to God for them, and speaking to them for God. I thank my God without ceasing, for your work of faith, and labour of love, and patience of hope. Be not weary in well doing, dear friends, for in due season we shall reap, if we faint not. Do not be impatient—wait on the Lord. The blessing will come. Use a few spare half hours in seeking after the lambs on the week days. This will prove to the parents that you are in earnest. To bring one child to the bosom of Christ would be a reward for all our pains in eternity. O! with what glowing hearts we shall meet in heaven those whom God has used us as humble instruments in saving! Meditate on Phil. i. 9. And may the Lord meet with you and the lambs on Sabbath day, and bless you, and do you good.

Farewell, dear fellow-labourers. Ever your affectionate friend and pastor, absent in body, not in spirit, &c.

TO A SOCIETY IN BLAIRGOWRIE FOR DIFFUSING THE
KNOWLEDGE OF THE TRUTH

Advices

DUNDEE, *March* 27*th*, 1841.

MY DEAR FRIEND,—I was happy indeed, to receive
your letter, and the Rules of your Society, which interested me very much. I would have answered you
sooner, but have been laid down by my heavenly
Father on a bed of sickness, from which I am just
recovering by his grace. Spared fig trees should bear
much fruit; pray that it may be so with me. Luther
used to say, that "*temptations, afflictions,* and *prayer,*
made a minister." I do trust that your society may
be greatly blessed, *first,* in the comforting, enlivening
and sanctifying of your own souls, and *then* in the
bringing others to know the same fountain, where you
have found peace and purity. Let Jesus come into
your meetings and sit at the head of the table. It is
a fragrant room when the bundle of myrrh is the chief
thing there. Let there be no *strife* among you, but
who shall be the lowest at his feet, *who* shall lean
their head most fully on his breast. Let all your
conversation, meditations, and readings, lead you to the
Lamb of God. Satan would divert your minds away
to questions and old wives' fables, which gender strifes.
But the Holy Spirit *glorifies* Jesus—*draws* to Jesus—
makes you cleave to the Lord Jesus with full purpose
of heart. Seek advance of personal holiness. It is for
this the grace of God has appeared to you. See Titus,
ii. 11, 12. For this Jesus died—for this he chose you
—for this he converted you, to make you holy men,
living epistles of Christ—monuments of what God can
do in a sinner's heart. You know what true holiness
is. It is *Christ in you the hope of glory.* Let Him
dwell in you, and so all his features will shine in your
hearts and faces. O! to be like Jesus! This is heaven
wherever it be. I think I could be happy among
devils, if only the old man were slain in me, and I
was made altogether like Jesus. But, blessed be God,

we shall not be called to such a trial, for we shall not only be like Jesus, but be with Him to behold His glory. Pray to be taught to pray. Do not be content with old forms that flow from the lips only. Most Christians have need to cast their formal prayers away, to be taught to cry, Abba. Arrange beforehand what you are to pray for. Do not forget *confession of sin*, nor *thanksgiving*. Pray to get your closed lips opened in intercession—embrace the whole world and carry it within the veil. I think you might with advantage keep a small book in which you might mark down objects to be prayed for. I pray God to make you very useful in the parish and in the world. Do all things without murmurings and disputings; see Phil. ii. 14, 16. Live for eternity. A few days more and our journey is done. O! fight hard against sin and the devil. The devil never sleeps. Be you also active for good. The Lord bless you and your dear minister. Pray for us. Pray for the dead parishes round you. Ever yours, &c.

LETTERS TO A SOUL SEEKING JESUS —NO. I
Seek to know your corruption.

DUNDEE, 1841.

DEAR FRIEND,—According to promise I sit down to talk with you a little concerning the great things of an eternal world. How kind it is in God that he has given us such an easy way of communicating our thoughts, even at a distance. My only reason for writing to you is, that I may direct your soul to Jesus, the sinner's friend. "This man receiveth sinners." I would wish much to know that you were truly united to Christ, and then, come life, come death, you will be truly and eternally happy. Do you think you have been *convinced of sin?* This is the Holy Spirit's work, and his first work upon the soul (John xvi. 8; Acts ii. 37; xxi. 29, 30.) If you did not know your body was dangerously ill, you would never have sent for your physician; and so you will never go to Christ, the heavenly physician, unless you feel that your soul is sick even unto death. O! pray for deep discoveries of your real state by nature, and by practice. The world will say you are an innocent and harmless girl; do not believe it. The world is a liar. Pray to see yourself exactly as God sees you; pray to know the worth of your soul. Have you seen yourself *vile*, as Job saw himself? Job xi. 3, 5; xiii. 5, 6—undone, as Isaiah saw himself? Isa. vi. 1, 5. Have you experienced any thing like Psalm li.? I do not wish you to feign humility before God, nor to use expressions of self-abhorrence, which you do not feel; but, O pray that the Holy Spirit may let you see the very reality of your natural condition before God. I seldom get more than a glance at the true state of my soul in its naked self. But, when I do, then I see that I am wretched, and miserable, and poor, and blind, and naked; Rev. iii. 17. I believe every member of our body has been a servant of sin—Romans iii. 13, 18—throat, tongue, lips, mouth, feet, eyes. Every faculty of our mind is polluted; Gen. vi. 5. Besides, you have long neglected the great salvation; you have been gainsaying and disobedient. O! that you were brought to pass sentence upon yourself, *guilty of all.* Hear what a dear believer writes of himself—" My wickedness, as I am in myself, has long appeared to me perfectly ineffable, and swallowing up all thought and imagination, like an infinite deluge, or mountains over my head. I know not how to express better what my sins appear to me to be, than by heaping infinite upon infinite, and multiplying infinite by infinite. When I look into my heart, it looks like an abyss infinitely deep, and yet it seems to me that my conviction of sin is exceedingly small and faint." Perhaps you will ask, why do you wish me to have such a discovery of my lost condition? I answer, that you may be broken off from all schemes of self-righteousness; that you may never look into your poor guilty soul to recommend you to God; and that you may joyfully accept of the Lord Jesus Christ who obeyed and died for sinners. O! that your heart may cleave to Christ. May you forsake all and follow Jesus Christ. Count every thing loss for the excellency of the knowledge of Christ. You never will stand righteous before God in yourself. You are welcome this day to stand righteous before God in Jesus. Pray over Phil. iii. 7, 9. I will try and pray for you. Grace be with you. Your friend in Jesus, &c.

TO THE SAME —NO. II

Seek the righteousness of Christ.

DEAR FRIEND,—I was glad to hear of your safe arrival, and that your health had not suffered by the voyage. I trust the Lord is dealing gently with your frail body, so that your mind may get leave freely to fix itself on Jesus Christ and him crucified. Above all, I pray that the Holy Spirit may sweetly and silently open your heart, to relish the way of salvation through the blood and obedience of Immanuel. Through this man is preached unto you the forgiveness of sins, and by Him all that believe are justified from all things; Acts xiii. 38, 39. You would be deeply concerned to hear that your room mate —— has been so suddenly and awfully called away. Should it not be a solemn warning to you? O! that you may be even now clothed in the righteousness of Jesus! so that, if you were called away, you may meet God in peace, and hear Jesus say, " Enter thou into the joy of thy Lord." In yourself you never will stand righteous before Jehovah. Psalm cxliii. 2, answers your case. " Enter not into judgment with me," must be your cry. In your nature, in your past life, in your breaking of the holy law, in your contempt and neglect of Jesus, in your indwelling sin, God can see nothing but what he must condemn. O! that you would be of the same mind with God about your own soul. Do not be afraid to look upon its loathsomeness. For God offers to clothe you in Jesus Christ. Romans v. 19. By the obedience of *one* shall many be made righteous

There is only *one* in all the world on whose face God can look and say, "He is altogether lovely." Jesus is that one. Now God is willing that you and I should *hide in Jesus*. I feel at this moment that he is my righteousness. Jer. xxiii. 6. This is his name whereby he shall be called, "the Lord our righteousness." I feel that the love of God shines upon my guilty soul through Jesus. This is all my peace. Your tears will not blot out sin. They do nothing but weep in hell, but that does not justify them; your right views of the gospel will not justify you; you must be covered with a spotless righteousness. Your change of heart and of life will not justify you, it cannot cover *past sins*—neither is it perfect. Your amended life is still fearfully sinful in Jehovah's sight, and yet nothing but perfect righteousness can stand before him. Jesus offers you this perfect righteousness; in him you may stand and hear God say, "Thou art all fair, my love." There is no spot in him. Do you thus look to Jesus? Do you believe the record that God has given concerning him! Do you receive Christ with open arms? Do you cry, "My Lord and my God," my surety, my all? Dear friend, do not tarry. Eternity may be near. *Now* is your best time, perhaps your only time, of closing with Christ. How many worlds would a lost soul in hell give for such an opportunity of cleaving to Christ as you have now. "He that hath the Son, hath life." This is all my prayer and desire for your precious, precious soul. Ever yours, in the gospel, &c.

TO THE SAME —NO. III

Joy in believing.

DEAR FRIEND,—I send you another line to tell you Jesus is *the way*. I would like much to hear how your weak body prospers, and whether your soul is resting under the apple tree (Song ii. 3;) but till some opportunity occurs, I must just content myself

with committing your soul and body into the hand of
Jesus, your faithful Creator. 1 Pet. iv. 19. We are
now looking forward to another communion season,
and I am busy instructing young persons for that holy
and blessed ordinance. I think you said you were a
good deal impressed at our last communion, and
wished that you had been one of those seated at the
table; perhaps you may never be permitted to sit at
the table on earth; perhaps your first communion
may be in glory. There is a text in Romans xv. 13,
which expresses all my desire for you, "Now the God
of hope fill you with all joy and peace in believing,
that you may abound in hope, through the power of
the Holy Ghost." You see here who is the author
of conversion—"The God of hope." He must open
your heart to attend to the things that are spoken.
The truths that are presented to you will not convert
your heart; the God of hope must breathe on your
heart and water it oft. Then see how he gives you
joy and peace—"in believing." When Jesus revealed
himself to Thomas, (John xx. 28,) Thomas cried out
with joy, "My Lord and my God!" If Jesus reveal
himself to you in all the glory of his person—the
completeness of his work and the freeness of his love—
you too will be filled with appropriating joyful faith,
and will cry, "My Lord and my God!" It is a difficult thing to explain what it is to believe—I suppose
it is impossible. But when Jesus unveils his matchless beauty, and gives you a sweet glimpse of his
matchless face that was buffeted and spit upon, then
the soul joyfully clings to him. This is believing,
and this is joy and peace in believing. The truest,
purest joy flows from a discovery of Jesus Christ.
He is the hidden treasure that gives such joy to the
finder. Matt. xiii. 44. Do you think that you have
found that treasure? Touching question! for if not,
you are poor indeed. But how much joy may you
have in Christ? "The God of hope *fill* you with all
joy." You need not be afraid to take the full joy
that Jesus gives. If you really come unto Christ, you
come unto the love of Jehovah, and that is a filling

love. The love of the creature does not fill the heart, but God's love coming full upon the soul gives fulness of joy (1 John i. 4.) It is holy love—sovereign love. I have been interrupted several times in writing this little note. I will not be long in writing you again. Do decide the question of your eternity. One thing is needful; have you closed with the great Mediator? Have you got saving knowledge of Jesus? Then only will death lose its power, and the grave become the bed of peaceful rest.

> " There is a land of pure delight,
>   Where saints immortal reign ;
> Infinite day excludes the night,
>   And pleasures banish pain."

Lean all your care for time and eternity on Jesus; that is the softest of all pillows—the bosom of our guardian Immanuel. I am ever yours, &c.

TO THE SAME —NO. IV

Taste that Christ is precious.

December, 1841.

MY DEAR FRIEND,—It is written, " *Unto you who believe, he is precious,*" and if you are a child of God you will know and feel what the words mean. 1 Peter ii. 7. At one time Christ was " like a tender plant" to you, and like "a root out of a dry ground." You saw " no form nor comeliness in him, no beauty that you should desire him." At that time you were at ease in Zion—you had no concern for your soul. Do you remember that time? Is it otherwise with you now? Have you been pricked in your heart by the Holy Spirit? Have you been made to see how impossible it is for man to be just with God? and has the Spirit drawn away the veil from the fair face of Immanuel, and given you an unfeigned glance at the brow that was crowned with thorns, and the cheek from which they plucked off the hair? Has the Spirit opened a window into the heart of Jesus, and

let you see the fountain-head of that love that " passeth knowledge ?" Then you will be able to say, " To
me *he is precious*." If you see plainly that all your
standing before God is in him, that he is your foundation stone—your fountain—your wedding garment,
then you will feel him to be precious. Most people
refuse to come to Christ. Read Luke xiv. 16, 24.
They all with one consent began to make excuse.
Why is this ? Just because they do not see and feel
that he is precious. But, O ! if you, my dear friend,
feel that he is your only righteousness—your only
fountain of living water—your high priest—your
shepherd—your advocate ; then you will say, " *He is
precious*." You will never say, " Have me excused." I carry to you the sweet invitation, " Come,
for all things are now ready." Jesus is ready to
wash and clothe you in his own blood and righteousness. The Holy Spirit is ready to come into
your heart and make it new. The Father is ready to
put his arms round your neck and kiss you. Luke
xv. 20. The angels are ready to give thanks for you,
and to love you as a sister for eternity. Now, will
you come, for *all things are ready ?* Are you now
saying in your heart, " I cannot but believe I am the
chief of sinners, and Jesus offers to be my refuge, my
mediator, my all in all ; I feel he is precious?" O
dear friend, I trust you do. This only will make
you happy in living, and blessed in dying. This is a
poor dying world. Man that is born of woman is of
few days and full of trouble. There is no part here
that death cannot take from us. But if you have
Christ, you have the only imperishable portion ! O !
may the Holy Spirit give you a firm hold of Jesus.
Then we shall meet in that sweet place where there
shall be no more death, neither sorrow nor crying,
neither shall there be any more pain. The Lord
deal kindly and gently with you, both in soul and
body. Farewell, dear friend.

Ever yours, &c.

TO THE SAME —NO. V

Be found in Christ.

December 8th, 1841.

My Dear Friend,—I send you another line to tell you of Him who is altogether lovely. I have a very dear boy in my parish, who is dying just now. He said to me the other day, " I have just been feeding for some days upon the words you gave me, ' His legs are like pillars of marble set upon sockets of fine gold,' (Song v. 15;) for (said he) I am sure he is able to carry me and all my sins.' You may say the same, if your eyes have been opened to see the beauty, fulness, freeness, and compassion of the Lord Jesus. Nothing but the hand of God can open your eyes to see your lost condition as it truly is. Flesh and blood cannot reveal him unto you, but my Father. O ! call upon him to do this for you. A spiritual discovery of yourself and of Jesus is better than a million of worlds to you, and to me also. Remember, you cannot be fair in yourself before God. Song i. 6, must be all your prayer—*"Look not upon me."* Take yourself at your best moments, you are but a vile worm in Jehovah's sight, and so am I. Remember, you may be " perfect in Christ Jesus." Allow yourself to be found in Christ. O ! what will come of you if you are found in yourself? Where will you appear? You will shrink back, and call on rocks and mountains to fall upon you and cover you. But if you are hiding in Jesus—if your eye and heart are fixed upon his wounds made by our sins—if you are willing to be righteous in his righteousness—to lie down under the stream of his blood, and to be clothed upon with the snowy fleece of the Lamb of God—then God will love you with his whole soul exceedingly. The pure, full love of God streams through the blood and obedience of Jesus to every soul that is lying under them, however vile and wretched in themselves. Have you tried—have you tasted the holy love of a holy God? Thy love is better than wine. It is better than all creature love or creature enjoyments. O ! do not live, —O ! do not die, out of this sweet, sweet, sin-pardoning, soul-comforting, love of God ! Remember, Jesus is quite willing to gather you under his wings. Matt. xxiii. 37. Put that beyond all doubt. Remember also, the present is your only time to be saved. Eccles. ix. 10. There is no believing, no repenting, no conversion in the grave—no minister will speak to you there. This is the time of conversion. We must either gain you now, or lose you for ever. O ! that you would use this little time. Every moment of it is worth a world. Your soul is very dear to me— dearer far to Jesus. Look to him and you will be saved. Ever yours, &c.

THE SAME —NO. VI

Go up, leaning on Jesus.

I have heard of you from ——, and have been praying for you, that your eye may rest on Jesus, and that your soul may lie in perfect peace under his blood shed for the sins of many. I have been thanking my Father, too, for dealing so bountifully with you. " He is the Father of mercies, and the God of all comforts." I will give you a sweet verse to meditate upon. " Who is this that cometh up from the wilderness, leaning upon the beloved ?" Song viii. 5. Do you think this is your position ? Truly this world is a wilderness if you have seen it rightly. It is a place of guilt and shame. Every natural heart is a wilderness—a dead place without a drop of living water—and then all natural hearts put together make up a wilderness world. The whole world lieth in wickedness. There are few that know and love Jesus, and these few are panting to get more of the living water. But if you have truly fled to Jesus, you are coming up from the wilderness. Now is our salvation nearer than when we believed. " The night is far spent, the day is at hand." Have you found Jesus truly ? Do you feel willing to be all vile, all hell-deserving in yourself, and to let God's dear Son be all your shield and righteousness? O! make sure of this. Never mind what *man* thinks of you. I would not give a straw for the opinions of men as to whether I was safe or no. It is not what man thinks of us that will cover us in the judgment day. O no! You must be in Jesus, sitting at his feet, allowing him to wash your stains away, allowing him to enwrap your guilty soul in divine righteousness. If you were lying at the bottom of the sea, no eye could see your deformities; so when the infinite ocean of Immanuel's righteousness flows over the soul, you are swallowed up as it were in Christ. Your blackness is never seen, only his fairness; and thus a God of truth can say, " Behold thou art fair; behold thou art fair my love. Thou art all fair my love; there is no spot in thee." Song iv. 1–7. Keep this always in memory; and when guilt comes on the conscience, as it will, lie down again beneath the righteousness of Jesus. Never lose sight of this. Jesus must be seen by the Father, instead of our guilty soul. It is no change in our black soul that is to be our covering. You must leave self, and stand in your elder brother. Hide behind him. Let the Father's eye fall on him, not on you. This is what Jesus wants. He died to be a shelter for such as you. This is what the Father wants; for he is not willing that any should perish. If you are seen by the Father a naked guilty sinner, you must die. There is no help for it. But if Jesus appears for you—if you hide in his wounds like the dove in the cliffs of the rock, and under his snowy raiment—then the Father himself loveth you, and now you are coming up from the wilderness. Every hour that strikes, that is an hour less between you and glory. O! do not grieve to part with the world if you are in Christ—an hour with Christ will make up for all your griefs and pains. Half an hour in the presence of our God will make us forget a lifetime of agony. " Leaning on her beloved!" Is this the position of your soul? Do you feel empty, weak, and helpless; and do you see Him mighty to save, able to save to the uttermost? His legs are like pillars of marble. This is Christ's glory, that he justifies sinners who have no righteousness, and sanctifies souls that have no inborn holiness. Let Jesus bear your whole weight. Remember he loves to be the only support of the soul. He is a jealous Saviour. He wants to be entirely trusted. There is nothing that you can possibly need but you will find it in him. *"All my springs are in thee."* Do you want righteousness? He has the spirit of a weaned child to give you; Ps. cxxxi. Do you want love? he is the fountain of love; all the promises of God in him are yea and in him amen. I am sure if you get a glimpse of him you would lay your head on his breast and die there. May the Spirit anoint your eyes to see him more and more, and soften your heart to lean on him. Those that have leaned on him through the wilderness shall sit with him on the throne. Rev. iii. 21. Farewell, dear soul! the Lord feed you sweetly, as he feeds the flowers, by silent drops of dew. Ever yours, &c.

TO M. S.

Trying dispensations.

DUNDEE, *February* 28, 1841.

DEAR FRIEND,—I have heard from J. S. of your brother's death, and I write a line to comfort you. There is no true comfort to be found but in Christ. He is a fountain of living waters, and you must go with your thirsty soul to him and drink. John vii. 37; Psa. lxiii. If your brother died in the Lord, then he is far better than if he were here. Phil. i. 23. If he died out of the Lord, you must be like Aaron when "he held his peace." Lev. x. 3. Be not moved by these afflictions, knowing that you were appointed thereunto. Seek more and more abiding peace in Christ. He is not only a Saviour, but a sympathizing elder brother.

Read the xi. of John, and Lamentations iii., and you will see what a compassionate bosom Christ has. Lean your head more and you will find rest. "Do not despise the chastening of the Lord." Inquire what change he would have wrought in you and in all your friends. Are there any who need to be awakened? let them listen to this warning. Are there any who need to be brought off from love of the world? let them hear the voice of God from your brother's grave, saying, "What shall it profit a man though he gain the whole world and lose his own soul?" Your brother, though dead, still speaketh. To you he says, "Lean on the beloved as you come up out of the wilderness. The Lord is at hand." Keep your eye fixed on Jesus. Pray much for his Spirit and likeness; and be ready for his coming.

Our communion is on Sabbath next. Your friend J. thought you would perhaps love to be here. Farewell for the present; may the Lord Jesus be very near you to comfort, and sanctify, and bless you. Ever yours, &c.

TO E. R., ASKING COUNSEL

A sight of corruption drives to Christ.

DUNDEE, 1842.

DEAR FRIEND,—I send you a hurried line, and may the Spirit accompany it with his divine power to your heart! It is a good thing to be shown much of the deceitfulness and desperate wickedness of your heart, provided it lead you to the Lord Jesus, that he may pardon and subdue it. Slightness and carnal ease are much more to be dreaded than discoveries of our leprosy.

The groans and triumphal song of a believer are not far separated, as you may see in Paul—Rom. vii. 24, 25—"O wretched man," and "I thank God," all in one breath. David felt the same—see lxxiii. Psalm. At one verse he feels himself a fool and a beast in the sight of a holy God, and in the very next verse he is cleaving to Christ with a song of unspeakable joy; ver. 22—24 Ah, there is a sweet mystery here—bitter herbs along with our passover Lamb. It is sweet to see ourselves infinitely vile, that we may look to Jehovah our righteousness, as all our way to the Father.

The sweet Psalmist of Israel felt this on his dying bed—2 Sam. xxiii. 5—" Although my house be *not so* with God, yet hath he made with me," &c. His house had been the scene of many a black sin; and now, when dying, he could not but confess that it was not right with God. Not a day he had lived appeared clean—not a moment. So may you say in the house where you live, and looking at the pollutions of your own heart, " Although my house be not so with God"—although my heart and life be not so, yet hath he made with me an everlasting covenant, ordered in all things and sure.

God makes that covenant with you, when he brings you to lay hold on Jesus as your surety—your curse-bearing, law-fulfilling surety. Then you are brought into the bond of the everlasting covenant, and all its blessings are yours—pardon, righteousness, consolation, grace upon grace life, love, the spirit of supplications—all are yours, and you are Christ's, and Christ is God's.

Pray to be made like Caleb, who had another spirit, and followed the Lord fully. Follow Christ all the day. He is the continual burnt-offering in whom you may have peace. He is the Rock that follows you, from whom you may have constant and infinite supplies. Give yourself wholly away to him. You are safe in no other keeping but in the everlasting arms of Jehovah Jesus.

Keep yourself from other men's sins. Do not go *to the end of the string*—that is, going as far as you can in dallying with temptation without committing open sin. Remember that it is our happiness to be under grace, and every sin will be bitterness in the end, and will take something out of your eternal portion of glory.

Grace be with your dear and much honoured minister, and with all that love Christ in sincerity. Never cease to pray for the parish, and for all parishes, that God would pour down his life-giving Spirit, to the conversion of perishing sinners and the glory of his own great name. I will remember you on the 12th of June.

May the Lord remember us.   Ever truly, &c.

———◆———

TO J. T.

A young boy anxious about his soul.

COLLACE, *Jan.* 27, 1842.

MY DEAR BOY.—I was very glad to receive your kind note, and am glad to send you a short line in return, although my time is much taken up.   You are very dear to me, because your soul is precious ; and if you are ever brought to Jesus washed, and justified, you will praise him more sweetly than an angel of light.   I was riding among the snow to-day, where no foot had trodden, and it was pure, pure white ; and I thought again and again of that verse, " *Wash me and I shall be whiter than snow.*"   That is a sweet prayer—make it your own.   Often go alone, and look up to Jesus, who died to wash us from our sins, and say, " *Wash me.*"   Amelia Geddie was one day dressed in a new white frock, with red ribbons in her bonnet, and some one said to her, " No doubt you will think yourself very trim and clean ?"   " Ah no," she said, " *I will never think that until I have the fine white robe of my Redeemer's righteousness put upon me.*" I am glad, my dear boy, you think that God is afflicting you to bring you to himself.   It is really for this that he smites you.   His heart, his hand, and his rod, are all inscribed with love.   But then, see that he does bring you *to himself.*   Do not delay.   The lake of fire and brimstone stretches beneath every soul that lives in sin.   There is no peace, saith my God, to the wicked.   If the Lord Jesus would but draw the curtain and let you see his own fair face, and his wounded side, and how there is room for the guiltiest sinner in him, you would be drawn to Jesus with the cords of love. I was preaching in Perth last Sabbath; when I came out a little girl came up to me, I think about three or four years old. She wanted to hear of the way to be saved. Her mother said she had been crying the whole night before about her soul, and would take no comfort till she should find Jesus. O! pray that the same spirit may waken you. Remember, Johnnie, you once wept for your soul too, and prayed and sought Jesus. Have you found him? or have you looked back, like Lot's wife, and become a hard, cold pillar of salt? Awake again and call upon the name of the Lord. Your time may be short, God only knows. The longest lifetime is short enough. It is all that is given you to be converted in. They are the happiest who are brought soonest to the bosom of Jesus.

Write me again. At present I must draw to a close. Give my kindest remembrances to your mamma, and to A. when you write. Tell him to write me. May you all meet at the table of Jesus above, and may I be there too, a sinner saved by grace. Ever yours, &c.

TO A. T.

On the death of his brother, the little boy to whom the preceding letter was written.

St. Peter's, *March* 1, 1842.

My Dear A.—I did not think I was to have answered your kind letter, in the time of bitter grief. But so it pleases Jehovah, whose will must be our will, if we would be happy. It is good for you to bear the yoke in your youth. This is the way God trains his saints, and especially his ministers. I saw your dear little brother twice on his dying bed, and indeed I could not believe he was dying, except that his calm eye was directed to the hills of immortality, and he seemed already to breathe some of the atmosphere of the world of sinless joy. I do trust and believe that he was a saved boy. You know I am rather slow of coming to this conviction, and not fond of speaking when I have not good evidence; but here, I think, God has not left us in doubt.

At Blairgowrie he used several times to speak to me about divine things, and the tear would gather in his eye when he said that he feared he had never been brought to Jesus. Once, when he had a sore throat, he told me he was not ready to die. But now he was quite different. The veil seemed to be lifted away from his heart, and he saw divine things simply and fully.

Over and over he told me that he was not afraid to die, for Christ had died. "How kind it was in God to send Jesus to die for sinners." He seemed tranquil and happy, even when the pain came on in his head and made him knit his brows. You have reason to mingle praise with your tears. Do not sorrow as one who has no hope. Only seek a right improvement of this bereavement. He is not lost but gone before, and we shall soon put off this clay cottage also. And soon we and he, made new, body and soul, shall meet the Lord in the air, and so be forever with the Lord. I was at your house on Sabbath night, and saw them all, sorrowful, yet rejoicing. Your dear little brother lies like a marble statue in the peaceful sleep of death, till Jesus' voice shall waken him. Happy boy! he shall hunger no more, neither thirst any more, neither shall the sun light on him, nor any heat. The days of his mourning are ended, and his eternity of love and holy joy is begun.

Improve this sharp wind, dear A., for you will soon lose the benefit, if not carefully sought after. Search out the Achan in your heart at such an hour. Let affliction strike heavy blows at your corruptions, your idolatries, and self-pleasing, and *worldly schemes.* Learn much of Christ at such an hour. Study him at the grave of Lazarus—John xi.; and at the gate of Nain—Luke viii. 11; and also within the veil—Rev. i. 18. Do not be ashamed to grieve deeply, but let your sadness find relief in the bosom that was pierced with the spear.

" Is any afflicted ? let him pray." Strange, Satan often tempts us to restrain prayer at such a time. Be very gentle towards the souls of your kindred now.

Remember D—— and R—— at the throne of grace. If God had taken them, where would they have been? Learn also that ministers must care for lambs. " Preach the gospel to every creature."

Pray for me, also, that I may do so, that I may be made a better man and a more faithful pastor of old and young. Ever yours, till we meet in glory, &c.

TO REV. D. CAMPBELL, OF LAWERS

Advice to a brother in sickness.

MY DEAR BROTHER,—Like yourself, I have been laid aside from the work of the ministry for two Sabbaths, but am now recovering.

I am truly afflicted to hear of your trouble, and yet I pray it may turn out to the furtherance of the gospel. The time of my absence from my flock in 1839 was more blessed to my people than even my presence had been. Our God can work through means or above them. He that puts the treasure into earthen vessels, often allows the vessels to be chipped and broken, that the excellency of the power may be of God and not of us. Fear not for your flock. The Chief Shepherd who sent you to them is faithful, and his name is the Mighty God. He can feed them with or without you. And none that are his can perish.

Use all prudent means for your recovery. Commit yourself entirely to God, and he will turn the shadow of death into the morning. I have been often brought very low, but it has been always good for me. In this way God educates his ministers, both for his temple below, and for being pillars in the temple above.

I do not think Broughty Ferry a safe place for you, if your lungs are at all affected. The air is damp, and east wind cold. If it is only your stomach that ails, then it will do well; but if you have any chest complaint, do not think of the east coast. Blairgowrie would be much more suitable; where you would have the kind care of a good Christian doctor, and the ministry of dear R. M.

I fear my illness will prevent me leaving home this summer; but I do not know. Your absence will make us pray more that your flock may not be forgotten.

Do not be afraid at leaving home. His compassions are new every morning. Great is his faithfulness. He doth not afflict willingly.

All grace be with you from the fountain of living waters. Ever yours, &c.

TO THE REV. H. BONAR, KELSO

Ministerial arrangements—Breathings after holiness.

August 18th, 1842.

MY DEAR HORACE,—I laid aside your note, and cannot find it again. I think you ask me for the second Sabbath in November, on my way back from London. I fear I must not do it, but abide by my former arrangement. Mr. Hamilton presses me hard to stay two Sabbaths, and I would have agreed, but am to elect elders on the second Sabbath of November. According to a new law of the church, the signed lists are read in a meeting of session on the third Sabbath after the intimation is given, so that I will need to be back, even though I should need to be in Edinburgh the week after. If spared then, I shall hold to our former arrangement.

We have had a very sweet season here during the concert, which was also our communion week. Andrew, Candlish, Cormick, Cumming, Milne, and Graham, from Ireland, all assisted me. We had meetings every morning.

Your scheme was very helpful; I enclose mine. About seven hundred people attended each morning;

and on the fast-day, and Sabbath too. Several souls have been deeply awakened.

I have great desire for personal growth in faith and holiness. I love the word of God, and find it sweetest nourishment to my soul. Can you help me to study it more successfully? The righteousness of God is all my way to the Father, for I am the chief of sinners; and were it not for the promise of the Comforter, my soul would sink in the hour of temptation.

Did you observe that the Charlinch revival took place in the week of the concert for prayer last year?

The trials of the Church are near. May we be kept in the shadow of the Rock. Farewell! May Jesus shine on you. Yours, &c.

TO THE REV. R. MACDONALD, BLAIRGOWRIE

Inward life—Words of counsel.

DUNDEE, 1842.

MY DEAR FRIEND,—This is Friday evening, and I do not know what to preach on Sabbath next, else I would have written you at greater length; but as I am to see you so soon face to face, there is the less need of communing with ink and pen.

I hope your health keeps good, and your labours abundant—that you have a continued interest in the blood which speaketh peace—a sense of forgiveness and acceptance in the beloved—that you feel "his right hand under your head," and the power of his indwelling Spirit dwelling in you and walking in you. These sweet experiences alone make the minister's life calm and serene, like this autumnal evening. Ah, how easy it is to speak or write about them. What a different thing to feel them. It is my constant desire, and yet I am constantly disappointed. I think I never was brought to feel the wickedness of my heart as I do now. Yet I do not feel it as many sweet Christians do, while they are high above it, and seem to look down into a depth of iniquity, deep, deep in their bosoms. Now, it appears to me as if my feet were actually in the miry clay, and I only wonder that I am kept from open sin. My only refuge is in the word, "I will put my Spirit within you." It is only by being made partakers of the *divine nature* that I can escape the corruption that is in the world through lust.

All things go on here much as they did. I cannot say that my sermons are much shorter, though I have tried to shorten them. My meeting is still the hour and half, nor do I see how I can shorten it. It is very well attended. A stranger started up and prayed one evening. I did not interrupt him, or take notice of it, but have though it best to forbid it. None but ordained servants should speak in churches.

I hope you have got all your preparations well forward. Deal faithfully by all that speak to you for the communion, especially the young. If you would have a clear conscience, none but those who are seeking really to close with Jesus Christ should be allowed to take the bread and wine, if a word of yours can help it.

Be decided in keeping back the scandalous. Stir up your elders to this. They are very apt to be remiss. May you have much grace given you at this time and peace—droppings of the Spirit, and refreshings of peace in the heart. I invite all who have any wish to speak to their minister before communicating, to do so. May you have much fruit at this time that shall appear many days hence. I have been surprised to find even a poor table service blessed. Expect much, and much will be given. Pray for me, for I am all but desolate.

Yours faithfully, &c.

TO ONE OF HIS FLOCK, WHO HAD BEEN APPOINTED TO THE CHARGE OF A FEMALE SCHOOL IN THE COUNTRY

Do what you can.

COLLACE, *July 25th*, 1842.

DEAR FRIEND,—I have been laid aside for a short time, and did not receive your letter till it was too late to send the communicant's line, which you desired. I have no doubt Mr. B. would give you a token, however, even without a line. I am truly glad to hear that you are so fully employed, and earnestly trust that your labours may be owned by God. Souls are perishing every day, and our own entrance into eternity cannot be far distant. Let us, like Mary, " do what we can," and no doubt God will bless it, and reward us openly. Sit under a living ministry if you can. Seek much personal holiness and likeness to Christ in all the features of his blessed character. Seek to be lamb-like; without which all your efforts to do good to others will be as sounding brass or a tinkling cymbal.

Pray for dear St. Peter's that the dew may never cease to fall there; continue in prayer and watch in the same with thanksgiving. Ever truly, &c.

TO ONE AWAKENED

Call upon a soul to choose Jesus.

DUNDEE, *Sept.* 1842.

MY DEAR G.—I was glad indeed to see by the line you sent me, that though your mind is dark and troubled you have not gone back to the world. Ah, it is a false deceiving world. It smiles only to betray. Fain would I lead you to taste the peace that passeth understanding, and that is to be found only in Jesus. You are quite wrong in thinking that I do not understand your misery. I know it well. It is true Jesus does give me peace. He washes me from all sin in his own blood. I often feel him standing by my side and looking down upon me, saying, "thou art mine." Yet still have I known more misery than you. I have sinned more deeply than you. I have sinned against more light and more love, and yet I have found mercy; why may not you? Remember what James Covey said: "Tell poor sailors that none of them need to despair, since poor blaspheming Covey found mercy." I was interrupted just while writing this, by a very little girl coming to ask, "what must I do to be saved?" Poor thing, she has been weeping till I thought her heart would break. She lives several miles off, but a companion was awakened and told her, and ever since she has been seeking Christ with all her heart. I was telling her that sweet verse, 1 Tim. i. 15 : "Christ Jesus came into the world to save sinners, of whom I am the chief." It will answer you also, dear friend. Christ Jesus was God's dear Son. He made all things, sun, moon, and stars, men, and angels. He was from all eternity in the bosom of the Father, and yet he came into the world. He did not say, "I will keep my throne and my happiness, and leave sinners to die and perish in their sins." No; "He came into the world." He became a babe, and was laid in a manger, for there was not room in the inn. The inn was like your heart; it was filled with other lodgers, and had no room for Jesus. He became "a man of sorrows and acquainted with grief." He bore our sins upon his own body on the tree. While we were sinners, "Christ died for us." Why did he do all this? Ah! it was "to save sinners." Not to save good people—not to save angels—but sinners. Perhaps you will say, "but I am too bad a sinner;" but Paul says, "of whom I am the chief." Paul was the chief of sinners, and yet he was saved by Christ. So Christ is willing and able to save you though you were the chief sinner on the face of the earth. If Christ came into this world and died to save such as you, will it not be a fearful thing if you die without being saved by him? Surely you have lived long enough without Christ. You have despised Jesus long enough. What has the world done for you, that you love it so much? Did the world die for you? Will the world blot out your sins or change your heart? Will the world carry you to heaven? No, no! You may go back to the world, if you please, but it can only destroy your poor soul. "She that liveth in pleasure is dead while she liveth," 1 Timothy v. 6. Read these words in your Bible, and mark them, and if you go back, that mark will be a witness against you before the great white throne, when the books are opened. Have you not lived long enough in pleasure? Come and try the pleasures of Christ—forgiveness and a new heart. I have not been at a dance or any worldly amusement for many years, and yet I believe I have had more pleasure in a single day than you have had all your life. In what? you will say. In feeling that God loves me—that Christ has washed me—and in feeling that I shall be in heaven when the wicked are cast into hell. "A day in thy courts is better than a thousand;" Psalm lxxxiv. 10.

I do not know what is to be the result of your anxieties. I do not know whether you will be drawn to Christ, or driven back into the whirlpool of a perishing world; but I know that all will soon be settled for eternity. I was in a very wicked family to-day, where a child had died. I opened my Bible, and explained this verse to them over the coffin of their little one, Heb. ix. 27, "It is appointed unto men once to die, but after this the judgment." Solemn words! we have only once to die, and the day is fixed. If you die wrong the first time, you cannot come back to die better a second time. If you die without Christ, you cannot come back to be converted and die a believer—you have but once to die. O! pray that you may find Christ before death finds you. "After this the judgment." Not, after this purgatory. No farther opportunity to be saved—"after this the judgment." As death leaves you, so judgment finds you. If you die unsaved, you will be so in *the judgment*. May I never see you at the left hand! If I do, you will remember how I warned you, and prayed for you, and besought you to come to the Lord Jesus.

Come to Jesus—he will in no wise cast you out. Your affectionate friend, &c.

TO A SOUL INQUIRING AFTER JESUS

The wise men—Guilt in us, righteousness in Jesus.

St. Peter's, *Monday, Sept. 18th,* 1842.

My Dear C.—I do not and cannot forget you, and, though it is very late, I have to write you a few lines to say, follow on to know Jesus. I do not know if you can read my crooked writing, but I will make it as plain as I can. I was reading this morning, Luke ii. 29, what old Simeon said when he got the child Jesus into his arms—" Now lettest thou thy servant depart in peace, according to thy word: for mine eyes have seen thy salvation." If you get a firm hold of the Lord Jesus, you will be able to say the same.

If you had died in your ignorance and sin, dear soul, where would you have been this night? Ah! how shall we sufficiently praise God if he really has brought you to the blood of the Lord Jesus Christ! Psalm xxxvi. 12, 13, will suit your case. If you all are really brought to Christ, it will be something like the case of the wise men of the east. Matt. ii. When they were in their own country, God attracted their attention by means of a star. They followed it, and came to Jerusalem, saying, " Where is he that is born King of the Jews? for we are come to worship him." Herod and Jerusalem were troubled at the saying. No one was seeking Christ but themselves. The world thought they were mad; but soon they saw the star again, and it led them to the house where the infant Saviour lay—his robe of state a swaddling band—his cradle the manger. Yet they kneeled down and called him, " my Lord and my God"—they got their own souls saved—and gave him gifts, the best they had, and then departed into their own country with great joy in their hearts, and heaven in their eye. So may it be with you. The most around you care not for Jesus. But you are asking, "Where is he?—we are come to be saved by him." None around you can tell. They think you are going out of your mind. But God is leading you to the very spot where the Redeemer is—a lowly, despised, spit-upon, crucified Saviour. Can this be the Saviour of the world? Yes, dear soul; kneel down and call him your Redeemer. He died for such as you and I. And now you may go away into your own country, again, but not as you came. You will carry with you joy unspeakable and full of glory. A young woman called upon me on Wednesday last, whom I had never seen before. She said she was a stranger from another part of Scotland; she came to this town about a year ago, and attended St. Peter's, and there, for the first time, learned that she was a sinner and needed Christ. About four weeks ago she found rest and joy at the Saviour's feet. I said to her, "Then you will bless God that he brought you from your own country to this place." She said, "I often do that." Another woman came the same evening, whom I had never seen. She said she had been married eight years to a wicked husband. One of her neighbours had brought her to our church, and now she feels that Christ has saved her soul.

Thus the work goes on—"The Lord added to the church daily such as should be saved." A young woman was with me to-night in great distress. She said, "I have a wicked heart within me that would sink a world." I said, "I am thankful to hear you complain of your wicked heart, dear friend, it is unsearchably wicked. There is not a sin committed on earth or in hell but has its spring and fountain in your breast and mine. You are all sin—your nature is sin—your heart is sin—your past life is sin—your prayers are all sin." O! that you would despair of being righteous in yourself. Then take the Lord Jesus for your righteousness. In him is no sin. And he stood for us, and offers to be your shield, your way to the Father. You may be righteous in Christ with a perfect righteousness, broad as the law, and pure as the light of heaven. If you had an angel's righteousness, you might well lay it down and put on Jesus. The robe of a blood-washed sinner is far whiter than that of an angel. Do not fear the frown of the world. When a blind man comes against you in the street, you are not angry at him; you say, He is blind, poor man, or he would not have hurt me. So you may say of the poor world, when they speak evil of Christians—they are blind. If they knew their sin, and misery, and the love of Jesus, they would cleave to him also. Fear not them which kill the body, and after that have no more that they can do. Keep close to the Lord Jesus. He is greater than all that can be against you—he is the Shepherd of his sheep—he will defend you from wolves. Pray for the Holy Spirit, dear friend. Ask him to come into your heart, and abide there. It is a mean dwelling for such a guest. Still he will make it clean and holy by dwelling in it. Ask him to teach you to pray; Rom. viii. 26, 27. He will give you "groanings that cannot be uttered." Ask him to change your heart and make it like that of Jesus. Ask him to write the law upon your heart, and to keep you in every time of need. I fear you are weary of my long sermons. Remember, if you are not saved, I will be a witness against you in the judgment day.

> Come, ye weary, heavy laden,
> Lost and ruined by the fall;
> If you tarry till you're better,
> You will never come at all.
> Not the righteous—sinners Jesus came to call.

Farewell! Write me soon all your heart.

Ever yours, till glory, &c.

TO THE SAME

Trials from a blind world—How the death of Christ is an atonement.

LONDON, *Nov. 5th*, 1842.

MY DEAR C.—I pray for you, that your faith may not fail. Hold fast by Jesus for a little while, and then we shall be for ever with the Lord, where the unbelieving will never be. I got safely up to town without stopping. The young man in the coach with us was Lord P. He and I were alone all night in the railway carriage, and I would fain have told him the way to be saved, but when morning dawned I lost him. I preached twice on Thursday, and once last night, and now I am preparing for to-morrow. I feel like John the Baptist, a voice of one crying in the wilderness. The mad world presses on like a bird hasting to the snare. They do not know that the dead are there, and her guests are in the depths of hell.

I thank God without ceasing when I remember you all—how God opened your eyes and hearts, and made you flee from the wrath to come and believe the record which God hath given concerning his Son. "Fear none of those things which thou shalt suffer." "Be thou faithful unto death, and I will give thee a crown of life;" Rev. ii. 10. Do not be surprised if worldly people mock you, and say all manner of evil against you falsely. Jesus told you it would be so. "If you were of the world, the world would love its own." You have been long enough of the world. Did the world ever hate you then? So now, when you have come out from among them, and are cleaving to Jesus, do you think they will love you? Remember Jesus loves you. God is for you, and who can be against you? Remember, all who have gone to heaven before you suffered the same things; see Rev. vii. 14, "These are they that came out of great tribulation."

You wish to understand more about Christ's death being an atonement. I shall try and explain. The curse which Adam by his sin brought upon us all,

was this, " Thou shalt surely die;" Gen. ii. 17. This
included the death of the body, the death of the soul,
and the eternal destruction of both in hell. This is
the curse that hangs over every unpardoned sinner.
And our sins have only added certainty and weight to
the awful curse, for the " wages of sin is death."
Now, when the Son of God said he would become
our Surety and Saviour, the Father said, " Thou must
die for them;" see John x. 17, 18. " I lay down my
life." " This commandment have I received from my
Father." It is true, Christ did not suffer eternal destruction in hell; but he was a person so glorious and
excellent—God's own Son—that his short sufferings
were equal in value to our eternal agonies. So that,
in the eye of law, and in God's account, Jesus has
suffered all that you and I were condemned to suffer.
Hence that sweet, sweet passage, Isa. xl. 1, 2, " Comfort ye, comfort ye, * * * for she hath received
(in Christ) of the Lord's hand double for all her sins."
Christ's dying for us is as much in God's account as
if we had twice over borne the eternal agonies of hell.
Hence that sweet song which God enable you and G.
to sing, Isa. xii. 1, " I will praise thee ; though thou
wast angry with me, thine anger is turned away, and
thou comfortedst me." Hence also that triumphant
question, Rom. viii. 34, " Who is he that condemneth?
It is Christ that died."

Keep looking then to Jesus, dear soul, and you will
have the peace that passeth all understanding. Whenever Satan accuses you, send him to the stripes of the
Lord Jesus. Deal gently and tenderly with your unconverted friends. Remember you were once as blind
as they. " He was despised, and WE esteemed him
not ;" Isa. liii. Honour your mother in the Lord.
Give her all reverence and obedience in things not
sinful. Ask —— to read and pray over Matt. xviii. 3, 6.
I would love much to visit the cottage on my return, but I fear I shall be kept in town till Friday,
so that I must travel night and day home. The Lord
bless you, and keep you cleaving to Christ the true
vine. You have found the pearl of great price. Go

and sin no more. "If any man draw back, my soul shall have no pleasure in him." God is able to keep you from falling. In his dear arms I leave you. Yours, &c.

TO A SOUL THAT HAD BEGUN TO SEE CHRIST

What you want in yourself is to be found in double measure in Christ.

DUNDEE, *Nov.* 1842.

MY DEAR FRIEND,—Why did you not write me a few lines? It would be occupation to you, and your soul might find rest, even when pouring itself out to another. I do trust you are seeking hard after Him whom your soul loveth. He is not far from any one of us. He is a powerful and precious Saviour, and happy are they who put their trust in him. He is the Rose of Sharon, lovely to look upon, having all divine and human excellencies meeting in himself; and yet he is the Lily of the Valleys—meek and lowly in heart, willing to save the vilest. He answers the need of your soul. You are all guilt; he is a fountain to wash you. You are all naked; he has a wedding garment to cover you. You are dead; he is the life. You are all wounds and bruises; he is the Balm of Gilead. His righteousness is broader than your sin, and then he is so free. Remember the word we read at the draw-well—"Whosoever will, let him take the water of life freely." Look at Isa. xl. 1, 2, "Comfort ye, comfort ye, my people." If you receive Christ as your surety, you have realized double punishment for all your sins. The sufferings of Christ for us were as honouring to God as if we had suffered eternal punishment twice over. If you will only open your arms to receive Christ as your surety, then your iniquity is pardoned. You will taste immediate forgiveness. Your warfare with the law and an accusing conscience will be immediately accomplished. If you will only lay hold on Christ now, you will feel the force of that sweet command, "Comfort ye, comfort ye;" double comfort, double peace, for in Jesus you have suffered double wrath. Pray over that verse; and may He who first made the light to shine out of darkness shine into your heart, to let you see the way of salvation clearly. Soon may you sing, " Thou wast angry with me; but thine anger is turned away, and thou comfortedst me." " O! to grace, how great a debtor!" You are always in my prayers, that God would reveal himself unto you. O the joy of being able to say, " My beloved is mine, and I am his." Ever yours, in the gospel, &c.

TO THE REV. P. L. MILLER, WALLACETOWN

A word in season to the weary.

Sept. 14, 1842.

MY DEAR PATRICK,—When I last saw Horatius, I agreed not to ask him at all at the autumn communion, but only in the spring. I know not well where to look, as A. is to undertake the Edinburgh communion.

Don't be cast down, except for sin. Lie low in self, and set both feet on the Rock of ages. The sun, by one blink, can give a smile to nature, so can the Lord's face give life to our dark souls. Numbers do not prove life always. Remember the well of Sychar. Get much of the hidden life in your own soul; soon it will make life spread around.

Try prayer when preaching fails. He can turn the water into wine. Farewell! Ever, yours in Jesus, &c.

TO THE REV. J. MILNE, PERTH

Another word in season to a brother.

September 24*th*, 1842.

MY DEAR BROTHER,—I long after you in the bowels of Jesus Christ. If I make you sorry, who is he that maketh me glad, but the same who is made sorry by me? I often try to carry you to Jesus, as the four friends did the palsied man, and I have been longing to hear you say that his word to you was—" Be of good cheer, thy sins be forgiven thee ;" and then, " arise and walk." I wonder often God does not hide his face from me and lay me low, yet he restores my soul after many falls. He holds me by my right hand, and I believe will bring me to glory, though the weakest and most inconstant of all his saved ones. We shall praise more loudly than other men, and love more ardently, and gaze upon his wounds more wistfully, and say—He gave himself for us. Cheer up, brother, and tell poor sinners what Jesus can do ; for if he could not save the vilest of them all, we had never preached the good news.

If I could be with you, how gladly would I ! But I do not see my way. I have promised to be in London the first Sabbath of November, which will take me soon away, and for a long time, from this poor flock.

Will you come to me on Monday the 17th, the last day of the concert for prayer ? I think of printing a similar tract to last year's, or perhaps the same, with improvements. Suggest something.

This is Saturday, and I am empty. O for fulness out of Him ! Why do we not take all out of Jesus ? Ever yours, till glory dawn, &c.

TO THE REV. J. MILNE, PERTH

Breathings of heart.

December 13th, 1842.

MY DEAR BROTHER,—We are to have the communion, if God permit, on 1st January, 1843. A. B. is to be with me. Could you come down on the Thursday or Friday previous, and give us a good and comfortable word in the evening, 29th or 30th December —either you choose, or both, if you prefer that ?

I preach at Newtyle to-night, and to-morrow evening at Lintrathen in a barn, and on Thursday at Kir-

riemuir. Pray for me, for I am a poor worm, all guilt
and all helplessness, but still able to say—In the Lord
have I righteousness and strength. When shall the
day break, and the shadows flee away? When that
which is perfect is come, then that which is in part
shall be done away. I long for love without any coldness, light without dimness, and purity without spot
or wrinkle. I long to be at Jesus' feet, and tell him I
am all his, and ever will be. Yours, till then, &c.

TO ONE WHO HAD LATELY TAKEN UP THE CROSS

Kept by God—Meeting with God.

St. Peter's, *Jan.* 31*st*, 1843.

My Dear M.—I was glad indeed, to hear that you
are prospering, and that you do not repent having
made Moses' choice—Heb. xi. 24, 25—of which I
used to tell you so often. Happy is that people whose
God is the Lord. You remember what Ruth said
when she clave to Naomi; "Thy people shall be
my people, and thy God my God." I have not got
your note by me, and it is late, but I will answer it
to-morrow. I only write a line to-night to strengthen
your faith—"that I may be comforted together with
you, by the mutual faith both of you and me;" Rom.
i. 12. I have been remaining quiet since I wrote you
last, that I may gather strength for the north. I
expect hard service, but I hope Jesus will be with
me. You remember the sweet promise Jacob got at
Bethel, while he slept at the foot of that wondrous
ladder, "Behold I am with thee, and will keep thee
in all places whither thou goest, for I will not leave
thee until I have done that which I have spoken to
thee of." That promise is to you and me as truly as
to Jacob. Therefore, do not fear though you may be
taken among those who are strangers to Jesus and his
love. There is a sweet promise; Ezek. xi. 16. I
have felt its preciousness in foreign lands. Jesus himself will be our sanctuary not made with hands. I

was preaching on Thursday last, on Rev. xix. 12 "On his head were many crowns;" trying to teach them the kingly office of the Lord Jesus. It was a very solemn night. On Sabbath I lectured on Heb. ix. 9, 10, and preached in the evening on Isa. xlix. 5 " Though Israel be not gathered;" showing that however many will be lost by unbelief, still Christ would not lose one beam of his glory. If all the world were blind, and said the sun was dark, that would not take away one bright ray from it. It was a very awful subject, and my heart yearned over poor lost sinners. Four little girls have come since, asking, " what must I do to be saved ?" Three of them were awakened before, and one very lately. A widow came last night whom I never saw before, to tell me that she had found the Lord Jesus. To-night we have been at a large meeting about the tracts which are distributed monthly to every house in town—a very sweet society. It is now late, and I am talking a little while with you as we used to do before retiring. Did you read Gen. xxxii. to-day ? What a solemn chapter. Do you ever come to a spot you can call Mahanaim, where the angels of God meet you ? I trust you are one of the heirs of salvation, and that the angels are sent forth to minister to you. Unconverted souls have no such privilege. You see Jacob was going on God's errand, at God's command (see xxxi. 3,) when the angels of God met him. O ! it is sweet to go on God's errands. How long we went Satan's, and the world's, and our own, " serving divers lusts and pleasures." Do you not feel your heart lighter now as you walk on the narrow way ? Is not a Christian's darkest hour calmer than the world's brightest ? Is not Jacob's prayer in his distress an interesting one ? (ver. 9–12.) He puts God in remembrance of his promise. This is what we should do—" The Lord which said unto me." And " thou saidst, I will surely do thee good." God commands us to do this; Isa. xliii. 26, " Put me in remembrance." It is a blessed way of praying, to pray upon a promise, and to plead, " Do as thou hast said." You remember "Faith's Plea," a little book Miss C. gave you. Who do you think the man was that wrestled with Jacob? Was it not Jesus, the sinner's friend? At the daybreak Jacob began to see his blessed features, and when his thigh was out of joint he could do nothing but hang upon him. This is what you and I should do. Say, "I will not let thee go except thou bless me." Are there not some spots that you can call Peniel, where you have met Jehovah-Jesus face to face? When you do get into his presence, O do not weary of it; do not soon let go your hold. I am sure we lose much by our slight hold on Jesus. I was telling an interesting story to-night. Thirty thousand Spaniards lately came over the Pyrenees into France, to escape the civil wars. Some Geneva youths determined to take the opportunity of providing them with Spanish Testaments. The London Society granted them ten thousand copies. With these they set off and distributed freely. But the Spanish priests had come over and would not allow the Spaniards to receive or keep them. Many were burned or torn; they called them "The plague." One Spanish youth bought a Testament—kept it—read it—believed on Jesus; and when his countrymen returned to Spain, he staid behind to hear more of these wonders of redeeming love. Was not this one precious soul worth all the expense and trouble a thousand times over? "Be not weary in well doing, for in due season we shall reap if we faint not." Be active for God; you have lost much time already. Do nothing rashly, nothing unfeminine—give no just cause for reproach, but do not fear ridicule or proud men's sneers. If they knew what you know, they would rather inquire, "O that I knew where I might find Him!" Meanwhile, good night. May He who never slumbers nor sleeps watch over you all, and keep you till your dying day! May Jesus be near you, and make you his own! I fear I must not visit Kelso this season. I leave for the north on Monday, and do not expect to be home till the 25th. I fear this cuts off all hope of my visiting R—— the time you mention. I do hope to be in England early

in the summer, but before that I do not see my way.
But I shall gladly leave myself in Jehovah's hand.
Present duty is ours; neither must we consult our
mere wishes. If I hear from you before I leave, I
shall try and send you another line. I am glad you
teach in the classes, and I think I see you telling all
you know. Remember Paul; when his heart was
changed, for thirty years he did nothing else than
serve Jesus. He laboured away in the service of Him
who died for him, and plucked him from the burning.
It is interesting to notice also, how often Paul told
them of his own conversion. He told it to the Jews;
Acts xxii.—then to Agrippa; Acts xxvi.—then to the
Galatians; Gal. i. 13—16; then to the Philippians;
Phil. iii. 4. I think this an example for us to do the
same, cautiously and wisely. John Newton once
preached in Newgate to the prisoners. He chose
1 Tim. i. 15, for his text, and told them his own history,
so that they wept and he wept. Pray for me still,
that my way may be made plain. This is one of the
blessings of having spiritual children, that you will
surely pray for me. Do not cease to pray for ——
that her eyes may be opened to see her true condition,
and that she may call upon Jesus before it be too late.
I must now leave you and write a little to others. I
preach at Wallacetown to-night. May the Master be
there! O he is a sweet Master! One smile from
Jesus sustains my soul amid all the storms and frowns
of this passing world. Pray to know Jesus better.
Have no other righteousness—no other strength but
only Jesus. Soon we shall see him coming in the
clouds of heaven. May you be kept faithful to death.
Ever your loving friend, &c.

TO M. B.

One of his flock who had felt deserted in soul.

PETERHEAD, *Feb. 7th*, 1843.

DEAR FRIEND,—I was very happy to hear from you.
I grieve to hear of your sorrow; but Job's sorrow was

deeper, and David's also, in the xlii. Psalm. If you cannot say, " I found Him whom my soul loveth," is it not sweet that you can say, " I am sick of love"—he is my beloved still, though he has withdrawn himself and is gone for a time ? Seek into the cause of your declension. See that it be not some Achan in your bosom—some idol set up in the corner of your heart. See that it be not some allowed sin—an unlawful attachment that is drawing you away from the bleeding side of Jesus, and bringing a cloud between you and that bright Sun of righteousness. When you find out the cause, confess it and bewail it in the ear of a listening God. Tell him all. Keep nothing back. If you cannot find out the cause, ask him to tell it you. Get it washed in the blood of Jesus. Then get it subdued. Micah vii. 19. None but the Lord Jesus can either pardon or subdue. Remember not to rest in a state of desertion. " I will rise now and go about the city." And yet do not think that you have some great thing to do before regaining peace with God. The work on which peace is given has all been done by Jesus for us. " The word is nigh thee." Christ is the end of the law for righteousness to every one that believeth.

The sunshine is always sweeter after we have been in the shade ; so will you find Jesus in returning to him. True, it is better never to wander ; but when you have wandered, the sooner you return the happier you will be. " I will go and return to my first husband, for then it was better with me than now." Hos. ii. 7.

Do not delay, but humble yourself under his mighty hand, and he will exalt you in due season. I have been speaking to-night in this place to a large and attentive audience on Zech. ix. 9. May you be enabled to apply it. Remember me to Mrs. K——, and also to all your fellow-servants whom I know and love in the truth. Tell N—— C—— to make sure that she is in Christ, and not to take man's word for it. Tell E—— L—— to abide in Jesus ; and tell her brother to take care lest he be a rotten branch of the true vine. Tell W——— J——— to be faithful unto death.

I have no greater joy than to know that my children walk in the truth. I am your loving pastor, &c.

TO THE REV. ALEX. GATHERER, DUNDEE

During his visit to the north.

ELLON, *Feb.* 20*th*, 1843.

DEAR FRIEND,—I was glad to hear from you in this far off land. I am deeply grieved to hear that fever still prevails. God is pleading hard with my poor flock. I am glad to hear of your preaching on such precious texts, and hope they were blessed to many. Never forget that the end of a sermon is the salvation of the people. I feel more and more that it is God's cause in which we are embarked. King Jesus is a good master. I have had some sweet seasons of communion with an unseen God, which I would not give for thousands of gold and silver. May you have much of his presence with you. Write me to Cruden, or, if immediately, to Captain Shepherd's, Straloch, New Machar. Ever yours, in Jesus, &c.

TO ONE WHO HAD MET WITH A BEREAVEMENT.

Sorrow of the world—Incidents.

March 8, 1843.

MY DEAR ———, I know you will be wearying to hear from me, but it has scarcely been in my power till now ; I have had so many things to do since my return. I trust Jesus is making known to you his power to calm the soul in the deepest trials. "Where is your faith?" he said to the disciples; and he says to you, "All things are possible to him that believeth."

I was much afflicted for your sakes to read the solemn letter you sent to me. Do you remember the words, "We must needs go through Samaria?" We are getting new light upon their meaning.

I was reading to-day about godly sorrow, and the sorrow of the world. Do you know the difference between these two?

Had this blow come upon you in your unconverted state, it would have wrought, perhaps, only the sorrow of the world—carnal sorrow—sorrow that drives us away from God—makes us murmur and complain of his dealings. Like Pharaoh, who turned harder every blow that God struck—even the loss of his first born only hardened him. But godly sorrow, or, more literally, "sorrow towards God"—grief that brings us to the feet of God—worketh repentance unto salvation, not to be repented of. It is used as an instrument to bring the humbled soul to cleave to Jesus. O may it be so with you. Humble yourselves under the mighty hand of God, and he shall exalt you in due season. Improve the season while it lasts. The farmer improves the seed time, to cast in the seed into the furrows. Now, when God has made long the furrow, by the plough of affliction, in your heart, O see that you let the Sower sow the good seed deep in your hearts. I trust H. B—— may be made a great blessing and comfort to you next Sabbath. May you all be enabled to meet with Jesus at his own table, and to tell him all your sorrows there, and ask grace to keep you in the evil day.

I would like well to be with you; but in body this may not be. In heart I am often with you, because I can say what I was reading to-day, " Ye are in my heart to live and to die with you." 2 Cor. vii. 3.

I preached twenty-seven times when I was away, in twenty-four different places. I was very, very tired, and my heart has beat too much ever since, but I am wonderfully well. I have " fightings without and fears within," just now. Do pray earnestly for me—as indeed I know you do. I wish you had been with me last night. When I was away, the people agreed to meet twice a week in the lower school room to pray for me; and, now that I have come back, we have continued the meetings. The school is quite crammed. Such sweet loud singing of praise I never heard, and many tears.

I stood by a poor socialist in the agonies of death to-day. He was quite well yesterday. He anxiously wished me to come and pray. O to be ready when the Bridegroom comes.

Farewell. Peace from above fill your soul, your friend and brother prays, &c.

ANOTHER TO ONE BEREAVED

Betake yourself to Him that is ever the same.

March 9th, 1843.

My Dear ———, I did not think I would have been so long in answering you in your time of sorrow, but I have been more than occupied. I earnestly trust that this sad bereavement may be greatly blessed by God to you. Pray that you may not lose this precious opportunity of giving your hand and heart for ever away to the Lord Jesus. May Hosea ii. 14, be fulfilled in you all. " Behold, I will allure her, and *bring her into the wilderness,* and speak comfortably unto her ;" and that clear promise (Ezek. xx. 35—37,) " I will cause you to pass under the rod, and I will bring you into the bond of the covenant." This solemn event shows you what I always used to tell you, *how short* your life is—what a vapour—how soon the joys that depend on the creatures may be dried up—that " one thing is needful "—and that Mary was wise in choosing *the good part which cannot be taken away from her.* You remember the first night you were in St. Peter's, I showed you this, preaching from Psalm xvi. 6, " The lines have fallen to me in pleasant places, and I have a goodly heritage." I am indeed, more than ever anxious about you, that you receive not the grace of God in vain. It is the furnace that tries the metal, and it is affliction that tries the soul whether it be Christ's or not. I am jealous over you with a godly jealousy, lest the furnace should show you to be reprobate silver. Do let me hear how your soul truly is—whether you can see the hand of a Father in this bereavement—and whether you are more than ever determined, through grace, to be the Lord's   How sweet, that *Jesus ever liveth.* He is the same yesterday, and to-day, and for ever. You will never find Jesus so precious as when the world is one vast howling wilderness. Then he is like a rose blooming in the midst of the desolation —a rock rising above the storm. The Bible, too, is more full of meaning. Have you ever prayed over that verse, (Lam. iii. 33.) *He doth not afflict willingly?* O precious book, that conveys such a message to the mourner's dwelling! And does not trial bring more meaning out of that verse, (Romans viii. 28,) "We know that *all* things work together for good to them that love God—to them that are the called according to his purpose?" The Bible is like the leaves of the lemon trees; the more you bruise and wring them the sweeter the fragrance they throw around. " Is any afflicted?—let him pray." Do you not find that prayer is sweeter now? The soul finds vent for his feelings toward God.—" *Call upon me in the day of trouble*—I will deliver thee, and thou shalt glorify me." When I had my fever abroad, Mr. Bonar whispered that verse into my ear. I had nearly lost all my faculties—I could remember nothing except that I was far from home ; but that verse kept sounding in my ears when I was nearly insensible ; " I called, and he delivered me."

Are you preparing to go to the Lord's table next Lord's day ? May you, indeed, have the wedding garment—righteousness without works—and see the King in his beauty—and give yourself away to him, saying, " I am my beloved's, and my beloved is mine." It should be a solemn sacrament to you. I can add no more. Write me soon, dear G——, and tell me all that is in your heart, and whether the voice of the Comforter does not say, " Be still !" when death has left so deep a silence in your family. Believe me ever your friend in Jesus. &c.

TO ONE COMPLAINING OF THE PLAGUES OF THE HEART

Passing on to glory.

ST. PETER'S, *March 8th*, 1843.

MY DEAR FRIEND.—I send a few lines to you in answer to yours. You complain of the plague of your own heart, and so you will till you die. You know little yet of its chambers of imagery. All that is ours is sin. Our wicked heart taints all we say and do; hence the need of continual atonement in the blood of Jesus. It is not one pardoning that will serve the need of our souls. We must have daily, hourly pardons. I believe you are in the furnace, but it is a short one. Soon the Bridegroom will come, and we shall be with him, and like him, and God shall wipe away all tears from our eyes. I burst through all the cobwebs of present things, and, his Spirit anointing my eyes, look at Jesus as one beside me. Blessed elder brother, with two natures—God and man —ever-living, never-dying, never-changing! I was preaching last Sabbath, on Heb. ix. 13, 14, " He through the eternal Spirit offered himself." It was very sweet to myself. In the afternoon I preached on Rev. ii. 4, 5, "I have this against thee, that thou hast left thy first love." I fear many of my people have done so; therefore it was very suitable. Several I see have felt it very deeply. In the evening I preached on Psalm lxxviii. 41—" They turned back, and tempted God, and limited the Holy One of Israel," —on the sinfulness of limiting God. It was a very sweet and solemn day. Meantime, stay your soul on God. " Thou wilt keep him in perfect peace whose mind is stayed on thee, because he trusteth in thee." A few more trials—a few more tears—a few more days of darkness, and we shall be for ever with the Lord. " In this tabernacle we groan, being burdened." All dark things shall yet be cleared up—all sufferings healed—all blanks supplied, and we shall find fulness of joy (not one drop wanting) in the smile and presence of our God. It is one of the laws of Christ's kingdom, " We must through much tribulation enter into the kingdom of God." We must not reckon upon a smooth road to glory, but it will be a short one. How glad I am that you have "received the word in much affliction, with joy of the Holy Ghost." Cleave closely to Jesus, that you may not have to say in a little, "O that I had affliction back again to quicken me in prayer, and make me lie at his feet.

> Trials make the promise sweet,
> Trials give new life to prayer;
> Trials bring me to his feet,
> Lay me low, and keep me there.

This land will soon be strangely convulsed, if God prevent not. The plans now preparing for carrying the gospel into every corner of the land are sweet indeed. If I be spared and strengthened, I go to London towards the end of April. My stay must be very short. It is also intended to send me to the General Assembly in May. My poor flock; how I yearn over them! So many of them careless, and judgment at the door! Mr. Burns comes to me to-morrow.

I must add no more, as I have work before me. May you experience more and more that, "When He giveth quietness, none can make trouble"—even as you once experienced the other, "When He hideth his face, who then can behold him?" Soon we shall see him as he is; then our trials shall be done. We shall reign with him, and be entirely like him. The angels will know us by our very faces to be brothers and sisters of Jesus.

Remember Jesus *for us* is all our righteousness before a holy God, and Jesus *in us* is all our strength in an ungodly world. Persevere ever to death; eternal life will make up for all. I was reading to-day, "God hath granted repentance unto life." Remember Barnabas's advice, "Cleave to the Lord;" not to man, but to the Lord. May He perfect all that concerneth you. Do not fear the face of man. Remember how small their anger will appear in eternity. Till then, believe me, your friend in gospel bands, &c.

PASTORAL LETTERS TO THE FLOCK OF ST. PETER'S.

FIRST PASTORAL LETTER

View of what God has done—how it should affect them.

EDINBURGH, *January* 30*th*, 1839.

To all of you, my dear friends and people, who are beloved of God, and faithful in Christ Jesus, your pastor wishes grace and peace from God the Father and Christ Jesus our Lord.*

As several of you have expressed a desire to hear from me, and as He who at first sent me to you to bear witness of the Lord Jesus has for many weeks withdrawn me, and still lays his afflicting but gentle hand on me, it has seemed good to me, not without prayer, to write to you from week to week a short word of exhortation. May the Holy Spirit guide the pen, that what is written may be blessed to your comfort and growth in grace.

God is my record how greatly I long after you all in the bowels of Jesus Christ; and the walls of my chamber can bear witness how often the silent watches of the night have been filled up with entreaties to the Lord for you all. I can truly say with John, " that I have no greater joy than to hear that my children walk in the truth ;" and though many of you were in Christ before me, and were living branches of the true vine before I was sent into the vineyard, yet believe me it is true of them also, I have no greater joy than to know, that you are more and more filled with the Holy Ghost, and bear more and more fruit to the glory of God the Father. " Herein

---

* He had begun to correct a copy of those Pastoral Letters for publication, at the earnest request of some of his friends. The few corrections made are all inserted. The chief alterations are in the fourth of the Pastoral Letters. He had got no farther than the seventh.

is the Father glorified that you bear much fruit."
You remember what Paul, when he was a prisoner
of the Lord, wrote to the Philippians, (i. 12,) "I
would that ye should understand, brethren, that the
things which happened unto me have fallen out rather
unto the furtherance of the gospel." I am very
anxious that you and I should understand the very
same, in the things which have happened unto me,
that we may vindicate God in all his dealings with
us, and "not despise the chastening of the Lord." I
know too well that there are many among you who
would feel it no grievance if all the Lord's ministers
were taken out of the way. Ah! how many are
there who would rejoice if they were for ever left to
sin unreproved, and to do what is right in their own
eyes. Still I am quite sure that to you, "who have
obtained like precious faith with us"—to you, who
are the Lord's people, the present is a season of affliction, and you feel as Naomi felt, that the hand of the
Lord has gone out against us. My present object in
writing you is shortly to persuade you that "it is
well"—"the Lord doeth all things well"—and that it
may be really for the furtherance of the gospel among
you. In many ways may this be the case.

First, With respect to myself. It does not become
me here to show what benefit it may be to me. Suf-
fice it to say, that it has been a precious opportunity
in which to reflect on the sins and imperfections of my
ministry among you. A calm hour with God is worth
a whole lifetime with man. Let it be your prayer
that I may come out like gold, that the tin may be
taken away, and that I may come back to you, if that
be the will of God, a better man, and a more devoted
minister. I have much to learn, and these words of
David have been often in my heart and on my lips.
" I know that thy judgments are right, and that thou
in faithfulness hast afflicted me ;" Psalm cxix. 75.
Ministers are God's tools for building up the gospel
temple. Now you know well that every wise workman takes his tools away from the work from time to

time, that they may be ground and sharpened: so
does the only wise Jehovah take his ministers oftentimes away into darkness and loneliness and trouble,
that he may sharpen and prepare them for harder
work in his service.   Pray that it may be so with
your own pastor.

Second, With regard to you, my dear brothers and
sisters in the Lord, this time of trial is for your furtherance.   Does not God teach you, by means of it, to
look beyond man to the Saviour, who abideth ever ?
Is not God showing you that ministers are earthen
vessels, easily broken, and fit only to be cast aside
like a broken pitcher out of mind ?   Is he not bidding
you look more to the treasure which is in them, and
which flows in all its fulness from Christ ?   It is
a sad error into which I see many Christians falling,
that of leaning upon man, mistaking friendship toward
a minister for *faith* on the Son of God.

Remember that before Moses was sent to deliver
Israel, his hand was made leprous, as white as snow,
to teach them that it was not the might of that hand
that could deliver Israel ; Exod. iv. 6, 7.   It has been
the fault of some of you to lean too much on man.
Now God is teaching you that, though the *cistern*
may break, the *fountain* abides as open and full and
free as ever—that it is not from sitting under any
particular ministry that you are to get nourishment,
but from being vitally united to Christ.   Ministers
" are not suffered to continue by reason of death, but
Christ, because he continueth ever, hath an unchangeable priesthood."   Hebrews vii. 23.

Third, With regard to those among you who are
almost, but not *altogether*, persuaded to be Christians,
does not this providence teach you to make sure of
an interest in Christ without delay ?   You thought
you would have the Saviour held up to you for an in-
definite number of Sabbaths, little thinking that your
Sabbaths and mine are all numbered.   Many a time
you have said to me in your heart, " Go thy way for
this time, when I have a more convenient season I

will call for thee." You did not think that a time might come when you may call for your teachers, and they be as silent as the grave.

I find many godly people here are looking forward to a time when God's faithful witnesses shall be put to silence, and anxious souls shall wander from sea to sea, seeking the word of God, and shall not find it. Be entreated, O wavering souls, to settle the question of your salvation *now*. Why halt ye between two opinions? It is most unreasonable to be undecided about the things of an endless eternity, in such a world as this, with such frail bodies, with such a Saviour stretching out his hand, and such a Spirit of love striving with you. Remember you are flesh—you will soon hear your last sermon. I call heaven and earth to record this day against you, that I have set before you life and death, blessing and cursing, there-fore, choose life, that thou and thy seed may live. Deut. xxx. 19.

Fourth, There is another class who are not of you, and yet are on every hand of you, "of whom I have told you often, and now tell you, even weeping, that they are the enemies of the cross of Christ, whose God is their belly, who glory in their shame, who mind earthly things." Ah! you would not believe if I were to tell you the great heaviness and continual sorrow that I have in my heart for you; and yet I hope my absence may be blessed even to you. Just think for a moment if God were to remove your teachers one by one—if he were to suffer the Church of our covenanted fathers to fall before the hands of her enemies—if he were to suffer Popery again to spread its dark and deadly shade over the land, where would you be?—you that despise the Sabbath, that care little for the preached word—you that have no prayer in your families, and seldom in your closets— you that are lovers of pleasure—you that wallow in sin? You would have your wish then—you would have your silent Sabbaths, indeed—no warning voice to cry after you—no praying people to pray for you— none to check you in your career of wickedness—none to beseech you not to perish. Learn from so small a circumstance as the absence of your stated minister, what may be in store for you, and flee now from the wrath to come. "It may be, ye shall be hid in the day of the Lord's anger." Zeph. ii. 3.

Finally, My brethren, dearly beloved and longed for, my joy and crown, abide all the more in Christ because of my absence, and maintain a closer walk with God, that when I return, as God gives me good hopes now of doing, I may rejoice to see what great things God has done for your souls. God feeds the wild flowers on the lonely mountain side, without the help of man, and they are as fresh and lovely as those that are daily watched over in our gardens. So God can feed his own planted ones without the help of man, by the sweetly falling dew of his Spirit. How I long to see you walking in holy communion with God, in love to the brethren, and burning zeal for the cause of God in the world! I will never rest, nor give God rest, till he make you a lamp that burneth—a city set upon a hill that cannot be hid. Now strive together with me, in your prayers to God for me, that I may come unto you with joy by the will of God.

The grace of our Lord Jesus Christ be with you. My love be with you all in Christ Jesus. Amen.

SECOND PASTORAL LETTER

Past times of privilege reviewed—privileges still remaining.

EDINBURGH, *February 6th*, 1839.

To all of you, my dear flock, who have chosen the good part which cannot be taken away, your pastor wishes grace, mercy, and peace from God our Father and the Lord Jesus Christ.

The sweet singer of Israel begins one of his psalms with these remarkable words—"I will sing of mercy and judgment; unto thee, O God, will I sing." This is the experience of all God's servants in time of trou-

ble. Even in the wildest storms the sky is not all
dark; and so in the darkest dealings of God with his
children, there are always some bright tokens for
good. His way with us of late has been "in the
sea, and his path in the deep waters." Yet some of
you may have felt that his own hand was leading us
like a flock; Psalm lxxvii. 19, 20. One great token
of his loving kindness has been the way in which
he has supplied the absence of your stated minister.
Ordained messengers, men of faith and prayer, have
spoken to you from Sabbath to Sabbath in the name
of the Lord. Awakening, inviting, comforting messages you have had; and even your meetings on
Thursday evenings he has continued to you; the
gates of the house of prayer, like the gates of the city
of refuge, have been as open to you as ever, inviting
you to enter in and behold by faith what Jacob saw
in Bethel, "the ladder set on earth, and the top of it
reaching into heaven," inviting you to meet with Him
with whom Jacob wrestled till the breaking of the
day. Think how often, in times of persecution, the
Apostles were constrained to leave the seed they had
sown, without leaving any one to water it, but "the
Lord on whom they believed." See Acts xiii. 50, 52,
and xiv. 23, and xvi. 40. How often, in times of persecution in the Church of Scotland, our faithful pastors
had to leave their few sheep in the wilderness, without any human shepherd to care for their souls, commending them to God, and to the word of his grace.
These times may come again. God may be preparing
us for such fiery trials. But he hath not yet dealt
so with us. He that tempers the wind to the shorn
lamb, and "who stays his rough wind in the day of
his east wind," has mingled mercy with judgment;
and even when he humbles us, gives us cause for
praise. "Oh, that men would praise the Lord for his
goodness, and for his wonderful works to the children
of men." Another mark of his loving kindness to us
is, his suffering me to pray for you. You remember
how the Apostles describe the work of the ministry
Acts vi 4. "We will give ourselves continually to

prayer and to the ministry of the word." Now, God is my record that this has been my heart's desire ever since my coming among you. I have always felt myself a debtor to you all, both to the wise and the unwise; so as much as in me is, I have been ready to preach the gospel unto you; but God has for a time withdrawn me from that part of the work among you. To me that grace is not now given to preach among you the unsearchable riches of Christ. (Oh, how great a grace it is! how wonderful that it should ever have been given to me!) Still he allows me to give myself unto prayer. Perhaps this may be the chief reason of my exile from you, to teach me what Zechariah was taught in the vision of the golden candlestick and the two olive trees, Zech. iv. 6., that it is not by might, nor by power, but by *His Spirit*, obtained in believing, wrestling prayer, that the temple of God is to be built in our parishes. I have hanged my harp upon the willow, and am no more allowed " to open to you dark sayings upon the harp," nor " to speak of the things which I have made touching the King," who is " fairer than the children of men." Still my soul does not dwell in silence. I am permitted to go in secret to God my exceeding joy; and, while meditating his praise, I can make mention of you all in my prayers, and give thanks for the little flock, who, " by patient continuance in well doing, seek for glory, and honour, and immortality." " If I forget thee, O Jerusalem, let my right hand forget her cunning. If I do not remember thee, let my tongue cleave to the roof of my mouth; if I prefer not Jerusalem above my chief joy." I feel it is another gift of grace, that I am suffered to write to you. You remember how often the Apostles cheered and strengthened the disciples, when absent from them, by writing to them.* What a precious legacy to the Church in all ages have these Epistles been! every verse, like a branch of the tree of life, bearing all

---

* 2 Cor. vii. 12.   Gal. vi. 11.   1 Thess. v. 27.   Heb. xiii. 22. Peter v. 12.   2 Pet i. 12—15; iii. 1.   1 John i. 4.   Jude 3.

manner of fruit, and the leaves for the healing of the nations. You remember how holy Samuel Rutherford, and many of our persecuted forefathers in the Church of Scotland, kept the flame of grace alive in their deserted parishes by sending them words of counsel, warning, and encouragement, testifying, not face to face, but with ink and pen, the gospel of the grace of God. I do feel it a great privilege that this door is open to me, and that, even when absent, I can yet speak to you of the things pertaining to the kingdom.

"This second epistle, beloved, I now write unto you, in both which I stir up your pure minds by way of remembrance; yea, I think it meet, so long as I am in this tabernacle, to stir you up by putting you in remembrance."

I. Abide in Him, little children, whom I have always preached unto you, that when he shall appear, we may have confidence and not be ashamed before him at his coming. Let every new sight of your wicked heart, and every new wave of trouble, drive your soul to hide in him, the Rock of your Salvation. There is no true peace but in a present hold of the Lord our righteousness.

II. Enjoy the forgiveness of sins—keep yourselves in the love of God. If you abide in Christ, you shall abide in his love—your joy let no man take from you. "These things write we unto you that your joy may be full."

III. Be ye clean that bear the vessels of the Lord. "He that (saith he) abideth in Him, ought himself also so to walk even as he walked." Ah, how many falls will I have to mourn over when I return, if God send me back to you—how many unseemly quarrelings and miscarriages among you, that are God's own —how many unlovely tempers among those who follow Him who is altogether lovely! O take heed, do not give the enemy cause to blaspheme; naming the name of Christ, depart from all iniquity.

IV. Continue in prayer. How many messages have been carried to you publicly and from house to house, and yet how little success. I bless God for all the tokens he has given us that the Spirit of God has not departed from the Church of Scotland—that the glory is still in the midst of her. Still the Spirit has never yet been shed on us abundantly. The many absentees on the forenoon of the Sabbaths—the thin meetings on Thursday evenings—the absence of *men* from all meetings for the worship of God—the few private prayer meetings—the little love and union among Christians—all show that the plentiful rain has not yet fallen to refresh our corner of the heritage Why is this? This is the day of Christ's power— why are the people not made willing? Let James give the answer: "Ye have not, because ye ask not." Hitherto ye have asked nothing in my name. Ask and ye shall receive, that your joy may be full. Finally, dear brethren, farewell. Day and night I long to come to you, but still God hinders me. Do not omit to praise him for all the great grace he has mingled in our cup of bitterness. "Seven times a day do I praise thee because of thy righteous judgments." When passing through the waters he has been with us, and in the rivers they have not overflowed us; and, therefore, we may be sure that when we pass through the fire we shall not be burned, neither shall the flames kindle upon us.

Now, may the God of peace himself give you peace always, by all means, and the grace of the Lord Jesus Christ be with your spirits. Amen.

THIRD PASTORAL LETTER

How God works by Providences.

EDINBURGH, *February 13th*, 1839.

To all of you, my dear friends and people, who are and shall ever be followers of the Lamb, whithersoever he goeth, your pastor again wishes grace and peace from God our Father, and the Lord Jesus Christ.

I long very much that this grace may again be given unto me to preach among you face to face "the unsearchable riches of Christ." "Oftentimes I purpose to come unto you, but am let hitherto." Still, I feel it a great privilege that, even in my retirement, I can send you a word to the end that you may be established. I feel as if one door was left open to me by the Lord. Believe me, it is the foremost desire of my heart that Christ may be glorified in you, both now and at his coming—that you may be a happy and a holy people, blessed and made a blessing. For the sake of variety, let me guide your thoughts to a passage of God's own word, and there I will speak to you as if I were yet present with you, and half forget that you are not before me.

In Job xxiii. 8—10, you will find these solemn words—"Behold, I go forward, but he is not there; and backward, but I cannot perceive him: on the left hand, where he doth work, but I cannot behold him; he hideth himself on the right hand, that I cannot see him. But he knoweth the way that I take: when he hath tried me I shall come forth as gold."

You all know the afflictions which came upon Job. "He was a perfect and upright man," and the greatest of all the men of the east, yet he lost his oxen and his asses, his sheep and camels, and his ten children in one day. Again, the breath of disease came upon him, and he sat down among the ashes. In all this Job sinned not with his lips. He blessed the hand that smote him — "What! shall we receive good at the hand of the Lord, and shall we not receive evil?" And yet, when his troubles were *prolonged*, he knew not what to think. Learn how weak the strongest believer is—a bruised reed; without Christ, we are, and can do nothing. When Job's brethren dealt deceitfully with him "as a brook"— when he felt God hedging him in, and God's arrows drinking up his spirit, then clouds and darkness rested on his path—he could not unravel God's dealings with his soul—then he cried, "Show me wherefore thou contendest with me!" He longed to get an explanation from God—" O that I knew where I might find him! that I might come even to his seat! Behold I go forward, but he is not there; and backward, but I cannot perceive him: on the left hand, where he doth work, but I cannot behold him: he hideth himself on the right hand that I cannot see him." You have here, then, in verses 8th and 9th, a child of light walking in darkness—an afflicted soul seeking, and seeking in vain, to know why God is contending with him. Dear friends, this is not an uncommon case; even to some of you God's providences often appear inexplicable. I hear that God has been at work among you, and " His way is in the sea." He has tried you in different ways; some of you by the loss of your property, as he tried Job; some of you by the loss of dear friends; some by loss of health, so that " wearisome nights are appointed you ;" some by the loss of the esteem of friends—aye, even of Christians. " Your inward friends abhor you." Perhaps more than one trouble has come on you at a time —wave upon wave, thorn upon thorn. Before one wound was healed, another came—before the rain was well away, " the clouds returned." You cannot explain God's dealings with you—you cannot get God to explain them—you have drawn the Saviour's blood and righteousness over your souls, and you know that the Father himself loveth you—you would like to meet him to ask, " Wherefore contendest thou with me ?" " Oh that I knew where I might find him." My dear afflicted brethren, this is no strange thing that has happened unto you. Almost every believer is at one time or another brought to feel this difficulty—" God maketh my heart soft, and the Almighty troubleth me." Is it in anger or is it in pure love that he afflicts me ? Am I fleeing from the presence of the Lord, as Jonah fled? What change would he have wrought in me ? If any of you are thinking thus in your heart, pray over this word in Job. Remember the word in the xlvi. Psalm, " Be still, and know that I am God." God does many things to teach us that *He* is God, and to make us wait upon him. And, still further, see in verse 10th what light breaks in upon our darkness—" But he knoweth the way that I take : when he hath tried me, I shall come forth as gold."

Observe, *first*, " *He* knoweth the way that I take." What sweet comfort there is in these words—*He* that redeemed me—*He* that pities me as a father—*He* who is the only wise God—*He* whose name is love—" *He* knoweth the way that I take."

The ungodly world do not know it—the world knoweth us not, even as it knew him not. A stranger doth not intermeddle with the joys or sorrows of a child of God. When the world looks on your grief with unsympathizing eye, you feel very desolate. " Your soul is exceedingly filled with the scorning of those who are at ease." But why should you? He that is greater than all the world is looking with the intensest interest upon all your steps.

The most intimate friends do not know the way of an afflicted believer. Your spirit is lonely even among God's children, for your way is hid, and the Lord hath hedged you in. Still, be of good cheer, the Father of all, the best of friends, knows all the way that you take.

You do not know your own way. God has called you to suffer, and you go like Abraham, not knowing whither you go. Like Israel, going down into the Red Sea, every step is strange to you. Still, be of good cheer, sufferer with Christ ! God marks your every step. " The steps of a good man are ordered by the Lord, and he delighteth in his way." *He* that loves you with an infinite, unchanging love, is leading you by his Spirit and providence. *He* knows every stone, every thorn in your path. Jesus knows your way. Jesus is afflicted in all your afflictions. " Fear not, for I have redeemed thee. I have called thee by my name, thou art mine. When thou passest through the water I will be with thee, and through the rivers they shall not overflow thee. When thou walkest through the fire thou shalt not be burned, neither shall the flame kindle upon thee."

Second, " When he hath tried me I shall come forth as gold." This also is precious comfort. There will be an end of your affliction. Christians must have " great tribulation," but they come out of it. We must carry the cross, but only for a moment, then comes the crown. I remember one child of God saying, that if it were God's will that she should remain in trials a thousand years, she could not but delight in his will. But this is not asked of us : we are only called " *to suffer a while.*" There is a set time for putting into the furnace, and a set time for taking out of the furnace. There is a time for pruning the branches of the vine, and there is a time when the husbandman lays aside the pruning hook. Let us wait his time—" he that believeth shall not make haste." God's time is the best time. But shall we come out the same as we went in ? Ah ! no, " we shall come out like gold." It is this that sweetens the bitterest cup ; this brings a rainbow of promise over the darkest cloud. Affliction will *certainly* purify a believer. How boldly he says it, " I shall come out like gold." Ah, how much dross there is in every one of you, dear believers, and in your pastor ! " When I would do good evil is present with me." O, that all the dross may be left behind in the furnace ! What imperfection, what sin, mingles with all we have ever done ! But are we really fruit-bearing branches of the true vine ? then it is certain that when we are pruned we shall bear more fruit. We shall come out like gold. We shall shine more purely as " a diadem in the hand of our God." We shall become purer vessels to hold the sweet smelling incense of praise and prayer. We shall become holy golden vessels for the Master's use in time and in eternity.

To the many among you who have no part nor lot in Christ, I would say, " See here the happiness of being a Christian in time of trouble." It is no small joy to be able to sing the xlvi. Psalm in the dark and cloudy day. I have often told you, and now tell you when I am far from you, " we are journeying to the place of which the Lord hath said, ' I will give it you ;'

come then with us, and we will do thee good, for God hath spoken good concerning Israel."

Finally, Pray that your pastor may come out of his trials like gold. All is not gold that glitters. Pray that every thing that is but glittering dross may be taken away, and that, if it be *His* will, I may come unto you like the fine gold of Ophir. "Continue in prayer, and watch in the same with thanksgiving, withal praying also for us, that God would open unto us a door of utterance to speak the mystery of Christ."

My chief comfort concerning you is, that "my God shall supply all your need according to his riches in glory by Christ Jesus." Brethren, farewell. Be perfect, be of good comfort, be of one mind, live in peace, and the God of love and of peace shall be with you.

The grace of the Lord Jesus Christ, and the love of God, and the communion of the Holy Ghost be with you all. Amen.

FOURTH PASTORAL LETTER

God the Answerer of Prayer.

EDINBURGH, *February* 20*th,* 1839.

To all of you, my dear flock, who are chosen in Christ before the foundation of the world, to be holy and without blame before him in love, your pastor again wishes grace and peace from God the Father and our Lord Jesus Christ.

There are many sweet providences happening to us every day if we would but notice them. In the texts which ministers choose, what remarkable providences God often brings about! I have often felt this, and never more than now. Some of you may remember that the last chapter of the Bible which I read to you in the church was 1st Kings xix., where we are told of Elijah going away into the wilderness for forty days and forty nights to the mount of God, where he was taught that it is not by the *wind,* nor the *earthquake,* nor the *fire,* that God converts souls, but by the still small voice of the gospel. May not this have been graciously intended to prepare us for what has happened? Another providence some of you may have noticed. For several Thursday evenings before I left you I was engaged in explaining and enforcing the sweet duty of believing prayer. Has not God since taught us the use of these things?—"Trials make the promise sweet"—"Trials give new life to prayer." Perhaps some of us were only receiving the information into the head; is not God now impressing it on our hearts, and driving us to practise the things which we learned? I do not now remember all the points I was led to speak upon to you, but *one*, I think, was entirely omitted—I mean the subject of answers to prayer. God left it for us to meditate on *now*. O, there is nothing that I would have you to be more sure of than this, that "God hears and answers prayer." There never was, and never will be, a believing prayer left unanswered. Meditate on this, and you will say, "I love the Lord because he hath heard my voice and my supplication." Psalm cxvi. 1.

First, God often gives the very thing his children ask, at the very time they ask it. You remember Hannah, (Samuel i. 10,) she was in bitterness of soul, and prayed unto the Lord, and wept sore. "Give unto thine handmaid a man child." This was her request. And so she went in peace, and the God of Israel heard and granted her her petition that she had asked of him; and she called the child's name Samuel, that is, "Asked of God." O that you could write the same name upon all your gifts! you would have far more joy in them, and far larger blessings along with them. You remember *David*, in Psalm cxxxviii.— "*In the day* that I cried thou answeredst me, and strengthenedst me with strength in my soul." You remember *Elijah*, 1 Kings xvii. 21—"O Lord, my God! I pray thee let this child's soul come into him again. And *the Lord heard the voice* of Elijah, and *the soul of the child came into him again*, and he revived." You remember *Daniel*, ix. 20, 21—"*While I was* speaking, and praying, and confessing my sin, and the sin of my people Israel, and presenting my supplication before the Lord my God for the holy mountain of my God; yea, whiles I *was speaking in prayer,* even the man Gabriel, being caused to fly swiftly, touched me about the time of the evening oblation." O what encouragement is here for those among you who, like Daniel are greatly beloved— who study much in the books of God's word, and who set your face unto the Lord to seek by prayer gifts for the Church of God! Expect answers while you are speaking in prayer. Sometimes the vapours that ascend in the morning come down in copious showers in the evening. So may it be with your prayers. Take up the words of David, Psalm v. 3, " My voice shalt thou hear in the morning; in the morning will I direct my prayer unto thee, and will look up." You remember, in Acts xii., Peter was cast into prison, " but prayer was made without ceasing of the Church unto God for him," and, behold, the same night the answer surprised them at the door. O! what surprises of goodness and grace God has in store for you and me, if only we pray without ceasing. If you will pray in union to Jesus, having childlike confidence towards God—having the spirit of adoption, crying, Abba, within you—seeking the glory of God more than all personal benefits, I believe that in all such cases you will get *the very thing you ask, at the very time you ask it.* Before you call, God will hear, and while you are speaking he will answer. O, if there were twenty among you who would pray thus, and persevere therein like wrestling Jacob, you would get whatever you ask! yea, the case of Daniel shows that the effectual fervent prayer of one such believer among you will avail much. " Delight thyself in the Lord, and he shall give thee the desires of thy heart." Psalm xxxvii. 4.

Second, God often delays the answer to prayer for wise reasons. The case of the Syrophenician woman will occur to you all; Matt. xv. 21—28. How anxiously she cried, " Have mercy on me, O Lord, thou Son of David. But Jesus answered her not a word."

Again and again she prayed, and got no gracious answer. Her faith grows stronger by every refusal. She cried, she followed, she kneeled to him, till Jesus could refuse no longer. "O woman, great is thy faith. Be it unto thee even as thou wilt." Dear praying people, "continue in prayer, and watch in the same with thanksgivings." Do not be silenced by one refusal. Jesus invites importunity by delaying to answer. Ask, seek, knock. "The promise may be long delayed, but cannot come too late." You remember, in the parable of the importunate widow, it is said, "Shall not God avenge his own elect, which cry day and night unto him, though he bear long with them? I tell you that he will avenge them speedily;" Luke xviii. 1—8. This shows how you, who are God's children, should pray. You should cry day and night unto God. This shows how God hears every one of your cries, in the busy hour of the day time, and in the lonely watches of the night. He treasures them up from day to day: soon the full answer will come down. "He will answer speedily." The praying souls beneath the altar, in Rev. vi. 9—11, seem to show the same truth, that the answer to a believer's prayers may, in the adorable wisdom of God, be delayed for a little season, and that many of them may not be fully answered till after he is dead. Again, read that wonderful passage, Rev. viii. 3, where it is said that the Lord Jesus, the great Intercessor with the Father, offers to God the incense of his merits, with the prayers of *all saints*, upon the golden altar which is before the throne. Christ never loses one believing prayer. The prayers of every believer, from Abel to the present day, he heaps upon the altar, from which they are continually ascending before his Father and our Father; and when the altar can hold no more, the full, the eternal answer will come down. Do not be discouraged, dearly beloved, because God bears long with you—because he does not seem to answer your prayers. Your prayers are not lost. When the merchant sends his ships to distant shores, he does not expect them to come back

richly laden in a single day—he has long patience.
"It is good that a man should both hope and quietly
wait for the salvation of the Lord." Perhaps your
prayers will come back, like the ships of the merchant,
all the more heavily laden with blessings because of
the delay.

*Third, God often answers prayer by terrible
things.* So David says, in Psalm lxv., " By terrible
things in righteousness wilt thou answer us, O God of
our salvation." And all of you who are God's children have found it true. Some of you have experienced what John Newton did when he wrote that
beautiful hymn, " I asked the Lord that I might
grow."* You prayed with all your heart, " Lord,
increase my faith." In answer to this, God has shown
you the misery of your connection with Adam. He
has revealed the hell that is in your heart. You are
amazed, confounded, abashed. You cry " O wretched
man that I am, who shall deliver me from the body
of this death?" You cleave to a Saviour God with
a thousand times greater anxiety. Your faith is increased. Your prayer is answered by terrible things.
Some of us prayed for a praying spirit, " Lord, teach
us to pray." God has laid affliction upon us. Waves
and billows go over us. We cry out of the depths.
Being afflicted, we pray. He has granted our heart's
desire. Our prayer is answered by *terrible things.*

*Fourth, God sometimes answers prayer by giving
something better than we ask.* An affectionate father
on earth often does this. The child says, Father,
give me this fruit. No, my child (the father replies,)
but here is bread, which is better for you. So the
Lord Jesus dealt with his beloved Paul, 2 Cor. xii.
7—9. There was given to Paul a thorn in the flesh,
a messenger of Satan to buffet him. In bitterness
of heart, he cried, " Lord, let this depart from me."
No answer came. Again he prayed the same words.
No answer still. A third time he knelt, and now the
answer came, not as he expected. The thorn is not

* Olney Hymns, book iii., hymn 36.

plucked away—the messenger of Satan is not driven back to hell; but Jesus opens wide his more loving breast, and says, "My grace is sufficient for thee, for my strength is made perfect in weakness." O! this is something exceeding abundant above all that he asked, and all that he thought. Ah, this is something better than he asked, and better than he thought. Surely God is able to do "exceeding abundantly above all that we ask or think." Ephes. iii. 20. Dear praying believers, be of good cheer. God will either give you what you ask, or something far better. Are you not quite willing that he should choose for you and me? You remember that even Jesus prayed, "Oh my Father, if it be possible, let this cup pass from me." That desire was not granted, but there appeared unto him an angel from heaven strengthening him. Luke xxii. 43. He received what was far better, strength to drink the cup of vengeance. Some of you, my dear believing flock, have been praying that, if it be God's will, I might be speedily restored to you, that God's name might be glorified; and I have been praying the same. Do not be surprised if he should answer our prayers by giving us something above what we imagined. Perhaps he may glorify himself by us in another way than we thought. "O! the depth of the riches both of the wisdom and knowledge of God! How unsearchable are his judgments, and his ways past finding out! For of him, and through him, and to him, are all things. To whom be glory for ever. Amen."

These things I have written that you may come boldly to the throne of grace. The Lord make you a praying people. "Strive together with me in your prayers to God for me." "I thank my God upon every remembrance of you, always in every prayer of mine for you all, making request with joy."

Now, the God of patience and consolation grant you to be like-minded one towards another, according to Christ Jesus. "The God of hope fill you with all joy and peace in believing;" and the God of peace be with you all. Amen.

FIFTH PASTORAL LETTER

What God has done, and the returns made.—Isaiah v. 4.

EDINBURGH, *February 27th*, 1839.

To all of you, my dear flock, who are washed, and sanctified, and justified, in the name of the Lord Jesus, and by the Spirit of our God, your pastor again wishes grace, mercy, and peace.

This is now the fifth time I am permitted by God to write to you. If *you* are not wearied, it is pleasant and refreshing to me. I wish to be like Epaphras, Coloss. iv. 12—"Always labouring fervently for you in prayer, that you may stand perfect and complete in all the will of God." When I am hindered by God from labouring for you in any other way, it is my heart's joy to labour for you thus. When Dr. Scott of Greenock, a good and holy minister, was laid aside by old age from preaching for some years before his death, he used to say—"I can do nothing for my people now but pray for them, and sometimes I feel that I can do that." This is what I also love to feel. Often I am like Amelia Geddie, who lived in the time of the Covenanters, and of whom I used to tell you. The great part of my time is taken up with bringing my heart into tune for prayer; but when the blessed Spirit does help my infirmities, it is my greatest joy to lay myself and you, my flock, in his hand, and to pray that God may yet make "the vine to flourish and the pomegranate to bud."

If you turn to Isaiah v. 4, you will find these affecting words—"What could have been done more to my vineyard, that I have not done in it? wherefore, when I looked that it should bring forth grapes, brought it forth wild grapes?"

Consider these words, my dear people, and may the Spirit breathe over them that they may savingly impress your souls. These words are God's pathetic lamentation over his ancient people, when he thought of all that he had done for them, and of the sad return which they made to him. We have come into the

place of Israel; the natural branches of the good
olive tree have been broken off, and we have been
grafted in. All the advantages God gave to Israel
are now enjoyed by us; and ah! has not God occasion to take up the same lamentation over us, that we
have brought forth only wild grapes? I would wish
every one of you seriously to consider what more God
could have done to save your soul that he has not
done. But, ah! consider again, whether you have
borne grapes, or only wild grapes.

First, Consider how much God has done to save
your souls. He has provided a great Saviour, and a
great salvation. He did not give man or angel, but
the Creator of all, to be the substitute of sinners. His
blood is precious blood. His righteousness is the
righteousness of God; and now "to him that worketh
not, but believeth on him that justifieth the ungodly,
his faith is counted to him for righteousness," Romans
iv. 5. Most precious word. Give up your toil, self-
justifying soul. You have gone from mountain to
hill—you have forgotten your resting place. Change
your plan. Work not, but believe on Him that justifieth the ungodly. Believe the record that God hath
given concerning his Son. A glorious, all perfect,
all divine surety is laid down at your feet. He is
within your reach—he is nigh thee—take him, and
live; refuse him, and perish! "What could have
been done more for my vineyard, that I have not
done in it?"

Second, Again, consider the ordinances God has
given you. He has made you into a vineyard. Scotland is the likest of all lands to God's ancient Israel.
How wonderfully has God planted and maintained
godly ministers in this land from the time of Knox to
the present day! He has divided the whole land into
parishes; even on the barren hills of our country he
has planted the choicest vine. Hundreds of godly
labourers he has sent to gather out the stones of it.
God has done this for you also. He has built a tower
in the midst of you. Have you not seen his own hand
fencing you round—building a gospel tower in the

midst of you, and a gospel vine press therein? And
has he not sent me among you, who am less than the
least of all the members of Christ, and yet "determined not to know any thing among you save Jesus
Christ, and him crucified?" Has not the Spirit of
God been sometimes present in our sanctuary? have
not some hearts been filled there with gladness more
than in the time that their corn and wine increased?
Have not some hearts tasted there the "love that is
better than wine?" "What could have been done
more for my vineyard that I have not done in it?"
Now, let me ask, what fruit have we borne—grapes or
wild grapes? Ah! I fear the most can show nothing
but wild grapes. If God looks down upon us as a
parish, what does he see? Are there not still a
thousand souls utter strangers to the house of God?
How many does his holy eye now rest upon who
are seldom in the house of prayer, who neglect it
in the forenoon! How many who frequent the
tavern on the Sabbath day! O! why do they bring
forth wild grapes? If God looks upon you as *families*, what does he see? How many prayerless families! How often, as I passed your windows, late at
eve or at early dawn, have I listened for the melody
of psalms, and listened all in vain! God also has
listened, but still in vain. How many careless parents
does his pure eye see among you, who will one day,
if you turn not, meet your neglected children in an
eternal hell! How many undutiful children! How
many unfaithful servants! Ah! why such a vineyard
of wild grapes? If God looks on you as *individual
souls*, how many does he see that were never awakened to real concern about your souls! How many
that never shed a tear for your perishing soul! How
many that were never driven to pray! How many
that know not what it is to bend the knee! How
many that have no uptaking of Christ, and are yet
cold hearted and at ease! How many does God
know among you that have never laid hold of the
only sure covenant! How many that have no "peace
in believing," and yet cry "peace, peace, when there

is no peace!" Jer. viii. 11. How many does God
see among you who have no change of heart and life,
who are given up to the sins of the flesh and of the
mind! and yet you "bless yourself in your heart,
saying, I shall have peace, though I walk in the imagination of my heart, to add drunkenness to thirst."
Deut. xxix. 19. Ah! why do you thus bring forth
wild grapes? "Your vine is of the vine of Sodom,
and of the fields of Gomorrah : your grapes are grapes
of gall : your clusters are bitter." Deut. xxxii. 32.
Ah! remember you will blame yourselves to all eternity for your own undoing. God washes his hands
of your destruction. What could have been done
more for you that God has not done? I take you all
to record this day, if I should never speak to you
again, that I am pure from the blood of you all. O
barren fig trees, planted in God's vineyard, the Lord
has been digging at your roots ; and if ye bear fruit,
well ; if not, then ye shall be cut down! Luke xiii.
6—9.

Now, I turn for a moment to you who are God's
children. I am persuaded better things of you, my
dearly beloved, and things that accompany salvation,
though I thus speak. Yet, what need is there, in these
trying times, to search your heart and life, and ask,
what fruit does God find in me?

What fruit of *self-abasement* is there in you? Have
you found out the evil of your connection with the first
Adam? Rom. v. 19. Do you know the plagues of
your own heart? 1 Kings viii. 38. The hell of corruption that is there? Jer. xvii. 9. Do you feel you
have never lived one moment to his glory? Rom. iii.
25. Do you feel that to all eternity you never can be
justified by any thing in yourself? Rev. vii. 14.

Consider, again, what fruit there is of *believing*, in
you. Have you really and fully uptaken Christ as
the gospel lays him down? John v. 12. Do you
cleave to him as a sinner? 1 Tim. i. 15. Do you
count all things but loss, for the excellency of the
knowledge of him? Mat. ix. 9. Do you feel the glory
of his person? Rev. i. 17. His finished work? Heb.

ix. 26. His offices? 1 Cor. i. 30. Does he shine like the sun into your soul? Mal. iv. 2. Is your heart ravished with his beauty? Song v. 16.

Again : what fruit is there in you of *crying after holiness ?* Is this the one thing you do? Phil. iii. 13. Do you spend your life in cries for deliverance from this body of sin and death? Rom. vii. 24. Ah! I fear there is little of this. The most of God's people are contented to be saved from the hell that is *without.* They are not so anxious to be saved from the hell that is *within.* I fear there is little feeling of your need of the indwelling Spirit. I fear you do not know the exceeding greatness of his power to us-ward who believe. I fear many of you are strangers to the visits of the Comforter. God has reason to complain of you, " wherefore should they bring forth wild grapes ?"

Again : what fruit is there of *actual likeness to God* in you? Do you love to be much with God? " To climb up near to God—Genesis v. 22—to love, and long, and plead, and wrestle, and stretch after him ?"* Are you weaned from the world?—Psal. cxxxi.—from its praise—from its hatred—from its scorn? Do you give yourselves clean away to God —2 Cor. viii. 5—and all that is yours? Are you willing that your will should be lost in his great will? Do you throw yourselves into the arms of God for time and for eternity? O, search your hearts and try them, ask God to do it for you, and " to lead you in the way everlasting !" Psa. cxxxix. 23, 24.

I am deeply afraid that many of us may be like the fig tree by the wayside, on which the hungry Saviour expected to find fruit and he found none. Ah! we have been an ungrateful vine, minister and people! What more could God have done for us? Sunshine and shade—rain and wind—have all been given us ; goodness and severity have both been tried with us,— yet what has been returned to him? Whether have the curses or the praises been louder rising from our

* See Brainerd's Diary, Part ii., April 4.

parish to heaven? Whether does our parish more resemble the garden of the Lord, or the howling wilderness? Whether is there more of the perpetual incense of believing prayer, or the "smoke in God's nose" of hypocrisy and broken sacraments?

"I write not these things to shame you, but as my beloved sons I warn you." If there be some among you, and some there are, who are growing up like the lily, casting forth their roots like Lebanon, and bearing fruit with patience, remember "the Lord loveth the righteous." He that telleth the number of the stars taketh pleasure in you; "the Lord taketh pleasure in his people; he will beautify the meek with salvation." Keep yourselves in the love of God. Go carefully through all the steps of your effectual calling a second time.

The Lord give you daily faith. Seek to have a large heart. Pray for me, that a door of utterance may be opened to me. Remember my bonds. Pray that I may utterly renounce myself, that I may be willing to do and to suffer all his will up to the latest breath!

May you all obtain mercy of the Lord now, and in that day to which we are hastening. The grace of the Lord Jesus be with your spirits. Amen.

SIXTH PASTORAL LETTER

Self-devotedness—what it ought to be.

EDINBURGH, *March* 6, 1839.

To all my dear flock over which the Holy Ghost hath made me overseer—to all of you who are of the Church of God, which he hath purchased with his own blood—your pastor wishes grace, mercy, and peace.

I thank my God without ceasing that ever I was ordained over you in the Lord. For every shower of the Spirit that ever has been shed upon us—for every soul among you that has ever been added to the Church—for every disciple among you whose soul has been confirmed during our ministry, I will praise God eternally. May this letter be blessed to you by the breathing of the Holy Spirit. May it teach you and me more than ever that we " are not our own, but bought with a price."

The most striking example of self-devotedness in the cause of Christ which I ever heard in these days of deadness, was told here last week by an English minister. It has never been printed, and therefore, I will relate it to you just as I heard it, to stir up our cold hearts, that we may give our ownselves unto the Lord.

The awful disease of leprosy still exists in Africa. Whether it be the same leprosy as that mentioned in the Bible I do not know, but it is regarded as perfectly *incurable*, and so infectious that no one dares to come near the leper. In the south of Africa there is a large lazar house for lepers. It is an immense space, enclosed by a very high wall, and containing fields, which the lepers cultivate. There is only one entrance, which is strictly guarded. Whenever any one is found with the marks of leprosy upon him, he is brought to this gate and obliged to enter in, never to return. No one who enters in by that awful gate is ever allowed to come out again. Within this abode of misery there are multitudes of lepers in all stages of the disease. Dr. Halbeck, a missionary of the Church of England, from the top of a neighbouring hill, saw them at work. He noticed two particularly, sowing peas in the field. The one *had no hands*, the other *had no feet*—these members being wasted away by disease. The one who wanted the hands was carrying the other who wanted the feet, upon his back, and he again carried in his hands the bag of seed, and dropped a pea every now and then, which the other pressed into the ground with his foot—and so they managed the work of one man between the two. Ah! how little we know of the misery that is in the world. Such is this prison house of disease. But you will ask, who cares for the souls of the hapless inmates?

Who will venture to enter in at this dreadful gate, never to return again? Who will forsake father and mother, houses and land, to carry the message of a Saviour to these poor lepers? Two Moravian missionaries, impelled by a divine love for souls, have chosen the lazar house as their field of labour. They entered it never to come out again; and I am told that as soon as these die other Moravians are quite ready to fill their place. Ah! my dear friends, may we not blush, and be ashamed before God, that we, redeemed with the same blood, and taught by the same Spirit, should yet be so unlike these men in vehement, heart-consuming love to Jesus and the souls of men?

I wish now to mention to you a proposal which deeply involves the happiness of you and me, and of which I believe most of you have already heard something. O! that you would trace the Lord's hand in it. O! that you would be still, and know that he is God. Let me go over some of the ways by which God has led us hitherto. When I came to you at the first it was not of my seeking. I never had been in your town, and knew only one family in it. I did not ask to be made a candidate. I was quite happy where I was labouring in the Lord's work. God turned your hearts to ask me to settle among you. It was the Lord's doing. Since that day " ye know after what manner I have been with you at all seasons," and how, as far as God gave me light and strength, " I have kept nothing back that was profitable unto you, but have showed you, and have taught you publicly, and from house to house." Ye know, also, some of you, in your blessed experience, that God has given testimony to the word of his grace, so that " our gospel came not to you in word only, but in power, and in the Holy Ghost, and in much assurance."

It is indeed amazing how God should have blessed the word when there was so much weakness and so much sin. But " who is a God like unto our God, that pardoneth iniquity, and passes by the transgressions of the remnant of his heritage?" We planted and watered, and God gave the increase. Ye are God's husbandry—ye are God's building. To him be the glory.

You know also that I have had some painful trials among you. The state of the mass of unconverted souls among you has often made my heart bleed in secret. The coldness and worldliness of you who are God's children has often damped me. The impossibility of fully doing the work of a minister of Christ, among so many souls, was a sad burden to me. The turning back of some that once cared for their souls pierced my heart with new sorrows. Still, I have had two years of great joy among you—unspeakable joy—in seeing souls added to the church of such as shall be saved. I may never be honoured to preach again, yet still to all eternity I shall praise God that he sent me to you—" For what is our hope, or joy, or crown of rejoicing? Are not even ye in the presence of the Lord Jesus Christ at his coming! For ye are our glory and joy." 1 Thess. ii. 19, 20. And should I lightly break up such a connection as this? Ah, no! My dear friends, I do not need all your affectionate letters to persuade me, that, if it were the Lord's will, my own vineyard is the happiest place in the world for me to be. Again and again other vineyards were offered to me, and I was asked to leave you; but I never for a moment listened to one of them, for ye were the seal of my ministry; and where could I be happier than where the Lord had blessed me, and was still blessing me? But God sent another message to me. He laid a heavy hand upon my body; I long struggled against it, but it was too much for me. For two months I have been an exile from you, and I have felt all the time like a widower, or like Jacob bereaved of his children. My constant prayer was, that I might be restored to you, and to the Lord's service. You prayed the same, and when it was not answered, I cried, " Wherefore contendest thou with me?" That word was sent in answer—" My son, despise not thou the chastening of the Lord, neither *be weary* of his correction." Prov. iii. 11. God seems plainly to shut the door against my returning to you at present. I am greatly better, yet still I am forbidden to preach. I am not even allowed to conduct the family devotions morning and evening; indeed, whenever I exert myself much in conversation, I soon feel the monitor within warning me how frail I am.

In these circumstances, the General Assembly's Committee on the Jews, have this day resolved that your pastor, accompanied by Dr. Black of Aberdeen, and my beloved friend, Andrew Bonar of Collace,* should travel for the next six months, to make personal inquiry after the lost sheep of the house of Israel.

They propose that we should go without delay to the Holy Land—that we should then return by Smyrna, Constantinople, Poland, Germany, and Holland. Now, I did not seek this appointment—I never dreamed of such a thing. "But he that hath the key of David, he that openeth and no man shutteth, and shutteth and no man openeth," he has thrown open this door to me, while he keeps the door of return to you still shut. My medical men are agreed that it is the likeliest method of restoring my broken health, and that I have strength enough for the journey. You know how my heart is engaged in the cause of Israel, and how the very sight of Immanuel's land will revive my fainting spirit. And if it be the will of God, I shall return to you, my beloved flock, to tell you all that I have seen, and to lead you in the way to the Jerusalem that is above.

I cannot tell you how many providences have been sent to me, every one convincing me, that it is God's will and purpose I should go.

The most cheering one to me is, that a young man has nearly consented to fill my place, and feed your souls during my absence, who is every thing I could wish, and who will make you almost forget that you want your own pastor. Nay, whatever happens, I

---

* The Rev. Dr. Keith, of St. Cyrus had not at that time joined the Deputation.

hope you will never forget me, but remember me in your families, and remember me in your secret prayers. You are all graven on my heart—I never can forget you. How wonderful have been God's dealings with us! For many reasons he has sent this affliction on us—for sin in me, for sin in you; but also, I am persuaded, that he might seek after "the dearly beloved of his soul," that are now in the hand of their enemies. His way is in the sea—his name is wonderful. I grieve to write so much about myself. I had far rather speak to you of "*Him* who is fairer than the children of men." May you look beyond all ministers to *Him*—may he be your guide even unto death! Once again I hope to write before I leave my home and my country. Till then, may all grace abound toward you, and peace be upon Israel. Amen.

SEVENTH PASTORAL LETTER

Unexpected calls to labour—Parting counsels to believers.

EDINBURGH, *March* 13*th*, 1839.

To all of you who are my brethren, and my companions in tribulation, and in the kingdom and patience of our Lord Jesus Christ, your pastor wishes grace, mercy, and peace.

It gives me great joy to address you once more; and if I could only grave on your heart some of those words which make wise unto salvation, my time and labour would be amply repaid. The providences of every day convince me that I have followed not my own will, but God's, in leaving you for a time. If the Lord permit, I shall come to you again, and, I trust, more fully taught by the Spirit—a holier, happier, and a more useful minister. I did not know when I last preached to you that I was to be so long parted from you; and though I felt a solemn tenderness stealing over my soul which I could not well account for, and eternity seemed very near, and your souls seemed very precious, yet the Lord was "lead ing the blind by a way which we knew not." I have been searching God's word to find examples of this, and I find them very many.

You remember *Abraham*, how he was living quietly in his father's house, in Ur of the Chaldees, when the Lord appeared to him, and said, " Get thee out of thy country, and from thy kindred, and from thy father's house, unto a land that I will show thee;" Gen. xii. 1. And he went out, not knowing whither he went. You remember *Jacob;* his mother said unto him, " Arise, flee thou to Laban, my brother, to Haran, and tarry with him *a few days.*" But the Lord meant it otherwise; and it was twenty years before Jacob came back again; Gen. xxvii. 43. You remember *Joseph;* his father sent him with a message to his brethren. Gen. xxxvii. 14. " Go, I pray thee, see whether it be well with thy brethren, and well with the flocks, and bring me word again." He expected to see him return in a few days; but God had another purpose with him. It was more than twenty years before he saw the face of Joseph again, till he said, " It is enough. Joseph, my son, is yet alive; I will go and see him before I die."

You will find the same method of dealing in the New Testament. How little *Peter* knew that morning when he went up to the house top to pray, that he was that very day to be sent away to open the door of faith to the Gentiles, Acts x. 9; and God said to him, " Arise, get thee down, and go with them, nothing doubting," verse 20. Again, you remember *Barnabas* and *Saul,* how happily they were engaged with the brethren at Antioch ministering to the Lord and fasting. Little did they think that the next day they would be sailing away to carry the gospel to other lands. As they ministered to the Lord and fasted, the Holy Ghost said, " Separate me Barnabas and Saul, for the work whereunto I have called them. And when they had fasted and prayed, and laid their hands on them, they sent them away." Acts xiii. 2, 13.

Once more, when Paul had preached the gospel in all the cities of Asia, and was come to Troas, on the sea coast, how little did he think that night when he laid his head upon his pillow, that, by the next day morning, the swift ship would be carrying him across the seas, to bear the message of salvation to another continent. "A vision appeared to Paul in the night: There stood a man of Macedonia and prayed him, saying, Come over into Macedonia and help us. And after he had seen the vision immediately we endeavoured to go into Macedonia, assuredly gathering that the Lord had called us for to preach the gospel unto them." Acts xvi. 9, 10.

Now has not God dealt with us in a similar manner? Although we are nothing in ourselves but evil and hell deserving creatures; yet, when accepted in the beloved, God cares for us. O! we err, not knowing the Scriptures, nor the power of God, when we think that God is indifferent to the least of all that are in Christ. We are fastened on the Redeemer's shoulder. We are graven on his breastplate, and that is on the Redeemer's heart. Surely he hath directed our steps. "O the depth of the riches both of the wisdom and the knowledge of God." In other circumstances, I suppose, I would not have listened to this proposal. I could not have torn myself away had I been in strength and usefulness among you, and indeed the expedition probably would never have been thought of.

But God, who chose *Israel* to be his peculiar treasure, can easily open up ways when *his set time* is come. I parted from you only for a *few days;* but God meant otherwise, and he will make it his own fixed time. And now, behold, I know that there are some of you among whom I have gone preaching the kingdom of God, who "shall see my face no more." "He that keepeth Israel" may preserve your pastor under his almighty feathers. I know you will pray for me as you have done in secret, and in your families, and in your meetings for prayer, "that the sun may not smite me by day, nor the moon by night;" but, if I should come back again, will I find you all where I left you? Alas! I know it cannot be so, "for what is your life? It is even a vapour;" and God is still crying, "Return, return, ye children of men."

For some among you, I give thanks unto the Father that he hath made you meet to be partakers of the inheritance of the saints in light; Col. i. 12. There are some among you from whom I have learned more than I taught you, "who have been succourers of many, and of myself also," Rom xvi. 2, and who have often reminded me of corn, when it was fully ripe. Shall we be surprised if the Son of Man puts in the sickle? Rev. xiv. 13, 16. Dear advanced believers, we may never meet again. I feel it almost wrong to pray that ye may be kept to comfort us on our return. It is wrong to grudge you "an entrance into perfect day," where you shall lay aside that body of death and sin which is your greatest grief; yet may the Lord spare you, and bless you, and make you a blessing, that ye may bear fruit in old age. O, fill up the little inch of time that remains, to his glory; walk with God; live for God. O, that every thought, and word, and action, might be in his favour, and to his praise. The Lord grant that we may meet again here, and with you be refreshed; but, if not, may we meet "where we shall walk with Christ in white." God, who knows my heart, knows it would be a hell to me to spend an eternity with unconverted, Christless souls; but to be with Christ and his people is heaven to me, wherever it is. There are many young believers among you, whom I may never meet again. It is hard to think of parting with you; the mother feels it hard to part with the sucking child. It was my highest delight in this world to see you growing day by day—to see your sense of the plague of your own heart deepening—to see you cleaving to Christ, with full purpose of heart—to see your "peace widening like a river," and to see your love burning higher and higher toward the throne of God. You are in my heart to live and to die with you. Still, *He* who at any time fed you by *me*, can as easily feed you by another. I commend you to the Lord, on whom you believe. Read 2d Peter iii. 17, meditate over it, pray over it; beware lest ye also, being led away with the error of the wicked, fall from your own steadfastness; but grow in grace.

The only way to be kept from *falling* is to *grow*. If you stand still you will fall. Read Prov. xi. 28, " The righteous shall flourish as a branch." Remember you are not a *tree*, that can stand alone; you are only " a branch," and it is only while you abide in *Him*, as a branch, that you will flourish. Keep clear your sense of justification; remember *it is not* your own natural goodness, nor your tears, nor your sanctification, that will justify you before God. It is Christ's sufferings and obedience *alone*. Seek to be made holier every day—pray, strive, wrestle, for the Spirit, to make you like God. Be as much as you can with God. I declare to you that I had rather be one hour with God, than a thousand with the sweetest society on earth or in heaven. All other joys are but streams; God is the fountain—" all my springs are in thee." Now, may the blessings that are on the head of the just be on your head. Be faithful unto death, and Christ will give you a crown of life; and if I never meet you again in this world, may I meet you as " pillars in the house of my God," where " you shall go no more out." Pray for me when you have access to the throne—when you have a heart for it. I will try and pray for you, that ye may endure to the end. I have a word more for those of you that are still unconverted, whom I may never see again in the flesh. My heart bleeds to think of parting with you; but I must defer this to my next letter, for I expect to write you again before I go. Farewell for the present, and may the grace of the Lord Jesus Christ be with your spirits. Amen.

EIGHTH PASTORAL LETTER

Warnings to the unsaved—Causes why so many among us are unsaved.

EDINBURGH, *March* 20*th*, 1839.

To all of you, my dear flock, who are dearly beloved and longed for, my joy and crown, your pastor wishes grace, mercy, and peace, from God our Father, and from our Lord Jesus Christ.

In my last letter I showed you that, in all human probability, there are many of you to whom I have preached the gospel of salvation to whom I shall never preach it again face to face. I cannot be blind to the many dangers that accompany foreign travel— the diseases and accidents to which we shall be exposed ; but if, through your prayers, I be given to you again, how many blanks shall I find in my flock ! How many dear children of God gone to be " where the weary are at rest," where the imperfect "are made perfect !" How many of you that have stood out against all the invitations of Christ, and all the warnings of God, shall I find departed, to give in your account before the throne ! It is to these last I wish now to speak. For two years I have testified to you the gospel of the grace of God. I came to you in " weakness, and in fear, and in much trembling ;" and if the case of the children of God, and of backsliding souls, has often lain heavy at my heart, I can truly say that your dreadful condition " settled like wine upon the lees," when you are about to be " turned upside down, as a man turneth a dish and wipeth it," has been a continued anxiety to me ; and sometimes, when I have had glimpses of the reality of eternal things, it has been an insupportable agony to my spirit. I know well that this is a jest to you— that you care not whether ministers go or stay ; and if you get a short sermon on the Sabbath day that will soothe and not prick your conscience, that is all you care for. Still, it may be, the Lord who opened Manasseh's heart, will open yours, while I go over solemnly, in the sight of God, what appear to be the chief reasons why, after my two years' ministry among you, there are still so many unconverted, perishing souls.

One cause is to be sought in *your minister.* In Malachi ii. 6, you will find a sweet description of a faithful and successful minister—" The law of truth was in his mouth, and iniquity was not found in his lips: he walked with me in peace and equity, and did turn many away from iniquity." This is what *we should* have done ; but the furnace brings out the dross, and afflictions discover defects unknown before. O, that I could say with Paul—" that I have been with you at all seasons serving the Lord with all humility of mind, and with many tears. Ye are witnesses, and God also, how holily, and justly, and unblamably, we behaved ourselves among you that believe." I am indeed amazed that the ministry of such a worm as I am should ever have been blessed among you at all; and I do this day bewail before God every sin in my heart and life that has kept back the light from your poor dark souls. O, you that can pray, pray that I may come back a holy minister—a shepherd not to lead the flock by the voice only, but to *walk* before them in the way of life. Looking back over my pulpit work, alas! I see innumerable deficiencies. I always prayed that I might " not keep back any thing that was *profitable* "—that I might not shun to declare the whole counsel of God—" that I might decrease, and Christ increase." Still, alas! alas! how dimly I have seen and set before you the " truth as it is in Jesus." How coldly have I pleaded with you to "save yourselves from this untoward generation !" How many things I have known among you " besides Christ and him crucified !" How often have I preached myself, and not the Saviour! How little I have " expounded to you in all the Scriptures the things concerning Jesus !" One error more has been in my private labours among you. How much fruitless intercourse have I had with you! I have not been like a *shepherd* crying after the lost sheep, nor like a *physician* among dying men, nor like a servant bidding you to the marriage nor like one plucking brands from the burning! How often have I gone to your houses to try and win your souls, and you have put me off with a little worldly talk, and the words of salvation have died upon my lips! I dared not tell you, you were perishing—I dared not to show you plainly of the Saviour. How often I have sat at some of your tables, and my heart yearned for your souls, yet a false shame kept me silent! How often I have gone home crying bitterly, " Free me from *blood-guiltiness*, O God, thou God of my salvation."

I turn now to the causes in you, dear children of God. You also have hindered in great measure God's work in the parish. *First,* by your want of *holiness*. " Ye are the light of the world." I have often told you that a work of revival in any place almost always begins with the children of God. God pours water first on " him that is thirsty, and then on the dry ground." But how little has " the word of the Lord sounded out from you!" I do not mean that you should have been loud talkers about religious things. " In the multitude of words there wanteth not sin, and the talk of the lips leadeth to penury." But you should have been " living epistles, known and read of all men." You know that a lighted lamp is a very small thing, and it burns calmly and without noise— yet " it giveth light to all that are within the house." So, if you had day by day the blood of Christ upon your conscience — walking a forgiven and adopted child of God—having a calm peace in your bosom, and a heavenly hope in your eye—having the Holy Spirit filling you with a sweet, tender, chaste, compassionate, forgiving love to all the world—O! had you shone thus for two years back, how many of your friends and neighbours that are going down to hell might have been saying this day, " Thy people shall be my people, and thy God my God." Think, my beloved friends, that every act of unholiness, of conformity to the world, of selfishness, of whispering and backbiting, is hindering the work of God in the parish, and ruining souls eternally. And what shall I say to those of you who, instead of emitting the sweet winning light of holiness, have given out only rays of darkness. " I have this against thee, that thou hast left thy first love. Remember, therefore, from whence thou art fallen, and repent, and do thy first works or else I will come unto thee quickly, and will remove thy candlestick out of his place, except thou repent."

Second—You have hindered God's work by your want of prayer. When God gives grace to souls, it is in answer to the prayers of his children. You will see this, on the day of pentecost, Acts ii. Ezekiel xxxvii. 9, shows that in answer to the prayer of a single child of God, God will give grace to a whole valley full of dry and prayerless bones. Where God puts it into the heart of his children to pray, it is certain that he is going to pour down his Spirit in abundance. Now, where have been your prayers, O children of God ? The salvation of those around you depends on your asking, and yet "hitherto ye have asked nothing in Christ's name." Ye that are the Lord's remembrancers keep not silence, and give him no rest. Alas ! you have given God much rest—you have allowed his hand to remain unplucked out of his bosom. It is said of John Welsh, minister of Ayr, that he used always to sleep with a plaid upon his bed, that he might wrap it around him when he arose in the night to pray. He used to spend whole nights in wrestling with God for Zion, and for the purity of the Church of Scotland ; and he wondered how Christians could lie all night in bed without rising to pray. O ! we have few Welshes now, therefore our Church is so dim, and our land a barren wilderness. Dear Christians, I often think it strange that ever we should be in heaven, and so many in hell through our soul-destroying carelessness. The good Lord pardon the past, and stir you up for the future. I learn that you are more stirred up to pray since I left, both in secret and unitedly. God grant it be so. Continue in it, dear children. Do not let it slip again.

Plead and wrestle with God, showing him that *the cause is his own*, and that it is all for *his own glory* to arise and have mercy upon Zion.

Last of all, think of the causes in yourselves, O unconverted souls ! Be sure of this, that ye will only have yourselves to blame if ye awake in hell. You will not be able to plead God's secret decrees, nor the sins of your minister, nor the carelessness of your godly neighbours—you will be speechless. If you die, it is because you *will* die ; and if you *will* die, then you must die.

Think, first, on your carelessness about ordinances. They are the channels through which God pours his Spirit. The Bible—prayer—the house of God— these are the golden pipes through which the golden oil is poured. How many of you utterly neglect the Bible ! You know not the blessedness of the man spoken of in the first Psalm. How many of you restrain prayer before God ! How many of you have dead, useless prayers, learned by rote ! And O ! how you despise the house of God ! Alas ! that Church shall rise against you in judgment. It was a door of the ark brought near to you. Two years and more its gates have been wide open to you, and yet, how you have slighted it ! Already, I seem to hear your loud wailing when you mourn at the last, and say, " How have I hated instruction, and my heart despised reproof, and have not obeyed the voice of my teachers !"

Think, *second, how you have been mockers.* It has been too common for you to make a mock of eternal things, and of godly people. When there have been anxious souls seeking the way to be saved, and they could not conceal their tears, you have called them hypocrites ! When some have got a new heart, and have changed their way of life, you have spoken scoffingly of them, and tried to bring them into contempt. Alas ! poor soul, look within. You have hardened your heart into an adamant stone. Look at Prov. xvii. 5, " He that mocketh the poor reproacheth his Maker." And, again, Isaiah xxviii. 22, " Now, therefore, be ye not *mockers*, lest your bands be made strong."

To sum up all. The great cause that I leave you hard is, that you " despise the Son of God." You see no beauty in him that you should desire him. You lightly esteem the rock of your salvation. You have not had a soul piercing look at a pierced Saviour. You have not seen the infinite load of sins that weighed down his blessed head. You have not seen how open his arms are to receive—how often he would have gathered you. You have not heard that sweet word whispered by the Spirit, " Behold me, behold me," which, when a man once hears, he leaves all and follows. You have trampled under foot the blood of the Son of God. Farewell, dear, dear souls. God knows that my whole heart prays that you may be saved.

Perhaps there are some of you that never would bend under my ministry, who will melt like wax before the fire under the word of the dear young minister who is to speak to you in my absence. May the Lord give him hundreds for my tens! I will often pray for you, and sometimes write to you when I am far away. If I reach Immanuel's land, I will say, " the Lord bless you out of Zion." And if you will not turn, remember I take God for a record that I am pure from the blood of you all.

Dear children of God, I now cast you on him who cast you on me when I was ordained over you. He said to me " feed my sheep"—" feed my lambs"—" feed my sheep." Now, when he sends me away, I would humbly return his own words to him, saying, O Shepherd of Israel—feed my sheep—feed my lambs—feed my sheep. Little children, love one another. Keep yourselves from idols. Bear me ever on your hearts. Pray that when I have preached to others, I may not be a castaway. Pray that I may save some.

Now the God of peace, that brought again from the dead our Lord Jesus Christ, that great Shepherd of the sheep, through the blood of the everlasting covenant, make you perfect in every good work to do his will, working in you that which is well pleasing in his sight, through Jesus Christ; to whom be glory for ever and ever. Amen.

My next, if God will, may be from England.

NINTH PASTORAL LETTER

Incidents of the way as far as Leghorn—Exhortations.

LEGHORN, *May 2d*, 1839.

To all of you, my beloved flock, who have received Christ, and walk in Him, your pastor wishes grace, and mercy, and peace, from God our Father, and from our Lord Jesus Christ.

My heart's desire and prayer for you every day is, that you may be saved. I am now far from you in the flesh, yet am I with you in the spirit. I thank my God without ceasing, for as many of you as have been awakened to flee from the wrath to come—have rested your soul upon the good word of God concerning Jesus —and have tasted the love of God. In every prayer of mine for you all, I ask that ye may continue in the faith, grounded and settled—that ye may be like trees, rooted in Christ Jesus—or like a holy temple built up on him who is the only foundation stone.

I expected to have written you from London, and again before leaving France, but we have travelled so rapidly, often day and night, and the fatigue was so great to my weak frame that I was disappointed in this: but I did not forget you night or day, and I know well I am not forgotten by you. Since I wrote you last, I have passed through many cities and countries, and seen many faces and things strange to me. Many lessons for my own soul, and for yours, I have learned. At present I must write you shortly.

We left London on the 11th of April, and next morning crossed the British Channel from Dover to Boulogne, and found ourselves on the shores of France. The very first night we spent in France, we were visited by a most interesting Jew, evidently anxious about his soul. He spoke with us for many hours, accepted the New Testament in Hebrew, and bade good-by with much emotion. We thanked God for this token for good. Pray for us that God may give us good success, that we may have the souls of Israel for our hire. From Boulogne we travelled to Paris, by day and by night, and spent a Sabbath there. Alas! poor Paris knows no Sabbath, all the shops are open, and all the inhabitants are on the wing in search of pleasures—pleasures that perish in the using. I thought of Babylon and of Sodom as I passed through the crowd. I cannot tell how I longed for the peace of a Scottish Sabbath. There is a place in Paris called the *Champs Elysées*, or Plains of Heaven—a beautiful public walk, with trees and gardens: we had to cross it on passing to the Protestant church. It is the chief scene of their Sabbath desecration, and an awful scene it is. O! thought I, if this is the heaven a Parisian loves, he will never enjoy the pure heaven that is above. Try yourselves by that text, Isaiah lvii. 13, 14. I remember of once preaching to you from it. Do you really delight in the Sabbath day? If not, you are no child of God. I remember with grief that there are many among you that despise the Sabbath—some that buy and sell on that holy day— some who spend its blessed hours in worldly pleasures, in folly and sin. O! you would make Dundee another Paris if you could. Dear believers, oppose these ungodly practices with all your might. The more others dishonour God's holy day, the more do you honour it, and show that you love it of all the seven the best. Even in Paris, as in Sardis, we found a little flock of believers. We heard a sweet sermon in English, and another in French. There are only two thousand Protestant hearers out of the half million that inhabit Paris, and there are fourteen faithful sermons preached every Sabbath.

We left the French capital on the 16th April, a lovely evening, with a deep blue sky above, and a lovely country before us, on the banks of the Seine. This would be a delightsome land, if it only had the light of God's countenance upon it. We travelled three days and three nights, by Troyes, Dijon, and Chalons, till we came to Lyons, upon the rapid river Rhone, in the south of France. The Lord stirred up kind friends to meet us. Lyons is famous as being the place where many Christians were martyred in the first ages, and where many were burned at the time of the Reformation, because they loved and confessed the Lord Jesus. God loves the place still. There is a small body of three hundred believers, who live here under a faithful pastor, Mr. Cordes. He cheered our hearts much, and sent us away with affectionate prayers. That day we sailed down the Rhone more than one hundred miles, through a most wonderful country. We hoped to have spent the Sabbath at Marseilles, but just as we entered the Mediterranean Sea, a storm of wind arose, and drove the vessel on a barren island, at the mouth of the Rhone. We all landed, and spent our Sabbath quietly on the desert island. It was your communion Sabbath; and I thought that perhaps this providence was given me that I might have a quiet day to pray for you. There were about twelve fishermen's huts on the island, made of reeds, with a vine growing before the door, and a fig tree in their garden. We gave tracts and books in French to all our fellow passengers, and to the inhabitants, and tried to hallow the Sabbath. My heart went up to God the whole day for you all, and for my dear friends who would be ministering to you. I tried to go over you one by one as many as I could call to mind. My longing desire for you was, that Jesus might reveal himself to you in the breaking of bread—that you might have heart filling views of the lovely person of Immanuel, and might draw from *him* rivers of comfort, life, and holiness. I trust your fellowship was with the Father, and with his son Jesus Christ. Many I know are ignorant of Jesus. I trembled when I thought of their taking the bread and wine. You know all my mind upon this. The next morning the storm abated, and we sailed over the tideless sea, and reached the beautiful harbour of

Marseilles by eight o'clock. We had conference with a faithful young minister, and with the Rabbi of the Jews. We also attended the synagogue the same evening. The Jews of France are fast falling into infidelity, especially the younger Jews. They do not love the law and the prophets as their fathers did. They are, indeed, the dry bones in Ezekiel xxxvii. Still God can make them live. It is our part to speak to them the word of the Lord, and to pray for the quickening Spirit.

True Christians in France are increasing. There are four hundred Protestant ministers, and nearly one half of these are faithful men, who know nothing among their flocks but Christ and him crucified. In some places Christians seem more bold and devoted than in Scotland. It is very pleasant to hear them singing the French psalms: they sing with all their heart, and are much given to prayer. O, my dear Christians, be like them in these things. May the same Holy Spirit, who has often visited you in times gone by, fill your hearts more than ever with praise and prayer.

Popery in France is waxing bolder. The first day we landed on the shore, it was evident we were in a land of Popish darkness. On the height above Boulogne, a tall white cross attracted our eyes. We found on it an image of our Saviour nailed to the tree, larger than life; the spear, the hammer, the nails, the sponge, were all there. It was raised by some shipwrecked fishermen; and sailors' wives go there in a storm to pray for their absent husbands. The Popish priests meet us in every street; they wear a three-cornered hat, black bands, a black mantle with a sash, and large buckles on their shoes; they have all a dark suspicious look about them. At the entrance of every village there is a cross, and the churches are full of pictures and images. I went into one church in Paris, the finest in France, where the crosses were all of pure silver, and there was a large white image of the Virgin Mary, holding the infant Jesus in her arms. Many rich and poor were kneeling on the pavement before the image silently praying. Gross darkness covers the people. A priest travelled one whole night with us in the coach. We argued with him first in French and then in Latin, trying to convince him of his errors, showing him his need of peace with God, and a new heart. In the cxxxvii. Psalm you will see that Babylon, or Popery, is "doomed to destruction;" and in Rev. xviii., you will see that her destruction will be very sudden and very terrible. O that it may come soon, for thousands are perishing under its soul-destroying errors. And yet remember what I used to read to you out of Martin Boos; and remember the saying of the Lord to Elijah, 1 Kings xix. There may be many hidden ones even in Babylon. The whole way through France we distributed French tracts. Many hundreds in this way received the message of life. In every village they came crowding around us to receive them. Pray that the dews of the Spirit may make the seed sown by the wayside spring up.

We were too late for the first vessel to Malta, and therefore resolved to sail into Italy. We left Marseilles on the 23d April, and landed in Genoa on the 24th. Genoa is one of the most beautiful towns in the world—the most of the houses and churches are of pure white marble, and from the sea, look like palaces; but Satan's seat is there—we dared not distribute a single tract or book in Genoa—we would have been imprisoned immediately. The Catholic priests, in there black dismal cloaks, and the monks with their coarse brown dress, tied with a cord, a crucifix and beads hanging round their neck, bare feet, and cowl, swarm in every street. I counted that we met twenty of them in a ten minutes' walk. Popery reigns here triumphant, yet the people "are sitting still, and at ease," living for this world only. O ! it is an awful thing to be at ease when under the wrath of God. Every place I see in Italy makes me praise God that you have the gospel so freely preached unto you. Prize it highly; do not neglect the wells of salvation that flow so freely for you.

The next day we sailed for Leghorn, where we

have been ever since. We are living in the house where the excellent Mr. Martin, once minister of St. George's, Edinburgh, died in 1834. We visited his grave. I prayed that, like him, we might be faithful unto the end. There are from ten thousand to twenty thousand Jews here. We went to the synagogue the night we arrived, and twice since; it is a beautiful building inside, capable of holding two thousand persons. The place where they keep the law, written on a parchment roll, is finely ornamented with marble; so is the desk where they read the prayers. Lamps are continually kept burning. One rabbi was chanting the prayers when we entered. Beside the ark there stood three rabbis, in the eastern dress, with turbans and flowing robes, and long beards. They were much reverenced, and many came to kiss their hand, and receive their blessing. One of them is from Jerusalem; we have had many interesting conversations with him. Every day we have met with several Jews; they are very friendly to us, and we try to convince them out of the Scriptures, that Jesus is the Christ. There are about two hundred and fifty Protestants here, and we have tried to stir them up also to care for their souls. Dr. Black preached to them in our hotel last Sabbath evening.

Hitherto the Lord hath helped us. To-morrow we sail from Italy to Malta, then for Egypt, and then for the Holy Land. Dear believers, it is a sweet consolation to me that your prayers go with me wherever I go. Often, perhaps, they close the mouth of the adversary—often keep back the storms from our vessel—often open a way to the hearts of those we meet —often bring down a sweet stream of the Spirit to water my thirsty soul. May I be enabled to make a sweet exchange with you, praying my heavenly Father to render double unto each of your bosoms what you pray for me! May my dear brother, who, I trust, fills my place among you, be made a blessing to you all— may his own soul be watered while he waters yours! Join him with me in your supplications. May he win many souls among you that I could never win.

This is Thursday evening. I trust you are at this moment met together in the prayer meeting. O! do not forsake the assembling of yourselves together. My heart is with you all. May the Spirit fill the whole church, and every heart, with his presence and power. My body is still far from being strong. I am more and more convinced that I did right in leaving you. I trust to be restored to you again in the fulness of the blessing of the gospel of Christ. "The will of the Lord be done."

My dear brother, who is with me, whom you know well, and who daily joins me in fervent prayers for you, sends his salutations. Remember me to all who are sick and afflicted. Alas! how many of you may be labouring and heavy laden, that I know not of; but Jesus knows your sorrows. I commend you to the good Physician.

My dear classes, I do not, and cannot forget—Psalm cxix. 9th verse, I pray may be written in your hearts.

My dear children in the Sabbath schools I always think upon, on the Sabbath evenings; *and on those* who patiently labour among them. The Lord himself give you encouragement, and a full reward.

To all I say, keep close to Christ, dear friends. Do not be enticed away from him; he is all your righteousness, and all mine; out of *Him* you have all your strength, and I mine. It pleased the Father that in *Him* should all fulness dwell.

The grace of the Lord Jesus Christ be with your spirits. Farewell.

TENTH PASTORAL LETTER

Incidents of the way in Palestine and other lands—Request.

BRESLAW, IN PRUSSIA *Oct.* 16*th*, 1839.

To my dear flock, whom I love in the Lord Jesus, grace, mercy, and peace, be multiplied from God the Father, and from his Son Jesus Christ.

I fear that many of you will be thinking hardly of your distant pastor, because of his long silence; and, indeed, I cannot but think hardly of myself. I little thought, when leaving Italy, that I would be in Europe again before writing to you. I did not know how difficult it is to write at any length when travelling in the East. From the day we left Egypt till we came to Mount Lebanon, for more than two months, we were constantly journeying from place to place, living in tents, without the luxury of a chair or a bed. In these circumstances, with my weak body, and under a burning sun, you must not wonder at my silence. At the foot of Mount Carmel I began one letter to you, and again in sight of the Sea of Galilee I began another, but neither did I get finished. Last of all before leaving the Holy Land, I set apart a day for writing to you; but God had another lesson for me to learn. He laid me down under a burning fever, bringing me to the very gates of death. Indeed, my dear people, I feel like *Lazarus*, whom the Lord Jesus raised from the tomb. I feel like one sent a second time with the message of salvation, to speak it more feelingly and more faithfully to your hearts, as one whose eye had looked into the eternal world. In all our wanderings you have been with me by night and by day. Every scene of Immanuel's land brought you to my remembrance, because every scene tells of Jesus Christ and him crucified. In the wilderness— in Jerusalem—beside the Sea of Galilee—at Smyrna —on the Black Sea—on the Danube—you have been all with me. I have, day and night, unceasingly laid your case before God. It has been one of my chief comforts, that, though I could not preach to you, nor come to you, I could yet pray for you. Perhaps I may obtain more for you in this way than I could have done by my personal services among you. Another joy to me has been, that I know all of you who pray, pray for me. This has been a lamp to me in many a dark hour. God has wonderfully preserved us through your prayers. In the south of the Holy Land, we were daily exposed to the plague. Every night we heard the wail of the mourners going about the streets of Jerusalem; yet no plague came near our dwelling. Near the Sea of Galilee, we were often in danger of being robbed and murdered by the wild Arabs; yet we passed unhurt through the midst of them. Sailing to Smyrna, your pastor was brought low indeed, in so much that I never thought to see you again; yet God sent his word and healed me. In Poland, the Sabbath before last, I was actually in the hands of robbers; but through God's wonderful mercy, I escaped safe. In every step of our journey, I am persuaded we have been watched over by our all-loving Father, who is the hearer of prayer. And the Lord shall deliver us from every evil work, and will preserve us unto his heavenly kingdom. I speak of these things only that you may give him the glory, and trust in him to your dying day. Sing the cxvi. Psalm in all your families. Another joy to me has been, that God has given you the dear brother who watches over you so tenderly. You know not what joy it gave me to hear of you all through him. The letter reached me at Smyrna, when I was so weak that I could not walk alone. It was like health and marrow to my bones, to hear that the Lord's work is not yet done in the midst of you, and that so many of you stand fast in the Lord, having your conversation in heaven. I have no greater joy than to hear that my children walk in the truth. It is not like common joy. All joys of this world are short and fading—they reach not beyond the dark boundary of the grave; but to rejoice over those whom the Lord has given me out of a perishing world—this is joy which God himself shares, and which reaches into the light of eternity. Ye are my joy and crown. In like manner, there is no sorrow like the sorrow of the pastor who has to weep over a backsliding people. I do tremble to return to you, for I know well I shall have deep sorrow from some of whom I expected joy. I fear lest I have to mourn over some branches that are without fruit, on the good vine tree; over some, who once gave their hand to the Saviour, but are now saying, "I will go after my lovers." Are there none of you who have left your first love, and broken the bands that bound you to follow Jesus? Shall I find none of whom I must needs say, "They went out from us, but they were not of us?" O, there is no sorrow like unto this sorrow. Had I been able, as I hoped, to have written you from all the chief places in our journeyings, I would have attempted to describe to you all I saw; but now there are so many countries to look back upon, that it would be in vain to attempt it. I do hope, that if the Lord bring us together again, I may be able to tell you many things of our wanderings, and especially of Immanuel's land, which may both refresh and improve you. Nothing that I have heard I keep back from you, if only it be for your souls' good and God's glory. Of the Holy Land, I can only say, like the Queen of Sheba, "that the half was not told me." It is far more wonderful than I could have believed. I shall always reckon it one of the greatest temporal blessings of my lot, that I have been led to wander over its mountains with the Bible in my hand, to sit by its wells, and to meditate among its ruined cities. Not a single day did we spend there without reading, in the land itself, the most wonderful traces of God's anger and of his love. Several times we went to the Mount of Olives, to the Garden of Gethsemane, to the Pool of Siloam, and to the Village of Bethany, and every stone seemed to speak of the love of God to sinners. These places are probably very little altered from what they were in the days when Jesus tabernacled among men, and they all seemed to say, "Hereby perceive we the love of God, because he laid down his life for us." We were four days in sight of the Sea of Galilee. I could not help thinking of you, my dear young people, for we used to go over the Sea of Galilee so often on the Monday evenings, and all the scenes of divine love it has been witness to. One day we rode through the Plain of Gennesareth, and passed the mouldering ruins of Capernaum, the Saviour's city, where his voice of mercy was so often heard, and where his hand was so often stretched out to heal. We asked in vain for Chorazin and Bethsaida. The wo which Jesus pronounced has fallen upon them.

O my dear flock, "how shall you escape if you neglect so great salvation?" See how desolate they are left that refuse him that speaketh from heaven. The free offer of a divine surety rings through your churches, now that God continues faithful teachers among you. Every Sabbath, and oftener, the fountain for sin is publicly opened for you, and souls all defiled with sin are invited to come and wash. But these mercies will not always last.

If you tread the glorious gospel of the grace of God under your feet, your souls will perish; and I fear Dundee will one day be a howling wilderness like Capernaum. I spent nearly the whole of August during my illness in Bouja, a village near Smyrna, under the care of tenderest friends, whom the Lord wonderfully provided for me in a strange land. You remember Smyrna is one of the Seven Churches in Asia to which the Saviour sent those quickening messages in the Revelation of St. John. I thought again and again of the happy Thursday evenings which I once spent with you in meditating on these Seven Epistles to the Churches. You know it is said of Samuel, even when he was a child, that God did not let one of his words fall to the ground, and the same is true to this hour of the very weakest of God's faithful ministers. What we have spoken to you is not like the passing wind which hurries on and leaves no trace behind. It is like the rain and snow—it will not return to God without accomplishing some end in your hearts, either melting or hardening. Smyrna is the only one of these churches where a pure golden candlestick is now to be found with the light burning. There is a small company who believe in Jesus. It was pleasant indeed to hear the gospel preached there in all its purity and power. Be you also faithful to death, and you shall receive a crown of life. Leaving Smyrna, we sailed past Troas and Bithynia, and visited Constantinople, the most beautiful city in the world, and yet the most miserable. Looking round from the deck of the vessel, I could count above ninety minarets, many of them pure marble, carved and gilded in the richest manner. These all form part of mosques, or temples, of the false prophet Mahomet. This religion is a singular invention of Satan; their Koran, or Bible, is a book filled with nonsense, and with much wickedness. All their belief is comprehended in the short saying, " Lo Ullah il Allah, Mahomed Rasal Allah "—" There is no God but God, and Mahomed is his prophet." They expect to be saved chiefly by making pilgrimages to Mecca, by abstaining from wine and pork, and by praying five times a day. Every day, at sunrise or sunset, we saw them at prayer; wherever they are, in the open street, on the top of the house, or on the deck of a ship, they take off their shoes, wash hands, face, and feet, spread their garment before them, and turning their face towards Mecca, pray, bending and kissing the ground, often fifteen and twenty times. They are rather pleased if you look at them. They are very proud of their own faith, and will not listen for a moment to the gospel of Jesus. It would be instant banishment or death if any missionary were to attempt their conversion. Ah! my dear flock, how differently you are situated. How freely salvation is offered to you—a faith that really saves you from your sins—that makes you love one another. For love is of God, and every one that loveth is born of God. If you are not growing humble and loving, be sure your faith is no better than a Mahometan's. You are not of God, but of the world. The next countries we visited were Wallachia and Moldavia. We sailed to them from Constantinople, across the raging waves of the Black Sea, and up the mighty river Danube. These are two singular countries, seldom visited by travellers; they are governed by two princes, and the established religion is of the Greek Church. I wish I could show you all that I have seen of the superstitions and wickedness practised among them, that you might give more earnest heed to the pure gospel that flows as freely as air and water, through our beloved land. One day, in Bucharest, the capital city of Wallachia, I was present at a festival on the prince's birth day. An immense crowd was present in their finest church, and all the nobles of the land. The service consisted of prayers and chanting by a number of priests, dressed in the most splendid manner. When all was over I staid behind to see a curious superstition. At one side of the altar lay an open coffin, highly ornamented; within I observed a dead body wrapped in cloth of gold; a dead withered hand alone was left out. This is said to be the body of St. Demetrius, lately found in a river, by the water parting asunder miraculously. Such is the tale we are told. I stood beside it when the worshippers approached the coffin in great numbers, men and women, rich and poor. First, they crossed themselves, and kneeled, kissing the floor three times. Then they approached reverently, and kissed the withered hand of the dead body and a cross that lay beside it. Then they gently dropped a small coin into a little plate at the dead man's feet, and after receiving a blessing from the priest, with three prostrations more to the ground, they retired. This is one specimen of their abominable worship of dead men. Do I tell you these things that you may be proud of your superior light? Ah! no. I write these things that those of you who live no better lives than they do may be convinced of your danger. What can you expect of these poor idolaters, but that they will live after the flesh, in rioting and drunkenness, in chambering and wantonness, in strife and envying? But are there none of you, my dear flock, for whom night and day my prayers ascend—are there none of you who do the same things, though you have the Holy Bible, and a freely preached gospel, and no superstition? Yet how many of you live an unholy life! Ah! remember Sardis—"I know thy works, that thou hast a name that thou livest, and art dead. Be watchful, and strengthen the things which remain, that are ready to die: for I have not found thy works perfect before God." The next kingdom we came through was Austrian Poland—the land of graven images. We came through its chief towns, Tarnapol, Brody, Lemburg, and from thence to Cracow, travelling many hundred miles. You would be amazed, as I have been, if you saw the abominable idolatry of this land. The Roman Catholic is the established faith; and the government are bitter persecutors of any who change. At every village there are numbers of crosses, of immense size, with the image of the Saviour. There are also statues of the Virgin Mary, and of other saints, as large as life, all along the roads. Often there are wooden boxes set up, full of images; often, in the middle of a square, there is a small covered chamber full of these idols, of wood and stone, which the poor people worship every day. The Bible is an unlawful book in this country. All our Bibles were taken away from us, even our Hebrew ones, that we might not preach to the Jews the glad tidings of a Saviour. Blessed be God, they could not take them from our memories and hearts. Should not this make you all pray for the coming of the day when the towers of Popery shall fall—the day when God shall avenge us on her; for the Bible which she hates so much, says, "Her plagues shall come in one day, death and mourning, and famine; and she shall be utterly burned with fire; for strong is the Lord God who judgeth her." Pray for that day, for it will be the same day when God will bind up the breach of his people Israel, and shall heal the stroke of their wound. It will be the day when the Lamb's wife shall come forth in all her loveliness, and when the Lord Jesus shall wear the crown of his espousals.

I began this letter to you in Cracow, the ancient capital of Poland, but now an independent state. We spent three days there, inquiring after the poor despised Jews. We had much intercourse with a faithful, prayerful missionary, who labours among them there; and on the Sabbath, we celebrated the Lord's Supper.

During the four years he had been in Cracow, the missionary had never once enjoyed the ordinance, for all around are sunk in popery or infidelity. We were but five souls in all, and yet we felt it very pleasant, when surrounded with them that hated us, and far from our homes, with the door of the chamber shut, to remember Jesus. My thoughts and desires were much towards you. I had greatly hoped to be present at your next Lord's Supper; but now I see it cannot be. My only comfort is, I have committed you to those who are beloved of the Lord, workmen that need not to be ashamed, whose names are in the book of life; and the chief Shepherd, I feel persuaded, will not leave you orphans, but will come to you and breathe upon you. May the Lord keep back from the table all who are not united to Christ; and may you, who are his own children, have communion with the Father and with his Son Jesus Christ!

Since yesterday morning, we have travelled one hundred and eighty miles nearer home. We are now in Breslaw, and we breathe more freely, for this is the Protestant kingdom of Prussia. It makes my heart light to think that I am really on my way to you. It has been a sweet work, indeed, to me to carry, with poor stammering lips, the word of salvation to the scattered sheep of the house of Israel; still, I do long, if it be the Lord's will, to feed once more the flock that was given me in the dew of my youth. Whether I shall be permitted, and how long, to take up so great a work again, my Master only knows; but if you wish for it as fervently as I do, solemnly agree, in the presence of God, on the night on which this letter is read to you, to these two things—1st. Strive, together with me, in your prayers to God for me, that it would please him to forgive and forget our past sins and short-comings—mine in carrying the message, yours in receiving it; and that he would really heal my body, and strengthen my soul, for again uptaking the blessed work of the gospel ministry among you, and that he would grant us a prosperous journey to come unto you. 2d. Solemnly agree, in the strength of the Lord Jesus, to break off your sins by righteousness, and your iniquities by showing mercy to the poor. The sin of one Achan troubled the whole camp of Israel. If any one of you who are God's children wilfully continue in some old sin, then it may be God's will, for your sake, to trouble our camp, and continue his chastening. See that no fleshly lust—no covetousness, which is idolatry—no hankering after the world and its unholy pleasures—no unlawful affection—be reigning in you. Clean out the old leaven from all your houses, so that we may meet again in peace, and be refreshed together by days of the Lord's presence, and of the Spirit's power, such as we have never seen before. This is the hearty desire and prayer of your affectionate pastor, &c.

TO THE MEMBERS OF A PRAYER MEETING

Parable of the Sower.

MY DEAR FRIENDS,—It has been a matter of great joy to me to hear that you meet together from time to time to read the word of God and pray—to pray for a blessing on yourselves and families, that you may be brought to the saving knowledge of the Lord Jesus Christ, and to pray for ministers that they may be filled with the Holy Spirit, and made insatiably greedy for the salvation of souls, and that the word of God preached on the Sabbath may rise and be glorified till the whole world bow the knee at the name of Jesus.

O! you that have had your eyes opened to see your lost condition by nature and by wicked works—you that have been drawn, by the Father, to believe in Jesus, to wash in the blood of the Lamb, and to put on the righteousness of God—O! pray with all your heart that your dear friends may be brought to take the peace you feel—that your enemies may be brought to the same Saviour, and that all the world may be brought to know him, whom to know is life eternal.

If you look at the xiii. chapter of Matthew, verse 3—9, you will see how much of our preaching is in vain, and what need there is to pray that God would open the hearts we speak to.

Many among you, I fear, are like the hard way-side, so that, when the seed falls, it cannot get into your hearts, and the devil plucks it all away. Verse 3—4. Is it not true that some of your hearts are like the footpath, trodden all the week by wicked thoughts? *"Free passage this way"* is written over your hearts— common worldly thoughts—busy covetous desires of money—malicious thoughts—impure, abominable thoughts. O who can tell what a constant thorough-fare of wicked imaginations is passing night and day through every unconverted mind! O look at Gen. vi. 5, and weep over the Bible description of your own hard hearts. Now, when you come to the church on Sabbath, your heart is like a footpath; the seed can-not fall in, it lies upon the surface. You do not un-derstand the minister. Perhaps he preaches of the desperate wickedness of the heart, and the danger you are in of going to hell, if you be not born again. You feel it to be a dry subject, and turn your head away. Perhaps he is preaching of the love of Jesus, in tasting death for every man; and that he will in no wise cast the vilest sinner out. Still, you feel no interest, and, perhaps, you fall asleep during the sermon. O you are the wayside hearers—the devil plucks all the seed away. When you turn your back on the church, you turn your back on divine things; and before you have got half way home, the devil has carried off every word of the sermon. Yea, often, I fear, before you have got a sight of your own cottage, or the trees before the door, the devil has filled your hearts with abominable worldly thoughts, and your tongue with evil talk, unworthy of the Sabbath. O Satan, Satan! what a cunning fiend thou art! Even when the hard hearts will not receive the word, thou wilt not suffer it to remain; lest it should come back in a time of sickness or danger, thou carriest all away.

Dear believers, pray that it be not so with you nor with your friends; pray for a soft heart and a retentive memory; and often speak together of the sermons you hear, and get them harrowed into your hearts, that Satan may be cheated, and your soul saved.

Many, I fear, among you, are receiving the seed into stony places (v. 6;) receiving the word for a while; but soon withering away in time of persecution. I fear there may be some among you who are charmed with something about the gospel, instead of cleaving in heart to Christ. I can imagine that some of the wounded Israelites, that were bitten by the serpent, were much taken with Moses, as he held up the brazen serpent, instead of looking at the serpent itself. Many are fond of ministers who are not fond of Christ. Read over Ezekiel xxxiii. 30—32, and pray that this be not your case.

Now, I will give you two marks, by which you may know whether you are one of these unfruitful hearers. 1st. The *rocky heart* will remain the same. If you find that your liking to the gospel is from the surface, from curiosity, or fancy, or love to a minister—if you find that your rocky heart has never been broken by conviction of sin—has never melted to flow towards Jesus—then you are an empty professor; you have a name to live, while you are spiritually dead.

2d. *You will endure for a while.* A really converted soul is like a branch. "I am the vine, ye are the *branches.*" It will cleave to it summer and winter. But if you have only a mock conversation, you will wither away when persecution comes. God knows how soon days of trial may come in Scotland. Be ye therefore ready. He that endureth to the end shall be saved. I fear, dear friends, that many of you receive the seed among thorns; v. 7. Look into your heart and see, when you read your Bible in the morning, how many cares and anxieties are dancing before your eyes, so that you can hardly see the page you are reading. How often you come to the house of God, and you see the minister preaching of eternal things with all his might, but your heart is stuffed full of cares, and plans, and pleasures. Alas, alas! the world has got the first hold of your heart, and so you can think of nothing else. What will it profit you if you gain the whole world and lose your own soul?

One thing is plain, that thorns and wheat cannot grow on the same spot of ground; so that, if you will keep to your thorns, you must burn with them. O dear souls, if you got but a glimpse of the beauty of Jesus, you would leave all and follow him. If you got but a taste of the sweetness of forgiveness, you would count every thing else but loss for the excellence of the knowledge of Christ. See how Matthew did? Mat. ix. 9. He was once as worldly as yourselves, and as greedy of money as any one of you; and yet a word from the sweet mouth of Christ made him leave all. Read that sweet command of Christ; Mat. x. 37, 38. O! pray to be made willing to leave all for Christ. He is kinder than father or mother— more precious than son or daughter. Take up your cross, then, and follow him.

Last of all, I trust there are some among you like the good ground (v. 8,) who receive the word into a heart broken up by the Spirit of God—watered by prayer—and who bear fruit unto *life eternal*. HAVE YOU HAD YOUR HEARTS BROKEN, dear friends? Has God ploughed up your hard, unbelieving hearts? Have you had real concern for your perishing soul? Have you been driven to your knees? Have you ever wept in secret for your sins? Have you been made to tremble under your load of guilt? Do you come thus to the house of God—*your heart like an open furrow, waiting for the seed?* Inquire earnestly whether the fallow ground of your heart has ever been broken up; Jeremiah iv. 3. *A broken heart alone can receive a crucified Christ.*

HAVE YOU UNDERSTOOD THE GOSPEL? Have you believed the record that God has given concerning his Son? Do you feel that it is true that God is love?— that Christ has died the just for the unjust?—that he is beckoning you to come to him? Do you believe on the Son of God? He that believeth shall be saved; he that believeth not shall be damned; Mark xvi. 16.

DO YOU BEAR FRUIT? Without holy fruit all evidences are vain. How vain would it be to prove to a farmer that his fields were good and productive, if they produced no corn! You might say to him, "Neighbour, your land is good; the soil is dry and well trenched." "O, but," he would say, "where is the yellow grain—where are the full ears falling before the sickle of the reaper?" Dear friends, you have awakenings, enlightenings, experiences, a full heart in prayer, and many due signs; but, if you want holiness, you will never see the Lord. If you are a drinker, a swearer, a liar, a lascivious talker, a wanton, a slanderer, you are in the broad way that leads to destruction.

Read Matthew vii. 21—23; and pray that you may not be deceiving your own souls. Dear believers, pray that you may bear fruit an hundredfold. Do not be content with bearing thirtyfold or sixtyfold; pray to be *sanctified wholly;* 1 Thess. v. 23. Pray that the whole lump may be leavened; Matt. xiii. 33. Pray that, day and night, in company or alone, Sabbath and week day, you may adorn the doctrine of God our Saviour in all things. I often pray for you all; and desire that in secret and in your families you will not forget me. Your friend and souls' well wisher, &c.

EVIDENCE ON REVIVALS

ANSWER TO QUERIES ON THE SUBJECT OF THE REVIVAL OF RELIGION IN ST. PETER'S CHURCH, DUNDEE.

Submitted to a Committee of the Presbytery of Aberdeen.

IN December 1840, the Presbytery of Aberdeen appointed a committee to inquire into the revivals which had recently occurred in different parts of the country, or were taking place at that time. The committee, besides hearing evidence *viva voce*, issued queries which were sent, amongst other ministers, to Mr. McCheyne. The following are copies of these queries and of his answers:—

"I. Have revivals taken place in your parish or district; and, if so, to what extent, and by what instrumentality and means?

" II. Do you know what was the previous character and habits of the parties?

" III. Have any who were notorious for drunkenness, or other immoralities, neglect of family duties, or public ordinances, abandoned their evil practices, and become remarkable for their diligence in the use of the means of grace?

" IV. Could you condescend on the number of such cases?

" V. Has the conduct of any of the parties been hitherto consistent; and how long has it lasted?

" VI. Have the means to which the revivals are ascribed been attended with beneficial effects on the religious condition of the people at large?

" VII. Were there public manifestations of physical excitement, as in audible sobs, groans, cries, screams, &c.?

" VIII. Did any of the parties throw themselves into unusual postures?

" IX. Were there any who fainted, fell into convulsions, or were ill in other respects?

" X. How late have you ever known revival meetings last?

" XI. Do you approve or disapprove of these meetings upon the whole? In either case have the goodness to state why.

" XII. Was any death occasioned, or said to be occasioned, by over excitement in any such case? If so, state the circumstances in so far as you know them.

" XIII. State any other circumstances connected with revivals in your parish or district, which, though not involved in the foregoing queries, may tend to throw light upon this subject."

ADDITIONAL QUERIES

" XIV. What special circumstances in the preaching or ministration of the instruments appear to have produced the results in each particular case which may have come under your notice?

" XV. Did any person or persons whom you described as the instruments in producing the effects above adverted to address children? At what hour? In what special terms? And what might be the age of the youngest of them?

MR. McCHEYNE'S ANSWERS

I. It is my decided and solemn conviction in the sight of God, that a very remarkable and glorious work of God, in the conversion of sinners and edifying of saints, has taken place in this parish and neighbourhood. This work I have observed going on from the very beginning of my ministry in this place in November 1836, and it has continued to the present time; but it was much more remarkable in the autumn of 1839, when I was abroad on a mission of inquiry to the Jews, and when my place was occupied by the Rev. W. C. Burns. Previous to my going abroad and for several months afterwards, the means used were of the ordinary kind. In addition to the services of the Sabbath, in the summer of 1837, a meeting was opened in the church on Thursday evenings for prayer, exposition of Scripture, reading accounts of missions, revivals of religion, &c., Sabbath schools were formed, private prayer meetings were encouraged, and two weekly classes for young men and young women were instituted with a very large attendance. These means were accompanied with an evident blessing from on high in many instances. But there was no visible or general movement among the people until August 1839, when, immediately after the beginning of the Lord's work at Kilsyth, the word of God came with such power to the hearts and consciences of the people here, and their thirst for hearing it became so intense, that the evening classes in the school room were changed into densely crowded congregations in the church, and for nearly four months it was found desirable to have public worship almost every night. At this time, also, many prayer meetings were formed, some of which were strictly private or fellowship meetings, and others, conducted by persons of some Christian experience, were open to persons under concern about their souls. At the time of my return from the Mission to the Jews, I found thirty-nine such meetings held weekly in connection with the congregation, and five of these were conducted and attended entirely by little children. At present although many changes have taken place, I believe the number of these meetings is not much diminished. Now, however, they are nearly all of the more private kind—the deep and general anxiety, which led to many of them being open, having in a great degree subsided. Among the many ministers who have assisted here from time to time, and especially in the autumn of 1839, I may mention Mr. Macdonald of Urquhart, Mr. Cumming, of Dumbarney, Mr. Bonar, of Larbert, Mr. Bonar, of Kelso, and Mr. Somerville, of Anderston. Some of these were present here for a considerable time, and I have good reason for believing that they were eminently countenanced by God in their labours.

As to the extent of this work of God, I believe it is impossible to speak decidedly. The parish is situated in the suburb of a city containing sixty thousand inhabitants. The work extended to individuals residing in all quarters of the town, and belonging to all ranks and denominations of the people. Many hundreds, under deep concern for their souls, have come, from first to last, to converse with the ministers; so that I am deeply persuaded the number of those who have received saving benefit is greater than any one will know till the judgment day.

II. III. The previous character of those who seem to have been converted was very various. I could name not a few in the higher ranks of life, that seem evidently to have become new creatures, who previously lived a worldly life, though unmarked by open wickedness. Many, again, who were before nominal Christians, are now living ones. I could name, however, far more, who have been turned from the paths of open sin and profligacy, and have found pardon and purity in the blood of the Lamb, and by the Spirit of our God; so that we can say to them, as Paul said to the Corinthians, " Such were some of you, but ye are washed, but ye are sanctified, but ye are justified," &c. I often think, when conversing with some of these, that the change they have undergone might be enough to convince an atheist that there is a God, or an infidel that there is a Saviour.

IV. It is not easy for a minister, in a field like this, to keep an exact account of all the cases of awakening and conversion that occur; and there are many of which he may never hear. I have always tried to mark down the circumstances of each awakened soul that applied to me, and the number of these from first to last, has been very great. During the autumn of 1839, not fewer than from six hundred to seven hundred came to converse with the ministers about their souls; and there were many more, equally concerned, who never came forward in this way. I know many, who appear to have been converted, and yet have never come to me in private; and I am, every now and then, meeting with cases of which I never before heard. Indeed, eternity alone can reveal the true number of the Lord's hidden ones among us.

V. With regard to the consistency of those who are believed to have been converted, I may first of all remark, that it must be acknowledged, and should be clearly understood, that many who came under concern about their souls, and seemed, for a time, to be deeply convinced of sin, have gone back again to the world. I believe that, at that remarkable season in 1839, there were very few persons who attended the meetings without being more or less affected. It pleased God, at that time, to bring an awfully solemn sense of divine things over the minds of men. It was, indeed, the day of our merciful visitation. But many allowed it to slip past them without being saved; and these have sunk back, as was to be expected, into their former deadness and impenitence. Alas! there are some among us, whose very looks remind you of that awful warning, "Quench not the Spirit."

Confining our view, however, to those who, as far as ministers could judge by the rules of God's word, seemed to be savingly converted, I may with safety say, that I do not know of more than two who have openly given the lie to their profession. Other cases of this kind may have occurred, but they are unknown to me. More, I have little doubt, will eventually occur ; for the voice of God teaches us to expect such things. Some of those converted have now walked consistently for four years ; the greater part from one to two years. Some have had their falls into sin, and have thus opened the mouths of their adversaries, but the very noise that this has made shows that such instances are very rare. Some have fallen into spiritual darkness ; many I fear have left their first love ; but yet I see nothing in all this but what is incident in the case of every Christian church. Many there are among us, who are filled with light and peace, and are examples to the believers in all things. We had an additional communion season at my return from the continent, which was the happiest and holiest that I was ever present at. The Monday was entirely devoted to thanksgiving, and a thank-offering was made among us to God for his signal mercies. The times were hard, and my people are far from wealthy, yet the sum contributed was seventy-one pounds. This was devoted to Missionary purposes. It is true that those whom I esteem as Christians, do often grieve me by their inconsistencies ; but still I cannot help thinking that, if the world were full of such, the time would be come when " they shall neither hurt nor destroy in all God's holy mountain."

VI. During the progress of this work of God, not only have many individuals been savingly converted, but important effects have also been produced upon the people generally. It is indeed amazing, and truly affecting to see, that thousands living in the immediate vicinity of the spot where God has been dealing so graciously, still continue sunk in deep apathy in regard to spiritual things, or are running on greedily in open sin. While many from a distance have become heirs of glory, multitudes, I fear, of those who live within the sound of the Sabbath bell, continue to live on in sin and misery. Still, however, the effects that have been produced upon the community are very marked. It seems now to be allowed, even by the most ungodly, that there *is* such a thing as conversion. Men cannot any longer deny it. The Sabbath is now observed with greater reverence than it used to be; and there seems to be far more of a solemn awe upon the minds of men than formerly. I feel that I can now stop sinners in the midst of their open sin and wickedness, and command their reverent attention, in a way that I could not have done before. The private meetings for prayer have spread a sweet influence over the place. There is far more solemnity in the house of God; and it is a different thing to preach to the people now from what it once was. Any minister of spiritual feeling can discern that there are many praying people in the congregation. When I came first here, I found it impossible to establish Sabbath schools on the local system; while, very lately, there were instituted with ease, nineteen such schools, that are well taught and well attended.

VII. VIII. IX. As I have already stated, by far the most remarkable season of the working of the Spirit of God in this place, was in 1839, when I was abroad. At that time, there were many seasons of remarkable solemnity, when the house of God literally became "a Bochim, a place of weepers." Those who were privileged to be present at these times will, I believe, never forget them. Even since my return, however, I have myself frequently seen the preaching of the word attended with so much power, and eternal things brought so near that the feelings of the people could not be restrained. I have observed at such times an awful and breathless stillness pervading the assembly; each hearer bent forward in the posture of wrapt attention; serious men covered their faces to pray that the arrows of the King of Zion might be sent home with power to the hearts of sinners. Again, at such a time, I have heard a half-suppressed sigh rising from many a heart, and have seen many bathed in tears. At other times I have heard loud sobbing in many parts of the church, while a deep solemnity pervaded the whole audience. I have also, in some instances, heard individuals cry aloud, as if they had been pierced through with a dart. These solemn scenes were witnessed under the preaching of different ministers, and sometimes occurred under the most tender gospel invitations. On one occasion, for instance, when the minister was speaking tenderly on the words, " He is altogether lovely," almost every sentence was responded to by cries of the bitterest agony. At such times I have seen persons so overcome, that they could not walk or stand alone. I have known cases in which believers have been similarly affected through the fulness of their joy. I have often known such awakenings to issue in what I believe to be real conversion. I could name many of the humblest, meekest believers, who at one time cried out in the church under deep agony. I have also met with cases where the sight of souls thus pierced has been blessed by God to awaken careless sinners who had come to mock.

I am far from believing that these signs of deep alarm always issue in conversion, or that the Spirit of God does not often work in a more quiet manner. Sometimes, I believe, he comes like the pouring rain; sometimes like the gentle dew. Still I would humbly state my conviction, that it is the duty of all who seek the salvation of souls, and especially the duty of ministers, to long and pray for such solemn times, when the arrows shall be sharp in the heart of the King's enemies, and our slumbering congregations shall be made to cry out, " Men and brethren, what shall we do ?"

X. XI. None of the ministers who have been engaged in the work of God here have ever used the name " revival meeting ;" nor do they approve of its use. We are told in the Acts that the apostles preached and taught the gospel daily ; yet their meetings are never called revival meetings. No other meetings have taken place here, but such as were held for the preaching and teaching of the gospel, and for prayer. It will not be maintained by any one, that the meetings in the sanctuary every Lord's day are intended for any other purpose than the revival of genuine godliness, through the conversion of sinners, and the edification of saints. All the meetings in this place were held, I believe, with a single eye to the same object. There seems, therefore, to be no propriety in applying the name peculiarly to any meetings that have been held in this place. It is true, indeed, that on week evenings there is not generally the same formality as on Sabbaths—the congregation are commonly dressed in their working clothes, and the minister speaks with less regular preparation.

During the autumn of 1839, the meetings were in general dismissed at ten o'clock ; although, in several instances, the state of the congregation seemed to be such as to demand that the ministers should remain still longer with them, that they might counsel and pray with the awakened. I have myself, once or twice, seen the service in the house of God continue till about midnight. On these occasions, the emotion during the preaching of the word was so great, that after the blessing had been pronounced at the usual hour, the greater part of the people remained in their seats, or occupied the passages, so that it was impossible to leave them. In consequence of this, a few words more were spoken suited to the state of awakened souls ; singing and prayer filled up the rest of the time. In this way the meeting was prolonged by the very necessity of the case. On such occasions, I have often longed that all the ministers in Scotland were present, that they might learn more deeply what the true end of our ministry is. I have never seen or heard of any thing indecorous at such meetings ; and, on all such occasions, the feelings that filled my soul were those of the most solemn awe, the deepest compassion for afflicted souls, and an unutterable sense of the hardness of my own heart. I do entirely and solemnly approve of such meetings, because I believe them to be in accordance with the word of God, to be pervaded by the Spirit of Christ, and to be ofttimes the birth places of precious never-dying souls. It is my earnest prayer that we may yet see greater things than these in all parts of Scotland.

XII. There was one death that took place in very solemn circumstances at the time of the work of God in this place, and this was ascribed by many of the enemies to religious excitement. The facts of the case, however, which were published at the time clearly show that this was a groundless calumny.

XIII. I have been led to examine, with particular care, the accounts that have been left us of the Lord's marvellous works in the days that are past, both in our own land and in other parts of the world, in order that I might compare these with what has lately taken place at Dundee, and in other parts of Scotland. In doing this, I have been fully convinced that the outpouring of the Holy Spirit at the Kirk of Shotts, and again, a century after, at Cambuslang, &c., in Scotland, and under the ministry of President Edwards, in America, was attended by the very same appearances as the work in our own day. Indeed, so completely do they seem to agree, both in their nature and in the circumstances that attended them, that I have not heard a single objection brought against the work of God now, which was not urged against it in former times, and that has not been most scripturally and triumphantly removed by Mr. Robe, in his Narrative, and by President Edwards, in his invaluable Thoughts on the Revival of Religion in New England:—" And certainly we must throw by all talk of conversion and Christian experience; and not only so, but we must throw by our Bibles, and give up revealed religion, if this be not in general the work of God."

XIV. I do not know of any thing in the ministrations of those who have occupied my pulpit, that may with propriety be called peculiar, or that is different from what I conceive ought to characterize the services of all true ministers of Christ. They have preached, so far as I can judge, nothing but the pure gospel of the grace of God. They have done this fully, clearly, solemnly ; with discrimination, urgency, and affection.

None of them read their sermons. They all, I think, seek the *immediate* conversion of the people, and they believe that, under a living gospel ministry, success is more or less the rule, and want of success the exception. They are, I believe, in general, peculiarly given to secret prayer; and they have also been accustomed to have much united prayer when together, and especially before and after engaging in public worship. Some of them have been peculiarly aided in declaring the terrors of the Lord, and others in setting forth the fulness and freeness of Christ as the Saviour of sinners; and the same persons have been, at different times, remarkably assisted in both these ways. So far as I am aware, no unscriptural doctrines have been taught, nor has there been a keeping back of any part of "the whole counsel of God."

XV. The ministers engaged in the work of God in this place, believing that children are lost and may through grace be saved, have, therefore, spoken to children as freely as to grown persons; and God has so greatly honoured their labours, that many children, from ten years old and upwards, have given full evidence of their being born again. I am not aware of any meetings that have been held peculiarly for children, with the exception of the Sabbath schools, the children's prayer meetings, and a sermon to children on the Monday evening after the communion. It was commonly at the public meetings, in the house of God, that children were impressed; often, also, in their own little meetings, when no minister was present.

March 26th, 1841.

SONGS OF ZION

TO CHEER AND GUIDE PILGRIMS ON THEIR WAY TO THE
HEAVENLY JERUSALEM

~~~~~~~~~~

THE BARREN FIG TREE

WITHIN a vineyard's sunny bound
An ample fig tree shelter found,
  Enjoying sun and showers;
The boughs were graceful to the view,
With spreading leaves of deep-green hue,
  And gaily blushing flowers.

When round the vintage season came,
This blooming fig was still the same,
  As promising and fair;
But though the leaves were broad and green,
No precious fruit was to be seen,
  Because no fruit was there.

"For three long years," the Master cried,
"Fruit on this tree to find I've tried,
  But all in vain my toil;
Ungrateful tree! the axe's blow
Shall lay thy leafy honours low;
  Why cumbers it the soil?"

"Ah! let it stand just one year more,"
The dresser said, "ti'l all my store
  Of rural arts I've shown;
I'll dig about its sluggish roots;
Perhaps 't will yet bear pleasant fruits;—
  If not, then cut it down."

386

How many years hast thou, my heart,
Acted the barren fig tree's part,
     Leafy, and fresh, and fair,
Enjoying heavenly dews of grace,
And sunny smiles from God's own face!
     But where the fruit? ah! where?

How often must the Lord have prayed
That still my day might be delayed,
     Till all due means were tried;
Afflictions, mercies, health, and pain,
How long shall these be all in vain
     To teach this heart of pride?

Learn, O my soul, what God demands
Is not a faith like barren sands,
     But fruit of heavenly hue;
By this we prove that Christ we know,
If in his holy steps we go—
     Faith works by love, if true.

August 14, 1834

"THEY SING THE SONG OF MOSES."

Dark was the night, the wind was high,
  The way by mortals never trod;
For God had made the channel dry,
  When faithful Moses stretched the rod.

The raging waves on either hand
  Stood like a massy tottering wall,
And on the heaven-defended band
  Refused to let the waters fall.

With anxious footsteps, Israel trod
  The depths of that mysterious way;
Cheered by the pillar of their God,
  That shone for them with favouring ray.

But when they reached the opposing shore,
  As morning streaked the eastern sky,
They saw the billows hurry o'er
  The flower of Pharaoh's chivalry.

Then awful gladness filled the mind
  Of Israel's mighty ransomed throng;
And while they gazed on all behind,
  Their wonder burst into a song.

Thus, thy redeemed ones, Lord, on earth,
  While passing through this vale of weeping,
Mix holy trembling with their mirth,
  And anxious watching with their sleeping.

The night is dark, the storm is loud,
  The path no human strength can tread;
Jesus, be thou the pillar-cloud,
  Heaven's light upon our path to shed.

And oh! when, life's dark journey o'er,
  And death's enshrouding valley past,
We plant our feet on yonder shore,
  And tread yon golden strand at last;

Shall we not see with deep amaze,
  How grace hath led us safe along;
And whilst behind, before, we gaze,
  Triumphant burst into a song?

And even on earth, though sore bestead,
  Fightings without, and fears within;
Ransomed to-day from slavish dread,
  To-morrow captive led by sin;

Yet would I lift my downcast eyes,
  On Thee, thou brilliant tower of fire—
Thou dark cloud to mine enemies—
  That Hope may all my breast inspire.

And thus the Lord, my strength, I 'll praise,
  Though Satan and his legions rage;
And the sweet song of faith I 'll raise,
  To cheer me on my pilgrimage.

Edinburgh, 1835

JEHOVAH TSIDKENU

"THE LORD OUR RIGHTEOUSNESS"

(The Watchword of the Reformers.)

I once was a stranger to grace and to God,
I knew not my danger, and felt not my load;
Though friends spoke in rapture of Christ on the tree,
Jehovah Tsidkenu was nothing to me.

I oft read with pleasure, to soothe or engage,
Isaiah's bold measure and John's simple page;
But e'en when they pictured the blood-sprinkled tree,
Jehovah Tsidkenu seemed nothing to me.

Like tears from the daughters of Zion that roll,
I wept when the waters went over his soul;
Yet thought not my sins had nailed to the tree
Jehovah Tsidkenu;—'t was nothing to me.

When free grace awoke me, by light from on high,
Then legal fears shook me, I trembled to die;
No refuge, no safety in self could I see,—
Jehovah Tsidkenu my Saviour must be.

My terrors all vanished before the sweet name;
My guilty fears banished, with boldness I came
To drink at the fountain, life-giving and free,—
Jehovah Tsidkenu is all things to me.

Jehovah Tsidkenu! my treasure and boast,
Jehovah Tsidkenu! I ne'er can be lost;
In thee I shall conquer by flood and by field,
My cable, my anchor, my breastplate and shield!

Even treading the valley, the shadow of death,
This watchword shall rally my faltering breath;
For while from life's fever my God sets me free,
Jehovah Tsidkenu, my death song shall be.

November 18, 1834

ON MUNGO PARK'S FINDING A TUFT OF GREEN MOSS IN THE AFRICAN DESERT

[" Whatever way I turned, nothing appeared but danger and difficulty. I saw myself in the midst of a vast wilderness, in the depth
of the rainy season, naked and alone, surrounded by savage animals, and men still more savage. I was five hundred miles from
the nearest European settlement. At this moment, painful as
my reflections were, the extraordinary beauty of a small moss in
fructification irresistibly caught my eye. I mention this to show
from what trifling circumstances the mind will sometimes derive
consolation; for though the whole plant was not larger than the
top of one of my fingers, I could not contemplate the delicate
conformation of its roots, leaves, and capsule, without admiration.
Can that Being, thought I, who planted, watered, and brought to
perfection, in this obscure part of the world, a thing which appears of so small importance, look with unconcern upon the
situation and sufferings of creatures formed after his own image?
Surely not. I started up, and disregarding both hunger and fatigue, travelled forward, assured that relief was at hand, and I
was not disappointed."—*Park's Travels.*]

The sun had reached his mid-day height,
And poured down floods of burning light,
　　On Afric's barren land;
No cloudy veil obscured the sky,
And the hot breeze that struggled by
　　Was filled with glowing sand.

No mighty rock upreared its head,
To bless the wanderer with its shade,
　　In all the weary plain;
No palm trees with refreshing green
To glad the dazzled eye were seen,
　　But one wide sandy main.

Dauntless and daring was the mind
That left all home-born joys behind
　　These deserts to explore—
To trace the mighty Niger's course,
And find it bubbling from its source
　　In wilds untrod before.

And ah! shall we less daring show,
Who nobler ends and motives know
　　Than ever heroes dream—

Who seek to lead the savage mind
The precious fountain-head to find
    Whence flows salvation's stream?

Let peril, nakedness, and sword,
Hot barren sands, and despot's word
    Our burning zeal oppose—
Yet, Martyn-like, we lift the voice,
Bidding the wilderness rejoice,
    And blossom as the rose.

Sad, faint, and weary on the sand
Our traveller sat him down; his hand
    Covered his burning head,
Above, beneath, behind, around—
No resting for the eye he found;
    All nature seemed as dead.

One tiny tuft of moss alone
Mantling with freshest green a stone,
    Fixed his delighted gaze—
Through bursting tears of joy he smiled,
And while he raised the tendril wild
    His lips o'erflowed with praise.

"O, shall not He who keeps thee green,
Here in the waste, unknown, unseen—
    Thy fellow-exile save?
He who commands the dew to feed
Thy gentle flower, can surely lead
    Me from a scorching grave!"

The heaven-sent plant new hope inspired—
New courage all his bosom fired,
    And bore him safe along;
Till with the evening's cooling shade
He slept within the verdant glade,
    Lulled by the negro's song.

Thus, we in this world's wilderness,
Where sin and sorrow, guilt, distress
    Seem undisturbed to reign,
May faint because we feel alone,
With none to strike our favourite tone
    And join our homeward strain.

Yet, often in the bleakest wild
Of this dark world, some heaven-born child,
   Expectant of the skies,
Amid the low and vicious crowd,
Or in the dwellings of the proud,
   Meets our admiring eyes.

From gazing on the tender flower,
We lift our eyes to Him whose power
   Hath all its beauty given;
Who, in this atmosphere of death,
Hath given it life, and form, and breath,
   And brilliant hues of heaven.

Our drooping faith, revived by sight,
Anew her pinion plumes for flight,
   New hope distends the breast;
With joy we mount on eagle wing,
With bolder tone our anthem sing,
   And seek the pilgrim's rest.

March, 1836

"I AM DEBTOR"

When this passing world is done,
When has sunk yon glaring sun,
When we stand with Christ in glory,
Looking o'er life's finished story,
   Then, Lord, shall I fully know—
   Not till then—how much I owe.

When I hear the wicked call
On the rocks and hills to fall,
When I see them start and shrink
On the fiery deluge brink,
   Then, Lord, shall I fully know—
   Not till then—how much I owe.

When I stand before the throne
Dressed in beauty not my own,
When I see thee as thou art,
Love thee with unsinning heart,
   Then, Lord, shall I fully know—
   Not till then—how much I owe.

When the praise of heaven I hear,
Loud as thunders to the ear,
Loud as many waters' noise,
Sweet as harp's melodious voice,
Then, Lord, shall I fully know—
Not till then—how much I owe.

Even on earth, as through a glass
Darkly, let thy glory pass,
Make forgiveness feel so sweet,
Make thy Spirit's help so meet,
Even on earth, Lord, make me know
Something of how much I owe.

Chosen not for good in me,
Wakened up from wrath to flee,
Hidden in the Saviour's side,
By the Spirit sanctified,
Teach me, Lord, on earth to show,
By my love, how much I owe.

Oft I walk beneath the cloud,
Dark as midnight's gloomy shroud;
But, when fear is at its height,
Jesus comes, and all is light;
Blessed Jesus! bid me show
Doubting saints how much I owe.

When in flowery paths I tread,
Oft by sin I'm captive led;
Oft I fall—but still arise—
The Spirit comes—the tempter flies;
Blessed Spirit! bid me show
Weary sinners all I owe.

Oft the nights of sorrow reign,
Weeping, sickness, sighing, pain;
But a night thine anger burns,
Morning comes and joy returns;
God of comforts! bid me show
To thy poor, how much I owe.

May, 1837

CHILDREN CALLED TO CHRIST

Like mist on the mountain,
    Like ships on the sea,
So swiftly the years
    Of our pilgrimage flee;
In the grave of our fathers
    How soon we shall lie!
Dear children, to-day
    To a Saviour fly.

How sweet are the flowerets
    In April and May!
But often the frost makes
    Them wither away.
Like flowers you may fade:
    Are you ready to die?
While "yet there is room"
    To a Saviour fly.

When Samuel was young,
    He first knew the Lord,
He basked in his smile
    And rejoiced in his word;
So most of God's children
    Are early brought nigh:
Oh, seek him in youth—
    To a Saviour fly.

Do you ask me for pleasure?
    Then lean on his breast,
For there the sin-laden
    And weary find rest.
In the valley of death
    You will triumphing cry—
"If this be called dying,
    'T is pleasant to die!"

Jan. 1, 1831

"THY WORD IS A LAMP UNTO MY FEET, AND A LIGHT UNTO MY PATH"

When Israel knew not where to go,
God made the fiery pillar glow;
By night, by day, above the camp
It led the way—their guiding lamp;
Such is thy holy Word to me
In day of dark perplexity.
When devious paths before me spread,
And all invite my foot to tread,
I hear thy voice behind me say—
"Believing soul, this is the way,
Walk thou in it." O gentle Dove,
How much thy holy law I love!
    My lamp and light
    In the dark night.

When Paul amid the seas seemed lost,
By Adria's billows wildly tossed,
When neither sun nor star appeared,
And every wave its white head reared
Above the ship; beside his bed
An angel stood, and "Fear not," said.
Such is thy holy word to me
When tossed upon affliction's sea;
When floods come in unto my soul,
And the deep waters o'er me roll,
With angel voice thy Word draws near
And says, "'T is I, why shouldst thou fear?
Through troubles great my saints must go
Into their rest, where neither woe
Nor sin can come; where every tear
From off the cheek shall disappear,
Wiped by God's hand." O gentle Dove
Thy holy law how much I love!
    My lamp and light
    In the dark night.

When holy Stephen dauntless stood
Before the Jews, who sought his blood,
With angel face he looked on high,
And wondering, through the parted sky,

Saw Jesus risen from his throne
To claim the martyr as his own.
Angelic peace that sight bestowed,
With holy joy his bosom glowed,
And while the murderous stones they hurled,
His heaven-wrapt soul sought yonder world
Of rest. "My spirit, Saviour, keep,"
He cried, he kneeled, he fell asleep.
Such be thy holy word to me
In hour of life's extremity!
Although no more the murdering hand
Is raised within our peaceful land—
The Church has rest, and I may ne'er
Be called the martyr's crown to wear:
Yet still, in whatsoever form
Death comes to me, in midnight storm
Whelming my bark, or in my nest
Gently dismissing me to rest,
O grant me in thy word to see
A risen Saviour beckoning me.
No evil then my heart shall fear
In the dark valley. Thou art near!
My trembling soul and thou, my God,
Alone are there; thy staff and rod
Shall comfort me. O gentle Dove,
How much thy holy law I love!
　　My lamp and light
　　In the dark night.

1838

FOUNTAIN OF SILOAM

Isaiah viii. 6

Beneath Moriah's rocky side
　　A gentle fountain springs,
Silent and soft its waters glide,
　　Like the peace the Spirit brings.

The thirsty Arab stoops to drink
　　Of the cool and quiet wave,
And the thirsty spirit stops to think
　　Of Him who came to save.

Siloam is the fountain's name,
  It means *"One sent from God;"*
And thus the holy Saviour's fame,
  It gently spreads abroad.

O grant that I, like this sweet well,
  May Jesus' image bear,
And spend my life, my all, to tell
  How full his mercies are.

Foot of Carmel, June, 1839

THE SEA OF GALILEE

How pleasant to me thy deep blue wave,
  O sea of Galilee!
For the glorious One who came to save
  Hath often stood by thee.

Fair are the lakes in the land I love,
  Where pine and heather grow,
But thou hast loveliness far above
  What Nature can bestow.

It is not that the wild gazelle
  Comes down to drink thy tide,
But He that was pierced to save from hell
  Oft wandered by thy side.

It is not that the fig tree grows,
  And palms, in thy soft air,
But that Sharon's fair and bleeding rose
  Once spread its fragrance there.

Graceful around thee the mountains meet,
  Thou calm reposing sea;
But, ah, far more! the beautiful feet
  Of Jesus walked o'er thee.

These days are past—Bethsaida, where?
  Chorazin, where art thou?
His tent the wild Arab pitches there,
  The wild reeds shade thy brow.

Tell me, ye mouldering fragments, tell
    Was the Saviour's city here?
Lifted to heaven, has it sunk to hell,
    With none to shed a tear?

Ah! would my flock from thee might learn
    How days of grace will flee;
How all an offered Christ who spurn,
    Shall mourn at last, like thee.

And was it beside this very sea
    The new-risen Saviour said
Three times to Simon, "Lovest thou me?
    My lambs and sheep then feed."

O Saviour! gone to God's right hand!
    Yet the same Saviour still,
Graved on thy heart is this lovely strand
    And every fragrant hill.

O! give me, Lord, by this sacred wave,
    Threefold thy love divine,
That I may feed, till I find my grave,
    Thy flock—both thine and mine.

Sea of Galilee, 16th July, 1839

TO YONDER SIDE

Luke viii. 22—25

Behind the hills of Naphtali
    The sun went slowly down,
Leaving on mountain, tower, and tree,
    A tinge of golden brown.

The cooling breath of evening woke
    The waves of Galilee,
Till on the shore the waters broke
    In softest melody.

"Now launch the bark," the Saviour cried,
    The chosen twelve stood by,

" And let us cross to yonder side,
  Where the hills are steep and high."

Gently the bark o'er the water creeps,
  While the swelling sail they spread,
And the wearied Saviour gently sleeps
  With a pillow 'neath his head.

On downy bed the world seeks rest,
  Sleep flies the guilty eye;
But he who leans on the Father's breast
  May sleep when storms are nigh.

But soon the lowering sky grew dark
  O'er Bashan's rocky brow;
The storm rushed down upon the bark,
  And waves dashed o'er the prow.

The pale disciples trembling spake,
  While yawned the watery grave,
" We perish, master—master, wake—
  Carest thou not to save?"

Calmly he rose with sovereign will,
  And hushed the storm to rest.
" Ye waves," he whispered, " Peace! be still!"
  They calmed like a pardoned breast.

So have I seen a fearful storm
  O'er wakened sinner roll,
Till Jesus' voice and Jesus' form
  Said, " Peace, thou weary soul."

And now he bends his gentle eye
  His wondering followers o'er,
" Why raise this unbelieving cry?
  I said, *To yonder shore.*"

When first the Saviour wakened me,
  And showed me why he died,
He pointed o'er life's narrow sea,
  And said, " *To yonder side.*"

" I am the ark where Noah dwelt,
  And heard the deluge roar—

No soul can perish that has felt
    My rest—*To yonder shore.*"

Peaceful and calm the tide of life
    When first I sailed with thee;
My sins forgiven, no inward strife,
    My breast a glassy sea.

But soon the storm of passion raves,
    My soul is tempest tossed;
Corruptions rise, like angry waves,
    "Help, Master, I am lost!"

"Peace! peace! be still thou raging breast,
    My fulness is for thee"—
The Saviour speaks, and all is rest,
    Like the waves of Galilee.

And now I feel his holy eye
    Upbraids my heart of pride;
"Why raise this unbelieving cry?
    I said, *To yonder side.*"

Begun at the Lake of Galilee, July 15th, 1839

ON THE MEDITERRANEAN SEA IN THE BAY OF CARMEL

O Lord, this swelling, tideless sea,
Is like thy love in Christ to me;
The ceaseless waves that fill the bay
Through flinty rocks have worn their way,
And thy unceasing love alone
Hath broken through this heart of stone.
The countless smile that gilds the deep
When sunbeams on the water sleep,
Is like thy countless smile of grace
When I am seen in Jesus' face.
No ebbing tide these waters know,
Pure, placid, constant in their flow;
No ebb thy love to me hath known
Since first it chose me for thine own.
Or if, perchance, at thy command,

The wave retiring leaves the sand,
One moment all is dry, and then
It turns to fill the shore again:
So have I found thy wondrous grace
Forsake my soul a little space;
Barren and cold, deserted, dry,
A helpless worm to thee I cry;
Thy face is hid a little while,
But with the morning comes thy smile,
Jesus once more his beauty shows,
And all my heart with peace o'erflows.

These deep blue waters lave the shore
Of Israel, as in days of yore!
Though Zion like a field is ploughed,
And Salem's covered with a cloud;
Though briers and thorns are tangled o'er
Where vine and olive twined before;
Though turbaned Moslems tread the gate,
And Judah sits most desolate;
Their nets o'er Tyre the fishers spread,
And Carmel's top is withered;
Yet still these waters clasp the shore
As kindly as they did before!
Such is thy love to Judah's race,
A deep unchanging tide of grace,
Though scattered now at thy command
They pine away in every land,
With trembling heart and failing eyes,
And deep the veil on Israel lies,
Yet still thy word thou canst not break,
"Beloved for their fathers' sake."

July 18th, 1839, *near Acre*

THE CHILD COMING TO JESUS

Suffer me to come to Jesus,
  Mother dear, forbid me not;
By his blood from hell he frees us;
  Makes us fair, without a spot.

Suffer me, my earthly father,
　At his pierced feet to fall;
Why forbid me? help me, rather
　Jesus is my all in all.

Suffer me to run unto him;
　Gentle sisters, come with me;
O that all I love but knew him,
　Then my home a heaven would be.

Loving playmates, gay and smiling,
　Bid me not forsake the cross;
Hard to bear is your reviling,
　Yet for Jesus all is dross.

Yes, though all the world have chid me,
　Father, mother, sister, friend;
Jesus never will forbid me!
　Jesus loves me to the end!

Gentle Shepherd, on thy shoulder
　Carry me a sinful lamb;
Give me faith, and make me bolder,
　Till with thee in heaven I am.

July, 1841

———◆———

OIL IN THE LAMP

FOR A SABBATH CLASS

Matthew xxv. 1—13

Ten virgins, clothed in white,
　The Bridegroom went to meet;
Their lamps were burning bright
　To guide his welcome feet.

Five of the band were wise;
　Their lamps with oil filled high;
The rest this care despise,
　And take their vessels dry.

Long time the Lord abode,
　Down came the shades of night;
The weary virgins nod,
　And then they sleep outright.

At midnight came the cry
　Upon their startled ear;
"Behold the Bridegroom nigh,
　To light his steps appear!"

They trim their lamps; in vain
　The foolish virgins toil:
"Our lamps are out, O deign
　To give us of your oil!"

"Not so"—the wise ones cry—
　"No oil have we to spare;
But swiftly run and buy,
　That you the joy may share.

They went to buy, when, lo!
　The Bridegroom comes in state·
Within those ready go,
　And shut the golden gate.

The foolish virgins now
　Before the gateway crowd;
With terror on their brow,
　They knock, and cry aloud:—

"Lord, open to our call!
　Hast thou our names forgot?"
Sadly the accents fall—
　"Depart, I know you not."

Learn here, my child, how vain
　This world, with all its lies;
Those who the kingdom gain
　Alone are truly wise.

How vain the Christian name,
　If still you live in sin:—
A lamp, and wick, and flame,
　No drop of oil within.

Is your lamp filled, my child,
    With oil from Christ above?
Has he your heart, so wild,
    Made soft and full of love?

Then you are ready now
    With Christ to enter in;
To see his holy brow,
    And bid farewell to sin.

Sinners! behold the gate
    Of Jesus open still;
Come, ere it be too late,
    And enter if you will.

The Saviour's gentle hand
    Knocks at your door to-day;
But vain his loud demand;
    You spurn his love away.

So at the Saviour's door
    You'll knock, with trembling heart;
The day of mercy o'er,
    Jesus will say—Depart!

1841